Negro Thought in America, 1880–1915

Negro Thought in America, 1880-1915

Racial Ideologies in the Age
of Booker T. Washington

BY AUGUST MEIER

Ann Arbor
The University of Michigan Press

Second printing 1964

Copyright © by The University of Michigan 1963

All rights reserved

Library of Congress Catalog Card No. 63-14008

Published in the United States of America by

The University of Michigan Press and simultaneously

in Toronto, Canada, by Ambassador Books Limited

Manufactured in the United States of America

by Vail-Ballou Press, Inc., Binghamton, N.Y.

To my parents

ACKNOWLEDGMENTS

Although, unfortunately, it will not be possible to mention all those individuals who proved helpful during the course of this study, I cannot refrain from acknowledging the assistance of those to whom I am especially indebted.

Thanks are due Professors David Donald, Richard Hofstadter, and especially my sponsor, Henry Steele Commager, for their many suggestions and their critical reading of the original manuscript, which was submitted as a doctoral dissertation at Columbia University. I owe especial gratitude to Benjamin Quarles, who read and made suggestions for about half of the chapters, and to Sherman Merrill, John Hope Franklin, Emmett Dorsey, and Herbert Hill for their critical reading of the entire manuscript.

Mrs. Jean Blackwell Hutson and the staff of the Schomburg Collection of the New York Public Library, and Mrs. Dorothy Porter and the staff of the Moorland-Spingarn Collection, Howard University, were particularly generous with their time and effort in many ways. The staffs of the Fisk University and Atlanta University libraries and of the Manuscripts Division of the Library of Congress were also very helpful.

The following were especially helpful on certain matters of interpretation: Charles S. Johnson, Arna Bontemps, Jitsuichi Masuoka, Inabel Burns Lindsay, Alain Locke, Elsie Lewis, Hylan Lewis, Robert Bone, Howard H. Bell, Leslie H. Fishel, Jr., W. E. B. Du Bois, Francis Broderick, Elliott Rudwick, Jack Abramowitz, Clarence Bacote, and Sterling Brown. Inabel Lindsay and Sterling Brown also supplied helpful introductions to other people, and W. E. B. Du Bois shared recollections of individuals and events that were exceedingly useful. Charles H. Thompson, Marquis James, Suzanne Carson Lowitt, and particularly Helena Hooker generously shared with me their unrivaled knowledge of the Booker T. Washington Papers.

Otelia Cromwell, Mary Church Terrell, Mae Miller Sullivan, Lilian Dancy Reid, J. C. Dancy, Jr., and the Methodist Board of Education kindly let me use manuscript materials in their possession. I am particularly indebted to William Shaw for letting me see a manuscript biographical sketch of William Jefferson White. Lilian Dancy Reid, Josephine Sherrill, and W. J. Trent, Sr., made available rare copies of the A.M.E. Zion Quarterly *Review,* and Warren Vann let me have an equally rare copy of the St. Luke *Herald.* Roscoe Lewis permitted me to consult his unpublished manuscript on ex-slave autobiographies, based on personal interviews.

Others who made significant suggestions were Armistead Pride, Nathaniel Tillman, L. D. Reddick, J. Saunders Redding, Mozell Hill, Lewis W. Jones, Edward Lewinson, Otto Klineberg, Harry T. Walker, Robert Hayden, Rayford Logan, Lucy Aiken, William Boyd, Lorenzo J. Greene, Flint Kellogg, and Benjamin Mays.

Special mention must be made of the award of an advanced graduate fellowship by the American Council of Learned Societies (and of subsequent stipends arranged by Charles S. Johnson and Fisk University and by the Morgan State College Faculty Research Grant Committee), which made possible the detailed research and interdisciplinary approach that were prerequisites to the scope and orientation of this book.

Finally, I must acknowledge a special debt to the work of Ralph J. Bunche, whose two memoranda dealing with Negro ideologies and organizations, prepared for the Carnegie-Myrdal study of the Negro in America, were indispensable for the original conceptualization and formulation of my research.

I am indebted to the editors of the following journals for permission to reprint excerpts from articles: *Midwest Journal, Phylon, Crisis, Journal of Negro Education, The Journal of Southern History,* and *The Journal of Negro History.*

METHODOLOGICAL NOTE

Naturally, in a study of this sort one is largely limited (by the material available) to the expressed ideas of the articulate, who are ordinarily among the prominent people, and usually of the favored social and economic classes. In the pages that follow reference is made to what appeared to be representative expressions of the varying points of view as expressed by the articulate members of the race. Wherever a point of view has appeared to be expressed by only a minority or to be expressed by a majority of the articulate, this has been clearly indicated. Some very prominent Negroes, however, did not express themselves publicly on their racial philosophy, and one can only infer that the articulate members of the race represented their points of view or the points of view of the less prominent members of the higher social and economic groups. The authors of quoted statements are identified only if they are of distinct prominence— usually with a nationwide reputation among Negroes. Some statements not identified by author are included because, even though expressed by minor figures, they appear to express especially well a certain point of view.

Considerable attention is given to institutional developments in the Negro community for several reasons. First of all, these institutional developments shed some light—more light than any other approach would—on the attitudes of the nonvocal, and they also reflect the unvocalized ideas of the articulate (as in the case of the development of segregated religious institutions during Reconstruction). In addition, as observed in Part Four, a discussion of them gives added depth to the discussion of the dominant racial philosophies of the period and illuminates their importance and pervasiveness as no other data can.

Finally, it should be pointed out that social thought does not exist independently of social forces and social institutions, but maintains a complex causal connection with them, both influencing their growth and direction, and in turn being influenced by them. No adequate understanding of Negro racial thought can be given without an analysis of the institutional developments in the Negro community and their interrelationship with the changing trends in Negro thought. Moreover, since social philosophy does not occur in a vacuum, it has been deemed necessary to relate Negro racial thought to currents in the larger stream of American social thought, to the changing conditions under which Negroes lived, and thus ultimately to the general political and economic background of the period.

CONTENTS

PART ONE

Prologue

I hope that the time is not far distant when . . . liberty in its true sense
will prevail in this country—when equal and exact justice shall be
meted out to all; when the American people shall have forgotten
their prejudices; when the lapse of ages shall have washed out
forever the virus of slavery from our hearts; when the genius of liberty
with all its glowing beauty shall extend its sway over this nation;
when there shall be no white, no black, no East, no West, no
North, no South, but one common brotherhood and one united people,
going forward forever in the progress of nations.

R. H. CAIN
Congressional Record, 43d Cong., 2d
sess., 1153.

CHAPTER I

THE HERITAGE OF RECONSTRUCTION

The Civil War and emancipation brought an abrupt shift in the hopes and aspirations of American Negroes. The decade of Reconstruction was characterized by a hopefulness that was in marked contrast to the deepening pessimism of the 1850's. In those years, abolitionist agitation notwithstanding, proscription and prejudice seemed to increase annually in the North, while the slave power appeared to achieve one victory after another—from the Fugitive Slave Law of 1850 to the Dred Scott decision seven years later. Whatever may have been the economic forces, sectional rivalries, and particularistic and nationalistic sentiments that caused and prolonged the Civil War, and whatever may have been the varying humanitarian, political, and economic motives of Reconstruction congressmen and their constituents, most Negro leaders viewed the situation as an irrepressible conflict between slavery and liberty and a struggle for the rights of man in fulfillment of the genius of the American democratic faith. "Slavery and free institutions," wrote Frederick Douglass, "can never live peaceably together . . . Liberty . . . must either overthrow slavery, or be itself overthrown by slavery." To articulate Negroes, the issues of Reconstruction were not tariffs and currency and railroad grants, or the hegemony of an industrial Northeast over an agrarian South and West. Rather they concerned the awarding of citizenship rights to Negroes and the vindication of American democratic institutions and their mission to the world. As a convention of Pennsylvania leaders declared in 1868:

The vote of one black man now—to-day—right here in his native land, is worth to the nation, to liberty, to the securing of our rights as American citizens, and the establishing of the Republic on the eternal foundations of truth and justice, more than is involved in the theory of civilization of all other parts of the world. It is America that you have to civilize, to Christianize, and compel to accept and practically apply to all men, without distinction of color or race, the glorious principles and precepts laid down in her immortal Declaration of Independence.

To build up a nation here, sacred in freedom, as an example to the world, every man equal in the law and equally exercising all rights, political and civil . . . is the surest way to civilize humanity.[1]

Republican politicians and aggressive northeastern industrialists might use the Negro vote and the Reconstruction amendments to consolidate their position and perpetuate their power, but to Negroes the issues were moral ones, based on the promise of American life, on the assumptions of the American faith that were rooted in the Declaration of Independence and the ethics of Christianity.

The most representative vehicle of thought among the articulate classes, during both the ante-bellum and Reconstruction periods, was the Convention Movement. Ever since 1830 Negro leaders had met irregularly in national and state conventions to formulate plans for the solution of the problems facing the race. The significance of the conventions derives from the fact that ordinarily they were attended and managed by the most distinguished leaders of the race—important clerics, editors, businessmen, orators, and, after the fourteenth amendment, officeholders. Broadly speaking—and at the risk of some oversimplification—one may say that their proposals had tended to emphasize moral suasion in the Garrisonian 1830's, had largely shifted to political action in the Liberty Party and Free Soil 1840's, and had shifted again to a predominating emphasis on self-help, racial solidarity, economic advancement and emigration in the disheartening 1850's.[2]

In the last months of the war, with victory in sight, almost one hundred and fifty leading colored men hopefully convened in Syracuse, New York, in October 1864, to draw up a program for the challenging days ahead. With Frederick Douglass presiding, they organized a National Equal Rights League, selecting the distinguished Ohio lawyer and abolitionist J. Mercer Langston for president. Taking their stand on the principles of American government, the Christian spirit of the age, and the justice of their cause, they protested against the many manifestations of prejudice.

Since the thirteenth amendment had not yet been passed, and since the majority of Northern states still failed to grant Negroes the ballot, their two chief demands were quite naturally abolition and political equality. To those who thought that Negroes should be satisfied with emancipation and with obtaining the rights to property and to testify in the law courts, they countered that in a republican country all rights "become mere privileges, held at the option of others, where we are excepted from the general political liberty." Although the noted abolitionist, recently turned emigrationist, Reverend Mr. Henry Highland Garnet, regarded continuing discrimination and prejudice as an argument for colonization abroad, and even declared that Negroes were a separate nationality in the United States, the optimistic majority were prepared to stake all on their American nationality. As native Americans they regarded any attempt to expatriate or colonize them abroad, or to concentrate them forcibly in one section of the United States, as unjust: "For here were we born, for this country our fathers and our brothers fought, and here we hope to remain in the full enjoyment of enfranchised manhood."

While addressing the nation on matters of abolition and citizenship, the convention spoke to the freedmen along moral, educational, and economic lines. It exhorted "them to shape their course toward frugality, the accumulation of property, and above all, to leave untried no amount of effort and self-denial to acquire knowledge, and to secure a vigorous moral and religious growth." To Negroes of all sections it recommended settlement on public lands.[3] Thus, in politics, morals, education, and economics the Syracuse convention enunciated the chief values and ideals in American culture as a program for the advancement of the race. Succeeding conventions, both state and national, for the most part simply played variations on these basic themes.

Among the numerous state conventions held in 1865 and 1866, some (perhaps as many as half) of those in the South exhibited a moderate, if not sycophantic tone. Conventions in North Carolina, Alabama, and Kentucky were noteworthy for stressing education, morality, economy, and industry rather than politics and civil rights in their attempt to be conciliatory toward the white South during the days of presidential reconstruction.

For example, the North Carolina convention held in the fall of

1865 counseled education and industry as means of elevating the race, and "most respectfully and humbly" appealed to the state constitutional convention not for political rights, but for just treatment, a chance for education and protection before the law. The delegates recalled that while hoping for Union victory, they had nevertheless been obedient and passive during the war. They saw no reason why emancipation should destroy the attachment for the white race which had previously existed and agreed that Negroes should merit the protection and sympathy of local whites by their industry, sobriety, and respectful demeanor. Behind the tactful façade, however, certain of the convention's leaders entertained radical sentiments. The presiding officer, the African Methodist Episcopal Zion missionary J. W. Hood, frankly declared that Negroes would contend for the right to testify in the courts, the right to be represented on juries, and the right to vote. And in spite of its mild words the convention upon adjournment resolved itself into a State Equal Rights League to secure the repeal of all discriminatory laws by means of political and moral suasion. The Kentucky convention in March 1866 was more accommodating. Waiving temporarily the ballot and the doctrine of equality before the law, it advised self-help, education, and economic and moral elevation as essential to the salvation and prosperity of any people.[4]

The triumph of the Radicals in the election of 1866, however, put an end to this conciliatory sort of convention. And with the passage of the fourteenth amendment, Negroes grew even more concerned with the exercise of political rights. Continued intimidation in the South and the expulsion of Negro members of the Georgia legislature formed the background for the preoccupation with political matters at the national convention held in Washington in January 1869. The delegates asserted that redress of grievances was possible only through suffrage—"the dearest treasure in the gift of any government,"— and they urged Negroes to petition Congress for the passage of the fifteenth amendment. The convention also asked Congress to pass a bill opening up to homesteading land grants forfeited by southern railroads.[5]

Since the National Equal Rights League was defunct, there having been no national convention since 1865, there was considerable debate at the Washington conference about reviving it. Some delegates thought that since Negroes now possessed all citizenship rights, legally speaking, the League was unnecessary. The crux of the matter was whether or not Negroes should have a separate organization to fight for their rights. This question had been discussed during the antebellum period, some individuals asserting that there should be no separate segregated Negro conventions. Yet circumstances appeared to make unified action and self-help on the part of Negroes necessary. The latter point of view, as we shall see, was strongest when conditions were at their worst, as in the 1850's or again in the late nineteenth and early twentieth century, but there was always a strain of this sort of thinking.

Douglass, for instance, at the Syracuse convention in 1864 had attempted to answer the question as to why Negroes met in a national convention by saying that unfavorable public sentiment made it necessary. The National Equal Rights League Convention in 1865, deploring "the lack of thorough combination and organized efforts" among Negroes, had declared that united action was needed for racial elevation. The discussion at Washington in 1869 waxed long and hot. Since 1865 conditions had improved considerably for the Negro, and there was less unity of opinion. Emancipation had become a fact as well as a proclamation, the thirteenth and fourteenth amendments had been adopted, and while prejudice and discrimination persisted, the residue of feelings of self-help and racial solidarity from the 1850's had largely disappeared. The noted abolitionist and well-to-do caterer of New York and Newport, George T. Downing, though he had attended the Syracuse convention, now thought a league would only produce evil effects. But others like A. M. Green of Philadelphia, an active leader in the Pennsylvania League, thought it a mistake to abandon a distinctive racial organization, since to do so would "disorganize our people upon a mere chimera of some brilliant imagination." [6]

There was a real basis for ideological conflict over this matter, and a very real paradox facing the Negro leaders. They were fundamentally struggling for integration into American society, for the elimination of segregation of any sort. Yet in creating a racial equal rights organization, which many deemed necessary for effective action for these rights and for uplifting Negroes economically and socially, they appeared to be creating a segregated movement in itself, to be fostering the very thing they were attacking. Independence and self-help were commonplace virtues in American culture, and no one could deny that in union there is strength. Yet the appeal for racial solidarity smacked of self-segregation, of a sort of nationalism, of furthering the system of "color caste." This paradox is one of the central themes in American Negro thought on the race problem. The outlook of the Reconstruction period was primarily integrationist, for it was a period when there was much sympathy and support among whites for the Negro cause and the passage of concrete legislation assuring Negroes of their citizenship rights. Later, as conditions took a turn for the worse, the theme of self-help and solidarity again assumed a major role. In 1869, however, the work of the League seemed in large part completed, at least on paper. And so the convention refused to revive the Equal Rights League, but satisfied itself with creating an executive committee to carry on its work.

The Washington convention of January 1869 marks the end of the first period of the Reconstruction convention movement. With the passage of the fifteenth amendment discussion shifted from agitation for political rights to other matters, and more emphasis was given to homesteading, migration from the South, civil rights, education, and economic problems. From 1869 to 1871 attention was devoted largely to the problems of Negro workers.

Negroes had displayed interest in the organized labor movement during the ante-bellum period. But both before and after the Civil War considerable enmity existed toward Negroes among white workers and unionists, and though colored workers were admitted to some craft unions, and at times to segregated locals, color prejudice was strong and exclusion common. The National Labor Union, formed in 1866, was more idealistic in its orientation, and Negro participation was in fact invited. But in view of the attitudes and practices of the constituent craft unions, the issue was too controversial to enable its leadership to insist upon integration of Negroes into the unions themselves. Consequently, Negro skilled workers, longshoremen, hod-carriers and waiters had organized their own protective and benevolent associations in the major northeastern and border cities.[7] Discouraged by the temporizing of the National Labor Union, the Baltimore Negro trade unionists, under the leadership of the ship-caulker Isaac Myers, took the initiative in calling a Colored National Labor Convention, which met in Washington in December 1869.[8] While many representatives from labor organizations attended, outside of Myers the actual leaders were the politicians, bishops, and perennial conventioneers.

The Convention insisted upon the right of labor to organize, but constantly harped on the theme that there was no real conflict between capital and labor and that indeed every man should strive to become a capitalist. In pursuit of this goal the delegates held that the masses should be encouraged to learn trades and professions and that they should be taught that all labor was honorable and a sure road to wealth, that habits of economy and temperance, combined with industry and education would elevate the race. Workers, therefore, should organize co-operative trade unions which would establish enterprises to employ Negroes unable to obtain jobs. The convention intimated that Southern farm workers would be justified in organizing to compel the planters to respect their claims to adequate pay and appealed to Congress for relief from the economic and political oppression of the planters and for the distribution of public lands in forty-acre lots. Protesting against the exclusion from apprenticeships and workshops practiced by trade unions, the delegates created a Colored National Labor Union that would, however, make no discrimination as to nationality or color, since it would be suicidal for members of the laboring class to be arrayed against each other. The convention also stressed the value of education and gave some attention to political rights. It summed up its outlook by declaring: "Our mottoes are liberty and labor, enfranchisement and education! The spelling-book and the hoe, the hammer and the vote, the opportunity to work and to rise . . . we ask for ourselves and our children." [9]

Thus, the labor convention really had the same basic outlook as the earlier conventions, though its emphasis was different. The participation of elite leaders in this convention and a similar convention held in 1871 showed their interest in the labor movement and their awareness that most Negroes were members of the working class, although like the white labor unions of the day, these conventions exhibited a characteristic petit-bourgeois psychology.

The Convention Movement from 1871 to 1873 was pretty much dominated by the politicians, and was concerned primarily with civil rights, the enforcement of the fifteenth amendment, and protest against the rising tide of discrimination and violence. The largest of the Reconstruction national conventions, held in Washington in December 1873, was devoted entirely to the question of civil rights. [10] However, in the closing years of Reconstruction, when it was becoming evident that the radical regimes were on the road to destruction, patterns of thought were shifting somewhat to a soft-pedaling of political and civil rights, and to a considerable emphasis upon self-help, racial solidarity, land-ownership, and migration from the South.

Representative of these trends was a convention of colored newspaper editors at Cincinnati in 1875. The convention's proceedings, presided over by Peter H. Clark, principal of the Colored High School in Cincinnati, stressed racial self-confidence and self-reliance, the need for intelligence and wealth, and called for united action to advance the welfare of the race. A reference to the denial of civil rights in a committee report caused considerable debate. A few delegates "could see no use of keeping up the same old whine." Others supported the statement on civil rights, one delegate asserting that the only way for Negroes to obtain their rights was to keep on asking for them. Apparently, the clause was permitted to pass, but it is significant that thus early was the pivotal ideological conflict between Booker T. Washington and his critics joined twenty years before the Tuskegeean became a nationally known figure at Atlanta. The convention, in fact, while protesting against discrimination, proposed as solutions not agitation and political activity, but education and the co-operative acquisition of landed wealth in the South or elsewhere.[11]

Broadly speaking, the Reconstruction convention movement was interested primarily in obtaining political and civil rights. Practically every convention also insisted upon the prime importance of education. While less important, the advocacy of thrift, industry, frugality, morality, land-ownership, and the acquisition of wealth was still a vital part of the program. In short, Negroes were striving forward in all areas of life in their attempt to gain integration into American society. If the characteristic view was that the franchise would be the guarantor of the Negroes' status in American society, there were some who claimed to recognize, as did Booker T. Washington and many others later, that it was largely through the cultivation of the petit bourgeois virtues and the obtaining of wealth that Negroes would win acceptance and even ease the path for political and civil rights. In general, racial unity and solidarity received but little emphasis until conditions clearly took a turn for the worse toward the end of the Reconstruction period.

While the elite leaders were talking of political rights, civil rights, and education, and to a lesser extent of land redistribution, thrift, and industry, what were the aspirations of the masses of Southern freedmen? The evidence indicates that their chief interests lay in land ownership, education, and politics—in approximately reverse order of importance to the preoccupations of the conventions and political leaders.

First and foremost, like oppressed peasants the world over, the freedmen wanted land. All of the sources, favorable and unfavorable to Negroes alike, agree upon the freedmen's intense desire to own their own farms. This propensity was, of course, in accord with the larger American faith of property and land ownership, of homesteading and western migration, of Yankee virtues and pioneer independence. As Vernon Wharton has put it: "Their very lives were entwined with the land and its cultivation; they lived in a society where respectability was based on ownership of the soil; and to them to be free was to farm their own ground." [12] The speeches of Reconstruction political leaders and equivocal federal land policy helped to stimulate the popularity of "forty acres and a mule," but the phrase spread rapidly because the desire for land was already present in the minds of the freedmen. The federal government failed the freedmen in this matter, but a significant number, even in the face of white opposition and the unwillingness of white landowners to sell to them, attempted to buy their own farms. Travelers from the North, Freedmen's Bureau agents, and missionaries reported enthusiastically upon evidence of progress in this direction, and upon examples of ex-slaves who were successfully emulating the "Yankee" qualities of thrift, industry, and sharp-dealing. Of interest also were co-operative efforts at buying farms. For example J. W. Alvord, Freedmen's Bureau superintendent of schools, cited as a not unrepresentative case ten freedmen who had "clubbed together with the proceeds of their crop and bought a whole Sea Island plantation of seven hundred acres . . . in cash." [13]

Nevertheless, because of adverse circumstances including lack of business experience, lack of money, white hostility, and crop failures, only the fortunate few with exceptional ability or luck became permanent landowners. The great masses had to be satisfied first with Freedmen's Bureau contracts, and later with various forms of tenancy, especially the sharecropping system which had begun to emerge in the conquered areas even before the close of the Civil War. The plantation system simply assumed a new form—it did not disappear; rather it probably increased in extent.[14] So acute was the desire to improve one's economic status by buying land or obtaining better rental and sharecropping arrangements that many Negroes, dissatisfied with conditions in the older states, moved southwestward to new lands, or migrated intrastate to newly opened areas.

The intense eagerness for obtaining land, the efforts in this direction, and the successes—limited though they were—accomplished against great odds, belie Booker T. Washington's stereotyping of Reconstruction as an era when Negroes began at the top in politics rather than at the bottom in practical economic realities. Indeed, as has been shown, even the political leaders recognized the importance of land ownership and economic independence.

If the sources are agreed on the desire for land ownership—and where that was impossible, for leasing land, rather than working as laborers—they also agree upon the freedmen's desire for education. Negroes, of course, shared in the American passion for common school education. Old and young flocked to the schools opened by Northern missionaries and the Freedmen's Bureau. Especially notable were the freedmen's own efforts at self-help in education—establishing schools, hiring teachers, and erecting buildings. In January 1867, for example, Alvord reported that South Carolina Negroes had raised a thousand dollars for their schools in December 1866; and that in Georgia ninety-six schools were supported in whole or in part by the freedmen who owned fifty-seven of the school buildings, and so forth. And in the middle of 1868, he reported that of 1831 day and night schools under Bureau supervision, 1325 were sustained in whole or in part by the freedmen, who owned 518 of the buildings.[15]

Furthermore, most sources agree that the freedmen took an enthusiastic part in politics. Again, political activity was at the core of the American tradition. Whatever role the Union League and other Northern agencies may have played, it is certain that the stimulus found an active response. Overwhelmingly, of course, the Negroes voted Republican.

For the masses, the interest in education, in land, and in politics were together, as Wharton has put it, "an integral part of the substance of freedom."[16]

While integration into American society was the expressed ideology of the Reconstruction period, the continued hostility of whites, particularly in the South, encouraged attitudes favoring group separatism.

These attitudes were not widely expressed in speeches and newspapers, but they were highly significant nevertheless, and were clearly evident in the institutional development of the Negro community. Such tendencies have always been present in Negro thinking, in spite of the desire for integration based upon the American equalitarian and democratic traditions, for at no time have Negroes been free from white prejudice and discrimination. In the same way that Negroes found it either necessary or desirable to have their own conventions, so in the face of an antagonistic white world, Negroes created their own segregated institutions and came to justify their existence.

The reasons that have led Negroes to favor their own segregated institutions are several, but they are ultimately rooted in the hostility of the white world in which they live. In the first place this hostility has forced Negroes to think of themselves as a group apart and has thus encouraged the development of a definite ethnocentrism. Negroes found it easier to associate with each other rather than with whites and discovered the value of group organizations to advance their mutual interests. White discriminatory and exclusionist policies were the direct cause of the establishment of segregated institutions such as the Negro churches and fraternities. Also, Negroes denied a place of leadership in the white world have encouraged the development and maintenance of segregated institutions where they would have the opportunity of achieving status and importance. Such institutions, once established, have a way of stimulating and perpetuating Negro ethnocentrism and of fostering attitudes favorable to group separatism. Individual leaders with vested interests in them are inimical to real integration. Others fear to compete and adjust in an uncertain white world. And the increased separation that these institutions encourage reinforces the mutual ignorance, suspicion, and hostility that exist between the Negro and white groups. Ordinarily, it is true, segregated institutions are justified as a temporary form of withdrawal that will vanish once prejudice and discrimination disappear. Yet the continuing uncertainties, discriminations, and psychological attitudes built up over the years perpetuate group consciousness and the justification of segregated institutions.

There is thus a mutual and interactive causal relationship between segregated institutions and ideologies and attitudes of withdrawal from the white world. On the one hand white hostility has led Negroes to regard the creation of their own institutions as either necessary or wise; on the other hand these institutions reinforce and perpetuate thinking favorable to group separatism. Segregated institutions, of course, have appeared most desirable in the periods of greatest oppression and discouragement, and it has been in such periods that this desirability was most often expressed overtly and became the core of a dominant ideological orientation. But some sentiment for them has existed even in periods when the ideal of immediate integration dominated ideological expression.

The segregated institutions of the Negro community had had their true beginning, not during the period of enthusiasm for the rights of man engendered by the American Revolution and the Enlightenment (though then as always some Negroes preferred to withdraw), but during the generation after the adoption of the Constitution when increasing proscription stimulated their development. Independent Baptist churches had appeared in southern towns during the Revolution, and Prince Hall had made efforts to found a Masonic lodge in Boston about the same time, but it was not until 1787 that the Negro Masons received their charter, and not until after the turn of the century that the African Methodist Episcopal (A.M.E.), African Methodist Episcopal Zion (A.M.E. Zion), and Northern Baptist denominations gradually emerged. The independent Negro churches had their greatest development in the North, though some also existed in the antebellum Southern towns, in spite of limitations upon the activities of free Negroes that inhibited their development. Mutual benefit organizations—at least as old as the Free African societies that appeared in Philadelphia, Newport, Boston, and New York between 1787 and 1810—appeared locally in almost all the cities, and in the North there were a number of fraternal organizations—most notably the Masons and the Oddfellows (the latter founded in 1843)—with memberships in several states.

During Reconstruction the widely expressed and dominant philosophy of integration did not entirely replace the tendency toward a separate group life. Thus, as the Union armies advanced southward, the Northern churches, Negro and white, began to proselyte among the freedmen. Baptist churches appeared everywhere and obtained the largest number of Negro communicants. The A.M.E. Zion Church was especially successful under the missionary zeal of J. W. Hood in North Carolina as early as 1864, and that state became the new center for this connection. The larger A.M.E. Church also spread rapidly throughout the South. Moreover, Negro members of the Southern white churches refused to accept any longer a position of inferiority, but preferred to establish their own religious organizations. The most important of these secessionist churches was the Colored Methodist Episcopal (C.M.E.) Church, which was established in a friendly withdrawal from the Methodist Episcopal Church South in 1870.

More difficult to trace is the story of the local mutual benefit and the national fraternal organizations. As before the war laboring groups organized occasionally and burial societies were very common. Moreover, the various national fraternal societies with both mutual benefit and social functions, such as the Masons, Oddfellows, Good Samaritans, Templars, Knights of Tabor, and Knights of Pythias expanded rapidly into the South.[17]

Both church and fraternity were especially important in the Negro community, far more so than in the white community in nineteenth-century America. It was in the church and fraternity that Negroes found unhampered opportunity for social life and for the exercise of leadership. A high proportion of distinguished Negro leaders have been ministers. Finally, the rapid growth of segregated religious and social institutions indicated that underneath the dominant Reconstruction philosophy of immediate integration, social realities were such as to encourage attitudes favorable to group separatism.

Yet, it cannot be overemphasized that the prevailing vocalized expression of thought during Reconstruction was characterized by a broad program for advancement based upon the equalitarian traditions in American culture. Negroes focused their attention upon becoming full-fledged citizens. The franchise, education, guarantees for civil rights, the acquisition of property and wealth, and the cultivation of morality were all designed to elevate Negroes and achieve their integration into American society. On the other hand, these things were not only instruments, but goals, for in themselves they would constitute assimilation of American culture, and acceptance in the "body politic." To characterize Reconstruction thinking, either on the part of the "leaders" or on the part of the masses, as devoted almost entirely to civil rights and political activity, or even to a false notion of the value of education, is to distort the picture. Reconstruction leaders constantly urged economic improvement as an essential method of achieving assimilation into American society. Their concern with the problems of the Negro workers and their groping moves toward co-operation with the white labor movement, indicate that they were acutely aware that the great majority of Negroes would have to start at the bottom and not at the top. The fact that they looked forward to a future of independent entrepreneurship for Negroes as well as whites simply shows that they had absorbed well the regnant American economic myth. In their constant emphasis upon hard work, thrift, industry, sobriety, and the acquisition of property and wealth, of independent farms and homesteads, they showed a concern for the economic side of life that has been overlooked in the stereotyping of Reconstruction. Yet it is important to remember that while the masses were primarily interested in landownership, the elite leaders, who had achieved some sort of economic security, were first and foremost interested in political and civil rights. A full citizenship, the fulfillment of America's promise, the practical application of her democratic faith were what Negroes wanted and hoped to win.

PART TWO

Ideologies in Transition: From the Compromise of 1877 to the Compromise of 1895

Twenty years have passed; the North is quiescent, the South is rejoicing, the negro is docile, the Anglo-Saxon is master of the situation, the negro has lost all of his aspirations for political preferment since Democracy reigns supreme in all the Southern States. He seems to have changed his course of procedure, has left the political arena, turned his attention to the cotton field, rice plantation, sugar crop and the best method of educating his children, refining his family relations, acquiring wealth by his industry and thus becoming a full-fledged American citizen through the only just and proper methods which give success in developing his manhood. It seems as if the negro had come here to stay. Quiet, happy, good-natured, he is making the South blossom as a rose. . . .

R. H. CAIN
"The Negro Problem of the South,"
A.M.E. *Review,* II (January, 1886),
145.

INTRODUCTION

The generation following the collapse of the Reconstruction governments and the Compromise of 1877 underwent a period of increasing prejudice and discrimination, especially in the South.[1] The
acceptance of white hegemony in the South by the federal government left Southern Negroes without any effective defense of their
political and civil rights. Through violence, fraud, and complicated
registration and voting procedures, Negro political influence was effectively curtailed in the Southern states. Alliances with independent
parties like the Populists helped to stave off complete political efface-
ment for a while, but only culminated in the final wave of race riots
and constitutional disfranchisement. Mississippi in 1890 and South
Carolina in 1895 were the first states to incorporate disfranchisement
provisions into their constitutions.

Meanwhile, first by custom and then by law, the Southern states
were evolving a system of race relations that achieved stable form
after the turn of the century. Throughout the South legal separation
of the schools—with discrimination in the distribution of school funds
—was provided for in the 1870's and 1880's. Railroad segregation
laws were enacted during the 1880's and 1890's. Usually, custom
preceded law in these matters, and universally segregated facilities
were unequal facilities.

The Southern race system also involved inequities in the administration of justice. The Supreme Court held that Negroes had the right
to sit on juries, but in practice they came to be almost entirely excluded. The convict lease system with its many abuses was greatly

expanded. And lynchings—most of them in the South—reached their peak in the 1880's and early 1890's, averaging about 150 a year during the two decades and attaining a maximum of 235 in 1892.

The completed racial system did not develop overnight, but piece by piece, until early in the twentieth century patterns of disfranchisement, segregation, and racial subordination were complete. As late as the 1880's distinguished Southerners were accepting Negro voting as an accomplished fact, and Negroes with first-class tickets rode with whites in first-class railroad cars in Virginia and South Carolina until almost the close of the century.

The picture for the North was not too bright either, though Negroes did maintain their political rights and, at least on paper, their civil rights. Public opinion in the North had never been altogether sympathetic with Negroes. Indeed, in 1865 only six Northern states permitted Negroes to vote on the same basis as whites, and only four more did so by the time the fifteenth amendment was passed. Having attained their political rights, Negroes came to hold posts in the legislatures and city councils and in a few cases on the bench in several areas in the North.

In the matter of civil rights Northern states generally came to give legislative support to the fourteenth amendment. Particularly after the Supreme Court declared the Civil Rights Act of 1875 unconstitutional in 1883, a number of legislatures enacted legislation prohibiting discrimination in places of public accommodation. Such laws, however, were often of little value in the face of hostile public opinion, relatively few cases came before the courts, and local custom, particularly in areas contiguous to the South, often acted as an effective deterrent to the exercise of the rights guaranteed by legislation. In regard to educational facilities, only four New England states admitted Negroes to schools on an equal basis with whites in 1865. Elsewhere, Negroes had been segregated in inferior quarters, where they were taught at all. By 1880 Negroes in the North had won recognition of their right to an education, and by 1900 had, on paper at least, achieved integration of pupils in public schools. This, however, was often accomplished at the expense of colored teachers, who were excluded from the mixed school systems; the laws themselves were generally ignored in the Ohio Valley and along the Mason-Dixon line.

Economically, Negroes were relegated almost entirely to menial occupations and unskilled labor, and in the South remained primarily agricultural tenants and laborers. After the withdrawal of federal protection, Negroes were more and more exploited and intimidated in their economic relationships as well as in their political relationships with whites. In some instances, their condition descended almost to a state of peonage. Urban employers and labor unions were discriminatory both in the North and in the South. White employers either failed to use Negro labor or relegated it to the worst jobs. Although in the mid-1880's the Knights of Labor included Negroes on a basis of equality, by the 1890's the A.F. of L. craft unions and the railroad brotherhoods were setting the pace with exclusionist policies and segregated locals, though a few unions, like the United Mine Workers (with almost two-thirds of its membership Negro) were racially democratic. The hostility of white organized labor was a leading factor in the decline of the number of Negroes in the skilled trades in the South after 1890, while in the North the employment situation became worse as immigrants replaced Negroes in domestic service toward the end of the century.

Unquestionably, there was increasing prejudice toward Negroes throughout the country. Even many abolitionists had been paternalistic rather than equalitarian in regard to Negroes, and it was not too difficult for men of this stripe to become easily disillusioned with the "lack of progress" of the freedmen or the "follies" of the Reconstruction governments. The majority of Northerners had never had any exalted notions of racial equality, and once memories of war had begun to fade, and the political and economic exigencies of keeping a solid Republican South (on the basis of an enfranchised Negro population) had passed, reconciliation and nationalism quite naturally became the order of the day. Reconciliation between the sections was correlated with a rising anti-Negro prejudice, and was accomplished largely at the expense of the Negroes, as the North acquiesced in discriminatory treatment by the South and even came to justify it. By the end of the century public opinion in the North had come to feel that Negroes were an inferior race, unfitted for the franchise, and that white domination was justified.[2]

The political situation and the attitude of the Republican party mirrored the changing attitudes and conditions. From championship of the Negroes' cause, the party shifted first to compromise and then to acceptance of the Southern race system. The Compromise of 1877 expressed what had actually been the underlying trend for several years—that the Republican party was simply unwilling to enforce the Reconstruction legislation in the South. President Arthur's administration courted anti-Negro white "independent" political groups in the South in an attempt to increase party strength. Not only did Republicans fail to halt outrages and disfranchisement, but it was a Republican Supreme Court that in 1883 declared the Civil Rights Act unconstitutional, and it was a Republican Congress that in 1890 repudiated campaign pledges by failing to pass the Lodge Federal Elections Bill and the Blair Federal Aid to Education Bill, which would have protected Negro political rights and improved Negro (as well as white) schooling in the South. Outside of Harrison's espousal of the Lodge Bill, Republican presidents grew increasingly silent on Negro rights, while the lily-white faction of the party made its appearance.

Correlated with these changes in the status of Negroes, and to a large extent causing them, were larger economic and social issues. The Compromise of 1877 was itself rooted in the growth of industrialism in the New South and in the increasing domination of Southern politics by industrial rather than agrarian interests, which ended the necessity of depending on Negro votes for an economic program favorable to the banking and industrial interests of the North which had come to control the Republican party. Northern capitalists, allied with and dominating Southern industry, not only found Negro votes unnecessary, but were interested in securing a stable, semiskilled labor force with which to exploit Southern resources and develop Southern industry rather than in securing justice and social reform for the benefit of the ex-slaves and their descendants.

By the 1890's, moreover, the new imperialism was reinforcing American racism. The acquisition of an overseas empire was especially significant for Negroes, because it was associated with exploitation of Filipinos, Puerto Ricans, and other colored peoples; and the racial significance of the white man's burden abroad was not overlooked by Southerners at home, nor were those who undertook this burden unaware of the implications of the Southern race system for their task. Certainly, Oriental exclusion, the Southern race system, the New Imperialism, and racist Social Darwinism all combined to give the close of the nineteenth century and the opening of the twentieth an interesting configuration in regard to racial relations.

The economic developments of the post-Civil War decades brought with them not only the triumph of industrial enterprise and the tendency toward monopoly and finance capitalism, but also the appearance of labor and agrarian reform movements that attempted to oppose or modify the economic drift. And in the struggle between the reformers and the dominant economic interests, the Negroes appeared to be among the losers. In their attitudes toward Negroes the reform movements ranged from enthusiastic espousal of the brotherhood of man and the solidarity of the oppressed to a strident prejudice and hatred of Negroes as economic rivals and as a scapegoat for the difficulties of the white working and small farmer classes. These contradictory tendencies were evident, for example, in the labor movement, from the National Labor Union, which equivocated and finally evaded the issue, through the Knights of Labor, which openly espoused the cause of the black worker, to the triumph of the A.F. of L., whose constituent unions usually discriminated. They were evident too, in the Southern Alliance and Populist Movement, which first organized Negroes into an allied, but separate Colored Alliance, then sporadically but enthusiastically identified the cause of the Negro farmer with that of the white farmer and formed alliances with Negro Republicans for political convenience (though often and ultimately usually basing a large part of its outlook on anti-Negro sentiment), and finally culminated in a violent wave of racial hatred and persecution. In fact, the rise of the lower class whites to political consciousness and power was related directly and indirectly to the disfranchisement and oppression of Negroes and the final codification of the Southern race system. The first big surge of Jim Crow laws came in the years 1887–91, when the Farmers' Alliance was becoming a power in the state legislatures, and in many states constitutional disfranchisement was an aftermath of the agrarian revolt, as members of both the radical agrarian and the conservative groups variously favored and opposed disfranchisement when it seemed to suit their interests to do so.[3]

The strongly economic, materialistic, laissez-faire, and Social Darwinist cast of late nineteenth-century American thought was to have a large influence upon Negro thinking. While Negroes never abandoned their emphasis upon the Christian and humanitarian and democratic elements in the American tradition, and though their outlook never became as secular as that of many of their fellow Americans, like the latter they more and more viewed wealth as the symbol of success, while political activity, from which they were largely de-

barred, sank into the background. What they did was to adopt the
ideas of the gospel of wealth and Social Darwinism and apply them
to their own racial situation. The story of the transition from the
broad approach of the Reconstruction period to a narrower emphasis
upon wealth and the frugal virtues, the creation of an independent
farming and business class, and racial solidarity in an impersonal
economic and Social Darwinist competition for survival that would
allegedly create (as even many Negroes often said), an "advanced
and progressive race out of a childlike backward race," is the story
this part aims to tell.

The changing outlook of Negroes took a number of different forms.
If the Republican party was becoming indifferent toward Negroes, a
few thought it would be profitable to divide their votes and form a
balance of power between the two major parties. If Republican indifference and Southern disfranchisement closed off political avenues of
advancement, then economic and moral development should be the
area for endeavor. If whites grew more hostile to Negroes, then Negroes must help themselves and band together to advance their cause.
If whites believed Negroes to be inferior, then Negroes must show
themselves the equals of whites—by publicizing their past achievements, by successfully running the race of Social Darwinist competition with the whites, and by cultivating a vigorous racial pride to
offset the "Anglo-Saxon consciousness of kind." If whites did not want
to bother with Negroes, then, many believed, it would be best to form
their own segregated institutions and communities, or even emigrate
to Africa. But above all, Negroes must stick together and help themselves.

The striking parallels in emphasis between white and Negro thought
in this period are in part coincidental; generally in periods of discouragement Negroes have adopted doctrines of self-help, racial solidarity, and economic development as better techniques for racial advancement than politics, agitation, and the demand for immediate
integration. Twice before this had occurred—once in the years of the
"Conservative Reaction" after the Revolutionary era, and again in
the 1850's. Negroes have always emphasized those elements in the
American tradition that seemed most applicable to their goal of attaining full recognition of their citizenship rights.

In the years after the Compromise of 1877 the swelling sense of
national unity between North and South was accomplished at the ex-

pense of the Negroes, their subordination in the American social order being the price paid for this compromise. And in this context, the development of American industrial capitalism and the alliance of Northern and Southern capital were important factors in the Compromise of 1877 and the subsequent subordination of Negroes on the Southern scene. Booker T. Washington's Atlanta Compromise of 1895, summing up—in a phraseology acceptable to the dominant elements of the New South—the shift in Negro thought from political to economic action, from immediate integration and protest to self-help, and from rights to duties; and uniting Northern and Southern whites and Negroes upon a common, even if ambiguous, platform, expressed Negro accommodation to the social conditions implicit in the earlier Compromise of 1877.

CHAPTER II

CHANGING ATTITUDES TOWARD POLITICAL ACTIVITY

Because of increasing disfranchisement in the South and Republican indifference in the North, the years between the Compromise of 1877 and the Compromise of 1895 were characterized by a growing disillusionment with political activity and with the Republican party. Negroes began to place more emphasis upon economic development and less on political action. By the 1890's some had come to favor the acceptance of literacy and/or property qualifications impartially applied to both races as a condition of voting in the South. A few publicly advocated accommodation to Democratic leadership in the South, while a distinguished minority in the North rebelled against the Republicans and seriously attempted co-operation with the party of Grover Cleveland. Nevertheless, it is important to emphasize that despite dissatisfaction most Negroes remained Republicans in their sympathies and that the tradition of political participation always retained considerable vitality.

Even during Reconstruction some Southern Negroes had supported the "Conservatives" or Democrats. Some of these were genuine conservatives because of their close connections with paternalistic upper-class whites, others were disillusioned with Republican corruption, and some were chiefly political opportunists. From time to time there were rumblings of dissatisfaction within Republican ranks. For example, Senator Blanche K. Bruce in 1876 received considerable support among Negroes when he criticized the party because the

Senate had failed to seat P. B. S. Pinchback; for a brief period he went so far as to advise Negroes to divide their vote in order to obtain the best political advantage.[1]

After Reconstruction Southern Negroes who stood with the Democrats tended to be of the old servant class, or successful, conservative farmers and businessmen who identified their interests with those of upper-class whites. As Mississippian Gilbert Myers, owner of five or six hundred acres of land and 108 head of cattle, all accumulated since the Civil War, told a Senate committee in 1879, he voted Democratic "because I sympathize with my own self, knowing that I expected to stay with them [sic] to make property if I could, and the South has always been kind to me. My master that I live with I nursed him and slept at his mother's feet and nursed at her breast, so I thought my interest was to stay with the majority of the country who I expected to prosper with." In South Carolina, a few Negro Democrats, generally conservative, unobtrusive artisans, were elected to public office during the late nineteenth century. George M. Mears, for example, last Negro Democrat in the state legislature (1882–92), was a free-born ship carpenter who, like a number of the ante-bellum free people of color, had been a Democrat ever since obtaining the right to vote.[2]

Nor were Negro Republican leaders always averse to working with the Democrats. Both expediency and disenchantment with the Republican policy inclined some of them toward political co-operation with paternalistic upper-class Southern whites, at the very time that conservative Democrats, alarmed at the threat posed by "independent" and agrarian political movements, courted the Negro vote. Furthermore, many Negroes, fearful of the lower-class whites and their leaders, who were often more virulent in their prejudice than the upper classes, preferred the Democrats to the white Independents whom the Arthur administration and Southern lily-white Republicans supported at the expense of the colored politicians. Though Negroes did participate to a significant extent in third-party movements, in the political warfare that followed many sided with the Democrats. In Virginia most Negroes at first voted for the Readjustors in the late 1870's and early 1880's; later the Conservatives made serious inroads into the Negro vote. The Populist Movement also resulted in large numbers "voting" Democratic, as whites applied economic pressure, physical intimidation, and fraud. In some cases Negroes voluntarily supported the Democrats. In Georgia, for example, the Democratic gubernatorial candidate of 1892, William J. Northen, appealed to Negroes on the basis of his antilynching stand. The majority of the state's Negro political leaders supported him, and one observer claimed that while Negroes voted on both sides, "of the state as a whole it may be said that Populism was defeated by the colored voters espousing the Democratic side." Moreover, during the 1880's and 1890's in the "black" counties of both Mississippi and South Carolina there appeared the practice known as fusion—of dividing the offices between Negro Republicans and white Democrats, so that the former held a seat or so in the legislature and a share of the less important local positions.[3] In Georgia, A.M.E. Bishop Henry Turner, noted for his ringing denunciation of the Democratic legislature which had expelled him and the other Negro members in 1868, was so disillusioned with the Republicans and so pleased with Cleveland's policy in regard to Negro officeholders, that he actively sided with the Democrats. His reward came when his fellow-Georgian Hoke Smith, Secretary of the Interior in Cleveland's second administration, appointed three of his close relatives to office.[4]

While the majority of Northern Negroes remained loyal to the Republicans, significant criticism and even some defections were evident in the North during the late 1870's and early 1880's. Among the voices raised were those of two former abolitionist leaders, Peter H. Clark and George T. Downing. Clark, a high-school principal in Cincinnati, had been a Republican from 1854 until he joined the Liberal Republicans in 1872. He insisted that his support for the Democrats was not at variance with his desire for full citizenship rights for Negroes. As he put it in 1885, he did not think it wise for the Negro vote to be "concentrated in one party," for if Negroes would vote with the Democrats when in accord with them on national and local issues much of the antagonism against Negroes would be dissipated.[5]

George Downing, active in the Underground Railroad, in the abolitionist movement, and in the struggle for citizenship rights in Rhode Island, was easily one of the most distinguished American Negroes of the time. As early as 1869 he had believed Negroes entitled to more consideration from the party which emancipated them. But it was not until 1883 that he finally broke with the Republicans, after satisfying himself that leading Northern Democrats favored racial justice. At that time he advocated a division of the colored vote, because he believed it would be better to have "more than one party anxious, concerned, and cherishing the hope that at least part of that vote may be obtained; because division would result in an increased support from all quarters." [6]

By 1883, in fact, considerable disaffection had appeared, due in large part to President Arthur's toying with anti-Negro white Independents in the South.[7] At the national Negro convention held in Louisville in 1883 a resolution endorsing the Republican party caused turbulent debate and was never acted upon. Frederick Douglass felt called upon to defend himself from charges of indifference to the Compromise of 1877, and the convention enthusiastically received his remarks when he called himself "an uneasy Republican," and urged Negroes to follow no party blindly. "If the Republican party cannot stand a demand for justice and fair play," he added, "it ought to go down." The Pittsburgh convention of April 1884 after sharp debate passed a compromise resolution declaring it inexpedient to endorse any party or presidential candidate.[8] In Pennsylvania a colored Independent party included men like the abolitionist Robert Purvis and William Still of Underground Railroad fame.[9] In Massachusetts, James M. Trotter, a former lieutenant in the famous 54th Massachusetts regiment, broke with the party and resigned his post as assistant superintendent of the registered letter department in the Boston post office—a political appointment he had held for eighteen years. Later, Cleveland appointed Trotter recorder of deeds for the District of Columbia, the highest post held by Negroes in that period. About the same time the Democratic governor Benjamin F. Butler, who had received a substantial Negro vote on the basis of his war record, appointed the Harvard Law School graduate and former member of the state legislature and of the Boston Common Council George L. Ruffin judge of the city court of Charlestown, making him the first Negro judge in the North. From then on the number of Negro "Independents" in Massachusetts gradually increased, and under the leadership of Trotter, Ruffin, and Downing New England possessed an active group of Cleveland Democrats.[10]

In New York there was also a small group of able Democrats, led by James C. Matthews, an Albany lawyer who in 1874 had opened the city's white schools to Negroes by instituting a legal suit. Like most of the leading figures in the Colored Democracy he was a former

Republican, but by the beginning of Cleveland's first administration he was regarded as the most prominent Negro Democrat. Also prominent in New York was another lawyer, T. McCants Stewart, a free-born Charlestonian who had taken his A.B. and LL.B. at the University of South Carolina during the Reconstruction before coming to New York to serve as pastor at Bethel A.M.E. Church. In 1885, returning dissatisfied after two years of teaching in Liberia College, he settled in Brooklyn, where he practiced law, served on the Board of Education 1891–95, and actively supported Cleveland. He thought it neither manly nor politic for Negroes to cling to the hem of the garments of the Republican party, to whom the Negroes owed no debt of gratitude for what was simply a war measure. Negroes should make their political decisions on the basis of the several major issues which concerned the country; solidarity in politics merely brought hatred from opponents and the contempt of friends. In the 1890's Cleveland's record of appointments was a favorite theme of Democrats in New York as elsewhere; and in addition, the Colored Democrats of the Empire State had come to argue that Negroes should support the Democrats partly because they were more sympathetic to labor than the Republicans were. As the platform of the New York State Cleveland League, of which James C. Matthews was the president, put it in 1892, the Democratic party was the "poor man's party . . . the exponent of labor, which is our lot." [11]

Two leading editors during the 1880's, W. Calvin Chase of the Washington *Bee,* and T. Thomas Fortune of New York were both highly critical of the Republicans and counseled a division of the vote, though political realities and perhaps campaign subsidies kept them in the Republican column at election times. To the highly volatile Chase, who had a varied career in government and newspaper work before taking over the *Bee* in 1883, it appeared that Negroes had been loyal to a party that had "deserted, disowned, and frowned upon the colored people of the South in 1876," and that thereafter had steadily ignored the cardinal principles of its campaign platforms. He charged that "the present managed Republican Party is a little, if anything, better than the hidebound slave-holding Democratic Party." A few months later, however, he regarded Democratic activities as ample evidence of the danger involved in making any concessions to the party. While in the spring of 1884 he regarded Negroes as the balance of power in the forthcoming election, by September he was enthusiastically supporting Blaine and accusing "the so-called Negro Democrats" of attempting to mislead an oppressed race. But scarcely was Cleveland elected than he urged Southern Negroes to divide their vote, and asserted that "it is the folly of the Republican Party which necessarily compels us to be independent." [12] Chase's erratic course, symptomatic of Negro discouragement in the face of growing Republican indifference, continued into the next century.

Far abler was Timothy Thomas Fortune, the leading Negro journalist from the middle 1880's until he sold the New York *Age* to Fred R. Moore and Booker T. Washington in 1907. A native of Florida, he had led a varied career in politics and teaching in his native state, Delaware, and Washington, D.C. (where he attended Howard University for a year), before coming to New York to undertake his editorial career in 1880. He was soon arraigning the selfish Republican party for its disastrous Reconstruction policy of "revolting peculation and crime," and for its "base ingratitude, subterfuge and hypocrisy to its black partisan allies," whom it left to the mercy of their enemies. While nothing but evil existed in the "Bourbon Democratic Party," still a Negro could be an independent Democrat. He supported Blaine in 1884 only because the Democratic policy was even worse than the Republican, and the election of Cleveland left him indifferent because neither party evinced any great concern for the Negro's welfare. Again in 1886 he urged Negroes to be active in all parties and to act on the motto *"Race first: then party."* Though the *Age* endorsed Harrison in 1888, it afterward criticized his administration for the defeat of the Lodge and Blair bills and for the lily-white movement in the party. Yet Fortune effectively posed the political dilemma facing Negroes when he asked in 1889:

> But where is the use of dwelling on the question now? The Southern white men have made up their minds to drive the Negro to the wall, and the Negro must oppose to the Democrats an unbroken front as long as this remains true. As long as the Republican Party stands for everything in this respect that the Democratic Party opposes the colored voters will remain in sentiment . . . Republicans as solid . . . as a Chinese Wall. . . . When the Democratic Party ceases to be a party of unmitigated cussedness the discussion of the question of a division of voters in the South will be in order.[13]

Negroes were pleased and impressed with Cleveland's generous policy in regard to officeholding. But, though a few organs like the

Indianapolis *World* were Democratic, by and large the Negro press remained loyal to but critical of the Republicans. Few went as far as Fortune and Chase in espousing independence. Representative of the abler journalists was Harry C. Smith, editor of the Cleveland *Gazette* and an active politician who served three terms in the state legislature (1894–98, 1900–1902), where he sponsored the Ohio Civil Rights Law of 1894 and the antilynching law of 1896. He constantly criticized the Republicans for their Southern policy. While Smith did not repudiate the party, and only rarely even intimated that a division of the vote might be advisable, a few weeks before the election of 1892 he went so far as to declare: "Let our newspapers tell the people . . . to stay in the ranks of the Republican Party, but act, politically, on election day, as did Hanna and his Republican followers in recent years here in Cleveland when they assisted in the election of Mayor John Farley and Mayor Tom L. Johnson, both Democrats." [14]

Usually, those who championed division of the vote, political independence, or support for the Democrats were forthright agitators for the rights of Negroes rather than accommodators or conciliators. This was even true of men like W. A. Pledger of Georgia who aligned themselves politically with conservative southern Democrats. However, at least two individuals are notable for enunciating this political program in an accommodating framework. One of them was C. H. J. Taylor, a lawyer and editor of the Kansas City *World,* who served briefly as minister resident in Liberia in 1887 and later became a lawyer and newspaper editor in Atlanta. Taylor's *Whites and Blacks* (1889), breathed a spirit of conciliation toward the white South. He was highly critical of Radical Reconstruction. Negroes, he maintained, had "voted in the white political scum they thought to be their dearest friends, but who . . . proved themselves their greatest enemies." All racial troubles, he continued, originated in politics. Political emancipation would come if Negroes ceased exhibiting prejudice toward whites and showed that they understood individual responsibility as citizens and that they appreciated favors conferred by Southern white men. If the Negroes were so stupid as to vote blindly with the Republicans rather than for the interests of their section, proving themselves unforgiving and refusing "the olive branch of political peace offered by Grover Cleveland . . . then by all means disfranchise them, and that speedily."

Another outstanding man who favored a division of the vote was J. C. Price, president of Livingstone College, Salisbury, North Carolina, and one of the top half dozen leaders between 1890 and his premature death in 1894. Price urged independence in politics as part of a mildly conciliatory policy toward the South. Writing in the *Independent* in 1891, he predicted that the last decade of the century would find the Negro "voting for good men and wise measures, rather than for mere partisans as such." Price thought highly of Cleveland and felt that since Democrats were dominant in the South, Negroes "as far as is consistent with the instincts of manhood . . . would do well to harmonize with that element . . . even at the sacrifice of nonessentials." [15]

Most Negro leaders, however, though increasingly critical of the Republican Party, never left it. They easily prevented an "Independent" convention called in 1888 from passing strong Democratic resolutions.[16] Frederick Douglass probably represented the typical development of Negro thinking on the problem in these years. In 1872 he had made his famous analogy that the Republican party was the deck, all else the sea; but as early as 1874 he was admitting that there was much to criticize. Disappointed in the treatment he received at Grant's hands, he nevertheless remained loyal and was appointed marshal of the District of Columbia by Hayes and recorder of the deeds by Garfield. Later, Harrison made him minister to Haiti. During election times he waxed bitter about Negro Democrats. Writing to D. A. Straker, formerly an important legal and political figure in South Carolina who had been critical of the Compromise of 1877 and who had espoused the cause of political independence but had made a qualified return to the Republicans by 1888, he said: "Few things pain me more than to hear any colored man talking of voting the Democratic ticket this fall. Such talk . . . is rank with treason to the . . . best interest of the colored race." Yet Douglass continued to have misgivings about the Republicans. Speaking before Washington's noted Bethel Literary and Historical Association in 1889 he held that past experience made Negroes doubtful that the Harrison administration and a Republican Congress would do anything about Negro rights. To Douglass it was purely a moral question. "The success of the Republican Party does not depend mainly upon its economic theories. . . . Its appeal is to the conscience of the Nation, and its success is to be sought and found in firm adherence to the humane and progressive ideas of liberty and humanity which called it into being." He was rather indifferent to Cleveland's victory in 1892, but he never left the party and he never urged Negroes to divide their vote.[17]

Actually, the turn of the decade marked the high point of Negro support for the Democrats before the elections of 1908 and 1912. Many might protest at Republican policy and praise Cleveland; even an official church organ like the A.M.E. Church *Review* might say on occasion that the only way to make the vote of the Southern Negro valuable was to divide it.[18] But in view of the final accomplishment of disfranchisement in the South, the increasing indifference of Northern opinion, the small size of the Negro population in the North, where independence might have been effective if there had been more Negro voters, and the traditional attachment of the rank and file and most leaders to the Republicans, the attempt to divide the Negro vote was doomed to failure.

At most only a significant minority had espoused the idea. And a number of these returned to the Republicans in the early 1890's. Downing in 1891 had become critical of the Democrats, though he continued to believe that Negroes should use both parties realistically rather than passively support the Republicans.[19] Fortune by the 1890's had turned his back on independence. The important Indianapolis *Freeman,* which since its founding in 1888 had supported the Democrats, in 1891 became a Republican paper. An important defection was T. McCants Stewart, who in 1895, upon being "frozen out" of a job by objecting Democrats, returned to the Republicans.[20] Another significant figure, H. C. C. Astwood of Louisiana, a former Republican and consul in Trinidad under President Arthur and appointed consul to Santo Domingo in Cleveland's first administration, angrily returned to the Republican Party when the Senate rejected his appointment as consul to Calais.[21] Indeed, much of the discouragement undoubtedly lay with Democratic appointment policy, the *Bee* reporting that Matthews would have succeeded John R. Lynch as fourth auditor of the Treasury if Secretary Carlisle had not objected. But the unfortunate realities of the situation were succinctly stated by a group of Wisconsin citizens in 1892, who, "being cognizant of the fact that we have not received that protection, recognition and justice at the hands of the Republican Party, guaranteed to us by the

Constitution of the United States, [are] yet unfailing in our devotion to this party and its principles." [22]

Increasingly, as disfranchisement grew and officeholding decreased, Negroes became disillusioned with politics and placed more and more emphasis on economic and moral development as a substitute for and as a prerequisite to political activity. In fact economic improvement was primarily regarded as a temporary accommodation to realities, and an indirect technique for achieving political rights, for it was widely held that if Negroes achieved high moral character and an imposing economic position, they would impress whites so favorably that they would be freely accorded their rights. For some individuals, but by no means all, this tactic was coupled with a conciliatory approach to the white South, and a tendency to soft-pedal Negro grievances, while blaming Negroes themselves for their low status in society. It was also associated, as will be demonstrated in the next chapter, with a philosophy of self-help and racial solidarity.

The drift of ideas became clear after the Democratic victory in 1884 resulted in the prospect of sharply curtailed political opportunities. In a symposium conducted by the A.M.E. Church *Review* on the Democratic return to power, Democratic supporters such as Downing, Clark, and William Still counseled attention to economic development. Downing asked if, instead of "unnecessarily and unprofitably antagonizing his neighbors," would it not be wiser for the Negro to concentrate on the acquisition of wealth and learning. Still observed that having found political action a broken reed, the Negro "of late has been taking less stock in politics and more in education and land. And upon the whole the present prospect of his becoming a success in the land of his nativity ... was never more favorable." Moreover, while Negroes should certainly air their grievances, he urged them "to make friends with thine adversary ... if it can possibly be done without a sacrifice of self-respect and manly character." [23]

The *Review* encouraged contributions of this sort in the following years, though it also supported the Lodge Federal Elections Bill, the agitation of the Afro-American League, and the Republican party. On one occasion it even maintained that in many localities where colored landowners "have been forcibly kept out of politics, they have turned attention to accumulating property, and so unjust treatment has proved a blessing in disguise. Christianity, morality, courage, and industry are sure to produce wealth, and any people who become strong in these qualities are sure to move upward among men." Other editors were also inconsistent. Thus, both Chase and Fortune in moments of discouragement urged Negroes to eschew politics. Fortune once wrote in words suggestive of his later friend Booker T. Washington:

No people ever became great and prosperous by devoting their infant energies to politics. . . . We were literally born into political responsibility . . . before we had mastered the economic conditions which underlie these duties. . . . We have not performed one single civil duty correctly because the economic condition of the race was so absolutely without foundation. . . . We began citizenship at the apex instead of at the base—began to rule men before we had learned to rule ourselves. . . . The moral, mental and material condition of the race must be properly looked after before we can hope to establish any sort of status in the politics of this country.

Usually, however, Fortune took a directly contrary position, as when he declared that since history showed that "industrial condition is regulated, directly or indirectly by the political condition of the people," disfranchisement was obviously the cause of the Negro's economic plight.[24]

Ex-Senator Blanche K. Bruce, a wealthy Mississippian, but a person who carefully looked after his own political preferment under Republican administrations until he died in 1897 (serving as Register of the Treasury and Recorder of the Deeds), while out of office in the 1880's lectured frequently on "The Race Problem," emphasizing "that the race needs now more than anything else . . . material and educational growth." Other advocates of the economics-before-politics point of view, such as C. H. J. Taylor, T. McCants Stewart, and Rev. J. W. E. Bowen combined it with an accommodating ideology toward Southern disfranchisement. Bowen, a professor at the Methodist Church North's Gammon Theological Seminary in Atlanta, in 1894 congratulated William Still upon his "refutation" of Douglass' advocacy of political activity and said that he himself had invariably seen that the solution could never be found in politics, that moral excellence, industry, and the power to contribute to the nation were to be the important factors in Negro progress. Indeed, he regretted that the Negro had been "dragged from the plow to the legislature," to become "drunken with the new wine of political power." [25]

On the other hand, considerable sentiment for political participation continued. While the individuals cited represented a substantial and growing body of thought among Negro leaders, political rights remained important in the thinking even of many who stressed economic development as a temporary substitute or prerequisite for political action. In discouraged moments a man like Chase might counsel avoiding politics, but he was an avid dabbler in politics and a frustrated office seeker. Both he and Fortune were notoriously inconsistent and often agitated on the question of political rights. Some editors, like Harry C. Smith of the Cleveland *Gazette,* consistently harped upon the importance of political activity. In the North in fact, Negro officeholding increased during the 1880's. In Illinois until the present, and in Massachusetts and Ohio until about 1900, Negroes sat regularly in the state legislature—usually one or two at a time.

Even in the South political participation continued to a remarkable extent and was temporarily reinvigorated by the agrarian revolt in the 1890's. Negroes sat in the common council of Richmond until 1896, and in the Georgia legislature into the twentieth century. In spite of lily-white efforts Negroes continued to hold leading positions in the Republican party in a number of Southern states. In South Carolina W. H. Deas, in Georgia W. A. Pledger, in Mississippi the James J. Hill-John R. Lynch-Blanche K. Bruce triumvirate, in Texas Norris Wright Cuney played important roles in party affairs. South Carolina sent a Negro representative to Congress through most of the 1880's and early 1890's; Virginia had one in the Congress of 1889–91; and George H. White was representing North Carolina as late as 1901.

Moreover, Negroes gave significant support to third party movements with a radical, agrarian tinge. The majority of Virginia Negroes sided with the Readjustors in the elections of 1879, 1881, and 1883, and elsewhere in the early 1880's an impressive minority supported the Greenbackers. Later, many participated actively in the Populist Movement, and in several states the Populists made definite appeals to the Negro vote. Although in some states, as in the case of the Greenbackers, Populists ran fusion tickets with the lily-white rather than the black-and-tan faction of the Republican party, and although a number of leading Negroes supported the Conservative Democrats rather than the third party, in North Carolina, at least, fusion was notable in that it resulted in the election of Negroes to Congress and to local offices. Because of deeply ingrained prejudice among the white Populists—a prejudice the Conservatives skillfully exploited in their attempt to undermine the agrarians—and because in most cases the majority of Negroes were either unable or unwilling to support them, the Populists became disillusioned with their policy of inter-racial co-operation. In short, the net result of the Populist revolt in the South, and the increased political activity which it brought about, seemed to be an embitterment of race relations, and the consolidation of the Southern race system, particularly the constitutional disfran-chisement of the Negro. Georgia's Watson in time turned from an enthusiastic supporter of Negro rights to a vicious Negrophobe. And in North Carolina the Democrats destroyed the fusion alliance by an appeal to white supremacy in the election of 1898. Its aftermath was the Wilmington, North Carolina, race riot that did so much to tempo-rarily disillusion Negroes with the value of political activity.[26]

So strong was the tradition of protest and political activity that articulate opinion was all but unanimous in support of the Lodge Federal Elections Bill of 1890. Protest meetings were held in various parts of the nation, urging passage of the bill. The Afro-American Press Association, representing newspapers from all parts of the country, at its meeting in 1891 expressed regret that the Senate had failed to pass it. The Colored Farmers' Alliance disagreed with the Southern Alliance by favoring the bill. Negroes in Congress supported the proposal, even after the bill's defeat.[27]

Shock and indignation greeted the action of Isaiah Montgomery, founder of the all-Negro town of Mound Bayou, and the lone Negro member of the Mississippi Constitutional Convention of 1890, be-cause of his frankly accommodating stand on the suffrage question. He said that it would be wise to reduce the Negro vote to the point where it would be much smaller than the white vote, by means of literacy and property restrictions, but implied that this would en-courage Negroes to obtain knowledge and wealth and thus permit them to slowly regain the franchise. His rationalization of disfran-chisement brought Montgomery the epithets of "traitor" and "Judas." As Fortune remarked, "No flippant fool could have inflicted such a wound upon our cause as Mr. Montgomery has done in this ad-dress." [28]

Yet the advocacy of literacy qualifications *applied equally to both races* was already gaining respectability. In the very year of Montgomery's address, two of the most distinguished Negro leaders in the country, Virginia Congressman J. Mercer Langston and J. C. Price, proposed such a restriction on the franchise, though at the same time they insisted upon full and equal citizenship rights for Negroes. So also did T. Thomas Fortune himself three years later.[29] Neither these men nor the Negro members of the South Carolina Constitutional Convention of 1895, who made the same proposal, however, were criticized as was Montgomery—probably because they were more explicit about their stand on equal citizenship rights and called for restriction on ignorant whites as well as Negroes.

In fact, the attitudes of the Negro delegates to the Constitutional Convention of 1895 in South Carolina are particularly instructive in this connection, for in this, the second state to enact constitutional disfranchisement, an able leadership had continued to participate in politics and strongly favored the exercise of the franchise. It was the lawyer and post-Reconstruction politician Thomas E. Miller, scion of a free Negro slave-holding family, graduate of Lincoln University, Pennsylvania, 1872, and a member of Congress 1889–91, who had led the opposition in the state senate to the elaborate registration and eight-box ballot law of 1882. An occasional Negro, however, approved this act, as did a conservative editor who wrote "Let the eight box law . . . stand [rather] than to risk the remanding of the state to the clutches of ignorance and rascality." Ex-Congressman Robert Smalls, collector of the Port of Beaufort, represented the viewpoint of most South Carolina leaders when in 1890 he denounced the history of elections in South Carolina since 1874 as "the history of a continued series of murders, outrages, perjury and fraud" and insisted on the right to vote—"a right secured by the organic law of the country." South Carolina's congressmen, Thomas E. Miller and George Washington Murray, both worked for a federal elections law during the early 1890's.

Negro political and religious leaders agitated frantically against disfranchisement during the campaign for the constitutional convention of 1895, appealing to the "better classes" and the national government for assistance. Six were elected to the convention, including Smalls and Miller. All spoke against the suffrage article of the constitution which effected Negro disfranchisement by strict residence qualifications, a poll tax, a literacy test (to which there were property and understanding alternatives), and a list of disfranchising crimes to which Negroes were supposedly especially prone. In their speeches they reviewed the Negroes' services to the country as workers and as soldiers, emphasized their constitutional rights, and attacked the doctrine of white supremacy and the fraudulent nature of the voting provisions. Especially notable, however, was their willingness to support a "straight literacy" qualification (or, as in the case of one of them, with an "an additional or alternative property qualification"), equally applied to both races.[30]

This stand was probably an appeal to those conservative whites who wanted to disfranchise poor whites as well as Negroes and was a tactic employed similarly by Booker Washington later in his appeals to the Louisiana and Alabama constitutional conventions. Moreover, it was a strategic position, for it cut the ground from under those who complained of Negro ignorance or feared Negro domination. It would have eliminated more Negroes than whites from the suffrage, while at the same time it would have saved face for the Negroes and would have held out the hope that as they acquired education and wealth they would be readmitted to the franchise. Such sentiments paved the way for the acceptance of literacy and/or property qualifications by many responsible leaders at the close of the century.

In conclusion then, the majority of Negroes (or at least Negro leaders) favored political participation and the Republican party during these years. A few—some consistently and some inconsistently—espoused the cause of the Democratic party and of dividing the vote, while most were becoming increasingly disillusioned about the Republicans. There was sentiment—particularly in the South—and increasingly vocal, for temporarily eschewing politics, or participating only to a limited extent. Some leaders during the early 1890's came to the conclusion that Negroes should support the idea of literacy and/or property qualifications equitably applied to both races as a device for undercutting white opposition to Negro voting, while holding out the theoretical opportunity for Negroes to vote at a future date, and there was growing interest, even among those who still believed in agitating for civil and political rights, upon developing on an economic and moral plane, so as to assimilate Negroes to white American culture, and thus break down prejudice and discrimination and pave the way for an unopposed re-entry into political life. Above all it must be emphasized that no segment of opinion favored the idea of a permanent or complete limitation upon the Negroes' political rights; rather the retreat from politics was regarded as temporary, and the solutions proposed were thought of as indirect techniques of attacking the race problem—as tactics that would ultimately pave the way for full political equality.

CHAPTER III

ECONOMICS, SELF-HELP, AND RACIAL SOLIDARITY

The years following Reconstruction were characterized by an increasing emphasis on economic activity as a factor in solving the race problem. This view was usually part of a larger complex of ideas that included racial solidarity and self-help. It was based upon the assumption that by the acquisition of wealth and morality—attained largely by their own efforts—Negroes would gain the respect of white men and thus be accorded their rights as citizens. This complex of ideas had been especially popular in the discouraging decade before the Civil War. Although Reconstruction leaders had placed some emphasis on landownership and the virtues of thrift and industry, they had advised racial solidarity and self-help only sporadically. But now, under the growing stresses of the New South, the whole complex was revived.

Prominent among early advocates of this point of view was the noted Episcopal divine, Alexander Crummell, rector of St. Luke's Church in Washington, D.C., and generally regarded as the leading nineteenth-century Negro intellectual. A native of New York, he received an A.B. from Queen's College, Cambridge, in 1853; and though he had earlier been highly critical of the American Colonization Society he went directly from England to Liberia, where he remained for twenty years as a pastor and a teacher noted for his militant espousal of nationalism and colonization. To Crummell in this period American race prejudice and divinely ordained race distinctions made the hope of a great future for Negroes in the United States nothing but a silly dream. Proud of his unmixed Negro ancestry, Crummell throughout his life firmly believed in the future destiny of the race.

Though turning his back on colonization after his return to the United States in 1873, Crummell was eminently fitted to express the philosophy of self-help, solidarity, and race pride. He also accepted the increasing stress on economic and social development in preference to politics and agitation. The close affinity between Crummell's Liberian nationalism and his later advocacy of racial solidarity is superbly illustrated by a sermon—delivered in 1875 and published in 1882—on "The Social Principle Among a People and Its Bearing on Their Progress and Development," the first part of which was practically a verbatim repetition of a sermon given in Liberia in 1859. By the social principle Crummell meant the principle of association which "binds men in unity and brotherhood, in races and churches and nations"—a principle responsible for the greatness of all successful nations. Ruin would follow if Negroes failed to combine their forces. Unfortunately, Negroes were noted for their lack of co-operative effort, particularly in business endeavor. Elaborating at considerable length in the 1875 sermon Crummell held that there were two "heresies" which Negroes must avoid: *"That the colored people of this country should forget as soon as possible that they ARE colored people,"* and *"That colored men should give up all distinctive efforts, as colored men, in schools, churches, associations, and friendly societies."* Until the time came when, in God's plan, prejudice would disappear, Negroes would be a distinct nation in this country, "a 'peculiar people' in this land." Consequently, it was folly to talk of the common heritage and destiny of the American nation. On the contrary Negroes must strive for footing and superiority along racial lines. He regarded his program as a temporary but necessary expedient for the ultimate extinction of caste; but the future of the race depended upon moral elevation, to be obtained through self-help, economic development, and racial organization. Instead of agitating, Negroes should work together, "not for idle political logomacy, but for industrial effort, for securing trades for youth, for joint-stock companies, for manufacturing, for the production of the great staples of the land, and . . . for mental and moral improvement." Organization was prerequisite to the attainment of character, and character in turn would provide power. In fact the acquisition of high, commanding, and masterly character would settle "all the problems of caste . . . though you were ten times blacker than midnight." [1]

Negro conventions of the late 1870's also placed their strongest emphasis on racial solidarity, self-help, and economic advancement. Except for preoccupation with the problem of migration growing out of the Kansas Exodus, the National Conference that met at Nashville in 1879 was typical of such conventions in its ideological outlook. The delegates, many of them the most distinguished leaders in the Negro community, were more concerned with self-help and economic development than with the decline of political and civil rights. It was recognized that

we are to a great extent the architects of our own fortune, and must rely mainly upon our own exertions for success. We, therefore, recommend to the youth of our race the observation of strict morality, temperate habits, and the practice of the acquisition of land, the acquiring of agriculture, of advancing to mercantile positions, and forcing their way into the various productive channels of literature, art, science and mechanics.

This theme preoccupied most speeches given at the convention, though there was some protest against the decline of civil and political rights. Representative was the address of a Chicago lawyer, Ferdinand Barnett, who complained of Negroes expecting more from Negro artisans and merchants than from white ones and insisted that "we must help one another. Our industries must be patronized and our laborers encouraged." Moreover, he urged racial organization to prosecute the "continued warfare for our rights. . . . We are laboring for race elevation and race unity is the all-important factor." [2]

Another delegate to the Convention, John Wesley Cromwell, editor of the *People's Advocate* of Alexandria and Washington, and formerly a missionary teacher and minor politician in Virginia during Reconstruction, was identified with this point of view during the following years. Cromwell, regarding wealth as the basis of American greatness, frankly took his cue from Henry Clay's neo-mercantilism. In 1883 he suggested a Negro American's Protective Policy by which Negroes would, on the basis of racial patriotism, award their work to colored men even where whites would perform it more cheaply, in order to build up colored tradesmen to the point where they could compete with the whites.[3]

The A.M.E. Church *Review,* the leading Negro magazine, gave a good deal of space to articles emphasizing the importance of economic and moral development, self-help, and racial solidarity. Benjamin Tucker Tanner, editor of the A.M.E. *Christian Recorder* 1868–84, and then of the *Review* until he became a bishop in 1888, urged his readers to imitate the Jews who, like Negroes persecuted and thrown back upon themselves, had become the "master of Europe" by advancing along economic lines. He also urged support for the colored press on a racial basis. Even if colored papers were not as well edited as white ones, he believed it to be "the business of every colored man to help make them so; not by a criticism of dubious worth, but by a cash subscription. The one remaining thing for us to do is to stand together." [4]

Of the major newspapers the Washington *Bee* was the most emphatic in its advocacy of economic solidarity and co-operation. The best way to build up Negroes economically, Chase said, was to patronize race business. At a meeting of the Bethel Literary and Historical Association in 1892, some of the most distinguished colored citizens of Washington—including the high-school teachers W. S. Montgomery (later assistant superintendent of schools) and Robert H. Terrell, Dr. Charles B. Purvis, surgeon-in-chief of Freedmen's Hospital, and Professor Kelly Miller of Howard University urged the value of business enterprise, especially of the "co-operative" sort such as banks and insurance companies. Another of the speakers at this meeting was the civic leader Andrew F. Hilyer, who had but recently taken the lead in forming the Union League of Washington in order to advance the "moral, material and financial interests of the colored people . . . by encouraging a spirit of practical cooperation among us." As J. Madison Vance, a New Orleans lawyer, expressed it in a speech in Boston in 1894, "the Negro confronts destiny. He must be the architect of his own fortune. He must demonstrate capacity and independence. . . . Let us stand on our own racial pride and prove our equality by showing the fruits of thrift, talent and frugality." [5]

Increasing interest in economic development and racial solidarity involved some in a conciliatory philosophy toward the white South, but other advocates of these ideas held strongly to doctrines of political rights and protest. For a decreasing minority, economics continued to be subordinate to politics. Fortune carried numerous items about business development, but seldom adverted to it editorially except in his most discouraged moments. The Cleveland *Gazette* frequently carried notices of racial economic enterprises, but criticized racial chauvinism in business enterprise; to Smith segregated business enterprises were no more a remedy for white discrimination than were segregated public schools.[6] Such views as his, however, were in the minority by the end of the century.

While Negro leaders generally were coming to subscribe to a philosophy of thrift and industry that envisaged the elevation of Negroes to an independent entrepreneurial status, there were those who expressed economic doctrines of a more radical tinge, and were more inclined toward economic solidarity among the laboring classes than toward economic solidarity within the race. The Colored Alliance claimed a membership of one million, a significant number participated in the Populist movement, and about 60,000 were members of the Knights of Labor at its height in 1886.[7] Not only did large numbers of Negro farmers and workers view the programs of the Alliance and the Knights and co-operation with members of the white working classes as a solution to their economic problems, but at least a few leaders and intellectuals expressed sympathy with trade unionism and radical economic ideas.

Occasionally, individuals with essentially petit bourgeois ideologies—like Frederick Douglass and John R. Lynch—recognized the evil of "wage slavery" and the essential unity of interests among white and colored workers. They stressed the importance of interracial labor unions in solving the Negro's economic plight, though insisting as John Lynch said, that Negroes should not identify themselves with violence, socialism, or anarchism. As a matter of fact the Knights of Labor received here and there some favorable comments in the Negro press; the *Gazette* for example urged Negroes to join the Knights. Chase and Fortune were also sympathetic, though other journals seemed generally opposed to labor unions.[8]

Like the Colored Farmers' Alliance, which expressed a single-tax philosophy, a small group of intellectuals—notably D. A. Straker, T. McCants Stewart, and T. Thomas Fortune—were influenced to a greater or lesser extent by the work of Henry George.[9] Of these it was Fortune who made the most thoroughgoing application of native reformist thought to the problems of the Negro during the 1880's. He believed that the working classes produced all the wealth of the world, but were exploited by the rich. "What are millionaires, anyway," he asked, "but the most dangerous enemies of society?" At the basis of economic and social miseries lay "land monopoly"—control by the few of the land which belonged to the whole people. After the Civil War, instead of breaking up large plantations as it should have done, and giving the freedmen forty acres and a mule, the American government by the act of emancipation added four millions to the laboring classes to work for the enrichment of vast soulless corporations and for a privileged class of individuals which had usurped the soil from which the working classes had to obtain their subsistence. Consequently, the land that had given birth to chattel slavery was in the hands of unrepentant rebels, "giving birth to *industrial slavery:* a slavery more excruciating in its exactions, more irresponsible in its machinations than any other slavery." Fortune held that Southern white and black workers would recognize their common cause and predicted that the future struggle in the South would be not between Negroes and whites but between capital and labor, between landlord and tenant. And in praising the Knights of Labor for including workers of all races, he saw an imminent conflict of labor against the "odious and unjust tyranny" of capital. "The revolution is upon us, and since we are largely of the laboring population, it is very natural that we should take sides with the labor forces in their fight for a juster distribution of the results of labor." [10]

Not until W. E .B. Du Bois was converted to socialism some twenty years later, did a distinguished Negro leader state with such intellectual vigor the thesis of class conflict and the identity of the interests of the black and white workers. Meanwhile, by the end of the decade, Fortune had veered away from his early radicalism to criticize the Farmers' Alliance and was expressing a program more in consonance with the American middle class tradition.

Fortune's shift of view heralded Negro disillusionment with the radical agrarian and labor movements. The leadership of the American Federation of Labor, which had first discouraged color discrimination, by the end of the century had come to terms with the exclusionist and discriminatory policies of many of its constituent unions.[11] Hopes of Populism had also miscarried. All in all the 1880's marked the high point of Negro interest in the labor movement, and the early 1890's the high point of Negro interest in radical agrarianism. A few intellectuals had been influenced by the doctrines of Henry George. But the passing of the Knights of Labor, the failure of Southern agrarians to wipe out the color line, and a parallel decline of radical leanings among the few outstanding men who had subscribed to them, combined to give Negro thought an even more conservative cast than it otherwise would have had at this time. Both the decline in political fortunes and the failure to achieve unity with the white working classes forced Negroes to turn their greatest efforts toward achieving wealth and middle-class respectability by their own efforts.

If some were groping toward the espousal of a segregated racial economy, others thought they saw advantages in separate schools and churches—at least temporarily until real equality and integration could be achieved. The argument among Negroes over mixed or segregated schools raged during the 1880's, especially in Ohio, where determined efforts resulted in public school desegregation in 1886. The chief issue was the fact that integration was usually at the expense of colored teachers, who were not employed in the mixed systems. Another argument for segregated schools was that Negro children would be taught better by colored teachers, and would be protected from white insults. It was a real dilemma that the Negro community in the North was facing.

So controversial was the matter that the noted Bethel Literary and Historical Association debated the issue for two nights during its first season (1881–82). J. W. Cromwell was among those favoring separate schools, while Dr. C. B. Purvis and George T. Downing led the opposition. The *Gazette* carried the story of the Ohio debate during the 1880's, editor Smith accusing Cincinnati high-school principal Peter H. Clark of defending segregated schools for his own private advantage. Smith stated the case for mixed schools trenchantly enough:

> If there is anything that causes us to advocate mixed schools, it is the unjust discrimination even in the selection of studies . . . where there are separate schools; also discrimination in the matter of salaries . . . , fewer number of school buildings. . . . Separate schools are hothouses of prejudice. . . . The strongest argument in favor of separate schools . . . is that they give employment to our intelligent men and women. True, but wherever mixed schools are possible . . . it is also possible to have mixed teachers.

Eventually, when the mixed school bill became law, Clark lost his job. Marshall W. Taylor, first Negro editor of the Methodist Church

North's *Southwestern Christian Advocate* commented: "We prefer separate schools with colored teachers to mixed schools without them, every time." The influential A.M.E. *Christian Recorder* was also concerned over the loss of jobs occasioned by the closing of segregated schools. Its editor, Benjamin F. Lee (a former president of Wilberforce University who was elected bishop in 1892), feared the campaign for mixed schools—schools that would teach little or nothing about Negro goodness or greatness, schools that would be taught chiefly by people unconnected with and not interested in the life of their Negro pupils.

In Washington Calvin Chase of the *Bee* denounced advocates of mixed schools for lacking confidence in teachers of their own race and claimed that segregated schools would be necessary until Negroes were accorded their full rights. He was ably supported by the high-school principal Francis L. Cardozo, a graduate of the University of Edinburgh, former secretary of state and state treasurer in South Carolina, and fourth auditor of the United States Treasury, 1879–84. Cardozo denied that the separate school would perpetuate color distinctions, but felt that by giving an incentive to study, employment to Negro teachers, and decent treatment to students, it would elevate the race. "The mere fact of separation does not necessarily involve inferiority," he said. He believed that the Jews, by devoting themselves to an internal development, had dissipated the prejudice against them; and he regarded the A.M.E. Church as having "done more for real equality" by developing a leadership that would be able to function in integrated situations than could have been accomplished if a separate church had never been formed. He advocated separate schools and churches only as a means to an end, but until Negroes could enter white institutions on terms of complete equality, he thought it preferable to maintain segregated institutions. Some were even more extreme. C. H. Phillips, editor of the Colored Methodist Episcopal *Christian Index* and later a C.M.E. bishop, urged self-segregation in both social and religious organizations. When in 1895 the Women's Press Club of Georgia withdrew from the National Federation of Women's Clubs because three Negro clubs had been admitted, he deplored "the growing disposition on the part of the Negro to force his way into white institutions where he is not wanted." It was his view that since the two races were "peculiarly constituted," separate institutions were an "absolute necessity." [12]

Not only did certain Negroes defend the segregated churches, but others were forced to accept segregation within the "white" churches, notably in the Episcopal and Northern Methodist denominations. As a whole Negro Methodists resented the policy of segregated conferences. In the Episcopal Church, where many dioceses kept the Negro congregations in a subordinate position, a Conference of Church Workers Among Colored People, organized under Crummell's leadership in 1883, proposed an independent Missionary Plan, under which the Negro congregations of a diocese would be directly responsible to the general conference, rather than existing as mere appendages to local white churches. Though Negroes were thus willing to accept segregation as long as they were accorded some status and control over their affairs, the general conference avoided the issue. In both churches, moreover, the question of a Negro bishop for the Negro members was also agitated unsuccessfully.[13]

Philosophies of economic chauvinism and separate institutions were part of a larger complex of ideas involving self-help, race pride, and group solidarity, though it must be emphasized that such ideas were usually regarded as being a tactic in the struggle for ultimate citizenship rights. As a matter of fact, the themes of race pride and unity grew greatly in popularity during the 1880's and 1890's. In 1883 the Bethel Literary Association held an exciting debate on the subject— a debate that would have been unlikely fifteen years later, when these ideas had become commonly accepted. Heated discussion developed over a paper with the thesis that in stressing race pride Negroes were apt to neglect the more important task of individual development. Cromwell thought that "the material defect in the individual theory is that white people will not let you get rid of the idea of race." Cardozo hoped that the two races would assimilate, but he frankly admitted that the colored people must work together as a unit until accorded their rights. And J. C. Price believed that in their upward struggle colored men should not lose sight of the fact that they were Negroes any more than the Irish, the Germans, or the French lost sight of their nationality. The A.M.E. *Review* devoted considerable space to the subject. A frequent contributor often emphasized race pride and independence and once said: "The race must furnish its own models, manifest its inherent virtues, display a manly prowess and conquer as others have done." And C. H. J. Taylor, while urging conciliatory attitudes toward the white South, complained that Negroes hated themselves, despised their own folk songs, bleached their skin, and straightened their hair. "We have no reason to complain," he said, "until we take more pride in our own." [14]

Accompanying this emphasis on race pride was an interest in race history. The Negro history movement had developed in the ante-bellum period out of two needs felt by Negroes in their subordinate status in the American social order: the need to assert and prove their equality with whites as one means of convincing whites of their worthiness for political and civil rights, and the need to give themselves a sense of dignity and pride of race to offset the inferiority doctrines of the whites and to stimulate a group solidarity. These two purposes were not necessarily unrelated, for it was often argued that Negroes needed racial pride and solidarity in order to organize effectively for the struggle for integration. On the other hand separatist and emigrationist movements have been characterized by strong historical interests.

Out of these two needs developed what we might call a cultural nationalism. The ethnic dualism pervading Negro thought is particularly evident among the vindicators and historians to be discussed. Those who looked upon their work as necessary to solidify the Negro group in its struggle for equality and at the same time to convince whites of the equality of races in order to open the door to full integration, ranged from amalgamationists to what we call today cultural pluralists—people who hold to the idea that all groups have, as ethnic entities, something distinctive to contribute to the totality of American culture and should therefore be accorded full participation in American democracy. Others emphasized the glories of the racial past as justification for maintaining racial integrity or for extreme nationalist and emigrationist movements like those of the 1850's or like that of Marcus Garvey after World War I.

Ante-bellum writers had developed various scriptural and historical arguments to document their thesis about Negro accomplishments and capacity—arguments that formed the foundation of Negro historical thought until World War I. Negroes, it was asserted, were descended from Ham, whose name meant black or swarthy. However, contrary to much white thinking, several Biblical arguments demonstrated that Negroes inherited no curse from Ham. Since Ham was a Negro, it followed that all his descendants were—and these included most of the civilized peoples of the ancient Near East. The oldest civilizations were those of Ethiopia—"hoary Meroe"—and Egypt, and European civilization is ultimately derived from them through Greece and Rome. They claimed that most great men of antiquity born in Africa and a number of others were frequently listed as Negroes—including Cyrus, Plato, Caesar, and, less often, Jesus. For the more recent past evidences of Negro ability were presented by such European writers as the ex-slave Juan Latino, sixteenth-century Latin professor at the University of Granada, Alexander Pushkin, Alexander Dumas, and Robert Browning. Toussaint l'Ouverture and the history of Haiti and Liberia proved the Negroes' capacity for self-government. Americans like Benjamin Banneker, Phyllis Wheatley, Richard Allen, Frederick Douglass, Harriet Tubman, and a host of talented ministers, abolitionists, and later on businessmen and political leaders, as well as Alexander Hamilton were cited as examples of Negro achievement. Moreover, Negroes had fought with valor and distinction in all of the nation's wars—from Bunker to San Juan Hill. Naturally, this has been a composite picture. Some authors emphasized the scriptural and antique; others the American and recent; some included both. Some made extreme claims; others did not.

Two important post-Emancipation historians, William Wells Brown (author of three works, culminating in *The Rising Son: Or the Antecedents and Advancement of the Colored Race,* 1874), and George Washington Williams, who did the first scholarly history of the Negro in the United States (*History of the Negro Race in America,* 1883), wrote to provide an argument for integration. Williams, a preacher, lawyer, and member of the Ohio legislature said his book was written in the hope "that the day will hasten when there shall be no North, no South, no Black, no White—but all American citizens, with equal duties and equal rights." Subsequent writers placed more emphasis upon race pride and solidarity in the study of Negro history. Such was the avowed purpose of William T. Alexander's *History of the Colored Race in America* which ran through several editions in the period; of Joseph E. Hayne, A.M.E. minister and author of *The Negro in Sacred History* (1887); and of Reverend Rufus L. Perry, a Baptist editor and minister in Brooklyn, who wrote *The Cushite: or the Children of Ham* (1887). E. A. Johnson, a Raleigh North Carolina lawyer, businessman and school principal, summarized this point of view very well in his rather popular *School History of the Negro*

Race in America: "It must, indeed, be a stimulus to any people to be able to refer to their ancestors as distinguished in deeds of valor, and particularly so to the colored people . . . a race of people once the most powerful on earth."

In general, there was an increasing interest in Negro history during this period. The Bethel Literary and Historical Association opened its first meeting with a paper on the Egyptians, and frequently thereafter entertained papers on historical topics. Of the journals, the A.M.E. Church *Review* was especially notable for its attention to historical matters. So strong was the interest in Negro history by the middle nineties that even the extreme assimilationist, Harry C. Smith of the Cleveland *Gazette,* could urge a reading of race history to give "a proper pride of race and self." As Straker summed it up: "There is enough history of the Negro race to make a Negro proud of his race. . . . Why not then teach the Negro child more of himself and less of others, more of his elevation and less of his degradation? This only can produce true pride of race, which begets mutual confidence and unity." [15]

At times the emphasis on race pride and solidarity approached a kind of nationalism. Writers frequently used the term nation or nationality in referring to Negroes. But the significance of this usage and the degree of ethnocentrism implied are often in doubt. Terms such as race and nation were used interchangeably in the confused pseudo-anthropology of the late nineteenth century. In spite of the fact that prejudice and discrimination made Negroes aware that they were a distinct ethnic group in American society, the American democratic and equalitarian traditions have served to discourage extreme forms of ethnocentrism. Thus, Negroes often loosely compared themselves to other races or nations or peoples. From time to time the words nation and nationality crept into declarations of Negro conventions and the like. Ordinarily, Negroes viewed themselves as a distinct group or nationality because they were set apart by other Americans, though they themselves actually wished to be accepted into American society. That the usage of the term "nationality" was often of the vaguest can be inferred from a statement of the extremely assimilationist Cleveland *Gazette* on January 9, 1886: "Like other nationalities constituting the American family, we have struggled for constitutional government and constitutional liberty." In any event all this is evidence of the essential ambivalence of Negroes in their identification with both race and nation. On the other hand, full-fledged nationalist sentiment, involving a complete repudiation of American society, had usually characterized emigrationist movements.

In the years between the Compromise of 1877 and the Compromise of 1895 emphasis upon group loyalty, race pride, and racial solidarity, upon a sort of cultural pluralism—all evidence of ethnocentrism or "nationalism,"—visibly increased. The idea of nationalism was frequently expressed, for example, in connection with the appeal to economic racial solidarity. In extreme form John H. Smythe, a Washington lawyer, expressed sentiments of racial separatism and distinctiveness. Smythe, a member of the North Carolina Constitutional Convention of 1875 and minister to Liberia 1875–85, in an address in 1887 complained:

> If there is any fault with us it is that we are always aping somebody else. . . . The negro has not this love for his country [Africa] and it is unfortunate; even his virtues and his vices are the white man's. Race allegiance is compatible with the highest patriotism. The Negro is now a distinct, and ever will be a distinct race in this country. Blood—not language and religion—makes social distinctions. We are therefore bound by every drop of blood that flows in our being, and by whatever of self-respect you and I individually and collectively possess, to make ourselves —not on the pattern of any other race, but actuated by our peculiar genius in literature, religion, commerce and social intercourse—a great people.[16]

Smythe then apparently viewed Negroes as a distinct nationality within American society, which should be keenly aware of its racial ties to Africa.

Smythe was also an outspoken opponent of intermarriage.[17] Indeed, related to this matter of racial pride and solidarity, were attitudes on the question of intermarriage. Generally, Negroes have regarded the prohibition of intermarriage as an insult to their dignity as men and citizens, but have opposed the practice in specific instances on the grounds of race pride. They have in fact been ambivalent toward the idea of ultimate amalgamation, and they have carefully distinguished between civil rights and "social equality." Frederick Douglass' second marriage, to a white woman, in 1884, caused considerable commotion, most Negro commentators opposing it. On the other hand, certain Negro leaders such as Fortune, Greener, Dr. C. B. Purvis (who himself had a white wife), Blanche K. Bruce, and Judge Ruffin rushed to his defense. Declared Ruffin:

The negro must go; his fate is sealed; he must be swallowed up and merged in the mass of Southern people. . . . This thought will not now be well received by the negro; his hope has been to build up his race, to vindicate his people. It will be less favorably received by the white man . . . , but, nevertheless, the merging . . . is inevitable.[18]

These views are related to the question of cultural assimilation and what we now call cultural pluralism. Although there was an increasing emphasis upon the positive values of racial separatism, some still actively championed immediate assimilation into American society, and eventual integration remained the avowed goal of most separatists. Men like George T. Downing optimistically looked forward to a time when Negroes would be fully accepted, and to the end of his life he predicted amalgamation as the ultimate solution. H. C. C. Astwood wanted an end to segregation at once in both church and school. He felt that Cardozo's ideas on the subject would "in the end create for the colored man the very position he seeks to escape from. Separate institutions are more injury to the colored race . . . than any other influence." [19] But such ideas were becoming more and more in the minority.

Broadly speaking, while all did not hold to the entire complex of ideas of race pride and solidarity, of economic development and self-help, of the value in segregated social institutions, each of these viewpoints was growing in popularity, and there was a marked tendency for them to cluster together. However, this complex of ideas was not necessarily held to the exclusion of interest in agitation for civil rights and political activity. While some, most notably Booker T. Washington, employed a philosophy of economy, morality, self-help, and solidarity as part of an accommodating technique, often these ideas were frankly declared to be a temporary detour, an indirect route to the goal of rights and integration, or a supplemental rather than an exclusive approach to the race problem. There was, of course, no contradiction between an ideology of cultural pluralism and fighting for full citizenship rights. Race pride, solidarity, and self-help were to be used directly in the struggle for the ballot and civil rights, since Negroes must do for themselves what whites were no longer willing to do. A significant number of important individuals subscribed to the whole, or nearly whole, spectrum of ideas ranging from assimilation to racial solidarity, from agitation and political activity to economy and morality, from the desirability of segregated institutions to the malignancy of Jim Crow laws. What distinguished their thought from that of the typical Reconstruction leader was a greater emphasis on economy and even more markedly on racial pride and solidarity and self-help.

A sampling of several distinguished individuals will illustrate these points. J. W. Cromwell and Calvin Chase not only advocated the middle-class virtues, economic nationalism, and all-Negro schools, but also agitated against injustices and urged political activity. The Indianapolis *Freeman* impartially advocated all types of action: editorials on August 30, 1890, for example, counseled racial unity, morality, education, good citizenship, "an intelligent use of our political advantages," thrift, investment in business, and opposition to Jim Crow cars. Jere Brown, a member of the Ohio legislature in the mid 1880's, urged racial unity to halt a movement for separate schools in Ohio in 1894. W. M. Alexander, secretary of the Baltimore Brotherhood of Liberty formed in 1885 to fight discrimination, counseled concerted action in business enterprises until their economic power would force recognition of the Negroes' citizenship rights. Benjamin F. Lee and C. H. Phillips, who favored segregated institutions, spoke out against legal segregation. Phillips actively entered into the fight against Jim Crow cars in Kentucky, spoke out against a Florida law forbidding interracial private schools, and favored the New York Civil Rights Bill. Crummell still minimized the value of political activity, still emphasized the development of moral character, and above all still insisted on the prime necessity of "social cohesion," the lack of which, he said in 1894, had proven the most formidable obstacle to the elevation of the race. He held that "no new people leap suddenly and spontaneously into senatorial seats or cabinet positions" and that the difficult road upward would entail arduous labor, patience, "quiet apprenticeship in humble duties" and the clear demonstration of ability. But he also denounced caste as "the canker of diseased souls," and by the close of the 1880's he was ready to say that "in this land the crucial test of the race-problem is the civil and political rights of the black man"; the nation, not the Negro, was on trial.[20]

D. A. Straker, who had moved from South Carolina to Detroit, in his *New South Investigated* (1888), roundly criticized political conditions, race prejudice, and economic oppression. He called the Democratic governments of the South a usurpation, and the exercise of citizenship rights there a mockery. Whites, he maintained, would have to be educated to the idea that Negroes were human beings, or the problem would never be solved. He also asserted that no people had ever risen to a high level of civilization simply upon their abstract rights. If Negroes desired to abolish discrimination, they would have to improve their condition, since "law inaugurates rights, but industry maintains and protects them." By being industrious like the Jews, the Negro could be the architect of his own future in the New South. As long as whites discriminated, Negroes should create their own business opportunities by employing and patronizing only members of the race. In short, mutual confidence, unity, industry, education, economy, and morality would solve the race problem. Elsewhere, Straker insisted that Negroes should no longer depend on others for their citizenship rights, but should unite to secure them for themselves.[21]

Benjamin Arnett, a Pennsylvania-born minister and politician who became an A.M.E. bishop in 1888, expressed a wide variety of ideologies. Active in the Pennsylvania convention movement during Reconstruction, he organized a Citizen's Joint Stock Company for mercantile business in connection with the work of the local leagues— the sort of co-operative enterprise that was more highly regarded later. Moving to Ohio he became active in politics and served a term in the legislature, where his most notable activity was in obtaining the repeal of the Black Laws in 1886. In supporting this bill he stressed the humiliation of segregation and the necessity for integrated schools and transportation, though he opposed intermarriage. He also supported a vigorous self-help philosophy. After the repeal of the Black Laws he told Negroes not to expect any more "pound cake from the Republican Party. . . . The opportunities, blessings and privileges of this day bring with them corresponding responsibilities; and to make this victory secure, our race must vindicate itself. . . ." Upon retiring from the legislature he gave a speech referring to the ancient glory of the race, when the Negro was "sovereign of the civilized world." He thought that the Negro had been a great success in politics, but would have to make his place secure by intelligence, industry, and character.[22] Arnett remained in politics and was widely regarded as President McKinley's chief adviser on Negro appointments.

William Wells Brown escaped from slavery to achieve note as an underground railroad agent, abolitionist, and author of the first novel by an American Negro. In *My Southern Home* (1880) he conceded that Negro politicians had been extravagant during Reconstruction, but stressed the positive achievements of the period, and the need for political rights. Negroes needed more self-reliance and "a high standard of moral, social and literate culture." Since all civilized races had risen through co-operation and combination, the final great struggle for the Negroes' rights lay with themselves. Unfortunately, Negroes, lacking proper race pride and confidence in each other, patronized white businessmen, though no race ever prospered or gained respect which lacked confidence in its own "nationality." Temperance, the cultivation of business, hard work, pluck, and manly independence would go a long way toward solving the race problem. He regarded amalgamation of Negroes and whites as unlikely in the forseeable future; the British, he averred, owed everything to their mixed blood, and all history demonstrated that isolated peoples make little or no progress, but that amalgamation was "the great civilizer of the races of man." [23]

Except for Brown's favorable attitude toward amalgamation, most articulate Negroes would have agreed with what he and Arnett said. For while economic advancement, self-help and racial solidarity were achieving ascendancy in the minds of Negroes, they maintained the goal of integration and citizenship rights before them.

CHAPTER IV

MIGRATION AND COLONIZATION

One possible solution to the economic and racial difficulties of Southern Negroes that received considerable attention was migration. Many recognized leaders of the race urged migration to other parts of the United States, and a few counseled emigration from the country.[1] But those who moved were almost entirely of the lower class. It will therefore be necessary to devote some attention to migration movements as indicative of the attitudes of this group, as well as to the statements of the more articulate.

The principal Negro migration between the Civil War and World War I was from one agricultural region to another within the South. There was some migration to the cities of the South and even of the North, and a trickle to the Far West, but the major trend was a movement from one Southern rural locality to another, gradually shifting the Negro population in a southwestward direction. Much of the migration was a continuous phenomenon. It appears that migration activity was especially strong between 1878 and 1881 and between 1888 and about 1890. In the first instance the migration included the dramatic Kansas Exodus from several Southern states, and some migration into Indiana and Arkansas; in the latter instance it was a general southward and southwestward migration to the Gulf states and Arkansas.[2] It is also noteworthy that the articulate classes were most active in their espousal of migration in 1879–80, and again about 1890, though their interest was primarily in migration *from* the South.

The migrants and would-be migrants uniformly cited oppressive conditions in the South—economic exploitation, political intimidation, injustice in the courts, and mob violence—as the reasons for their desire to move. Benjamin "Pap" Singleton, who called himself the *"whole cause of the Kansas immigration,"* had turned his attention to that state after high prices had caused the failure of his efforts to encourage landownership among the economically oppressed Negroes in Tennessee. Before the Senate committee investigating the exodus, Singleton asserted: "When the white man will think that equal rights . . . is a violation of his . . . dignity, then I am going to leave." In Louisiana a movement, started as early as 1874 by one Henry Adams, complained of lawlessness and exploitation on the part of landlords and the denial of all the rights of freemen. By 1878 and 1879 it had become the spearhead of a large-scale migration sentiment in Louisiana and neighboring states from Alabama to Texas. In 1889 a North Carolina "emigration" convention considered the situation in that state more precarious than at any time since emancipation, criticized the state's landlord and tenant act, blamed the Farmers' Alliance for keeping wages low and attacking the Negro's political rights, and complained of unjust juries. Economic depression, it declared, intensified the desire to move.[3]

Those race leaders who favored migration—though they did not migrate themselves—used similar arguments. Once the Kansas Exodus was under way a national convention meeting at Nashville in 1879 enthusiastically and almost unanimously supported the exodus. The convention reviewed the proscription Negroes suffered—abridgement of political rights, low wages, and the crop-lien system—and held that the desire for suffrage and freedom from terrorism were central causes of the movement. Later, the Afro-American League, formed in 1890, advocated migration to the Northwest as an antidote to the persecution encountered in the South.[4]

Though the majority of Northern leaders appear to have favored the Exodus, Southern leadership was distinctly divided on the question. True, Southerners played the leading roles at the Nashville convention, but there is considerable evidence to support the thesis that the comfortable classes and many political leaders were satisfied to stay where they were and even discountenanced the migration of the masses. The Senate committee investigating the Kansas Exodus heard the testimony of some of them. They included well-to-do farmers like a Louisiana citizen who had accumulated five or six hundred acres since the war, and another who voted with the Democrats; and a

Mississippian who, though a Republican, was a member of the county board of supervisors and owned 160 acres of land. They certainly had no reason to leave. Two North Carolina Reconstruction politicians, James H. Harris and James E. O'Hara (who was later a member of Congress), both testified that Negroes should remain in the state. O'Hara, generally known as conciliatory toward white Southerners, minimized the hardships facing Negroes in North Carolina. "I do not know," he said, "of any state in the American Union where there is a better feeling between the white and colored people than in North Carolina." In general North Carolina politicians, merchants, editors, and ministers consistently opposed migration from the state because their wealth and position depended upon the presence of a substantial Negro population. The situation was similar in South Carolina, where Robert Smalls and most of the other Negro politicians, many of them substantial landholders, were inimical to migration schemes which would deprive them of political influence.[5]

Thus economically prosperous individuals with land and businesses in the Southeast, and political leaders who depended for their careers on a large Negro vote, largely opposed the migrations. Moreover, none of the well-to-do or eminent Southern Negroes appear to have migrated themselves, even where they agreed that others should do so. And when they did support migration they usually came to it belatedly, as in the case of the Kansas Exodus, well after the movement was under way.

The principal, if not the entire, impetus for migration came from among the lower classes. The leaders of the 1879 migration, for example, were all otherwise obscure men. And ordinarily those distinguished race leaders who did support migration favored movement out of the South to the lands of the West and Northwest, while, except for the Kansas Exodus, the actual migration was chiefly southwestward. These facts suggest that, even though the migrants and would-be migrants spoke of political repression and mob violence—and these undoubtedly played some role—their principal motivation was economic, the other arguments being to a considerable extent rationalizations.

Indeed, the migration of Southern Negroes appears to have been always principally in response to economic conditions, as they moved into places where there were better opportunities—to the cities to some extent, especially after 1880, and primarily from one farm to another. It will be remembered that Singleton agitated for migration to Kansas only after his efforts at encouraging Tennessee Negroes to become landowners had failed. In North Carolina the short crop of 1878 produced an economic crisis precipitating the migration that ended up in Indiana. Henry Adams and his Louisiana group clearly stated the largely economic basis of their desire to move. And while Wharton believes that political conditions and racial violence played a part, drought, low prices, and the worst epidemic of yellow fever in the history of central and southwestern Mississippi resulted in the economic disaster that precipitated the migration to Kansas. William Pickens, a future field secretary of the N.A.A.C.P., in later years recalled the depressed economic conditions that caused his "industrious but improvident" family to leave South Carolina for Arkansas in 1888.[6] Moreover, the wave of migration that included the Kansas Exodus came at the close of the depression of 1873, when cotton prices were lowest,[7] and the migration activity in 1888–90 was correlated with the agricultural unrest associated with the rise of the Farmers' Alliance. One careful student concluded that the chief cause of Negro migration in Georgia before 1910 was discontent with land tenure, Negroes tending to go where they could rise from farm laborer to become either sharecroppers, cash renters, or landowners. Charles S. Johnson found that there was no correlation between racial persecution and migration; in some cases Negro population increased markedly in the very counties where there were large numbers of lynchings. As Johnson concluded in his survey of Negro migration between 1865 and 1920:

> Reasons are one thing; motives another. . . . Persecution plays its part —a considerable one. But when the whole of the migration of southern Negroes is considered, this part seems to be limited. It is indeed more likely that Negroes, like all others with a spark of ambition and self-interest, have been deserting soil which cannot yield returns in proportion to their population increase.[8]

If economic drives were paramount in Negro migration, while other grievances played their role, certain observers believed they saw additional socio-psychological forces. As in other areas of Negro life, economic advancement, self-help, and racial solidarity were closely intertwined. Both Kelly Miller and W. E. B. Du Bois, observing the increasing tendency of Negroes to become concentrated in certain counties of the Deep South, ignored the greater productivity of the land in those counties, and suggested that discriminatory conditions compelled Negroes to flock together and to seek security and social and economic progress among themselves.[9] While neither Du Bois nor Miller cited concrete evidence to prove their interpretation of the census returns, evidence of a sort does exist to support them—notably in the all-Negro towns in the Far West, in towns such as Mound Bayou in Mississippi, and in the attempt to create an all-Negro state in Oklahoma Territory in the 1890's. Ideologically, these all-Negro communities were characterized by a chauvinistic rationalization of racial separation. They emphasized racial solidarity to solve the Negro's problems and envisaged a Utopian society where Negroes could live untouched by discrimination and undertake their own elevation without white assistance or interference.

That feelings of ethnocentrism did sometimes characterize interest in migration is suggested by the efforts toward emigration from the country. Interest in colonization in tropical lands abroad had had a long ante-bellum history and had enjoyed its greatest vogue in periods when the outlook seemed the most discouraging, particularly during the decade preceding the Civil War, when the emigration conventions represented a full-blown nationalist movement. By the time of the Civil War, almost every Negro leader of consequence, according to one authority, either favored or was at least open to the idea of colonization in Africa or one of the Caribbean lands. Colonizationists characteristically thought in terms of an independent state where Negroes would enjoy the rights of free men and citizens, a state that would redeem Africa for civilization and by noteworthy achievement glorify the Negro race in the eyes of the world. The basic tenets of these colonizationists, rooted in the liberal and democratic nationalist tradition of the United States, was perhaps best summed up by Alexander Crummell, when he described Liberia as "this spot dedicated to nationality, consecrated to freedom, and sacred to religion." [10]

The Civil War did not entirely eliminate colonization efforts. Even during Reconstruction significant interest was manifested, mostly by people of lowly origins, and the number of migrants ran into the thousands. Thereafter, there were always some who thought of emigration—chiefly to Liberia—as the best solution of their difficulties. As in the case of the internal migration two chief peaks of activity came in the late 1870's and around 1890. This suggests that the two movements were related. The Louisiana Negroes under the leadership of Henry Adams had intended to seek a refuge on foreign soil if unable to obtain territory in the United States. Agitation for African emigration was one of the factors in the ferment that preceded the Kansas Exodus from Mississippi. A South Carolina Liberian Joint Stock Company's ill-fated expedition with 206 migrants in 1878 was the climax of a frenzy of interest in colonization just prior to the sizeable migration to the West from that state in 1879–80. Singleton, disillusioned over the race's future in the United States, during the first half of the 1880's was variously urging emigration to Canada, Cyprus, or Liberia. In Georgia the height of the colonization sentiment was reached in 1892. Early in 1891 the Colonization Society reported that never in its history had applications been so "numerous and urgent." [11] Not only did emigration associations appear at one time or another in nearly all Southern states, but *The African Repository* also reported some among the migrants to the West.

As in the case of the internal migration, the lower classes were chiefly involved. The American Colonization Society constantly tried to insist that its migrants had some education, belonged to a Christian Church, and were industrious if not skilled workmen, but it is clear from statements and letters in *The African Repository* that almost without exception the migrants were barely literate, poverty-stricken individuals, who needed aid to go to Liberia. Thus, only a few were able to migrate—either by paying their own way or by depending on the limited funds of the society. But the number of emigrants is no index to the sentiment for colonization, as most of those who expressed a desire to go were never able to do so.

Letters from would-be migrants to the American Colonization Society indicated that the economic motive may have been the predominating one, though verbal explanations included dissatisfaction with political and social conditions and nationalistic leanings. A Texan declared in 1887 that "we greatly desire now to go to the land of our forefathers and make it our home," because "low wages and high rents, and a despair of doing better in the future compel us to emigrate." Others had more inclusive viewpoints. Would-be migrants in both North and South Carolina in 1877 and 1878 cited outrages and political intimidation as well as economic grievances. An Arkansas group in 1877 urged settlement in Liberia, "where we will be permitted more fully to exercise those faculties which impart to man his dignity, and to evidence to all who despise, ridicule and oppress our race, that we possess with them a common nature . . . and thereby to prove that we are capable of self-government." Some, including Singleton, suggested highly nationalistic sentiments. An appeal from a Kansas African Emigration Association in 1887 expressed economic discontent and the desire to establish a "United States of Africa . . . for the elevation of the African and for the perpetuity of our race, which is here losing its identity by intermixture." [12]

Racial leaders of distinction were generally far less sympathetic toward settlement in Africa than they were with migration to the West and Northwest. Most unusual was the attitude of the Wilberforce Professor W. S. Scarborough, who having previously opposed migration of any sort, in 1890 counseled the scattering of the Negro population throughout the United States, and if that proved impossible mass migration to Africa or any place beyond American influence.[13] Yet in a few instances highly distinguished Negroes did favor colonization. The South Carolina Liberian Exodus Association was directed by leading citizens like Reverend R. H. Cain and Martin R. Delany, though an English traveler reported that "the upper class do not go themselves, but preach to their countrymen the advantage of going." Both Congressman Cain (who in 1880 was elevated to a bishopric in the A.M.E. Church) and Dr. Delany, an ante-bellum abolitionist, editor and physician, who had served as a major in the Union Army, had allied themselves with the Conservatives against the corrupt Radical Republicans in the state. They now insisted that the hopelessness of the struggle in this country made it desirable for Negroes to emigrate to Africa. Delany, one of the most prominent colonizationists of the 1850's reiterated his former ideology. "Where," he asked, "is a more fit place to seek new homes than in the land of their fathers and mothers, especially provided for them by nature?" But at the time of the 1890 colonization agitation, most of the state's leaders were opposed, though a Charleston minister did urge emigration on the ground that amalgamation was neither possible nor desirable and that it was impossible to obtain citizenship rights in the United States.[14]

Easily the leading advocate of African colonization during the late nineteenth and early twentieth centuries was the noted Bishop Henry M. Turner. Born in South Carolina, he was preaching in Baltimore when appointed the first Negro army chaplain. After the war he entered Georgia politics, and after the expulsion of the Negro members of the Georgia legislature in 1868 he devoted himself to church affairs, becoming a bishop in 1880. He became an advocate of emigration at least as early as 1874, and two years later he and Jabez P. Cambell, also a bishop in the A.M.E. Church, were elected vicepresidents of the American Colonization Society. Turner felt deeply honored by this recognition from an organization deemed by most Negroes, even many colonizationists, as inimical to them.

To Turner there was no worthwhile future in the United States; only the creation of their own nationality would bring prosperity and manhood to the Negroes. God had brought them to America to enable them to absorb the Christianity and the mechanical skills of the white race, which they were to use in the religious and cultural redemption of the ancestral continent. The Civil Rights Decision of 1883 gave him endless ammunition for his cause. He continually harped upon the "abominable decision" of the Republican Supreme Court—"really a conclave of human donkeys"—that had "made the ballot of the black man a parody, his citizenship a nullity and his freedom a burlesque," a condition compared with which the Russian serfs were lords. In contrast to the United States, he wrote in 1892 from Liberia: "One thing the black man has here, that is manhood, freedom, and the fullest liberty; and feels as a lord and walks the same way." So disgusted was he that he once said he cared nothing for the United States, "wish it nothing but ill and endless misfortune, wish I would only live to see it go down to ruin and its memory blotted from the pages of history. A man who loves a country that hates him is a human dog and not a man." [15]

The vast majority of articulate Negroes definitely opposed emigration as a solution to the race problem, though they did maintain an ethnic identification with Africa. Only rare individuals like Downing regarded Africa as of no more concern to him than it was to whites. Considerably more numerous were those like Bishop Benjamin Arnett and T. McCants Stewart who encouraged commercial relationships— and, in a relatively few instances, a limited migration—as a means of Christianizing Africa and creating a prosperous republic that would reflect credit on the race. Stewart, for example, upon returning to the United States in 1885 after spending two years in Liberia, denied being a colonizationist, but stressed commercial relations. Believing that Negroes would always remain within the American nation— though as a distinct people—he advised simply a voluntary movement of self-supporting people with sufficient capital "to build up a new Christian Negro Nationality in the 'Fatherland,' " that would cause Negroes everywhere to be respected.[16] The majority of the articulate appear to have expressed their racial ethnocentrism by an interest in African history and—more commonly—in the evangelization and civilizing of the continent. Most of the writers in a symposium sponsored by the A.M.E. Church *Review* on the subject in 1885, and most of the speakers at a conference on Africa sponsored by the Gammon Theological Seminary in Atlanta ten years later, thought that Negroes had a special interest and responsibility toward Africa.[17]

But while there existed a widespread identification with Africa, opposition to colonization dominated the articulate, even those who insisted that any who wished to emigrate had the right to do so. Men like T. Thomas Fortune, George T. Downing, and Harry C. Smith consistently berated the idea. At a convention called by Turner in 1893 the delegates were so strongly anti-colonizationist that they rejected any resolution favoring emigration. Turner was often attacked in scathing terms by his contemporaries. As Bishop Benjamin F. Lee said in 1893 Turner "speaks of the United States as Hades and of Africa as Eden; yet even he still holds his residence in Hades, only paying Eden a brief visit once a year." [18] Sentiment was so strongly anti-colonizationist that at least one man deemed it advisable to mask his feelings on the matter. Charles N. Grandison, president of the Methodist Church North's Bennett College in North Carolina, secretly believed colonization in Africa to be the only solution of the race problem. And at the time of Turner's 1893 convention Grandison was the only one of a large group of leaders polled by the Indianapolis *Freeman* who was open to the suggestion of large-scale colonization, and he expressed himself most circumspectly, to the effect that though colonization seemed impractical and impossible, its advocacy should not be considered a crime.[19]

Thus, articulate Negroes ranged from wholehearted advocacy to complete opposition to colonization. More espoused opposition, but the majority agreed that American Negroes had a special interest in and responsibility for elevating the condition of the ancestral continent, both for humanitarian reasons and to prove to the world the capacity of the Negro race. Even leaders who, like Benjamin F. Lee, preferred segregated racial institutions did not carry ethnocentrism to the extreme of favoring emigration, but maintained that Negroes should remain in the United States and struggle for their citizenship rights.[20] Among the oppressed masses of the South, there appeared to be considerable incipient interest in emigration to Africa—an interest usually expressed in terms of escape from oppressive conditions, and probably primarily economic in motivation, but that at times included a vision of a glorious national future in the land of their forefathers.

In certain important respects the colonization and internal migration movements were similar and closely related. Peaks of interest in both coincided closely in time, and among the masses they were often viewed as alternate courses of action. In both cases economic considerations were probably the chief motivation. However, while it is impossible to gauge the actual interest in these solutions to the race problem, clearly they were more attractive to the masses than to the leaders, especially colonization abroad. Ethnocentrism was associated to some extent with both migration and colonization; it was especially characteristic of the latter.[21] The ethnocentric character of the thinking of certain migrants and would-be migrants to the West and to Africa in no way contradicts the assertion that economic conditions were the chief cause of this interest. In the same way that dissatisfaction with economic difficulties in Italy and Germany between the two World Wars were largely responsible for, and found expression in the extremely nationalistic Fascist ideologies, so here too the drive toward economic security was overlaid by compensatory Utopian and nationalistic rationalizations of creating a national state in Africa or a separate community in the United States where Negroes would, by themselves, lead satisfying and successful lives—rationalizations that gave important psychological satisfactions to the economically frustrated.

Finally, both phenomena expressed a desire for human dignity, the right to exist as self-respecting citizens. But it is significant that in the period under discussion the emigrationist variant of Negro ethnocentrism was never as widespread—among the leaders at least—as it had been in the late 1850's. The chief hope of American Negroes, even those who glorified segregated institutions and racial pride and solidarity lay in the achievement of full citizenship rights in the United States.

CHAPTER V

PROTEST AND ACCOMMODATION

While the years following the Compromise of 1877 witnessed increasing emphasis on economic development, self-help, racial solidarity, and race pride, the Reconstruction emphases on the franchise, political activity, and civil rights continued. Moreover, the Reconstruction concern with common school education became important in the newer complex of ideas. Editor Benjamin Lee of the *Christian Recorder* summed up articulate opinion on this when he declared that "the combined forces of opposition cannot prevent us [from advancing] so long as we have the road to books and schools open to us. Even the snub that has been given to our political condition is as nothing compared with what it would be to shut against us the doors of schools." [1]

The vitality of the protest tradition was clearly demonstrated by the national and state conventions. In comparison with the late 1870's, the convention movement displayed increasing concern over the franchise, civil rights, mob violence, and Republican policy. The national convention at Louisville in 1883, though it regarded the abolition of the crop-lien system, education, and sound moral training as paramount, also bitterly complained

that many of the laws intended to secure us our rights as citizens are nothing more than dead letters. In the Southern States, almost without exception, the colored people are denied justice in the courts, denied the fruit of their honest labor, defrauded of their protective rights at the ballot-box, shut out from learning trades, cheated out of their civil rights . . . and left . . . an inadequate opportunity for education and general improvement.

State conventions held the same year in Arkansas, Texas, and South Carolina expressed similar feelings. The one held at Charleston outspokenly protested against partial jury trials, short school terms, limitations on the suffrage, the "pernicious" convict lease system, and the Republican party's discriminatory policy in the awarding of public offices; and they called the South Carolina regime "the most damnable form of State Government to which a free people have ever been subjected." [2]

Spasmodic state and regional conventions and civil rights organizations characterized the North, especially New England, but more remarkable were the occasional evidences of activity in the Southern and border states. Baltimoreans in 1885 formed a Brotherhood of Liberty to "use all legal means within our power to procure and maintain our rights." This organization grew out of two successful legal cases involving steamboat discrimination and a law prohibiting Negroes from practicing at the Maryland bar. The organization obtained additional school facilities, agitated on lynching, and served as a legal redress society. In 1888 over 350 Georgia Negroes, including the state's most eminent leaders, in convention went on record as favoring the Blair Bill, temperance and industrial education, and as opposing the chain gang, discrimination by common carriers, lynch law, disfranchisement, and inequities in the jury system.[3]

By the late 1880's the demand for a national convention to deal with pressing problems became vigorous. Rival groups had been talking of such a meeting since 1887. Finally, in 1890 there were two major conventions. At Chicago in January, T. Thomas Fortune founded the Afro-American League (for the history of this important organization see Chapters VIII and X). In February a group of 445 men, on the whole an older group than those at the Chicago meeting and including all the leading politicians, gathered in Washington. J. C. Price, just elected president of the Afro-American League, was named chairman of the convention by acclamation. The delegates enumerated the usual grievances, explained that oppression compelled them to meet in a separate convention to find ways to remedy the evils facing the race, and established a Citizens' Equal Rights Association. Though the convention did not concern itself much with self-help and economy, a pamphlet issued by the Equal Rights Association stressed the standard view that good conduct, education, and the acquisition of wealth would bring respect and thus break down the barriers to full citizenship rights. Both the American Citizens' Equal Rights Association and the Afro-American League became inactive due to internal frictions and rivalry between them, and except for an unsuccessful meeting called by Bishop Turner in 1893 the Washington meeting in 1890 proved to be the last Negro convention.[4] Thus, the Convention Movement came to a close after an irregular existence of over sixty years, beginning with the first National Convention of the Free People of Color in Philadelphia in 1830. Its spirit continued in the Afro-American League, which, revived in 1898 as the Afro-American Council, met annually for about ten years thereafter.

Although sentiment increased in favor of "voluntarily" segregated schools and social institutions, legally enforced segregation in transportation and places of public accommodation caused considerable agitation, even on the part of those who favored separate group institutions. The outcry against the Civil Rights Decision of 1883 was practically universal. Speaking at an indignation meeting in Washington, Douglass called the decision a shocking sign of "moral weakness in high places," a calamity arising from the "autocratic" power of the Court that made the country appear "before the world as a nation utterly destitute of power to protect the rights of its own citizens." Particularly in the North, Negroes actively opposed the tendencies toward legalized segregation and campaigned for the civil rights laws that most of the Northeastern states passed. In Ohio, editor H. C. Smith constantly harped on the evils present in all sorts of discrimination, legal and illegal, while in the state legislature Jere A. Brown and Benjamin W. Arnett played an active role in the introduction and passage of the Civil Rights Act of 1886.

Northern editors also constantly agitated against discrimination and segregation in the South. One incident in which an A.M.E. bishop was forced out of a first-class train coach prompted Fortune to denounce the Southern railroads for giving respectable Negro travelers miserable accommodations in smoking cars "where the vilest of impudent white scum resort to swear, to exhale rotton smoke and to expectorate pools of stinking excrementation of tobacco." [5] And in the South too, at first at least, there were some protests against railroad segregation and against compelling Negroes with first-class tickets to ride in inferior accommodations.

The matter of separate but equal facilities came before the Interstate Commerce Commission shortly after it was established in 1887. Two men, President W. H. Councill of the state school at Huntsville, Alabama, and A.M.E. minister W. H. Heard of Charleston, formerly a Reconstruction politician in Georgia and South Carolina (and later minister to Liberia, 1895–98, a noted emigrationist, and a bishop from 1908), brought cases before it on the basis of the nondiscrimination section of the act. Both men charged that they had been forcibly ejected from first-class railroad coaches. The commission, citing *U.S.* v *Buntin,* 1882, a circuit court decision sustaining racial segregation in Ohio on the basis of the separate but equal doctrine, explicitly held that segregation itself was not unlawful, but that Negroes who bought first-class tickets were entitled to first-class accommodations. Though a few were skeptical, on the whole the reaction in the Negro press was favorable to these decisions, since it was believed that the requirement of equality of accommodations would prove so burdensome that the railroads would end segregation. Fortune enthused over the "sweeping decision" and predicted that "of course these old Bourbon roads will now stop their foolishness because their pocketbooks will squeal."

What happened was that the Commission's order went unenforced, and after the second Heard case the states, beginning with Georgia and Louisiana in 1890, passed Jim Crow railroad car laws theoretically providing for separate but equal facilities but actually fastening inferior accommodations on Negroes for the next two generations. Negroes continued to protest. The Afro-American Press Convention in 1890 denounced railroad segregation, and all discrimination practiced in places of public amusement and accommodation as an "unjust infamy" contrary to the spirit of American institutions.[6] Negro members of the Louisiana and Arkansas legislatures bitterly opposed the segregation bills introduced in their states in 1890–91. As late as 1892 Negro leaders and editors in Georgia urged Governor Northen to force the railroads to supply equal accommodations, and in the same year some Atlanta citizens staged what was apparently a successful boycott of the streetcars after the city council passed a Jim Crow law.[7]

During the 1880's and 1890's there was a universal protest against lynchings and other forms of mass violence. In a typical statement H. T. Johnson, editor of the *Christian Recorder,* writing of a Texas holocaust in 1893, pointed out that whites who raped Negroes went unpunished, bemoaned the public support accorded lynchers, and asked: "Where and when has the Christianity of the land recorded its protest against mob violence, lynchings and outrages?" Easily the most famous of the anti-lynching crusaders was Ida Wells. Her Memphis newspaper, *Free Speech,* was destroyed by angry whites in 1892, and she was forced to flee the city on account of her outspoken editorials. Thereafter, she campaigned ceaselessly on the issue both in the United States and abroad.[8]

In view of the increasing indignities involved in segregation and mob outrages, some went so far as to preach violent retaliation. For example, Fortune in 1883 urged that Negroes put off first-class coaches should defend themselves; one could not be killed in a better cause, and "one or two murders growing from this intolerable nuisance would break it up." Even a North Ohio conference of the A.M.E. Church resolved in 1889 that if neither the state nor national government would stop lynching in the South "then the only thing that remains to our people there is to let the law of self-defense have its course." And a writer in the A.M.E. Church *Review* in 1893 urged a secret association to arm Negroes and organize them for self-defense.[9]

Others, however, believed that the Negroes' supposed docility and meekness made them all the more deserving of constitutional rights. Many cited the slaves' loyalty to their masters during the Civil War as a special basis for consideration. A writer in the *Christian Recorder* alleged that Negroes, unlike Indians, had always been "humble, obedient, respectful and never revengeful." They were not anarchists or communists but loyal Americans who had fought the nation's wars and quietly accumulated property. Editor H. T. Johnson, ordinarily outspoken in criticism of racial injustice, in 1894 combined an emphasis on "The Heritage of the Meek" with the notion of innate racial differences. Among Negroes, he said, "abideth hope and charity" which would make them "mighty to the pulling down of the fiercest oppositions."

Just as the ethics of the Sermon on the Mount appealed to the lowly of the Greco-Roman world, so it also appealed to many American Negroes oppressed in the late nineteenth century. Others of a religious bent emphasized the role of God and trusted in Him to solve the race problem. Many may have expressed this sentiment largely for rhetorical effect, but occasionally at least, it was a substitute for action. Thus a writer in the A.M.E. Church *Review* in 1895 thought that since "we have tried all the courts of the land with no avail; now let us try the Court of Heaven, with . . . an unshaking confidence in HIM, with patience to wait until a change comes." To the inarticulate masses the idea of looking to God for the ultimate solution of the race problem probably had stronger appeal than it did to the more sophisticated, and their ministers often expressed this notion in their sermons. It was widely held that in God's plan Negroes would emerge victorious from the struggle with their oppressors to enjoy a glorious future as a result of their sufferings. According to many authorities, the spirituals, with their origins in slavery, also reflect the resignation and passivity of the deeply religious "folk" Negro. The religion of the masses was largely otherworldly and compensatory, and even where it expressed hope for better worldly conditions, it emphasized the role of a transcendent God whose ways were inscrutable but ultimately just.[10]

The majority of articulate Negroes did not adopt this accommodating approach. While this was an era of growing emphasis on self-help, it was not unusual for prominent leaders to see the race problem as a white rather than a Negro problem. Fortune felt that Negroes had permitted themselves to be deceived by the subterfuge that the color of the Negro had created "a great and appalling 'race problem' " that would be difficult to solve. The real problem he said, was "not the Negro but the Nation. . . . It is whether the republic shall be a republic in fact or a stupendous sham."

Fortune represented the protest tradition at its trenchant best, but it was Smith of the *Gazette* whose ideas were most consistently in accord with the older Reconstruction traditions and aspirations. Not only did he constantly agitate against outrages and segregation, and for the franchise, justice, and equality, but he displayed little interest in the newer currents of dividing the vote, economic chauvinism, race pride and solidarity, and substituting economics for politics. He was one of the few who opposed segregated racial institutions and enterprises and favored integration at all costs. Yet the Negro press as a whole did not adopt an accommodating position. Fifty editors—many from the South—attending the 1890 meeting of the Afro-American Press Association complained of segregation and denounced the franchise laws of the Southern states as intended "to defeat the ends of justice, and to perpetuate the undemocratic infamy of minority and caste rule." [11]

Yet Frederick Douglass was still the greatest living symbol of the protest tradition during the 1880's and early 1890's. During his previous career—especially during the late 1840's and the 1850's—he had seen no contradiction between agitation for political and civil rights and an emphasis on the middle-class virtues, economic independence, self-help, race pride, and racial solidarity. By gaining the respect of the white man, Negroes would better attain their constitutional rights. Meanwhile, oppression and discrimination compelled Negroes to think and act as a "nation within a nation." For Douglass, of course, such a program was no substitute for agitation and direct action against the American race system, and he never espoused the idea of segregated schools and churches. After the Civil War Douglass continued to place more emphasis on the gospel of wealth and racial co-operation than did most of his contemporaries, and he held these ideas in an attenuated form in the early 1880's. Speaking in 1880 in phrases suggestive of Booker T. Washington's speeches (though Douglass never employed Washington's flattery of the white South), he said:

Neither we, nor any other people will ever be respected till we respect ourselves, and we will never respect ourselves till we have the means to live respectably.... A race which cannot save its earnings ... can never rise in the scale of civilization.... This part of our destiny is in our own hands.... If the time shall ever come when we shall possess in the colored people of the United States, a class of men noted for enterprise, industry, economy and success, we shall no longer have any trouble in the matter of civil and political rights. The battle against popular prejudice will have been fought and won.... The laws which determine the destinies of individuals and nations are impartial and eternal. We shall reap as we shall sow.

To be viewed in proper perspective these words should be considered along with a much different statement which appeared in the *North American Review* in 1881. In this article Douglass said that economic and judicial discrimination, denial of admission to places of public accommodation, and disfranchisement made the Negro the victim of a prejudice "calculated to repress his manly ambition, his energies, and make him a dejected and spiritless man."

Ridiculing the inconsistencies of the color line, he pointed out that Southerners "shrink back in horror from contact with the negro as a man and a gentleman, but like him very well as a barber, waiter, coachman or cook." He was not ashamed, he said in 1883, of political ambition: "We shall never cease to be despised and persecuted while we are known to be excluded by our color from all important positions under the Government." [12]

Curiously, during the 1880's and 1890's, as Negro thought generally veered from emphasis on civil rights, political activity, and immediate integration to doctrines of self-help, racial solidarity, and economic advancement, Douglass' thought moved in the opposite direction to a position more consistently assimilationist and of protest than at any previous time. No longer did he express interest in self-help, race solidarity, and the gospel of wealth. He more and more stressed assimilation as the solution to the race problem and declaimed against race pride and solidarity. One may surmise that this shift was connected with his second marriage in 1884. In the face of considerable criticism from Negroes for an alleged lack of race pride for marrying a white woman, Douglass asked: "What business has any man to trouble himself about the color of any other man's wife? Does it not appear violently impertinent—this intermeddling?" [13] This marriage, like the jealousy of leaders old and new, was among the causes of the decline of his position of leadership. And his ideas, which he expressed vigorously, were less and less in accord with the major trends of Negro thought. Douglass had always desired assimilation, and on various occasions he had expressed his belief that racial intermixture was inevitable. But as a widely reprinted address given in 1889 showed, he had discarded some of his earlier doctrines.

In this speech, which is representative of Douglass' views in the late years of his life, he omitted any mention of self-help and the gospel of wealth and protested vigorously against disfranchisement, discrimination in education and justice, and economic exploitation. He insisted that it was not a problem that Negroes were to solve themselves. It was not the Negro who was on trial. "The real question is whether American justice, American liberty, American civilization, American law, and American Christianity can be made to include . . . all American citizens." Admittedly, Negroes could in part combat prejudice through acquiring education and respectable character. But Douglass then went on to name, even though he knew that he ran the risk of incurring displeasure, errors committed by Negroes which contemporaries usually listed as virtues—race pride, race solidarity, and economic chauvinism. First among them was the greater prominence recently being given "in all our books, papers and speeches," to the encouragement of race pride, to which Negroes were "inclining most persistently and mischievously." Douglass found nothing to be either proud or ashamed of in a gift from God, and he perceived no benefit to be derived from the cultivation of race pride; on the contrary it was building on a false foundation. Besides, what were Negroes fighting against, if not race pride? Another error was the doctrine that racial union was essential if Negroes were to gain the respect of whites. Douglass held that "our union is our weakness," that the result of separate schools, churches, and benevolent and literary societies was a cultural provincialism peculiar to the race's condition as an oppressed people. Moreover, "a nation within a nation is an anomaly. There can be but one American nation . . . and we are Americans." Negroes should yield as little as possible to the circumstances that compelled them to maintain separate neighborhoods and institutions.[14]

Thus were the full implications of Douglass' basically protest and assimilationist philosophy brought to their logical conclusion. Interestingly enough, he was on good terms with Booker T. Washington,[15] though since Douglass had moved in opposition to the main direction of Negro thought in this period their ideologies were poles apart.

It is difficult to measure the full extent of accommodating tendencies from the literature. A substantial proportion of Southern ministers, public school officials, and propertied elements undoubtedly used such an approach. When the Atlanta *Constitution* in 1890 interviewed a number of the most prosperous Negroes in Atlanta about their views on the Lodge Bill, it was able to report that—for white ears at least—these men, several of whom were well-to-do merchants with white customers, were either indifferent or opposed to the proposed legislation.[16] Generally speaking Southern ministers, as shall become apparent later, took a rather "conservative" approach to the race question. Among the educators the most notorious accommodator was William Hooper Councill, who had become widely known for his unctuous sycophancy by the early 1890's. Of the editors consulted only Marshall W. Taylor of the *Southwestern Christian Advocate* was really accommodating in tone. Taylor, whose term of office spanned the middle 1880's, usually ignored the existence of the color line in the Methodist Church, North, defended segregated institutions, urged self-help and character development, and opposed violence and retaliation.

Some of the politicians also expressed themselves in a conciliatory tone when the occasion appeared to demand it. P. B. S. Pinchback, collector of customs at New Orleans, in 1885 opined that legislation had been attempted and found to be inadequate, so that only time and the general education of the masses of both races could eradicate the evil.[17] John M. Langston, regarded during his lifetime as second in importance as a leader only to Frederick Douglass, was the epitome of inconsistency. The son of a Virginia planter, he had been educated at Oberlin and had become a lawyer and noted abolitionist orator. Like Peter H. Clark, William Wells Brown, and others, he temporarily followed the ideological winds into an espousal of colonization during the years before the Civil War.[18] Subsequently, he led a distinguished career that included two terms as minister to Haiti, the presidency of the Virginia Normal and Collegiate Institute at Petersburg, and election to Congress in 1888. Either political ambition or party loyalty caused him to explain away the Compromise of 1877 as Pacific Reconstruction, which would be advantageous to the Negro since he could now spend all his energies in becoming educated, prosperous, and self-reliant, living in harmony with Southern whites, recognized as a man and a citizen. But in 1879 he encouraged the migration from the South as the only solution for escaping from Southern oppression. Again, speaking in Nashville in 1886 he enthused over conditions in the South where, he asserted, the whites were more and more according Negroes their rights, while Negroes were dividing their vote. The Negro problem, he said, would be solved by the Negro himself through the cultivation of intelligence, virtue, and wealth, "with good understanding in a wise community of interest with those who today are the masters of knowledge, power and wealth." Three years later he asserted that there could be no compromise connected with the fearless advocacy of the race's rights. As American citizens and in justice to themselves, Negroes could demand nothing less than their full citizenship rights. Until his death in 1897 Langston pursued this rather erratic course, alternating militancy with conciliation.[19]

On the whole, the accommodators were almost entirely in the South. William Still's conciliatory views during the 1880's were clearly exceptional for a Northerner. Men like Isaiah Montgomery and Marshall W. Taylor would not have functioned as leaders in the North. Not all Southern leaders were accommodators, nor were all Northern leaders equally in the protest tradition.

Southern leaders as a matter of fact continued to include a surprisingly militant group. Professor W. H. Crogman of Clark University at Atlanta, a native of the British West Indies who had become the first Negro instructor at a school of the Methodist Church, North (Claflin College, 1870), and the first Negro assistant secretary of the church's general conference, emphasized both the importance of industry and thrift and the supreme value of the inalienable rights of the Declaration of Independence. Addressing the National Education Association in 1884, he lashed out against segregation and discrimination, denouncing bitterly the contrast between the ideals children were taught in school and the realities Negroes were compelled to face in society. Later, he was less forthright. Speaking in Georgia in 1889 he conceded that Negroes would "prefer to see the government controlled by those more capable of governing," but insisted that the Negroes asked for an equalization of rights and privileges such as belonged to them under the fundamental law of the land. Also at Atlanta was a student named James Weldon Johnson, a native of Florida who would later become famous as an author and N.A.A.C.P. official. Giving the prize oration at Atlanta University in 1892 Johnson expressed a similar range of ideologies. Since caste proscriptions were based on the dogma of Negro inferiority, the Negro must gain the respect of whites by acquiring education and wealth. Yet history showed that the respected peoples are those who refuse to submit to oppression, and half the sufferings of the race would disappear if the Negro asserted himself more and fought lynching by physical resistance. W. A. Pledger, the leading Negro politician in Georgia, frequently worked with conservative Democrats politically, but was known for his forthright stands and his refusal to modify his tone in the face of threats and intimidation. Of the same stripe was John Mitchell, Jr., editor of the Richmond *Planet* and a member of the

Richmond City Council. He was noted as a fearless editor, who "would walk into the jaws of death to serve his race." [20]

Less militant, but nevertheless far from an extreme accommodator, was J. C. Price, president of Livingstone College, North Carolina, one of the top handful of race leaders during the early 1890's. A freeborn North Carolinian, he took an A.B. and a B.D. at Lincoln University in the late 1870's. He founded Zion Wesley College in 1881, later changing its name to Livingstone. Like Washington, who founded Tuskegee at about the same time, Price established himself primarily as an educator.

Central in Price's philosophy was a vigorous racial pride that emphasized self-help as an important factor in the solution of the race problem. He applied the principle of racial co-operation to the building of Livingstone College. The catalogue of 1884–85 declared that only Negroes could actually do the work of educating the race, and Price told the general conference of 1888 that while philanthropic contributions were welcome, "Livingstone College stands before the world today as the most remarkable evidence of self-help among Negroes in this country." [21] After being elected president of the Afro-American League in 1890 Price explained its value by saying that only through association would a race rise to any degree of eminence or power. Referring to Crummell's "social principle" he asserted that combination would help both material advancement and the struggle for citizenship rights. Price believed too that education would play a leading role in solving the race problem, both by changing white attitudes and by preparing Negroes for the franchise—Price agreeing that educational qualifications for voting were acceptable. Education would stimulate intelligence and industry, and no people thus gifted could be denied their inalienable and constitutional rights.[22]

Yet Price also maintained that the race problem was not of the Negro's making because the white South regarded the freedman as no better than a slave. Though conceding that the Negroes were not ready for the suffrage in 1867, he frankly stated that the real crux of the problem was the question of citizenship rights. He also vigorously protested out of bitter personal experience against the "cruel discrimination" in public transportation. The Southern question he continued, "is simply this—how long can we deny to men their inalienable constitutional rights, the denial of which they most keenly feel?" Yet he believed that the South, providentially the home of the

Negro, would solve the problem; and he declared that the Negro was ready to live peaceably with the Southern white man "under any conditions save those which violate the very instinct of his being and imply the surrender of his manhood and God-given rights." The Negro was willing to make any terms that are reasonable, and fair; "but compromise that reverses the Declaration of Independence, nullifies the Constitution, and is contrary to the genius of the republic, ought not to be asked." He expressed confidence in the better class of Southern whites, which he said was increasing, though still in the minority. Time and patience, he concluded, would be important factors in the solution of the race problem.[23]

Just what did Price mean by a "reasonable" solution? He expressed a willingness to see an educational qualification for voting and during the early 1890's advocated a division of the Negro vote. After Cleveland's re-election he urged co-operation with the Democrats "as far as is consistent with the instincts of manhood . . . even at the sacrifice of nonessentials." [24] Just what these nonessentials were he did not say, but like Washington, he urged moral and economic development and self-help as the key to Negro elevation, though unlike Washington he clearly avowed his belief in citizenship rights. His chief compromise lay in urging the acceptance of any reasonable *modus vivendi* for the immediate future and his proposal to divide the vote.

By 1890 Price was in a position to achieve national leadership. He had considerable support among philanthropists such as Collis Huntington, and Southern whites such as Josephus Daniels (whose newspaper was later largely responsible for stirring up the Wilmington riot of 1898). He had a program embracing all the major doctrines held by Negroes at that time, combined with a mildly conciliatory tone toward the white South. To these were added a magnificent oratorical ability. In the opening weeks of 1890 he was dramatically and unexpectedly made president of both the Afro-American League and the National Equal Rights Convention. Writing the members of the former, Price, who has gone down in history as a conciliator of the white South, threw down the gauntlet in ringing terms: "If we do not possess the manhood and patriotism to stand up in the defense of these constitutional rights, and protest long, loud and unitedly against their continual infringement, we are unworthy of our heritage as American citizens and deserve to have fastened on us the wrongs of which many of us are disposed to complain." [25]

Within two years both organizations had decayed and Price never achieved the influence which the conventions of 1890 had so auspiciously indicated. And five years later he was dead. Du Bois afterward recalled him as one who "had sought a way of honorable alliance with the best of the Southerners," and as one who had for a time arisen "as a new leader, destined it seemed, not to give up, but to re-state the old ideals in a form less repugnant to the white South. But he passed away in his prime." [26] Probably Price, whom some believe would have occupied the Tuskegeean's prominent position if he had lived, was better known than Washington in the early 1890's. Certainly he was among Negroes, for unlike the accommodating Tuskegeean who kept away from race conventions, Price was active in the national arena. However in view of the increasing militance of Southern opinion, it is likely that by 1895 Price's philosophy, with its unmistakable presentation of the Negro's goals, would have been an anachronism from the point of view of effective alliance with Southern whites.

It is apparent that in spite of an increasing emphasis on self-help and racial solidarity and moral and economic development, in spite of growing tendencies toward a conciliatory tactic, the basic protest tradition retained much of its vitality, even to some extent in the South. Its importance should not be underestimated. Even a man like C. H. J. Taylor, who during the 1880's had been noted for his accommodating attitude, could in 1893 declare it the duty of the convention which Bishop Turner had called to see that steps were taken to secure a better recognition of the Negroes' rights. In a poll of leading Negroes made by the Indianapolis *Freeman* just prior to this convention, Booker T. Washington was the only one queried who did not mention civil and political rights at all, but simply advised the convention to urge Negroes to "settle quietly down and get money and property and acquire character and education." Others mentioned these things, but they also counseled agitation for civil and political rights.[27] The explanation of Washington's prominence lies then less in his voicing the aspirations of the American Negro community than in other factors.

PART THREE

The Significance of Booker T. Washington

I believe the past and present teach but one lesson,—to the Negro's friends and to the Negro himself,—that there is but one way out, that there is but one hope of solution; and that is for the Negro in every part of America to resolve from henceforth that he will throw aside every non-essential and cling only to the essential,—that his pillar of fire by night and pillar of cloud by day shall be property, economy, education and Christian character. To us just now these are the wheat, all else the chaff. The individual or race that owns the property, pays the taxes, possesses the intelligence and substantial character, is the one which is going to exercise the greatest control in government, whether he lives in the North or whether he lives in the South.

BOOKER T. WASHINGTON
Future of the American Negro (Boston, 1899), 132.

CHAPTER VI

THE RISE OF INDUSTRIAL EDUCATION IN NEGRO SCHOOLS

The eminence of Booker T. Washington, it is commonly believed, was the influence chiefly responsible for the vogue of industrial and agricultural education in Negro schools in the generation before World War I. Yet a careful analysis of the evidence reveals that Washington simply brought to a climax a trend well under way before the middle 1890's, when he emerged as a figure of national reputation. How, then, did the temporary ascendancy of industrial education in Negro schools come about? What social and intellectual influences brought it to pre-eminence?

Stemming from the educational theories of Europeans such as Pestalozzi and Fellenberg, the sentiment for agricultural and industrial education found congenial soil in the Yankee traditions of morality, thrift and industry, economic independence, and material success and enjoyed its first considerable vogue in the United States during the second quarter of the nineteenth century. After the Civil War, under the impact of industrialization, it was transformed from a reformist fad into a widely practiced form of education. Yet it always remained an all-inclusive concept, elusive of narrow definition as to both its content and its purpose. Some thought of it as a pedagogical technique of acquiring simple manual skills and dealing with concrete objects as aids in teaching. Many thought of the mental discipline that would come from manual training and learning trades. Large numbers advocated manual labor schools in which youths would acquire an economically useful trade or mechanical skill and could earn part or all of their way through school. Related to this was the idea that modern society needed skilled factory workers and scientific farmers. And on a more advanced level industrial education was thought to include technological and engineering schools. Teaching of domestic science was introduced at an early date. Most of the theorizing had strong moral overtones about inculcating habits of thrift and morality and a feeling for the "dignity of labor." By some, industrial education was viewed as a means for helping the laboring classes to rise in the world, while others viewed it as a type of instruction suitable for adjusting them to their subordinate social role. This paradox was remarkably like the one that characterized theorizing about Negro education a half century later. For many the various definitions overlapped, and few made clear distinctions between them. Yet it was this very inclusiveness that enabled the term to serve so effectively as a platform for Negro education in the years before World War I.[1]

Some anti-slavery leaders had sporadically displayed interest in industrial education for Negroes since the late eighteenth century, and sentiment for it received a vital quickening with the emergence of militant abolitionism and the Negro Convention Movement in the 1830's. The early Negro conventions not only exhibited interest in the value of economy and industry, but they also supported the proposals of white abolitionists for a Negro manual labor college. While there was much talk of the moral and pedagogical value of manual labor schools, Negro thinking was largely motivated by economic realities. The antagonism of white skilled labor, exclusion from apprenticeships in the trades, the growing competition of immigrants for the menial occupations and services traditionally performed by Negroes, combined with a rising emphasis on self-help and racial solidarity, and upon moral uplift and economic development that characterized Negro thought as a result of the increasingly proscriptive legislation and the public sentiment of the 1850's, underlay the strong preoccupation with such schools at the national Negro conventions in 1853 and 1855. Using the very arguments that Booker T. Washington was to make famous half a century later both Frederick Douglass and the highly important Rochester Convention of 1853 held that economic progress, based on mutual self-help and racial co-operation, was a practical program for racial elevation and the achievement of citizenship rights, for when Negroes became valuable to society they would be respected; and therefore for the present they needed trade schools more than liberal arts colleges.[2]

The rise of industrial and agricultural education in Negro schools was part of a national (and world-wide) movement that included the manual labor colleges of the 1830's and 1840's, the early technical schools like Rensselaer, Lawrence, and Sheffield, and finally the spectacular growth of scientific subjects and technological institutions in higher education, and of manual training, vocational education, and home economics in the public schools after the Civil War. Moreover, the Morrill land-grant college act of 1862 gave a definite fillip to industrial and agricultural education, though its direct effect upon Negro education was for the most part long delayed. Less than half a dozen schools—Hampton, Claflin, Alcorn, Prairie View, and for several years Atlanta University—received land-grant funds before 1890, when a new act made it mandatory that Negroes receive a share of the assistance made available to each state.

Meanwhile, the Freedmen's Bureau commissioners and missionary school teachers, many of whom were familiar with the idea of manual labor schools from their abolitionist days, pushed forward the cause of industrial education. Thoroughly imbued with the importance of the values of thrift, industry, and morality, they believed it their duty to inculcate these values, which, they were fond of pointing out, neither the system of slavery nor the culture of the ante-bellum South had encouraged. As early as 1864 and 1865 various societies established "industrial schools" where trades such as sewing and shoemaking were taught "to develop ideas of self-dependence and self-support, which have been crushed out by slavery." [3] Indeed, elementary household arts were undoubtedly taught in many of the freedmen's schools, while the male students helped with the janitorial and repair work. However, domestic training and odd jobs on the campus were the extent of industrial training in most of the schools until after 1880, for while the idea of manual labor schools was popular, monetary difficulties created obstacles. Moreover, many of the freedmen's friends were anxious to prove that Negroes possessed the capacity for the most advanced intellectual endeavor.

While the Freedmen's Bureau and the various missionary groups exhibited some interest in industrial education, and while two states —Mississippi at Alcorn College and South Carolina jointly with the Methodist Church's Freedmen's Aid Society at Claflin College—were developing a reasonably effective program of mechanical and agricultural training, the most influential single agency fostering industrial education during Reconstruction was the American Missionary Association. An anti-slavery missionary society before the war, it enthusiastically took up the education of the freedmen. Because from the first its name has been practically synonymous with the finest in liberal arts education for Negroes, the Association's role in the rise of industrial education has ordinarily been overlooked. Yet between 1868 and 1871 at Hampton Institute in Virginia, at Atlanta University in Georgia, and at Tougaloo College in Mississippi, the Association inaugurated ambitious programs of industrial education.

It was Samuel Chapman Armstrong who, beginning in 1868, created at Hampton Institute (originally operated under American Missionary auspices) the first markedly successful agricultural and industrial school for Negroes. Certainly it was the most influential. Armstrong was the first to see the possibilities of using industrial education as a strategic ground of compromise between the white South, the white North, and the Negro. Sharing the traditional Puritan and Yankee outlook of the other missionary teachers and Freedmen's Bureau agents, Armstrong in addition brought to his work a conservative racial bias and a belief in the value of industrial education for "dependent" and "backward" races. To men of Armstrong's stamp, the colored races were slothful, backward, lascivious, and inferior and would remain so until they had assimilated the values and skills of Yankee civilization. For Armstrong the means of Negro advancement in a competitive, capitalist civilization lay essentially in combating what seemed to him to be shiftlessness, extravagance, and immorality, in working hard, buying land, saving money, creating stable Christian families, and learning trades. He urged Negroes to stay in the South, with their "best friends," the Southern whites, and to remain farmers, though striving to become independent landowners. He felt that Negroes should eschew politics and the demand for civil rights. These, he implied, would come when Negroes had acquired property and high moral standards—a process that would likely take centuries. Basically, Negroes were to help themselves, with guidance from whites of Armstrong's outlook.

This program of "uplift" by its very emphasis on moral and economic progress, and by relegating full citizenship rights to a distant and hazy future, made Armstrong's views easily translatable into terms acceptable to Southern whites. And as Armstrong saw, here too, was a program that would appeal to Northern capitalists who desired an end to the disorders of Reconstruction and the creation of a stable and trained labor supply. Seeming to accept an inferior status for Negroes—at least for the foreseeable future—Armstrong's outlook had a strong appeal because it was couched in philanthropic and paternalistic terms of uplift that salved the conscience of conservative Southerners and of Northerners—many of them former abolitionists —who had no genuine belief in racial equality. Above all it was couched in the platitudes of the day—in terms of laissez faire and the gospel of wealth, of uplifting backward races not really equal to whites (especially popular after Social Darwinism became the vogue), of self-help, morality, and economic independence—that appealed to the average middle and upper-class American. In short, Armstrong clearly perceived and made the first steps toward the Tuskegee Compromise which Booker Washington consummated between Negroes and "the best white people," North and South, at Atlanta, a quarter century later.

Armstrong viewed industrial education primarily as a moral force, but also emphasized the learning of trades for a future livelihood. Less important was the idea of students earning their way through school, for as Armstrong pointed out, no trade school could be fully self-supporting. He thought, however, that it was important for students to work for pay and thus support themselves at least in part, in order to inculcate the spirit of self-help, thrift and economic independence. Armstrong placed especially strong emphasis on agricultural education.[4]

Hampton was not the only Negro school with mechanical and agricultural training during the early 1870's. Moreover, during the latter part of the decade Mrs. Fanny Jackson-Coppin, principal of the Philadelphia Institute for Colored Youth, long noted for its classical curriculum, started her campaign for a manual trades department, and shortly introduced courses that culminated in an elaborate industrial program. And about 1880 Clark University at Atlanta introduced industrial work, the students making a few "cheap buildings" the first year.[5] Thus, by the time Tuskegee was founded in 1881, a significant number of influential institutions had inaugurated programs of industrial and agricultural education.

Finally, during the 1880's industrial education became the vogue in both Negro and white schools. This decade witnessed the widespread introduction of industrial arts in the white high schools, accompanied by a sharp debate over their value and culminating in the triumph of their advocates. As far as Negro education was concerned, in addition to this general trend, the Hampton philosophy appealing to conservative Northern and Southern whites gained in popularity. And more directly, the policy of the million dollar John F. Slater Fund, established in 1882, was of crucial importance in Negro education in the direction of industrial and agricultural training.[6]

Beginning its work in 1883 the Slater board, well aware of Armstrong's work, decided to give preference in its appropriations to institutions which gave instruction in trades and other manual occupations "that will enable colored youth to make a living, and to become useful citizens." In response to the program of the Slater fund and with its aid many Negro schools quickly instituted industrial and agricultural departments. By the school year of 1887–88 the fund was spending $42,500 annually to aid such programs in a maximum of forty-one schools. Though in his report to the trustees in October 1883, Attitucs G. Haygood, the fund's agent, had noted extensive opposition to industrial education, by 1886 he wrote that there were few schools that did not give it a place. Truly, the fund had "set forward incalculably the cause of industrial education in the best schools for colored people in the South." [7]

It is noteworthy that Haygood appropriated most of the funds to schools generally regarded as in the tradition of liberal rather than industrial education. Of course few attending Negro schools in this period were in the college departments, and industrial and agricultural training, like normal training, was generally limited to work on the elementary and high school level. Furthermore, few schools developed programs as elaborate as those of Tuskegee and Hampton or some of the land-grant colleges after 1890. Some paid lip-service to the idea rather than instituting an effective program which would have been too expensive for them. At times the program consisted mostly of manual training and home economics, with perhaps printing or shoemaking or gardening thrown in. Nevertheless, some of these schools that have been regarded as liberal arts institutions had rather elaborate industrial and agricultural programs. Printing was especially popular because it was financially remunerative; but many other industries, including bricklaying, masonry, forgework, carpentry, blacksmithing, shoemaking, wagon-making, cabinet-making, farming, and animal husbandry were established in the various schools.

A sampling of the work at certain of these schools that have not ordinarily been considered industrial institutions proves illuminating. Especially notable was the development in Atlanta, which with five colleges and a theological school was the leading center of Negro higher education in the country. While the Atlanta Baptist College (later Morehouse College) for men did not institute trades until the 1890's, the Atlanta Baptist Female Seminary (later Spelman College) had an excellent program in domestic arts, printing, and nursing. Methodist Clark University went in for sewing and dressmaking, printing, blacksmithing, advanced carpentry, a profitable carriage shop, and even simple engineering. Most elaborate was the development at Congregationalist Atlanta University, which in the early 1880's was doing extensive work in domestic arts and nursing and lesser work in agriculture and carpentry. In 1887 twelve wood-turning lathes run by steam power and other wood machinery and twelve forges and anvils for iron work had been secured. By 1889 the school had a printing office and was requiring students in all departments —including the college—to pursue some agricultural or industrial work. In 1891 it introduced a special mechanical course independent of the other departments, equipping the Knowles Industrial Building with an 18 horsepower engine, engine lathe, drill press, and emery grinder, and installing ten Goodyear shoe machines to train operatives in the shoe trade. It is no wonder that in 1886 Haygood commented that "the Atlanta University has committed itself heartily to the principle of industrial training." [8]

Fisk University was largely going through the motions on the matter of industrial education, but the same cannot be said of two other American Missionary Association schools, Talladega College and Tougaloo. At the latter, which opened in 1870 as a normal and industrial school like Hampton, from the very first those who wished might earn their way through school either on the farm or in the kitchen, as well as learn a practical trade or the art of domestic economy. During the 1880's student labor built a workshop and residence hall, special attention was given to stock raising and dairying, strawberries were raised and sold in Chicago, and the especially complete line of industries included tinning, blacksmithing, wagon-making, carpentry, painting, and steam-power sawing.[9]

Not only white denominational boards and in a few cases the states, but Negroes themselves made significant contributions during the late 1880's. The A.M.E. Church established institutions such as the Beaufort Normal and Industrial Academy in South Carolina and the Kittrell Normal and Industrial School in North Carolina. Price introduced industrial education at Livingstone, though he was chiefly interested in a high-grade liberal and theological curriculum. Socially prominent women in Washington directed the work of the Washington School for Colored Youth and were responsible for inaugurating industrial education in the public schools there with the support of the editor Calvin Chase and the high-school principal F. L. Cardozo. In 1886 some New Jersey Negroes organized an industrial school at Bordentown (later taken over by the state). The work of Fanny Jackson-Coppin has already been noted. Equally significant was the work of Lucy Laney who in 1886 laid the foundation for the Haines Normal and Industrial Institute in Augusta, Georgia.[10]

The white presidents and denominational boards responsible for most of the schools aided by the Slater Fund were enthusiastic in regard to industrial education. In their minds it served a variety of functions. It supplied a pedagogical aid for mental development; it served as a moral discipline inculcating habits of thrift and industry, a sense of the dignity of labor, and a feeling of economic independence; it prepared students to earn their living through the trades; it developed efficient and virtuous housewives and farmwives; and it was generally regarded as a fundamental instrument for the elevation of Negroes. Only a few schools had all of these objects in view. Training for the trades remained a largely unachieved goal because few schools could afford it. The moral and pedagogical note was a strong one, and was the chief rationale for industrial education as far as educators were concerned.

Behind the ideological rationale for industrial education, however sincere it was, lay other, more mundane considerations. As Haygood hinted in his report to the Slater Fund trustees in 1886: "There is more kindly feeling among Southern white people toward these schools than heretofore, and the influence of the Slater Fund has helped much in bringing about this better state of things. . . . That the Slater Fund has aided in raising funds, North as well as South, for the use of colored schools is certain." Five years later Haygood was even more emphatic: "But for the friendship won to some of these schools through the industries fostered by the Slater money, they would, by this time have ceased to be." [11]

In these few sentences Haygood went to the heart of the matter. Industrial education would buy Southern good will and Northern philanthropy. Here was concrete evidence of the insight of Armstrong's plan of compromise between North, South, and Negro. Here was the essence of Booker Washington's educational compromise in practice almost a decade before he became nationally known at Atlanta. Northern capitalists and philanthropists had no exalted idea of Negro equality, but felt a sense of noblesse oblige and wanted a supply of trained labor available for the industrialization of the South [12] and saw in industrial education an eminently "practical" method of educating Negroes. They simply did not appear to be aware that industrial education was equipping Negroes with skills that were being outmoded by the progress of the industrial revolution and preparing them for lives as small individualistic entrepreneurs at a time when the philosophy of economic individualism was becoming obsolete. Nor did the proponents of industrial education, steeped in the American agrarian myth of the glories of the yeoman farmer tradition, recognize the economic forces encouraging farm tenancy and urbanization. Conservative white Southerners either interpreted or misinterpreted industrial education as a device for preventing Negro advancement to the level of whites.

Informed philanthropic opinion had by 1890 given up the notion of training Negroes for specific trades and planned instead to give them general skills which would prepare them for rural living or for participating as semiskilled laborers in the industrialization of the South. Negroes were to be "uplifted" to the extent that they would adopt middle-class virtues and thus be a docile and stable laboring force.[13] It is one of the ironies of history that neither Hampton nor Tuskegee took the first step in offering Negroes the technical training necessary for effective competition in an industrial age. It was Howard University, noted for its high grade of liberal education, which in 1915 introduced engineering on a collegiate level in its newly reorganized School of Manual Arts and Applied Sciences.[14]

Negroes who supported industrial education from 1870–90 were motivated in part by the same reasoning as were white administrators. In addition, with the increasing proscription and discrimination, Negroes were turning as they had in the 1850's to self-help and economic and moral development. Part of this program was again industrial and agricultural education.

From the early 1870's Negro conventions and conferences frequently displayed an interest in industrial education. In 1890 the Afro-American League at its initial meeting, discussing the importance of thrift and morality, urged the establishment of such institutions rather than reliance exclusively on academic schools. Educators in Negro schools meeting in Washington in the same year insisted upon the necessity of both higher and industrial education. Considerable friction between the advocates of the two types had already been engendered, and the president of Atlanta University deprecated the slighting remarks passed by both sides.[15]

More eminent individuals were also coming to favor industrial education. J. W. Cromwell had been among its early supporters since the 1870's. Alexander Crummell, who had advocated agricultural and mechanical training along with education in the higher branches back in his abolitionist days, now preached the dignity of labor and the superiority of rural life and denounced the disproportion involved in overemphasis on higher education "to the neglect of the solid and practical" as a great evil. Yet he did not want to be misunderstood, for he was "exceedingly anxious" for the creation of a class of superior men and women trained in the higher culture. W. H. Crogman criticized liberal education for not preparing young men for useful lives and like Crummell stressed that all could not become professional men. Fortune was an enthusiastic proponent, who believed that classics, theology, science, and the professions were not yet suitable for the poverty-stricken Negro. "Many a colored farmer boy or mechanic has been spoiled to make a foppish gambler or loafer, a swaggering pedagogue or a cranky homiletician" by liberal education. Had the vast sums of money spent on higher education been spent for primary schools and schools of applied science, the race would have been much better off, both mentally and materially. Fortune believed in more than mere industrial training, and on one occasion sharply criticized a white Georgia bishop for urging it as appropriate for Negroes to the exclusion of the "calamity" of higher education.[16]

John R. Lynch concluded that Negroes had a duty to give their children an industrial education so that they might contend for admission into labor unions. T. McCants Stewart regarded it as a necessity if Negroes were to be a force in the skilled trades, and he spoke in terms of racial business co-operation. J. W. E. Bowen, who was well versed in educational philosophy, presented all of the standard arguments and thought that "applied to the Negro this new departure is fraught with incalculable good." It was no wonder then that that weathervane of public opinion, J. Mercer Langston, felt it politic as a congressman to introduce a bill to provide for the establishment of a national industrial university for the education of colored people.[17]

It is apparent that in the 1880's and 1890's as in the 1850's, industrial education was part of a larger complex of ideas emphasizing self-help and economic and moral development. Most of those cited here combined these ideas with an emphasis on racial solidarity. Significantly, pedagogical values, agricultural education, and manual training were a secondary consideration for articulate Negroes outside of strictly educational circles; primary were the instilling of moral values and the acquisition of a definite trade. This is particularly significant, because informed white opinion had come to hold that moral training, home economics, farming, manual training, and simple skills useful in rural areas were just about all most of the schools should offer.[18] Paradoxically, it was this very gap between white and Negro opinion that made it possible for industrial education to be acceptable to both groups.

There was always some opposition to the idea of industrial education for Negro youth. Most, even Washington himself, would have agreed that both types of education were necessary and that the problem was, as Kelly Miller said so often during the opening years of the next century, a matter of "ratio and proportion." Yet by the 1890's most of the Negro schools had programs of varying merit. By the time Haygood retired from the Slater Fund in 1891 he could assert that from being practiced in a mere half dozen schools in 1882, industrial education had come to the point where every important Negro school recognized the utility and necessity of industrial training. To be sure the Slater Fund was not solely responsible for the vogue of industrial education; a number of schools offered agricultural and mechanical training without benefit of Slater Fund largess. Yet its influence should not be minimized. As Atlanta University's W. E. B. Du Bois put it in 1902—scarcely a year before he launched his attack on Booker T. Washington: "Perhaps the greatest single impulse toward the economic emancipation of the Negro has been the singularly wise administration of the John F. Slater Fund." [19]

After 1890 two new developments affected the course of industrial education in Negro schools. As a result of the second land-grant college act, state industrial schools for Negroes were established throughout the South. The Slater Fund inaugurated a new policy under J. L. M. Curry's direction, concentrating its contributions upon a few institutions. By the late 1890's the number of schools receiving aid had been reduced from almost forty in the last years of Haygood's agency to ten or a dozen. Moreover, by 1901–2 over half of the money allocated went to Hampton and Tuskegee.[20] In spite of heroic efforts on the part of private schools and missionary organizations, Curry's policy simply weakened or destroyed the industrial programs in other institutions. In the Atlanta schools, except for Spelman, the effect was catastrophic. Even the strong departments at Atlanta University were suspended in 1894–95 for lack of funds.

After Curry died in 1903 Wallace Buttrick of the General Education Board took over the work of the Slater Fund and some improvement in the industrial program of the neglected schools took place. Nevertheless Curry's policy had worked irreparable harm in the majority of schools the Fund had formerly aided. Thus, when industrial education was enjoying its greatest vogue, due in large part to the eminence of Washington, it was markedly declining in institutions where it had existed for fifteen or more years. True, there flourished a group of newer schools, labeled industrial to obtain funds, but often doing work of inferior quality. At the time of World War I, in spite of strong philanthropic and ideological forces behind it, a federal survey found industrial work in Negro schools less well developed than in white schools, and that, in over half of the Negro schools offering industrial and manual training, work was inadequately or poorly done.[21] Apparently, few were ready to foot the bill for this particularly expensive form of education when it was proposed for Negroes, even though it was regarded as peculiarly fitted for them.

More significant than the torrent of words favoring industrial education were two ironic facts. Tougaloo College, begun as an industrial and normal school, and one of the few institutions to enjoy the uninterrupted largess of the Slater Fund during Curry's agency, inaugurated its college preparatory department in 1893–94, and its college department about 1901. And Spelman Seminary, even more favored by the Slater Fund and a leading center of industrial work, started its college about 1896.[22]

The reasons for the decline of industrial education in the very schools where it had enjoyed its earliest vogue, were largely financial, though the development of liberal higher education at Spelman and Tougaloo when industrial education was enjoying its greatest popularity suggests that certain leaders on denominational boards and certain college administrators had a larger vision as to the future of Negro education. It is evident from the reports of the Freedmen's Aid and Southern Education Society of the Methodist Church, for example, that desperate efforts were made to maintain industrial departments in the face of all difficulties, but as Slater funds were withdrawn, and as buildings burned down, industrial programs grew less and less substantial.[23] And the loss of Slater funds, so useful, as Haygood pointed out, in attracting additional contributions, undoubtedly was accompanied by increasing difficulties in obtaining other funds. As Kelly Miller said in 1902, "colored Universities have almost without exception added on industrial courses, largely for the sake of gaining the favor of northern philanthropists," who were becoming more and more committed to industrial education. Yet it appears that the vogue of Tuskegee and other strictly industrial schools was so great that the institutions which had strong liberal arts traditions in addition to their industrial departments were finding it harder and harder to obtain funds. Expensive industrial and agricultural work was bound to suffer in such a situation. In 1915 Hampton had an endowment of $2,709,344, and Tuskegee one of $1,942,112, while the best endowed of the liberal arts institutions, Lincoln University, Pennsylvania, had only $700,000. Du Bois as late as 1917 bitterly attacked Hampton for "her illiberal and seemingly selfish attitude toward other colored schools . . . decrying their work, criticizing and belittling their ideals, while her friends continually seek to divert to Hampton the already painfully meager revenues of the colored colleges." [24] A large part of the ideological conflict between the two types of education in the years after 1895 seems due to competition for funds.

But this has carried us beyond our story. By 1890 the ascendancy of industrial education had been established. Booker T. Washington was then one of the better-known Negro educators, yet he had not achieved a real national recognition. His influence, therefore, was scarcely of fundamental importance in creating the vogue for industrial education.

Washington, in fact, showed little or no originality in his program.

He exhibited a Pestalozzian enthusiasm for learning by doing and for teaching with concrete objects and the experiences of actual life.[25] His students erected buildings, worked their way through school, and learned trades which were intended to make them useful artisans (though most of them actually employed their skills in teaching). He summed up his point of view succinctly when he said in 1899: "First, we have found the industrial teaching useful in giving the student a chance to work out a portion of his expense while in school. Second, the school furnishes labour that has economic value and at the same time gives the student a chance to acquire knowledge and skill while performing the labor. Most of all, we find the industrial system valuable in teaching economy, thrift, and the dignity of labour and giving moral backbone to the students." He would not, he said, limit Negroes to industrial and agricultural education. But he felt that a material foundation, especially in farming, and the cultivation of the economic virtues were the only basis on which to erect a higher life. "I would set no limits to the attainment of the Negro in arts, in letters or statesmanship. . . . I plead for industrial education and development for the Negro not because I want to cramp him, but because I want to free him." [26]

Finally, Booker T. Washington was well aware of the function of industrial education as a platform of compromise between the white North, the white South, and the Negro. As early as 1884 he pointed out that many Southern whites objected to Negro education because educated Negroes did not work as manual laborers. "Just here is where the great mission of Industrial Education coupled with the mental comes in. It . . . secures the cooperation of the whites, and does the best possible thing for the black man." Elsewhere he said: "It was this training of the hands that furnished the first basis for anything like united and sympathetic interest and action between the two races at the South and the whites at the North and those at the South." [27]

These ideas had been in the minds of educators in Negro schools several years before Washington became famous. Both in pedagogical matters and in the social compromise which he effected, Washington derived his inspiration directly from Hampton Institute and Samuel Chapman Armstrong, who had erected the first successful model. The Slater Fund had been the chief impetus in advancing the cause of industrial education during the 1880's. By 1890 it was the vogue.

And at the zenith of this vogue Booker T. Washington stepped forth as its most potent symbol.

As is by now clear, this vogue was largely due to the fact that industrial education attracted support from a wide spectrum of opinion. And this was possible because of the large variety of interpretations to which it was susceptible. Industrial education in the 1890's appealed to many Negroes in the face of worsening conditions. It appealed to most Southern and many Northern whites because it appeared to relegate Negroes to an inferior position. It was accepted by philanthropists such as Oswald Garrison Villard of the N.A.A.C.P., who were sincerely interested in the welfare of the Negro. It also appealed to philanthropists less concerned with Negro rights, but who were impressed by the practicality of such a program for uplifting a "backward race" and creating a semiskilled labor force to exploit Southern resources. It appealed to a public opinion that saw pedagogical, economic, and moral values in its practice. It fitted the spirit of the age. All of these accounted for its vogue. And in 1895 when Washington made his famous Atlanta address, he emerged rather suddenly as a famous man and as *the* national Negro "leader," not because he was original in his proposals, but because his program had already become the core of the thought of influential groups in the North, in the South, and among Negroes.

Industrial education among Negroes had a long history before Washington emerged as a figure of national stature. A generation before he founded Tuskegee, Negroes advocated industrial education for very much the same reasons that he did, except that they did not phrase their ideas in terms of accommodation acceptable to an oppressive white community. Significantly, its espousal had always been associated with a program of self-help and racial solidarity. It was most popular with Negroes when increasing discrimination and failure to obtain the franchise and civil rights by agitation made them feel compelled to turn to such an indirect program as their only alternative if they were to prosper in the United States. In the 1880's converging and inter-related trends made industrial and agricultural training an ascendant form of Negro education which temporarily eclipsed liberal and higher education. Booker T. Washington became great and powerful not because he initiated a trend, but because he expressed it so well.

CHAPTER VII

BOOKER T. WASHINGTON: AN INTERPRETATION

Booker T. Washington had assiduously cultivated a good press and from time to time had received the attention accorded leaders who were, as the phrase went, "succeeding." Yet it was with relative suddenness that he emerged at the Atlanta Exposition in September 1895 as a figure of national reputation and the acknowledged leader of Negroes in America.

To Washington the solution of the race problem lay essentially in an application of the gospel of wealth, and he opened and closed his address that memorable afternoon with references to material prosperity. He urged Negroes to stay in the South, since when it came to business, pure and simple, it was in the South that the Negro was given a man's chance. Whites were urged to lend a helping hand in the uplifting of the Negroes in order to further the prosperity and well-being of their region. Coupled with this appeal to the self-interest of the white South was a conciliatory phraseology and a criticism of Negroes. Washington deprecated politics and the Reconstruction experience. He criticized Negroes for forgetting that the masses of the race were to live by the production of their hands and for permitting their grievances to overshadow their opportunities. He grew lyrical in reciting the loyalty and fidelity of Negroes—"the most patient, faithful, law-abiding and unresentful people that the world had seen." He denied any interest in social equality when he said: "In all things that are purely social we can be as separate as the five fingers, yet one as the hand in all things essential to mutual progress." In con-

100

clusion he asked for justice and an elimination of sectional differences and racial animosities, which, combined with material prosperity would usher in a new era for "our beloved South." [1]

Washington's emphasis upon economic prosperity was the hallmark of the age. The pledges of loyalty to the South and the identification of Negro uplift with the cause of the New South satisfied the "better class" of Southern whites and Northern investors; the generalities about justice to the Negro, of interracial co-operation in things essential to mutual progress, coupled with a denial of interest in social equality, encompassed a wide range of views that could be satisfied by ambiguous phraseology. Washington's generalized references to justice and progress and uplift soothed the pallid consciences of the dominant groups in the nation and at the same time allowed the white South to assume that justice could be achieved without granting Negroes political and civil rights. Yet a careful reading of the address indicates that it could also be interpreted as including ultimate goals more advanced than white Southerners could possibly support. Negroes must begin at the bottom, but surely Washington believed that eventually they would arrive at the top. Most Negroes interpreted social equality as meaning simply intimate social relationships which they did not desire, though most whites interpreted it as meaning the abolition of segregation. Even though Washington said that "it is important and right that all privileges of the law be ours; but it is vastly more important that we be prepared for the exercise of these privileges," and that "the opportunity to earn a dollar in a factory just now is worth infinitely more than the opportunity to spend a dollar in an opera house," his Negro supporters emphasized the future implications of his remarks, and his statement that "no race that has anything to contribute to the markets of the world is long in any degree ostracized." Unlike Negroes, the dominant whites were impressed by his conciliatory phraseology, confused his means for his ends, and were satisfied with the immediate program that he enunciated.

Washington captured his audience and assured his ascendancy primarily because his ideas accorded with the climate of opinion at the time. His association with industrial education, his emphasis upon the economic, and his conciliatory approach were undoubtedly important reasons why he was selected to speak on this prominent occasion. As Charles S. Johnson has suggested, Washington was effectively manipulating the symbols and myths dear to the majority of Americans.[2] It cannot be overemphasized that Washington's philosophy represents in large measure the basic tendencies of Negro thought in the period under consideration. Armstrong at Hampton had expressed the identical program as a ground of compromise between the white North, the white South, and the Negro. Indeed, it is clear that the chief source of Washington's philosophy was his experience at Hampton Institute, for he unmistakably bore the stamp of its founder.

How much the youthful Washington was shaped by his Hampton experience it is hard to say. He later recounted his strenuous efforts to obtain an education while working in the salt and coal mines at Malden, West Virginia, his lessons of cleanliness, thoroughness, and honesty as the servant of the wife of Yankee General Lewis Ruffner, and his bold trip, largely on foot, of five hundred miles from his home to Hampton. These were all evidences of the self-reliant personality that was his. Consequently, Yankee, Puritan, industrious Hampton and this ambitious and industrious youth of sixteen, who presented himself at its doors in the fall of 1872, clicked from the first. "At Hampton," he wrote later, "I found the opportunities . . . to learn thrift, economy and push. I was surrounded by an atmosphere of business, Christian influences, and the spirit of self-help, that seemed to have awakened every faculty in me." [3]

Armstrong was undoubtedly the most influential person in Washington's life, and his viewpoint contained the major ingredients of Washington's philosophy. Yet Washington was not fully committed to the Hampton idea when he left the school in 1875. He taught for two years in his home town in West Virginia, attended briefly the liberal arts Wayman Seminary in Washington, toyed with the idea of a political career, and started the study of law. Like the majority of his future students he at no time seriously considered practicing a trade for a livelihood. All questions were settled, however, when he was asked to return to Hampton to teach in 1879. Then, in 1881 Washington set forth to establish his own school at Tuskegee, Alabama, on the meager appropriations that resulted—paradoxically enough—from a political deal on the part of an ex-Confederate colonel who solicited Negro votes by promising to introduce a bill for a Negro industrial school in the legislature.[4] From then until 1895 Washington was engaged in building the school—a story of trial and success in the best Hampton tradition.

In discussing Washington's ideology it will be necessary to examine both his overtly expressed philosophy of accommodation and his covertly conducted attack on racial discrimination. His conciliatory approach was an important factor in his achieving eminence, and his continued ascendancy in Negro affairs, due as it was to the support of dominant white elements, depended upon his playing this tactful role to the fullest extent. Yet his very prominence brought him into situations that led to secret activities that directly contradicted the ideology he officially espoused.

In comparison with other figures in this study, Washington's expressed ideology remained remarkably consistent throughout his public life.[5] There appear to have been no significant changes in his publicly stated outlook except for a somewhat more accommodating attitude after 1895 than before, and except for a growing emphasis upon racial solidarity and economic chauvinism after the turn of the century. Through the years he was conciliatory in manner toward the white South, emphasized the ordinary economic and moral virtues, claimed that he regarded political and civil rights as secondary and ultimate rather than as primary and immediate aims, held up Negro moral and economic progress to public view, even while criticizing the weaknesses of Negroes and insisting that they should shoulder much of the blame for their status and the primary responsibility for their own advancement, and optimistically insisted that race relations were improving.

The central theme in Washington's philosophy was that through thrift, industry, and Christian character Negroes would eventually attain their constitutional rights. To Washington it seemed but proper that Negroes would have to measure up to American standards of morality and material prosperity if they were to succeed in the Social Darwinist race of life. Just as the individual who succeeds can do something that the world wants done well, so with a race. Things would be on a different footing if it became common to associate the possession of wealth with a black skin. "It is not within the province of human nature that the man who is intelligent and virtuous, and owns and cultivates the best farm in his county, shall very long be denied the proper respect and consideration."[6]

Consequently Negroes, he felt, must learn trades in order to compete with whites. He blamed Negroes for neglecting skills acquired under slavery, for the loss of what had been practically a monopoly of the skilled labor in the South at the close of the Civil War. He feared that unless industrial schools filled the breach, the next twenty years would witness the economic demise of the Negro. He was often critical of higher education. He never tired of retelling the anecdotes about the rosewood piano in the tumble-down cabin, or about the young man he found sitting in an unkempt cabin, studying from a French grammar. He denied that he intended to minimize the value of higher education, and his own children in fact enjoyed its advantages, but practical education, he believed, should come first in the rise of a people toward civilization. Occasionally, he praised higher education, but he often cited cases of college graduates who were accomplishing nothing, and once at least he referred to "the college bacillus." [7]

Fundamentally, Washington did not think in terms of a subordinate place in the American economy for Negroes. Though his language was ambiguous, he thought in terms of developing a substantial propertied class of landowners and businessmen. There was, as he often put it, a great need for "captains of industry." He felt a deep sympathy with the wealthy, and he preferred to talk most of all to audiences of businessmen who, he found, were quick to grasp what he was saying. In all this he was thoroughly in accord with the New South philosophy. He praised Robert C. Ogden of Wanamaker's (a trustee of Tuskegee and Hampton and chairman of the General Education Board) and H. H. Rogers, the Standard Oil and railroad magnate, as men whose interest in uplifting the Negro was partly motivated by their desire to develop one of the neglected resources of the South.[8]

Part of Washington's outlook toward capital and the New South was his antagonistic attitude toward labor unions. He recollected that before the days of strikes in the West Virginia coal mines where he had worked, he had known miners with considerable sums in the bank, "but as soon as the professional labor agitators got control, the savings of even the more thrifty ones began disappearing." To some extent, he felt, the loss of the Negro's hold on the skilled trades was due to the unions. He boasted that Negro labor was, if fairly treated, "the best free labor in the world," not given to striking. Later, writing in the *Atlantic Monthly* in 1913, Washington, though still basically hostile, appeared somewhat more favorable toward unions. He admitted that there were cases in which labor unions had used their influence on behalf of Negroes even in the South, and he knew of instances in which Negroes had taken a leading part in the work of their unions. Nevertheless, he felt that unions would cease to discriminate only to the extent that they feared Negro strikebreakers.[9]

Exceedingly important in Washington's outlook was an emphasis on agriculture and rural landownership that has ordinarily been overlooked. He constantly deprecated migration to cities where, he said, the Negro was at his worst and insisted that Negroes should stay on the farmlands of the South. Since all peoples who had gained wealth and recognition had come up from the soil, agriculture should be the chief occupation of Negroes, who should be encouraged to own and cultivate the soil. While he called Negroes the best labor for Southern farms, he optimistically looked forward to an independent yeomanry, respected in their communities.

Also associated with Washington's middle-class and Social Darwinist philosophy were the ideas of the value of struggle in achieving success, of self-help, and of "taking advantage of disadvantages." As he put it, "No race of people ever got upon its feet without severe and constant struggle, often in the face of the greatest disappointment." [10] He turned misfortune into good fortune, and middle-class rationalization of the strenuous life into an accommodating rationalization of the Negro's status. Paradoxical as it might seem, the difficulties facing the Negro had on the whole helped him more than they had hindered him, for under pressure the Negro had put forth more energy which, constructively channeled, had been of untold value.

While whites had some responsibility, the most important part in the Negro's progress was to be played by the Negro himself; the race's future recognition lay within its own hands. On the negative side this emphasis on self-help involved a tendency to blame Negroes for their condition. Washington constantly criticized them for seeking higher rather than practical education, for their loss of places in the skilled trades, for their lack of morality and economic virtues, and for their tendency toward agitation and complaint. But in its positive aspects this emphasis involved race pride and solidarity. Negroes should be proud of their history and their great men. For a race to grow strong and powerful it must honor its heroes. Negroes should not expect any great success until they learned to imitate the Jews, who through unity and faith in themselves were becoming more and more influential. He showed considerable pride in the all-Negro communities. At times he espoused a high degree of racial solidarity and economic nationalism. On one occasion he declared: "We are a nation within a nation." While Negroes should be the last to draw the color line, at the same time they should see to it that "in every wise and legitimate way our people are taught to patronise racial enterprises." [11]

If emphasis upon racial pride and self-help through economic and moral development formed one side of Washington's thinking, another was his insistence that interracial harmony and white good will were prerequisite to the Negro's advancement. In appealing to whites Washington spoke in both moral and practical terms. Southern whites should aid Negroes out of economic self-interest and should act justly since to do less would corrupt their moral fiber. Washington constantly reiterated his love for the South, his faith in the Southern white man's sense of justice, his belief that the South afforded Negroes more economic opportunity than the North. In 1912, answering the question "Is the Negro Having a Fair Chance?" he did go so far as to admit the existence of the standard grievances, but declared that nowhere were there ten million black people who had greater opportunities or were making greater progress than the Negroes of the South; nowhere had any race "had the assistance, the direction, and the sympathy of another race in all its efforts to rise to such an extent as the Negro in the United States." Washington devoted one whole book, *The Man Farthest Down* (1912), to the thesis that American Negroes were better off than the depressed classes in Europe. In general, Washington appealed to the highest sentiments and motives of the whites and brushed lightly over their prejudices and injustices in an attempt to create the favorable sentiment without which Negro progress was doomed. He frequently referred to the friendship Southern whites exhibited toward Negroes and constantly cited examples of harmonious relations between the races. At a time when Mississippi was notorious for "whitecapping" (the attacking of business establishments owned by prosperous Negroes who were then run out of town), he opined that "there, more than anywhere else, the colored people seem to have discovered that, in gaining habits of thrift and industry, in getting property, and in making themselves useful, there is a door of hope open for them which the South has no disposition to close." He was incurably optimistic in his utterances—as he said, "We owe it not only to ourselves, but to our children, to look always upon the bright side of life." [12]

Washington constantly deprecated protest and agitation. Leading virtuous, respectable lives and acquiring wealth would advance the race more than any number of books and speeches. Speaking at the Afro-American Council in July 1903 he urged patience and optimism:

In the long run it is the race or individual that exercises the most patience, forbearance, and self-control in the midst of trying conditions that wins . . . the respect of the world. . . . We have a right in a conservative and sensible manner to enter our complaints, but we shall make a fatal error if we yield to the temptation of believing that mere opposition to our wrongs . . . will take the place of progressive, constructive action. . . . Let us not forget to lay the greatest stress upon the opportunities open to us, especially here in the South, for constructive growth in labor, in business and education. . . . An inch of progress is worth more than a yard of complaint.[13]

While Washington never changed his basic ideology, before 1895 he tended to be more frank, though always tactful, regarding the Negro's goals. In 1894, for example, he admitted that conventions and organizations whose aims were to redress certain grievances were "right and proper," though they should not be the chief reliance of the race, and went on to declare that if his approach did not in time bring every political and civil right then everything, even the teaching of Christ, was false. As conditions grew worse Washington became more rather than less conciliatory. The outstanding exception to his general policy was his address at the Jubilee celebration held in Chicago after the Spanish-American War, where with President McKinley in the audience, he made one of his famous *faux pas*. Reviewing the valorous deeds of Negroes in the military history of the United States, especially in the recent war, he contended that a race that was thus willing to die for its country should be given the highest opportunity to live for its country. Americans had won every conflict in which they had been engaged, "except the effort to conquer ourselves in the blotting out of racial prejudice. . . . Until we thus conquer ourselves I make no empty statement when I say that we shall have a cancer gnawing at the heart of this republic that shall some day prove to be as dangerous as an attack from an army without or within." This statement aroused considerable ire in the Southern press, and Washington characteristically qualified his remarks. He explained that he seldom referred to prejudice because it was something to be lived down rather than talked down, but since that meeting symbolized the end of sectional feelings he had thought it an appropriate time to ask for "the blotting out of racial prejudice as far as possible in 'business and civil relations.' " [14]

On the three major issues of segregation, lynching, and the franchise, the Tuskegeean expressed himself with characteristic circumspection. Prior to the Atlanta address he had made it clear that he opposed segregation in transportation. Speaking in 1884 he had said that "the Governor of Alabama would probably count it no disgrace to ride in the same railroad coach with a colored man." As late as 1894 he urged Negroes to follow the example of Atlanta citizens who had boycotted the newly segregated streetcars and predicted that such economic pressures would make it respectable for both races to ride in the same railway coach as well. But after 1895 he held that separate but equal facilities would be satisfactory. As he once put it: "All . . . parts of the world have their own peculiar customs and prejudices. For that reason it is a part of common-sense to respect them." [15] And he did respect the customs of other parts of the world. He accepted President Roosevelt's dinner invitation in 1901 after careful consideration. He was on intimate terms with distinguished philanthropists and was entertained in circles in the North and abroad that few white Southerners could have entered. Yet he declared that the objection to the Jim Crow car was "not the separation, but the inadequacy of the accommodations." Again, speaking in 1914 on the matter of municipal segregation ordinances, Washington stirred up a hornet's nest of criticism by remarking: "Let us, in the future, spend less time talking about the part of the city that we cannot live in, and more time in making the part of the city that we can live in beautiful and attractive." Yet in a posthumously published account of "My View of Segregation Laws" Washington—or his ghostwriter—tactfully gave his reasons for condemning them, and in a most unusual concluding statement openly declared that segregation was "ill-advised" because it was unjust and all thoughtful Negroes resented injustice. There was no case of segregation, he said, that had not widened the breach between the two races. That Negroes did not constantly express their embitterment, he added, was not proof that they did not feel it.[16]

Even on lynching Washington expressed himself rarely, but when he did his statements received considerable attention. He generally emphasized the harm lynching did to the whites—to their moral fiber, to economic conditions, and to the reputation of the South—and at the same time counseled Negroes to cultivate industry and cease the idleness that led to crime. Yet he could be forthright in his condemnation of mob violence. "Within the last fortnight," he said in a statement issued to the press in 1904,

three members of my race have been burned at the stake; one of them was a woman. No one . . . was charged with any crime even remotely connected with the abuse of a white woman. . . . Two of them occurred on Sunday afternoon in sight of a Christian church. . . . The custom of burning human beings has become so common as scarcely to excite interest. . . . There is no shadow of excuse for departure from legal methods in the cases of individuals accused of murder.[17]

Ordinarily, Washington did not discuss politics, but there were occasions when he did admit that "I do not favor the Negro's giving up anything which is fundamental and which has been guaranteed to him by the Constitution. . . . It is not best for him to relinquish his rights; nor would his doing so be best for the Southern white man." He was critical of Reconstruction, when Negroes had started at the top instead of the bottom, in the senate instead of at the plow, and had been the unwitting instruments of corrupt carpet-bagger politicians. "In a word, too much stress had been placed upon the mere matter of voting and holding political office rather than upon the preparation for the highest citizenship." Washington's solution to the question of political rights was suffrage restriction applied to both races—a notion that had been growing in popularity since about 1890. "The permanent cure for our present evils will come through a property and educational test for voting that shall apply honestly and fairly to both races." In a letter to the Louisiana Constitutional Convention of 1898 he outlined his views. He was, he said, no politician, but had always advised Negroes to acquire property, intelligence, and character as the basis of good citizenship, rather than to engage in political agitation. He agreed that franchise restrictions were necessary to rid the South of ignorant and corrupt government, but suggested that no state could pass a law that would permit an ignorant white man to vote and disfranchise ignorant Negroes "without dwarfing for all time the morals of the white man in the South." In 1899, in referring to the disfranchisement bill before the Georgia legislature, he had forcefully declared that its object was to disfranchise the Negroes. Yet three years later he became notorious for his defense of the disfranchisement constitutions: "Every revised constitution throughout the Southern States has put a premium upon intelligence, ownership of property, thrift and character," he wrote in a general letter to the press.[18] But his hope that these qualifications would be equitably applied remained unfulfilled, and after 1905 Washington no longer rationalized about the disfranchisement constitutions, as he had done, but simply held that the acquisition of character, wealth, and education would break down racial discrimination.

All in all, in viewing Washington's philosophy, one is most impressed by his accommodating approach. By carefully selected ambiguities in language, by mentioning political and civil rights but seldom and then only in tactful and vague terms, he effectively masked the ultimate implications of his philosophy. For this reason his philosophy must be viewed as an accommodating one in the context of Southern race relations. In the context of the Negro thinking of the period, perhaps the most significant thing in his philosophy was his emphasis upon self-help and racial solidarity.

In certain quarters Washington did not like to be considered an extreme accommodator. Writing to Francis J. Garrison of the New York Evening *Post* in 1899 he said that he hesitated to appear on the same platform with W. H. Councill, who "has the reputation of simply toadying to the Southern white people." In a letter to the noted author and lawyer, Charles W. Chesnutt, he denied that he was interested only in education and property, and he enclosed two recent statements he had made on the franchise and lynching. True, he spoke only when he thought it would be effective, rather than agitating all the time, but "I cannot understand what you or others want me to do that I have left undone." He conceded that agitation had its place; justice he believed would be attained both through education and agitation. "You will assist in bringing it about in your way and those of us who are laboring in the South will do something to bring it about in our way." [19]

Although overtly Washington minimized the importance of the franchise and civil rights, covertly he was deeply involved in political affairs and in efforts to prevent disfranchisement and other forms of discrimination.

For example, he lobbied against the Hardwick disfranchisement bill in Georgia in 1899. While his public ambiguities permitted Southern whites to think that he accepted disfranchisement if they chose to, through the same ambiguities and by private communications Washington tried to keep Negroes thinking otherwise. In 1903 when the Atlanta editor Clark Howell implied that Washington opposed Negro officeholding, he did not openly contradict him, but asked T. Thomas Fortune to editorialize in the *Age* that Howell had no grounds for placing Washington in such a position, for it was "well understood that he, while from the first deprecating the Negro's making political agitation and office-holding the most prominent and fundamental part of his career, has not gone any farther." [20] Again, while Washington opposed proposals to enforce the representation provisions of the fourteenth amendment (because he felt that the South would accept reduction in representation and thus stamp disfranchisement with the seal of constitutionality), he was secretly engaged in attacking the disfranchisement constitutions by court action. As early as 1900 he was asking certain philanthropists for money to fight the electoral provisions of the Louisiana constitution. Subsequently, he worked secretly through the financial secretary of the Afro-American Council's legal bureau, personally spending a great deal of money and energy fighting the Louisiana test case.[21] At the time of the Alabama Constitutional Convention in 1901 he used his influence with important whites in an attempt to prevent discriminatory provisions that would apply to Negroes only.[22] He was later deeply involved in testing the Alabama disfranchisement laws in the federal courts in 1903 and 1904. So circumspect was he in this instance that his secretary, Emmett J. Scott, and the New York lawyer Wilford Smith corresponded about the cases under pseudonyms and represented the sums involved in code. Washington was also interested in efforts to prevent or undermine disfranchisement in other states. For example, in Maryland, where disfranchisement later failed, he had a Catholic lawyer, F. L. McGhee of St. Paul, approach the Catholic hierarchy in an attempt to secure its opposition to disfranchisement and urged the Episcopal divine George Freeman Bragg of Baltimore to use his influence among important whites.[23] Washington contributed money generously to the test cases and other efforts, though, except in the border states, they were unsuccessful. In 1903 and 1904 he personally "spent at least four thousand dollars in cash, out of my own pocket . . . in advancing the rights of the black man." [24]

Washington's political involvement went even deeper. Although he always discreetly denied any interest in politics, he was engaged in patronage distribution under Roosevelt and Taft, in fighting the lily-white Republicans, and in getting out the Negro vote for the Republicans at national elections. He might say that he disliked the atmosphere at Washington because it was impossible to build up a race whose leaders were spending most of their time and energy in trying to get into or stay in office,[25] but under Roosevelt he became the arbiter of Negro appointments to federal office. Roosevelt started consulting Washington almost as soon as he took office, and later claimed that Washington had approved of his policy of appointing fewer but better-qualified Negroes.[26] Numerous politicians old and new were soon writing to Tuskegee for favors, and in a few cases Roosevelt consulted Washington in regard to white candidates.[27] Ex-Congressman George H. White unsuccessfully appealed to Washington after the White House indicated that "a letter from you would greatly strengthen my chances." Scott reported that the President's assertion to one office seeker that he would consider him only with Washington's endorsement, had "scared these old fellows as they never have been scared before." Washington had at his disposal a number of collectorships of ports and internal revenue, receiverships of public monies in the land office, and several diplomatic posts, as well as the positions of auditor of the Navy, register of the Treasury and recorder of the deeds. As Roosevelt wrote to a friend in 1903, his Negro appointees "were all recommended to me by Booker T. Washington." [28] Furthermore, Roosevelt sought Washington's advice on presidential speeches and messages to Congress and consulted him on most matters concerning the Negro. Every four years also Washington took charge of the Negro end of the Republican presidential campaign.[29]

If Washington reaped the rewards of politics, he also experienced its vicissitudes. From the start he was fighting a desperate but losing battle against the lily-white Republicans. His correspondence teems with material on the struggle, especially in Louisiana and Alabama, and in other states as well. As he wrote to Walter L. Cohen of the New Orleans land office on October 5, 1905: "What I have attempted in Louisiana I have attempted to do in nearly every one of the Southern States, as you and others are in a position to know, and but for my action, as feeble as it was, the colored people would have been completely overthrown and the Lily Whites would have been in complete control in nearly every Southern State." Later, troubles came thick and fast after Taft's inauguration. The new president appointed fewer Negroes to office and did not consult Washington as much as Roosevelt had done. Not until 1911, after desperate efforts at convincing the administration of the need for some decent plums in order to retain the Negro vote, was it finally arranged to make a few significant appointments, most notably that of W. H. Lewis as assistant attorney general—the highest position held by a Negro in the federal government up to that time.

In areas other than politics Washington also played an active behind-the-scenes role. On the Seth Carter (Texas) and Dan Rogers (Alabama) cases involving discrimination in the matter of representation on juries, Washington worked closely with the lawyer Wilford Smith and contributed liberally to their financing.[30] He was interested in preventing Negro tenants who had accidentally or in ignorance violated their contracts from being sentenced to the chain gang.[31] He was concerned in the Alonzo Bailey Peonage Case, and when the Supreme Court declared peonage illegal, confided to friends that he and his associates had been working at the case for over two years, securing the free services of some of the best lawyers in Montgomery and the assistance of other leading white people. Yet Washington characteristically interceded to reduce the sentence of the convicted man, who was soon released.[32]

Of special interest are Washington's efforts against railroad segregation. At Washington's suggestion Giles B. Jackson of Richmond undertook the legal fight against the Jim Crow Law in Virginia in 1901.[33] When Tennessee in 1903 in effect prohibited Pullman accommodations for Negroes by requiring that such facilities be entirely separate, he stepped into the breach. He worked closely with Napier in Nashville and enlisted the aid of Atlanta leaders like W. E. B. Du Bois. This group, however, did not succeed in discussing the matter with Pullman Company president Robert Todd Lincoln, in spite of the intercession of another railroad leader, William H. Baldwin, president of the Long Island Railroad, an important figure in the Pennsylvania and Southern systems, and Washington's closest white friend. And, though Washington wanted to start a suit, the Nashville people failed to act.[34] Again, in 1906, employing the Howard University Professor Kelly Miller and the Boston lawyer

Archibald W. Grimké as intermediaries, Washington discreetly supplied funds to pay ex-Senator Henry W. Blair of New Hampshire to lobby against the Warner-Foraker Amendment to the Hepburn Railway Act.[35] This amendment, by requiring equality of accommodations in interstate travel, would have impliedly condoned segregation throughout the country, under the separate-but-equal doctrine. The amendment was defeated, but whether due to Blair's lobbying or to the protests of Negro organizations is hard to say.

Thus, in spite of his accommodating tone and his verbal emphasis upon economy as the solution to the race problem, Washington was surreptitiously engaged in undermining the American race system by a direct attack upon disfranchisement and segregation, and in spite of his strictures against political activity he was a powerful politician in his own right.

Comparable to Washington's influence in politics was his position with the philanthropists. He wielded an enormous influence in appropriations made by Carnegie, Rosenwald, the General Education Board, and the Phelps-Stokes and Jeanes Funds. Negro schools that received Carnegie libraries received them at Washington's suggestion, and even applied for them upon his advice.[36] Contributors sought his advice on the worthiness of schools; college administrators asked his advice on personnel. His weight was especially appreciated by the liberal arts colleges. Washington accepted a place on the boards of trustees of Howard University in 1907 and of Fisk University in 1909. In the case of Fisk he proved exceedingly helpful in attracting philanthropic contributions.[37] So complete was Washington's control over educational philanthropy that John Hope, president of Atlanta Baptist College, and a member of the anti-Bookerite Niagara Movement, found the doors of the foundations entirely closed to him. Only through the intercession of his friend Robert Russa Moton, a member of the Hampton circle and Washington's successor at Tuskegee, was Hope able to obtain Washington's necessary endorsement of his school to philanthropists such as Carnegie.[38]

Washington's popularity with leading whites and his power in philanthropic and political circles enhanced his prestige and power within the Negro community. His influence was felt in multifarious ways beyond his control over philanthropy and political appointments. His power over the Negro press was considerable and in large measure stifled criticism of his policies. His influence extended into the Negro churches, and his friendship and assistance were eagerly sought by those seeking positions in the church. Between 1902 and 1904 and perhaps longer, Washington controlled the avowedly protest Afro-American Council, the leading Negro rights organization prior to 1905. Whether or not Washington was a "benevolent despot" as one recent biographer has asserted,[39] is an open question, but that he wielded enormous power over the Negro community is undeniable.

It was this quasi-dictatorial power as much as anything else that alienated W. E. B. Du Bois from Washington and his program. Once Washington had achieved eminence he grew extremely sensitive to adverse criticism from Negroes. From the first some had opposed his viewpoint, and while many rushed to his support after he became the puissant adviser to Theodore Roosevelt, somehow "the opposition" (as Washington often referred to his critics) grew apace. Objections were raised to the arbitrary power of the "Tuskegee machine," as Du Bois called it, and to Washington's soft-pedaling of political and civil rights. From 1903 on Washington found himself increasingly under attack. He used every means at his disposal to combat his critics—his influence with the press, placing spies in the opposition movements, depriving their members of church and political positions. The high point of the attack on Washington, the formation of the National Association for the Advancement of Colored People in 1909–10, came at the very time when his political power was slipping, and after 1913 he had no political influence at all, while the N.A.A.C.P. was becoming stronger. By the time he died Washington had lost much of his power.

Washington's struggle against the various protest groups is interesting in that they had the same ultimate goal as he did, and came out frankly for the very things for which he was working surreptitiously. Yet Washington appears to have regarded them as more dangerous to the welfare of the race than "friends" like Carnegie, Taft, and Roosevelt, who were not genuine equalitarians and who thought Negroes should not emphasize politics and civil rights. Washington sincerely believed that his program would be the most effective in the long run, but he did not object too much to militance and agitation in the newspapers that supported him. His attacks upon "the opposition" suggest that something more than tactics or ideologies was at stake. It appears that Washington feared the effect of his critics on his personal power and prestige. He did not object to protest too much as long as it was not aimed at him and his policies. As he wrote R. C. Ogden, "wise, conservative agitation looking toward securing the rights of colored people on the part of the people of the North is not hurtful." [40]

It would appear to this author that a large part of Washington's motivation was his desire for power. To a large extent he had to be satisfied with the substance rather than the symbols of power. His desire for power and prestige, however, does not necessarily indicate insincerity or hypocrisy. It is usually hard to distinguish where altruism ends and self-interest begins. So thoroughly and inextricably bound together in Washington's mind were his program for racial elevation and his own personal career, that he genuinely thought that he and only he was in the best position to advance the interests of the race.

Thus, although Washington held to full citizenship rights and integration as his objective, he masked this goal beneath an approach that satisfied influential elements that were either indifferent or hostile to its fulfillment. He was not the first to combine a constructive, even militant emphasis upon self-help, racial co-operation and economic development with a conciliatory, ingratiating, and accommodating approach to the white South. But his name is the one most indissolubly linked with this combination. He was, as one of his followers put it, attempting to bring the wooden horse within the walls of Troy.

Washington apparently really believed that in the face of an economic and moral development that assimilated Negroes to American middle-class standards, prejudice would diminish and the barriers of discrimination would crumble. He emphasized duties rather than rights; the Negro's faults rather than his grievances; his opportunities rather than his difficulties. He stressed means rather than ends. He was optimistic rather than pessimistic. He stressed economics above politics, industrial above liberal education, self-help above dependence on the national government. He taught that rural life was superior to urban life. He professed a deep love for the South and a profound faith in the goodness of the Southern whites—at least of the "better class." He appealed more to the self-interest of the whites—their economic and moral good—than to their sense of justice.

The ambiguities in Washington's philosophy were vital to his success. Negroes who supported him looked to his tactfully, usually vaguely worded expressions on ultimate goals. Conservative Southerners were attracted by his seeming acceptance of disfranchisement and segregation, and by his flattery. Industrialists and philanthropists appreciated his petit bourgeois outlook. Washington's skillful manipulation of popular symbols and myths like the gospel of wealth and the doctrines of Social Darwinism enhanced his effectiveness. Terms like "social equality," "civil relations," "constitutional rights," "Christian character," "industrial education," and "justice" were capable of a wide variety of interpretations. The Supreme Court, for example, did not appear to think that the fourteenth and fifteenth amendments prohibited segregation and the use of various subterfuges that effected disfranchisement. Washington shrewdly used these ambiguities, and they were an important source both of his popularity and of the acrimonious discussion over his policy that occupied Negroes for many years.

Washington did not appeal to all groups. Extremists among white Southerners liked him no more than did the Negro "radicals." Men such as Governor Vardaman of Mississippi and the author Thomas Dixon, who feared any Negro advancement, opposed the Tuskegeean's program of elevation and uplift. Washington basically appealed to conservative, propertied elements both North and South. His stress upon the economic rather than the political was parallel to the New South philosophy of emphasizing industry rather than politics as a way of advancing the South in the councils of the nation. Yet he also capitalized on the myth of the small farmer, and the romantic agrarian traditions of the South. His call for a justly applied property and educational test that would disfranchise ignorant and poor Negroes and whites alike, and enfranchise the propertied, taxpaying, conservative Negroes, met the approval of important elements in the Black Belt plantation and urban areas of the South, who had no more love for the "poor whites" than Washington did. Again, Washington espoused a Social Darwinism of competition between individuals and races, of uplifting backward races, that was congenial to his age. He conveniently put Negro equality off into a hazy future that did not disturb the "practical" and prejudiced men of his generation. At the same time, by blaming Negroes for their condition, by calling them a backward race, by asserting that an era of justice would ultimately be ushered in, by flattering the whites for what little they had done for Negroes, he palliated any pangs of conscience that the whites might have had.

His program also appealed to a substantial group of Negroes—to those Negroes who were coming to count for most—in large part to a rising middle class. In fact, stress upon economics as an indirect route to the solution of the race problem, interest in industrial education, the appeal to race pride and solidarity, and denial of any interest in social equality were all ideas that had become dominant in the Negro community. The older upper-class Negroes in certain Northern centers, who had their economic and sometimes their social roots in the white communities, were less sympathetic to Washington. But to self-made middle-class Negroes, and to lower middle-class Negroes on the make, to the leaders and supporters of Negro fraternal enterprises, to businessmen who depended on the Negro community for their livelihood, Washington's message seemed common sense. Interestingly enough, this group, especially in the North, did not always express Washington's conciliatory tone, but assumed that Washington was using it to placate the white South.

To what extent Washington directly influenced Negro thought is difficult to evaluate. Washington was acceptable to Negroes partly because of the prestige and power he held among whites, and partly because his views—except for his conciliatory phraseology—were dominant in the Negro community throughout the country, and his accommodating approach was general throughout the South. Then, too, his Negro supporters read a great deal into his generalizations about eventual justice and constitutional rights. The fact that Negroes tended to see in his words what they already believed would appear to minimize his direct influence. Yet his prestige, the teachers sent out by Tuskegee and her daughter schools, and the widespread publicity generated by the National Negro Business League of which Washington was the founder and president, undoubtedly had a significant impact on Negro thought, reinforcing tendencies already in the foreground.

PART FOUR

The Institutionalization of Self-Help and Racial Solidarity, 1880–1915

Lifting as We Climb.
> Motto of the National Association of Colored Women.

Self-Help is Our Motto.
> The Farmers' Improvement Society of Texas.

CHAPTER VIII

AGENCIES OF PROPAGANDA, PROTEST, AND SOCIAL WELFARE

By the last decade of the century it was clear that the main themes in Negro thinking on the race problem were that for the most part Negroes must work out their own salvation in a hostile environment and that, furthermore, they must be united in their efforts at racial elevation. Even in the North Negroes felt they were, as the phraseology of the time went, being forced back upon themselves. This emphasis on self-help and solidarity tended to stress the economic approach, but it was also applied to efforts of protest and agitation. Frequently, as in Washington's case, this philosophy was associated with a flattering approach to the white South. But always it expressed—implicitly if not explicitly—a determination to succeed and participate in the "promise of American life."

Beyond the utterances of men active in public life, these doctrines found expression in the institutional life of the Negro community. Schools inculcated them, farmers' conferences throughout the South urged them, Negro businessmen's organizations made them the core of their platform. Fraternal societies and social welfare agencies attempted to put these ideals into practice. Banks, insurance companies, and Negro business generally appealed to them. Independent Negro organizations of protest and agitation insisted upon them as the foundation of their own work. The all-Negro towns represented their epitome. And beneath the varied developments, stimulated by and at the same time encouraging the ideals of self-help and solidarity,

121

lay a rising Negro entrepreneurial class dependent on the Negro market.

These institutional developments will be surveyed in this section. They show clearly the pervasiveness of the doctrines of self-help and racial solidarity—the keynote of Negro thought in the Age of Booker T. Washington—and they are especially significant because they come closer than statements of eminent individuals to indicating the outlook of Negroes as a group. Linked with the patterns of thought, these institutional developments both stimulated and reflected them.

It would be erroneous to attribute too great a role to Hampton and Tuskegee as sources of the philosophy of self-help and racial solidarity during the half century after the Compromise of 1877. Yet their influence, especially in fostering the cluster of ideas that coupled self-help and racial solidarity with economic development and moral virtue—and often with an accommodating tone—was enormous. Both Armstrong and Washington worked hard at reaching the public through the press and other agencies. Of vital importance was the stream of teachers that they sent into all parts of the South, thoroughly imbued with the gospel according to Hampton and Tuskegee. An ambitious few built their own schools and these, like those founded by others, and like Tuskegee itself, were generally regarded as examples of self-help, even though they were ordinarily largely dependent on white philanthropy.

Both institutions, moreover, held well-publicized annual conferences—an important instrument of propaganda. Especially noted were Tuskegee's Negro Farmers' Conferences, instituted in 1890. Such conferences were not original with Washington, but he made them famous.[1] According to Washington:

> The matters considered at the conference are those that the coloured people have it in their own power to control—such as the evils of the mortgage system, the one-room cabin, buying on credit, the importance of owning a home and of putting money in the bank, how to build schoolhouses and prolong the school term, and to improve their moral and religious condition.

In a skillful adaptation of religious revival technique, Washington would call on members of the farmers' conference to recite their successful experiences. One man told of his efforts failing year after year, because of the sharecropping mortgage. "Last year," he said, "I lived on corn meal, and bought nothing I could do without, and this year for the first time in my life I am free!" The resolutions of the 1900 Conference, which were typical, maintained that more and more Negroes should "work out our own destiny through the slow and often trying processes of natural growth rather than by any other easy, sudden, or superficial method," and expressed the standard Tuskegee ideology about industry, economy, character, and the white South.[2] Local farmers' conferences, modeled on Tuskegee's, became enormously popular among Tuskegee satellite schools and others; 150 were held in 1899 alone. Always the emphasis was on thrift and hard work and penurious economy, on struggle and success. The self-help note was dominant, and publicists described the conferences by such titles as "Negro Self-Uplifting" or "Self-Help Among Negroes."

Similar in spirit to the Tuskegee Conferences, and like them attended by eminent figures from the entire nation, was the annual Hampton Conference, organized in 1897. Considerable stress was placed on self-help in social welfare activities, and beginning in 1904 on co-operative insurance ventures and building and loan associations as forms of collective endeavor calculated to elevate the masses. An outgrowth of the spirit of the Hampton Conferences was the Negro Organization Society of Virginia, established under Hampton Institute auspices in 1909. This organization of organizations which claimed to represent 85 per cent of the Negroes of the state, preached a gospel of interracial and intraracial co-operation along the usual Hampton-Tuskegee line, and gave special attention to propagandizing for better health and sanitation.[3]

Similar in outlook to the Tuskegee Conferences was the Farmers' Improvement Society of Texas, organized about 1890 by R. L. Smith, a politician and school principal. Inspired in part by the trend toward self-help and solidarity and in part by the white agrarian organizations then at their peak, the society first improved the homes of village and rural Negroes in the Oakland, Texas, area, and then branched out into improving farming methods, paying sick and death benefits, and co-operative buying and selling. Its strongest efforts were directed at fighting the evils of the sharecropping system by inspiring Negroes to raise their own foodstuffs, to buy co-operatively, to purchase only for cash, and to become independent owners or cash-renters. By 1909 the movement had spread over Texas and into Oklahoma and Arkansas. It had 21,000 members, a co-operative business of $50,000 a year, and subsidiary institutions such as an agricultural college and a bank. Smith believed that improved family morals, thrift, industry, and the pooling of individual financial resources, welded together by the feeling of solidarity arising from the organization's efforts, would bring about a self-reliant manhood and womanhood, which was the chief aim of the society. Elsewhere, similar organizations appeared, like the Black Belt Improvement societies organized by the Tuskegee daughter schools, Snow Hill Institute in Alabama and Utica Institute in Mississippi. At the latter, the principal, W. H. Holtzclaw, encouraged landownership by forming a company to buy land and resell it to ambitious tenant farmers. Holtzclaw went unusually far along the road of racial solidarity by establishing a "community court of justice," which handled all misdemeanors that occurred within the Utica Institute colony, thus decreasing the expensive litigation carried on in the public courts.[4]

No organization was as influential in stimulating the philosophy of self-help and racial solidarity as the National Negro Business League, which Washington organized in 1900 to encourage the development of Negro business. Local leagues were formed, but the organization was really run from Tuskegee and backed by funds supplied by Andrew Carnegie.[5] So successful was the League that 1200 attended its 1906 meeting at Atlanta. At this meeting the delegates in typical Tuskegee spirit reaffirmed their faith in the progress that the race had made and could make in business, declared their belief that like all races Negroes must depend for their elevation mainly on their ability to make progress in constructive, visible directions by laying a foundation in economic growth, and resolved that Negroes should emphasize their successes and opportunities more than their failures and grievances. Notable in these resolutions, as in those of the Farmers' and Hampton Conferences, was the conspicuous absence of interest in political and civil rights.[6]

The annual meetings were enthusiastic. There was frequent applause as speakers recounted their rise from poverty to wealth; an emphasis on success, and an aura of optimism. As a speaker at the 1915 meeting put it: "You men who have achieved success in business had confidence in yourselves . . . as well as confidence that the people of your community would patronize and support you. . . . I believe it is the mission of the League to teach these two lessons, confidence and co-operation." A commonplace at League conventions was the assertion that anyone who tried could succeed. In 1914 a prosperous Okmulgee merchant, who had arrived in Oklahoma as a homesteader in 1891 with $69 in his pocket, insisted that "any Negro with ambition and industry, backed by character . . . will positively succeed. . . . Work will accomplish anything." It was often asserted that there were advantages in the disadvantages of segregation and discrimination. As the Baptist clergyman-businessman R. H. Boyd from Nashville said in 1903: "These discriminations are only blessings in disguise. They stimulate and encourage rather than cower and humiliate the true, ambitious, self-determined Negro." [7]

The League's attitude was characterized by a definite dualism. It asserted that the economic laws of laissez faire were blind to color differences and that economic usefulness and success were the best way to eliminate prejudice, but it also vigorously propagandized for Negro support of Negro business.

Representative of those who thought prejudice was no bar to the success of a Negro businessman whose products were as good as those of his white competitors was a Florida citrus grower who reported that he had no difficulty marketing his produce. "Whenever you are able to produce good oranges, tangerines, and grapefruit, I find it makes no difference whether you are a white man or a black man in finding a market." He was especially proud of the fact that the bank cashier who a dozen years earlier had refused to lend him twelve dollars had recently offered to let him borrow any amount he needed without a single endorsement. The Chicago clubwoman Fannie Barrier Williams felt a new pride and confidence in the future of the race, because Negro businessmen were opening up new and respected ways of contact. "If you can obtain and hold the acquaintance and confidence of the business world," she asserted, "you will be in a position to conquer more prejudice than we have yet been able to estimate." The League's paid organizer, Fred R. Moore, expressed the peculiar value of self-help and solidarity most pungently. He would, he said at the 1904 convention,

require every person who joins a local league to pledge himself to support all worthy enterprises managed by men and women of the race, and when I found him doing otherwise I would fire him out of the organization. . . . All business enterprises should be supported, how else can we expect to be respected . . . if we do not begin to practice what a great many of us preach? How can we otherwise succeed? Some would say that this was drawing the color line. I do not believe it. Jews support Jews; Germans support Germans; Italians support Italians until they get strong enough to compete with their brothers in the professions and trades; and Negroes should now begin to support Negroes. Don't delay this, but begin today.

The white man, he continued, would respect Negroes if they were organized in support of each other and thus demonstrated faith in the capacity of the race. Instead of constantly appealing to whites Negroes should create their own opportunities. "What a mighty power we shall be when we begin to do this, and we shall never be a mighty power until we do begin."

Ten years later the Kansas Cities' Business League, according to Washington one of the most flourishing Negro business leagues, reported striking success in the practical application of this philosophy. It boasted of the fifty new colored business enterprises resulting from efforts based on the doctrine that "our race's future will be largely what we ourselves make it." A vigilance committee ferreted out those who failed to patronize Negro enterprises, and the League had put on such a campaign that it was accounted "almost a crime" for a Negro who amounted to anything at all to patronize a white establishment for any article or service that could be obtained in a Negro place of business. By developing "a race-patronizing spirit" in this way the local league felt that it had accomplished "an immense amount of practical good." One might question the necessity of such extreme tactics in view of the assumption that whites would patronize worthy Negro businessmen. Yet, as S. H. Hart, president of the Capital Trust Company of Jacksonville, said, "some of the most influential members of the white race," were depositors in his bank, but nevertheless "it is just as necessary to have our own banks and trust companies, as it is to have our own physicians, lawyers and teachers." [8]

In spite of the talk about better relations between the races being the League's objective, practically speaking, most attention centered upon the short-range objective of achieving Negro support of Negro enterprise. This was due to the very nature of the situation. More than ever Negro business had to depend upon Negro support as white patronage of Negro barbers, caterers, and so forth declined beginning around 1890. When Negroes patronized white enterprises,

Negro businessmen found it necessary to appeal to them on a racial basis for their own salvation. This was all the more imperative because Negroes usually lacked the capital and business training necessary to compete effectively with white entrepreneurs even for Negro business, and because they faced discrimination from white lending agencies. This economic necessity was reinforced by, and in turn strengthened, the widely held philosophy of Negro advancement through racial solidarity and co-operation.

This Negro chamber of commerce was not the only business and professional organization to appear in response to the Negroes' peculiar status in American society and their exclusion from white groups. Editors were the first to organize; they formed an association in 1880. Teachers came next in 1889, and doctors followed in 1895. Illustrative of the rising tide of racial separatism in the North was the failure of a state Negro medical society formed in Ohio in 1897 [9] and the subsequent success of the National Medical Association when it began to organize in the same state in 1904. After 1900 the Tuskegee spirit found expression in a number of professional and business societies, subsidiary to the Business League. In 1903 came the National Bar Association, in 1906 the National Negro Bankers' Association, in 1907 the National Association of Funeral Directors, in 1913 the National Negro Retail Merchants' Association. Most of these organizations were formed in conjunction with Business League Conventions, and they were led by men identified with Washington and his point of view.

Fundamentally opposed to the philosophy of the Business League, and yet reflecting the same spirit of racial self-help and co-operation were the feeble attempts to form Negro labor unions. These were organized generally in occupations in which Negroes had obtained a substantial place but where the unions had excluded them from membership. Negro longshoremen had created successful unions in Charleston, Baltimore, and other Southern ports as early as the Reconstruction period, but it was not until after 1910 that colored longshoremen organized their own unions in the Hampton Roads area, where they maintained an active life until absorbed by the International Longshoremen's Association in 1917. The National Association of Afro-American Gas Engineers and Skilled Laborers, organized about 1900, lasted several years and was recognized by the Pittsburgh

Central, but never had more than three locals. More important were the succession of railway unions—from the Colored Men's Locomotive Firemen's Association founded about 1902 to the Railway Men's International Benevolent and Industrial Association, founded in 1915. The pre-World War I union with the longest career has been the National Alliance of Postal Employees, originally organized by Negro railway mail clerks in 1913, two years after the Railway Mail Association had excluded them.

While self-help and racial solidarity as defense reactions to white exclusion and hostility were most characteristic of economic and social welfare activities and were frequently employed as part of a conciliatory tactic that appeared to absolve whites of responsibility for the Negro's condition, they were also associated with organized protest movements. The theme of self-help through organized protest was not new. The convention movement had formed a more or less continuous effort of this sort. Moreover, the ascendancy of Washington did not entirely inhibit protest organizations—many of them ephemeral—formed on a regional and local level. There were in fact numerous temporary protest, protective, and legal-rights organizations and many—though not all—explicitly expressed ideologies of self-help and racial solidarity. An Arkansas minister in 1888 reported the existence of a Negro Legal Aid Society of the United States which insisted that justice could be secured only through unity and therefore aimed to bring the whole race together to a vital interest in its welfare. The brochure of a Negro Protective League in Pennsylvania in 1914 insisted upon the necessity of an organization to obtain the race's rights, such as every other nationality had. "In organization there is strength, and only with organization can we withstand the attack made upon our every right and privilege." In a somewhat different category there was talk of establishing a Negro political party; and one—the National Liberty Party—actually appeared in 1904.[10]

But the organization that best exemplified the philosophy of racial self-help and solidarity in protest and agitation was the Afro-American League, the brain-child of T. Thomas Fortune, founded in 1890, which persisted with varying success for almost two decades. In its comprehensive platform, in the wide sources of its membership (at one time or another almost all Negroes of prominence were connected with it), and in its attempt to serve as a meeting ground for all leading Negroes to discuss racial problems, it was clearly a continuation of the Convention Movement.

As early as 1887 Fortune had concluded that since the whites were determined to leave the colored man to fight his battles alone, Negroes must attack the problem themselves and organize a Protective League. Not until 1889, however, was Fortune able to effect the organization of local leagues; by then the idea proved so popular that they appeared in forty or more cities ranging from Boston to San Francisco and from Albany, New York, to Albany, Georgia, with the majority concentrated in the Northeast and Midwest. At the first national convention held in Chicago in January 1890, Fortune set the tone in a militant address. He defended agitation, even revolution, as necessary for progress and the preservation of rights. "It is a narrow and perverted philosophy which condemns as a nuisance agitators," he declared. He excoriated the nation for betraying the Negro, who must "fight fire with fire. . . . It is time to face the enemy and fight inch by inch for every right he denies us." A separate Negro convention was justified because whites drew the color line first: "Let us stand up like men in our own organization where color will not be a brand of odium." With this emphasis on race solidarity for agitation, Fortune combined the current philosophy of race organization for economic salvation. He proposed an Afro-American bank, a bureau of industrial education, and a bureau of co-operative industry, in order to stimulate the business potentialities of the race. Trained artisans, farmers, and laborers were more valuable, he said, than "educated lawyers, agitators, and loafers." He also proposed a "bureau of emigration" to scatter Negroes throughout the country.

The convention's proceedings and resolutions echoed Fortune. A letter from the former North Carolina Reconstruction judge, Albion Tourgee, was referred to the appropriate committee only after heated opposition from those who did not want to take suggestions from white men. The League's constitution provided for a politically nonpartisan body whose objectives were to protest and take legal action against disfranchisement, inequitable distribution of school funds, exclusion from juries, barbarous prison conditions, lynchings, and segregation on public carriers, and to encourage migration from the "terror-ridden sections." Perhaps the League's ideology was epitomized in the address of J. E. Bruce, a free-lance journalist who later belonged to the inner circle of the Garvey Movement, who in addressing the Washington, D.C. League, asserted:

The solution of the problem is in our own hands. . . . The Negro must preserve his identity. . . . Unity and harmony of sentiment and feeling are the levers that must of necessity overturn American caste-prejudice. In organization, cooperation and agitation, the Negro will come nearer the solution of the white man's problem than by merely submitting to injustice.[11]

In spite of hopeful beginnings, the League soon declined; by 1893 the national body and most of the local leagues were defunct. In 1898, however, it was revived as the Afro-American Council, under the leadership of Fortune and the A.M.E. Zion bishop, Alexander Walters. It expressed the same basic philosophy as the earlier League.[12] Though its constitutional objectives were never modified, its resolutions tended toward the conciliatory Hampton-Tuskegee spirit when the organization passed under the control of Washington after the turn of the century. The Council finally petered out about 1908, the victim of the ideological controversy between Washington and his critics. Its history underscores the vitality of the protest tradition which never became even a minor current; even in its most conservative years the Council protested in unmistakable, if tactful phrases against the grievances Negroes suffered. Above all its chief significance from an ideological point of view lies in its frank espousal of self-help and racial solidarity in the area of protest and agitation.

By far the oldest of the institutions embracing a racial philosophy of self-help and solidarity were the church and the mutual benefit society or fraternity. They are of particular importance for this study because in view of their mass base, their activities probably reflect the thinking of the inarticulate majority better than any other organizations or the statements of editors and other publicists.

It would be difficult to overemphasize the role of the church in Negro life in the age of Booker T. Washington. Negro clerics exercised an enormous influence in politics, in education, in social welfare activities, in fraternal organizations, and in business enterprises, though this influence did decline significantly during the twentieth century. As one scholar observed about 1909 in describing the situation in Pennsylvania, a minister was on the board of almost every incorporated business in the state, the largest building and loan association was founded by a clergyman, the great majority of the benevolent and insurance societies and most of the private schools had grown directly out of church activities, a number of the largest political rallies were held in churches, and clergymen were among the most powerful political leaders, the only Negro member of the State Republican Committee being a Baptist minister.[13]

As observed in Chapter III, Negroes were compelled to rationalize their acceptance of a segregated church life. Those within the predominantly white denominations appealed for equal status and recognition as separate units of their churches. J. W. E. Bowen in 1912 asked for Negro bishops in the Methodist Church, North, because the true and permanent elevation of a race to the level where it would exhibit race initiative, race pride, self-support, and active participation in the duties and privileges of citizenship would have to come from within. Distinguished clerics in the A.M.E., A.M.E. Zion, and colored Baptist churches came to regard the segregated church almost as a positive good. A.M.E. Zion Bishop J. W. Hood, writing in 1895, held that remaining in white churches would have dwarfed the Negro. Excluded from opportunities elsewhere, Negroes received from their churches trained leaders, especially important because "to care for the spiritual welfare of a people you must be one of them." A church of their own, for whose support they were completely responsible, provided the freedmen with a lesson in the importance of self-reliance which they could not have obtained so quickly in any other way. Not until prejudice disappeared would the African church have accomplished its special task. Of a similar turn of mind were other noted clergymen, including the celebrated Daniel A. Payne, senior bishop in the A.M.E Church until he died in 1895, and E. C. Morris, founder and for many years president of the National Baptist Convention.[14]

In the activities they sponsored, as well as in their public utterances, Negro clergymen exemplified their belief in the value of organized effort to uplift the race. Perhaps their most noteworthy efforts were in education. The A.M.E. Church, which had acquired Wilberforce University in 1854, after the war embarked upon an ambitious program beginning with Allen University and Morris Brown College in 1880, and by 1907 had twenty-five schools. A year later it was reported that out of twenty-three institutions of higher learning for Negroes sponsored by the American Baptist Home Missionary Society, fourteen were owned by Negroes themselves. The A.M.E. Zion and C.M.E. Churches each maintained one college (Livingstone and Lane respectively) and a number of other schools.[15] Institutions such as Morris Brown and Livingstone stressed the self-help, racially co-operative quality of their activities. At times Negro Baptists objected to the influence of their white co-religionists, and in Atlanta, for example, some attempted unsuccessfuly to secede from Atlanta Baptist College and form an independent school.[16]

The churches also exhibited some achievement in the area of group business enterprise. Of the major denominations all but the Baptists had previously established a publishing house. That of the A.M.E. Sunday School Union illustrated the ideological justification of such enterprises when it described one of its volumes as an effort to stimulate Negro literature and declared with pride that practically all of the work on the book had been done by Negroes in a building belonging to them.[17] The Baptists established their publishing house unusually late. It was not until about 1895 that the several rival groups fused in the National Baptist Convention, and not until 1896 that the National Baptist Publishing Board was founded, though even then support for it was not unanimous. Earlier there had been a distinct division of opinion as to the desirability of using the literature of the American Baptist Publication Society, there being those who believed that it was time for the Negro Baptists to "begin the cultivation of free manhood" by assuming their own responsibilities, and those who believed it better to remain, in their publications and educational interests, under the care of the white Baptists. Morris, sponsoring the proposal in 1893 as a means of race employment and race development, declared that the solution of the race problem would depend largely upon what Negroes proved able to do for themselves. Prerequisite to this was race pride, and he was persuaded that there was no better way to cultivate this quality than for Negroes to inaugurate enterprises of their own.[18]

Some churches also entered into social welfare work, being especially active in promoting temperance organizations, old folks' homes, orphanages, and mutual benefit societies, and less often sponsoring employment bureaus, industrial classes, lecture bureaus, slum missions, and homes for servant girls. In 1898 after surveying seventy-nine churches in nine Southern cities, Du Bois found twenty-nine engaged in some sort of benevolent and social work. By and large the Presbyterian and Congregational churches, attracting the well-to-do, and less evangelistic than other denominations, did the most elaborate "institutional work." Reverend Matthew Anderson of Berean Presbyterian Church in Philadelphia, a graduate of Oberlin College and Princeton Theological Seminary, and—though he did not ordinarily engage in agitation—a militant believer in the Christian gospel of human dignity and brotherhood, spelled out the rationale of such activities from the point of view of one who had done notable work along these lines. Speaking at the Hampton Conference in 1900 he stressed the battle against ignorance and improvidence by the Negroes' own efforts, co-operative racial business, and industrial education as the solution to the race problem.[19]

Related to the social welfare activities of the churches was the program of the Y.M. and Y.W.C.A. Here, too, increasing segregation was the rule, and because of white hostility it was encouraged by many Negroes. The work of the Colored Men's Department of the Y.M.C.A. began in response to a petition of Richmond Negro pastors when the International Congress met there in 1875, though segregated branches had appeared earlier in both North and South. By 1900 even in Boston certain Negroes were agitating for a segregated branch. Though the idea aroused considerable resentment in "radical" circles, the development of colored Y's was greatly facilitated just before World War I by the philanthropy of Julius Rosenwald, who encouraged self-help among Negroes in Chicago, New York, and other cities, by supplying matching funds (one-fourth in Chicago) if Negroes raised the rest for buildings.[20]

Negro churches were the principal—though not the only—source of social welfare activity between the close of Reconstruction and the 1890's, but were thereafter outstripped by the secular charities which enormously improved welfare work both quantitatively and qualitatively. Behind this secular development were the growing feeling of race solidarity and self-help, urbanization, the increasing resources for welfare action that urbanization made possible, and the maturation of the white charity movement beginning with the National Conference of Charities and Correction in 1874. The quarter century before World War I witnessed a remarkable development of welfare activity. Du Bois recorded the upsurge in his Atlanta University publications in 1898 and particularly in 1909; Fannie Barrier Williams, writing of the Chicago scene in 1905, saw a new spirit of determined self-help and self-advancement in race organization there; and a student of the Boston scene observed that ameliorative activities to aid the unfortunate of the race had risen to importance there as Negroes were more and more forced back on their own efforts.[21]

Du Bois, reviewing developments down to 1909, found Negroes engaged in general charity, women's clubs, old folks' homes, orphanages, hospitals, social and literary clubs, libraries, day nurseries, kindergartens, and settlement houses. The most successful work was being done in old folks' homes and orphanages, of which there were fully a hundred by 1913, almost all of them dating since the 1890's or later. Social settlements and nonprofit hospitals appeared in the 1890's. Though these obtained their chief support from whites, they were ordinarily promoted and conducted by Negroes and were therefore regarded as examples of self-help.[22] Negro women displayed considerable interest in seeking to protect decent lower-class girls and rescue fallen women. The White Rose Industrial Association organized in New York in 1898 "to establish and maintain a Christian, non-sectarian Home for Colored Working Girls and Women, where they may be trained in the principles of practical self-help and right living," engaged in a variety of settlement activities and maintained travelers' aids in New York and Norfolk to guide girls coming from the South in search of employment and to protect them from unscrupulous employment agencies that exploited them and even forced some into prostitution. But the most extensive work along these lines and the most effective employment bureaus were those conducted by interracial organizations, whose work was enhanced and co-ordinated by the National Urban League formed in 1911, with a board consisting mostly of conservative whites and Negroes such as Booker T. Washington but administered almost entirely by Negroes.[23] "Not Alms, but Opportunity," was its slogan of independence and self-help.

During and after World War I the Urban League, supported by white philanthropy, forged to the front as the leading welfare agency among Negroes, but in the preceding two decades the organized women's clubs dominated the field. As one student has suggested, no single force illustrated the co-operative and group activity that more and more characterized welfare work among Negroes better than the undertakings of the women's clubs. Such groups had existed here and there since antebellum times, but their real development followed the organization of the white General Federation of Women's

Clubs in 1890 and was clearly associated with the growing racial solidarity and self-help. As the Chicago clubwoman Fannie Barrier Williams enthused: "The Negro woman's club of to-day represents the New Negro with new powers of self-help." [24]

Between 1890 and 1895 colored women's clubs appeared in the principal cities and in 1896 the National Association of Colored Women was organized. The biennial national meetings stressed social welfare services. Thus, unlike the white clubs, the Negro clubs were less interested in individual than in racial self-improvement, and regarded it as their duty to uplift the race and its less fortunate members, under the motto "Lifting as We Climb." Certain local clubs illustrate the scope of activities. The Washington and Chicago clubs maintained kindergartens, day nurseries, sewing and cooking classes, mothers' meetings, and penny savings banks; the Chicago group in addition helped friendless and homeless girls and ran an employment bureau. The Phyllis Wheatley Club of New Orleans, one of the most active in the South, sustained a training class for nurses and contributed to an orphans' home. The Alabama Federation did especially notable work in supporting the Mt. Meigs Reformatory. Throughout the land there were literary clubs that often engaged in charitable work, and the maintenance of old folks' homes and orphanages was an especially important activity. Rather rare were civil rights and protest activities, such as efforts in Louisiana and Tennessee to repeal the Jim Crow laws, or the Women's Loyal Union formed in New York in 1892 to help Ida Wells in her antilynching crusade.[25] While in view of their humble financial resources, it is likely that only the strongest clubs were carrying on effective charitable activities, the philosophy of self-help and solidarity motivating their work was of considerable significance.

Related to this welfare work was the activity of the Civic Reform movements, many or most of which were rather ephemeral. A number of these were concerned with lessening crime and reforming criminals and juvenile delinquents. Especially well known was the work of the Baltimore Colored Law and Order League, instituted after the Atlanta riot in order to lessen Negro crime, the alleged cause of that holocaust. As characteristic of the new century as the Baltimore Brotherhood of Liberty was of an earlier age, it revealed the shift in emphasis. The principal accomplishment of this organization was a mildly successful campaign to reduce the number of saloons in Negro areas. A Texas Law and Order League encouraged thrift, industry, payment of taxes, and practical work in farming and trades. To cite a Northern example, a Michigan Co-Operative League was formed in 1905 to encourage high moral, physical, and educational standards, to get individuals to live up to their responsibilities as citizens, and to restrain crime. In 1906 it created a Michigan Co-Operative Realty Company to build homes and purchase desirable property for Negroes.[26]

In a somewhat different category were the self-help cultural societies related in part to the self-education and self-culture movement in the nation at large, to the vogue of forums, lectures, and the Chautauqua. Church literary groups and a few libraries had existed even before the Civil War, but in the late nineteenth century literary and art clubs sprouted all over the country, especially among women. At the same time there flowered a definite literature of self-culture written by and for Negroes.[27] Excluded from Southern libraries, Negroes to some extent undertook to furnish their own facilities, and churches and women's clubs (sometimes with public assistance) organized libraries and reading rooms. Groups in several cities maintained regular lecture bureaus, and numerous churches had lyceums, discussion groups, and debating societies. The most famous and one of the earliest was the Bethel Literary and Historical Association of the Metropolitan A.M.E. Church in Washington, founded in 1881. Colored theaters began to appear around 1900. Philadelphia boasted an orchestra; Theodore Drury produced grand opera between 1900 and 1906 in New York and afterward in Boston; and Washington had its well-known Coleridge-Taylor Choral Society founded in 1901.[28] From 1908 the colored musical and art clubs held national conventions annually for several years. Especially notable from the cultural point of view were the founding of the American Negro Academy in 1897, with the objective of fostering cultural activities, and such historical associations as the Negro Historical Society of Philadelphia (1897), the Negro Society for Historical Research (1911), and the Association for the Study of Negro Life and History (1915).

As old as the Negro church, and second only to it in importance as a self-help and co-operative institution was the fraternal and mutual benefit society. It is customary to distinguish between the secret order and the purely mutual benefit society, in that the former stressed ritual and social elements, while the latter emphasized uplift. Actually, there is no sharp dividing line between them. Both were often quasi-religious in outlook, and many societies took religious titles such as the Mosaic Templars of America, the Nazirites, the Galilean Fishermen, the Order of St. Luke, and so forth. Many were founded or led by ministers, or grew out of church benevolent associations.

The heyday of the small, local mutual benefit society was in the 1880's, and by the end of the century it was no longer able to compete with the larger and more strictly insurance society.[29] The membership and wealth of the larger insurance societies increased rapidly with the 1890's. While they grew largely at the expense of the small associations, they indicated a significant development in self-help and racial solidarity in an institutional form. The Oddfellows, the largest of the secret orders in the age of Booker T. Washington, had grown from eighty-nine lodges and about 4000 members in 1868 to 1000 lodges and 36,853 members during the next eighteen years (1868–86); they doubled their lodges to 2047 and almost tripled their membership to 155,537 in the next ten years; and more than doubled their lodges again and almost doubled their membership in the eight years between 1896 and 1904. Though less spectacular, other fraternal organizations such as the Colored Knights of Pythias (organized in 1880), the Mosaic Templars of America (formed in 1882), the Masons, and the Elks (founded in 1898) had a similar development.[30]

Easily the most famous of the nonsecret fraternal insurance societies, though representative in its operations, was the United Order of True Reformers. Founded in Virginia in 1881 as a fraternal benefit society by the Reverend William Washington Browne, a former slave, ex-school teacher, and temperance reformer, it was incorporated in 1883 as the Grand Fountain of the United Order of True Reformers and became a full-fledged mutual-benefit stock company. By 1907 it claimed a membership of 100,000. Its bank (which rivaled the claims of the Capital Savings Bank of Washington as being the first Negro bank), organized in 1888, by 1903 had 10,000 depositors. The bank's failure in 1910 led to the demise of the society in 1911. Other activities, in addition to the insurance features, included an old folks' home, a real estate department, a Mercantile and Industrial Association (which maintained stores in five cities), a weekly paper, and the Westman Farm, which sought to enter commercial agriculture and create a Negro community. All of these enterprises were outgrowths of and subsidiary to the fraternal order and reflected the burgeoning sentiment of racial self-help and solidarity along economic and social lines.[31] Also in Virginia was the Independent Order of St. Luke, founded during the Civil War, and taken over in a floundering condition about 1900 by Maggie L. Walker, who raised its membership from 1000 to 20,000 in seven years. Typically, it had several offshoots—a real estate association, a savings bank, a retail store, a printing plant, and a newspaper—and spread into neighboring states. The St. Luke *Herald's* editorials could protest vigorously, and held that "all of the unfair methods against the Negro, civil, political, educational, commercial and religious will sooner or later teach him the lesson of racial unity and cooperation." [32]

Representative of the sentiment behind these welfare and fraternal activities were speeches given at a meeting sponsored by the Douglass Relief Association of Washington in March 1898. Ex-Congressman John R. Lynch devoted himself to the employment problem and suggested co-operation on business and other lines as something that demanded the support of all who deplored current conditions. A local businessman praised Booker T. Washington, urged co-operation and thrift and the application of business principles, and held that "nothing could be gained by disunited elements, everything by unity of action." [33]

Thus, in all phases of life, behind the walls of segregation, the majority of Negroes had come to believe in the necessity of banding together and building counterparts to white institutions—whether cultural, welfare, religious, educational, economic, or purely social—though a very vocal minority still opposed them. Excluded from white professional social circles, six Philadelphia doctors organized the exclusive Sigma Pi Phi in 1904. Within the next ten years six of the eight Negro college fraternities and sororities were organized—the first being the Alpha Phi Alpha at Cornell University in 1906. There continued to be strong sentiment for segregated schools which would offer opportunities for Negro teachers and protect students from contacts with hostile white children—a movement that did not go unopposed.[34] In extreme form this tendency became institutionalized in the gropings toward what Du Bois enthusiastically referred to as a "group economy," and in the all-Negro communities.

CHAPTER IX

THE DEVELOPMENT OF NEGRO BUSINESS AND THE RISE OF A NEGRO MIDDLE CLASS

From the late 1880's there was a remarkable development of Negro business—banks and insurance companies, undertakers and retail stores. Connected with the gradual urbanization of American Negroes, this development was all the more significant because it occurred at a time when Negro barbers, tailors, caterers, draymen, blacksmiths, and other artisans were losing their white customers. Depending upon the Negro market, the promoters of the new enterprises naturally upheld the spirit of racial self-help and solidarity.

A tiny entrepreneurial class had existed even during the antebellum period, and this group increased after the Civil War. In Louisiana and South Carolina a free Negro slave-owning elite had owned sizable plantations. In various cities free Negro artisans, grocers, barbers, caterers, hotel owners, and coal dealers had acquired considerable wealth. In a number of places Negroes played a leading or dominant role in certain trades into the twentieth century. In Atlanta the leading barbers and certain important contractors and real estate dealers were Negroes well after 1900. In Charleston Negroes dominated the butcher's trade and barbering, formed the backbone of the shoemaking trade, and were among the city's most prominent contractors until after World War I. And in several cities, most notably Philadelphia, colored entrepreneurs dominated the catering business until late in the nineteenth century.

By the 1880's and 1890's a few Negroes were worth hundreds of thousands and occasionally as much as half a million dollars. Thomy Lafon, a New Orleans merchant, moneylender, and real estate dealer since before the Civil War left an estate of half a million when he died in the 1880's. In 1894 Wiley Jones, a owner of a streetcar line in Pine Bluff, Arkansas, was reputed to have a fortune of $200,000 obtained in farming, horsetrading, liquor selling, and transportation.[1] The largest of these earlier fortunes was that of R. R. Church of Memphis, who from Reconstruction to the time he died in 1912 was reported to have amassed over a million dollars out of speculation and investment in Memphis real estate. As a matter of fact the bulk of most of the fortunes was probably made out of investments in real estate and white corporations. Thus, in Washington, even though some of the city's most distinguished citizens were connected as early as the 1880's with the Capital Savings Bank, a survey of thirty-five of the community's well-to-do Negroes in 1898 revealed that the chief source of wealth of these professional and businessmen and government employees was real estate acquired by themselves or their parents. Only twelve had any investments in colored business, though all invested in white business; not one had grown rich by the patronage of Negroes.[2]

There was a real burgeoning of Negro enterprise after 1890 and especially after 1900, though it was based more on the Negro market than were the earlier enterprises. According to the National Negro Business League, the number of business enterprises had risen from 20,000 in 1900 to 40,000 in 1914. In that period banks had risen from 4 to 51; undertakers from 450 to 1000; drug stores from 250 to 695; retail merchants from 10,000 to 25,000.[3] Perhaps the most celebrated of these newer enterprises was that of the millionaire, Madame C. J. Walker, a St. Louis laundress who had invented the first successful hair-straightening process.[4]

As was stated earlier, these businesses were more and more based on the Negro market. As the century drew to a close, Negro businessmen serving whites encountered increasing prejudice, while the internal combustion engine spelled the doom of the livery stable and the blacksmith shop, and businesses of larger capitalization drove the small caterer and drayman out of business. The ideology of Negro support for Negro business had been growing since the 1870's partly because it served the interests of newspaper editors, bankers, and other business and professional men who depended on the Negro community for their support. Other factors encouraging the appeal to race pride and the ideal of a "group economy" were the generally rising philosophy of self-help and racial solidarity, the inexperience of Negro businessmen, the difficulties involved in obtaining credit from white banks, the discrimination practiced by white insurance companies and real estate firms, exclusion from white restaurants, hotels, and places of amusement, the gradual elimination of skilled workers from employment, and the competition offered by the economically stronger white retail businesses in Negro neighborhoods.[5] All these forced Negroes to fall back on the ideal of helping themselves by co-operative efforts, and many were led to believe that only racially developed and supported business would solve their economic and other problems. The appeal to racial pride and solidarity was only natural. Du Bois regarded the "group economy" as the final effort of Negroes to secure a permanent foothold in the business world. In some cases "the group economy approaches a complete system," he asserted, "Negroes serving their own needs in almost every activity." [6]

This appeal to economic solidarity, this growth of a segregated group economy involved an increase in the number of petty businessmen (barbers, tailors and cleaners, restaurateurs, grocers, etc.) serving the needs of the growing urban ghetto, and the development of what contemporaries referred to as "co-operative" business—cemetery associations, building and loan associations, insurance companies, and banks. Many businesses of this sort were closely related in social philosophy and historical origins to the welfare, fraternal, and religious agencies described in the preceding chapter. This was especially true of the cemetery associations, the insurance associations, and the banks that first appeared in the closing years of the nineteenth century, organized or led by ministers and ordinarily outgrowths of mutual benefit societies and fraternities.[7]

Examples of what contemporaries referred to as "co-operative" businesses were not lacking in previous years,[8] but their number rose sharply in the last decades of the century and during the early years of the twentieth century. During the 1880's and 1890's exclusion from "white" cemeteries and difficulties encountered in borrowing from white lending agencies, played an important role in the creation of cemetery and building and loan associations, which Du Bois regarded as the chief co-operative businesses of those years. For example, between 1883 and 1890 at least half a dozen building and loan associations appeared in Pennsylvania and Virginia. In Pennsylvania the first one was the Century founded in 1886; twenty years later the number in that state had reached ten. Successful realty companies also appeared—one in New York, the largest Negro enterprise in the city before it collapsed in 1910–11, was capitalized at half a million, employed over 200 people, and did an annual business of $200,000. Illustrative of the outlook of these enterprises was that of an early one, the Industrial Building and Savings Company of Washington, organized in 1885, and parent of the Capital Savings Bank. Presenting their views before a public meeting of the Bethel Literary Society in 1892, spokesmen for it emphasized that Negroes must make their own opportunities, accumulate money and material possessions, and in order to do these things must support their own enterprises.[9]

The development of Negro insurance is especially significant, because insurance enterprises are today the most important of Negro business enterprises. From the first days of the Republic church beneficial societies and mutual benefit and fraternal organizations had made sickness and death payments and assisted the widows and orphans of deceased members. Some church-related societies existed into the twentieth century and occasionally evolved into full-fledged insurance companies like the Afro-American Industrial Insurance Society organized by the Baptist minister J. Milton Waldron of Jacksonville in 1901. It was, however, the larger fraternal benefit societies that paved the way in the 1880's and 1890's for the regular insurance companies. This development was stimulated not only by the general popularity of self-help and racial co-operation, but more directly by the discriminatory premiums charged by white insurance companies, beginning with the Prudential in 1881, and rationalized on the basis of the Negroes' higher mortality rates.[10] The first center of Negro insurance was in Virginia, where it was developed by fraternal benefit societies such as the Order of St. Luke and the True Reformers. Inspired by the success of these nonsecret benevolent associations, the secret orders stepped up their insurance features, and the regularly chartered mutual aid and beneficial societies specializing in weekly sickness and health insurance appeared (the first one being the Mutual Benefit Association of Baltimore, 1885). The final step in the evolution of Negro insurance was the development of the legal reserve company, the first one being organized in Mississippi in 1909; four years later the important North Carolina Mutual and the Standard Life Insurance Company of Atlanta both became legal reserve companies.[11]

Related also to the fraternal organizations was the development of banking. After the failure of the Freedmen's Bank in the panic of 1873, the first two Negro banks were the True Reformers (Richmond) and the Capital Savings (Washington), both founded in 1888. By 1900 there were four Negro banks (one other having failed). Thereafter, the number increased rapidly, Washington reporting 56 banks in 1911, though many of these failed in the business recession that occurred just before World War I. As Abram Harris has pointed out almost all of the early institutions were established to serve as depositories for the Negro fraternal organizations. The importance of the fraternities is suggested by the fact that in 1907 the first and third largest banks in both paid-in capital and deposits were the True Reformers and the Mechanics Savings Bank—the latter founded in Richmond in 1903 as the depository of the Knights of Pythias.[12]

The philosophy associated with these banking institutions is illustrated by one of the leading ones—the Alabama Penny Savings & Loan Company of Birmingham, the fourth Negro bank organized (1890), and in 1907 the second largest both in capital and deposits (though it failed in 1915). Its stated aim was to encourage the saving and accumulation of money in order to demonstrate the capacity of the race by the successful maintenance of banking institutions. Its founder and president, the Reverend W. R. Pettiford, a free-born North Carolinian and former teacher, educated at the State Normal School at Marion, Alabama, was a prominent Baptist preacher, real estate dealer, and civic leader, closely associated with the Negro hospital in Birmingham. While he did not disdain to engage in political activity, this close associate of Booker T. Washington and president of the Negro Bankers' Association held that no race could make any substantial progress unless it developed very largely along business lines. In discussing the subject "How to Help the Negro to Help Himself," Pettiford stressed the economic virtues and enthusiastically urged the development of racial business and the education of the Negro masses to the point where they would patronize race businessmen. "Any class or race of people who fail to get this in their minds and act upon it are past redemption." [13]

In comparison with banking and insurance, Negro enterprises in manufacturing and transportation were of small importance, and they were usually short-lived. Of particular interest were the instances of Negro transit enterprises established to counter the streetcar segregation laws passed beginning around 1900. A Nashville company raised $20,000 to run a line of carriages. Cheated by an automobile company, and then let down by an electric company which refused to supply the promised current, it gave up only after an unsuccessful attempt to build a power plant. Elsewhere, similar attempts against streetcar segregation were enthusiastically described by the A.M.E. Church *Review* as encouraging examples of racial solidarity and economic co-operation in the face of discrimination.[14]

This development of Negro enterprise was an urban development, for the segregated residential areas in cities of the New South and the North (residential patterns in older Southern cities tending to remain mixed) created the Negro market which the Negro businessmen could exploit. Perhaps the most striking development of all occurred in Durham, North Carolina, where Negro enterprise flourished with unparalleled vigor. The Fitzgerald brickyards had been in operation since the 1870's. Best exemplifying the changing character of Negro business was the life of John Merrick and his North Carolina Mutual Life Insurance Company; here one observes the evolution of Negro insurance from the quasi-religious fraternal society through the chartered mutual aid association to the legal reserve company. A former slave, brickmason, and hod carrier, Merrick came to Durham in 1880 as a barber and soon became the personal barber of the future tobacco magnate Washington Duke—a friendship that paid dividends through the years. In 1883 Merrick was one of a group which bought outright a quasi-religious fraternal order, the Royal Knights of King David. Then in 1898 the business went through two reorganizations, with Merrick, Dr. Aaron McDuffie Moore, and the grocer Charles C. Spaulding emerging as the trio that ran its affairs. After 1905 the company expanded rapidly, and by 1915 it had entered twelve other states and the District of Columbia. Merrick and his associates also founded two drug stores, the Mechanics and Farmers Bank (1908), the Merrick-Moore-Spaulding Real Estate Company (1910), and somewhat later the short-lived Durham textile mill.

Other Durham enterprises of the early twentieth century included a lumber mill, an iron works, and an unsuccessful hosiery mill. Merrick, the chief figure in Durham's economic development, regarded it as his mission to teach Negroes "the importance of self-help and to reveal their opportunity in the world of finance and the building of co-operative enterprises. Steady employment, economy, business initiative, careful investment and subordination of politics were his themes." Booker T. Washington perceived in this city a model not only of Negro economic self-help, but of co-operation between the best classes of both races, which indeed it was, with institutions from the bank and insurance company to the Lincoln Hospital receiving the active support of Carr and the Dukes. Thus did New South capitalists engender New Negro capitalists, so that in the 1920's E. Franklin Frazier could speak of Durham as the "capital of the Black Middle Class." [15]

In other places in the South, such as Atlanta, comparable developments occurred without the assistance of white philanthropy. Northern cities also experienced the shift in the market and character of Negro business enterprises. In Philadelphia these multiplied rapidly, though white patronage diminished. In 1898 there were three building and loan associations in the city; in 1914 there were eight. In 1898 there were seven newspapers and magazines; in 1907 there were twenty. Ten industrial insurance companies were formed between 1900 and 1914. In 1899 Du Bois was predicting the demise not only of the colored caterers (which occurred) but also of the colored barbers, most of whom were serving whites; in 1907 he found barbers more numerous than ever, but catering to Negroes. Another student in 1907 reported that there had been a rapid rise of the professional and entrepreneurial classes (particularly the retail merchants) in the preceding two decades, and especially since 1900. "Within the past twelve months," he pointed out, "there have been incorporated two realty companies, one land investment company, four building and loan associations, one manufacturing company, besides a number of other small concerns." To a large extent the economic base of the newer enterprises lay in the Southern migrants, the Negro population of Philadelphia doubling—mostly by migration—between 1900 and 1915.[16]

On the whole the evidence indicates that this movement toward a segregated economy was strongest in the South, with its more extreme patterns of segregation and discrimination—though business enterprise was by no means evenly distributed throughout the South's cities. In 1907, of the sixty-seven insurance companies named in an admittedly incomplete listing compiled by Du Bois, all but nine, and all of the principal ones, were in the former slave states. Only two Northern cities had Negro banks before World War I—Philadelphia and Chicago. In the North, segregated economic institutions and sentiment for them were weakest in such cities as Boston and Cleveland, where abolitionist traditions lingered longest, and where some Negroes enjoyed white economic support and social contacts. Yet the ideology of a "group economy" as part of the philosophy of self-help and racial solidarity was widespread; even in Boston the changing attitude of the whites did much to encourage it. So pervasive was this doctrine of the "group economy" that not only did the National Negro Business League and its philosophy find ready acceptance, but Du Bois' Atlanta University Conference could also, as it did in 1899, urge Negroes to enter business life not merely to assimilate the race to the civilization of the age, but also as a "farsighted measure of self-defense," that would make for wealth and mutual co-operation. It counseled the support of Negro enterprise "even at some slight disadvantage. We *must* co-operate or we are lost." [17]

So in spite of the fact that at no time has more than a small proportion of Negro business gone to Negro entrepreneurs who were competing with economically more powerful white firms, in spite of the fact that a truly segregated economy was impossible because the basic industrial and credit facilities were in the hands of whites and because the Negro masses had white employers, though even enthusiasts like Du Bois were aware of the limitations of what Drake and Cayton have described as the "Dream of a Black Metropolis," nevertheless what E. Franklin Frazier has called the twin social myths of the success of Negro business and the advisability of a segregated economy grew markedly in popularity and came to dominate the outlook of American Negroes, especially the members of the entrepreneurial class.[18]

Closely allied with the idea of a "group economy" was the ideology underlying the establishment of the all-Negro communities. These were an institutionalized expression, in extreme form, of the ideological patterns of self-help and racial solidarity. Such communities had existed since ante-bellum times, but their heyday began during the 1880's. Though many efforts were abortive, a significant number of such settlements were created. Though chiefly in the South, they were scattered across the country from Whitesboro, New Jersey —founded by a group of North Carolinians under the leadership of ex-Congressman George H. White when disfranchisement spelled the end to Negro political influence in the state—to Allensworth, California, founded in 1908 by the former army chaplain, Lieutenant-Colonel Allen Allensworth.[19]

Unique in its comprehensiveness, but representative of many ideas of the period, was the "industrial settlement" at Kowaliga, Alabama, established about 1897 by William Benson, a graduate of Howard University, who aimed to erect a stable community of landowning farmers able to minister to their own needs for skilled craftsmen. The Kowaliga School was outwardly of the usual industrial type; its principal aim was to raise the general level of community life— to make good housewives rather than servants, to equip youth with useful farm skills that would encourage them to stay out of the cities where they would meet the competition of white mechanics and union discrimination. Benson's Dixie Industrial Company, incorporated in 1900, bought large tracts of land which it sold on easy terms to members of the community, conducted timber, saw mill, and retail store operations, and constructed a fifteen-mile railroad. Benson thought of the project as one through which Northern philanthropy could encourage the spirit of self-help among Negroes. He appears to have been on the verge of success when he died.[20]

Most famous of all were the attempt to create a predominantly Negro state in Oklahoma and the town of Mound Bayou. The chief leader in the former movement was E. P. McCabe, who had come to Kansas from the East in the late 1870's. Engaging in the land business and in politics he rose to the position of state auditor in 1882. Motivated in part by the Republican refusal to renominate him for office, McCabe became deeply imbued with the idea of the separation of the races and campaigned for an all-Negro state. So thoroughly did he work that in 1892, the year after Oklahoma was opened to settlement, there were seven Negro towns in the territory. Though McCabe failed to realize his dream of a Negro-dominated commonwealth with black senators, governors, and congressmen, the migration continued for a number of years, reaching its climax about 1910. Of the twenty-five towns that were eventually established the earliest was Langston (1891), and the most famous was Boley (1898).[21]

Even more celebrated was Mound Bayou, Mississippi, founded in 1887 by Isaiah T. Montgomery, a former slave of Jefferson Davis' brother, who would soon become noted for his defense of disfranchisement in the Mississippi Constitutional Convention of 1890. The community's other leading citizen was Charles Banks, a graduate of Rust University at Holly Springs and a former Clarksdale merchant who had moved to Mound Bayou in 1903, where he founded a bank, a cottonseed oil mill, and a loan and investment company. An important Masonic leader, and one of the chief figures in the Business League, he was described by Washington as the most influential Negro businessman in the country.[22] In addition to the enterprises led by Banks the town boomed with a sawmill, a Farmers' Co-Operative Mercantile Company, real estate ventures, a newspaper, a Normal and Industrial Institute, and a light and power company.

The psychology of both Mound Bayou and the Oklahoma towns revealed a chauvinistic rationalization of racial separatism, accompanied by an emphasis upon racial pride and solidarity. Both Banks and Montgomery were good friends of Washington, who took a deep interest in their community, and both enunciated the typical Tuskegee philosophy, though they were avid dabblers in politics.[23] A citizen of Langston saw developing in the Oklahoma communities "a type of Afro-American citizenship different from that found elsewhere," characterized by "the consciousness of the power that ensued from close communal life and co-operation." At the 1914 Business League Convention Boley proudly pointed to its self-government and its Negro officials, its $150,000 high school, its cement sidewalks and attractive residences, its Masonic temple, its electric light plant and waterworks, and its eighty-two business concerns (including a bank, three cotton gins, and a telephone system), as indicative of what Negro self-help and racial co-operation could accomplish.[24]

Yet behind the facade of optimism and self-assurance, behind the assertions of prosperity and success, there lay a story of vicissitude and ultimate failure. Boley's citizens entertained high hopes for political participation in the affairs of the state and county when Oklahoma achieved statehood; threat of effective Negro political action was, however, met by disfranchisement legislation. And a few years later the economic dreams of Boley's inhabitants began to dissolve when the town's economy was undermined by the cotton depression of 1913–14. Mound Bayou, ironically, had obtained substantial white philanthropic investment through the influence of Booker T. Washington. Yet its hopes also floundered when faced with the depression and the machinations of local white people.[25] The all-Negro communities remained small towns that were more significant as a symptom of a certain racial philosophy than as a solution to the race problem in America.[26]

Now these ideas of racial solidarity, self-help, and group economy do not appear to have been shared evenly by all segments of the Negro community. There were many complaints, especially around 1900, that Negro business was not supported sufficiently, and particularly that it was supported by the "middle" and "lower" classes, but not by the "upper class." As one editor said in 1899, the Negro businessman had to contend with the indifference of the "best class" of Negroes. Experience, he felt, had revealed that the poor class of people were more inclined to support race enterprise than the professional men. Du Bois, in commenting on Andrew Hilyer's report to the Hampton Conference in 1898 about the scanty support given Negro business by wealthy Negroes, felt it was natural that those with wealth should be guided by monetary considerations, while the lower and middle classes were "more influenced by considerations of race pride and social advance." [27]

Certainly those who depended on the Negro market supported a racial economic chauvinism. Those who had acquired their money from white customers and investment in white business tended to think more in terms of economic assimilation into the white community. In Northern cities such as Cleveland, Boston, and Chicago a distinct upper crust declined to patronize Negro business to World War I and after.[28] Yet after 1900 complaints about the failure of the upper class to support Negro business seem to have declined. It appears likely that in many cities the older group of well-to-do Negroes, losing its white customers, was on the decline or coming to appeal to Negro customers and that the more successful of the newer entrepreneurs who depended entirely on the Negro market were gradually coming to form the backbone of the upper stratum of Negro society. In the 1930's Frazier found the ideal of economic chauvinism widespread in all classes among Washington Negroes and concluded that "it is from the upper class that there has emanated the idea that the Negro could solve his economic problems by building a segregated economy." [29]

This discussion poses the problem of the development of the class structure among Negroes and its relationship to social thought. It is a question beset with many difficulties because of the paucity of evidence, the dynamic nature of the class structure in the United States, and the different patterns of class structure in different regions, in individual cities, in urban and rural areas, and in the Negro and white communities. The usual procedure has been to describe a Negro upper class and a Negro lower class in various communities, and to classify a range of intermediate individuals in a middle class, though the criteria for upper or middle class vary from community to community and from city to city.[30]

Social stratification among Negroes appeared before the Civil War. Among the slaves there were distinctions between house servants and skilled artisans on the one hand and field laborers on the other —distinctions that were to a large extent correlated with skin color and that were carried over into freedom. In the ante-bellum North a group of artisans, barbers, tradesmen, and the higher type of personal and domestic servants, along with occasional caterers, coal dealers, and other businessmen constituted an upper class. A more elaborate class structure emerged in some of the principal Southern cities, where one found a comfortable group of free Negroes, mostly of mixed ancestry, who were skilled artisans and made social distinctions on the basis of skill, income, and family background. The most elite families were those that possessed considerable property including slaves and could claim aristocratic white ancestry or absence of a tradition of slavery.[31] For some time after emancipation the ante-bellum free Negroes and their descendants enjoyed a higher social status than the freedmen; until recently the light-skinned aristocracies of cities like Charleston, St. Louis, New Orleans, and Washington maintained an exclusive position, and even today there is still some correlation—though much diminished—between skin color and class status.[32]

After emancipation social differentiation proceeded at an accelerated rate. In rural areas a pattern developed ranging from farm laborers through share tenants and cash renters to landowners. Proportionately fewer Negroes than whites owned farms, and only the lucky ones (often with the assistance of former masters or other patrons, along with hard work) had succeeded in becoming substantial landowners, though there were rare Negro families with plantations of over a thousand acres.[33] In the small towns a simple structure developed. In a group of Georgia, Alabama, and Virginia towns surveyed by Du Bois about 1898, the upper class consisted of a handful of ministers, teachers, blacksmiths, carpenters, shoemakers, tailors, restaurateurs, barbers, retail merchants, postal employees, clerical workers, a small percentage of the domestic workers, and a miscellaneous assortment of other artisans. Some towns, but not all, boasted physicians and lawyers and building contractors. On the whole these artisans and entrepreneurs depended on the white market; in one town two Negro barbers monopolized the town's business, and the leading meat market and restaurant were in the hands of colored men. The rest of the population were lower-class laborers. Representative of the smaller Northern cities was New Haven, where in the generation before World War I, outside of the leading ministers and a rare doctor or lawyer, the upper class consisted of a few carpenters and mechanics, and somewhat below them barbers, coachmen, cooks, butlers, and waiters.[34]

In the larger cities during the late nineteenth century upper-class status was accorded to a group that ranged from headwaiters, Pullman porters, coachmen, and butlers in prominent families, through draymen, blacksmiths, tailors, barbers, and postal employees, to coal dealers, hotel owners, caterers, and physicians, lawyers, teachers and certain ministers. By the twentieth century the artisan-entrepreneur and domestic servant group were passing from upper-class status (though as late as the 1920's Pullman porters in many places enjoyed considerable social status if they were of good family background, and older postal workers of good family are accorded some respect in certain cities at the present time). This development involved (1) a decline in the social status of the artisans and respectable domestics as the economic differentiation of the Negro community increased with the appearance of a larger business and professional class; and (2) the disappearance of the entrepreneurs who catered to the white market, and their replacement by a newer class of entrepreneurs dependent on the Negro market. Some entrepreneurs— mostly the newspaper publishers and undertakers, and some of the grocers, barbers, and so forth—had always depended on the Negro market. And some families of the older upper class turned from catering for whites to serving Negroes, like the descendants of the hotel owner W. H. Wormley in Washington, who became professional people. But from the available evidence it appears that most entrepreneurs and professional men who based their living on the Negro community were originally not from upper-class families but were socially mobile individuals, gradually coming to achieve upper-class status in most cities by the 1930's. The development occurred at varying rates in different cities; and in some cities the descendants of the older upper class have retained higher status than in others. A few examples will illustrate the situation.[35]

In Charleston, which was out of the mainstream of the New South's economic development, the ante-bellum aristocracy of artisans, contractors, barbers, postal employees, butchers, and professional people for many years enjoyed their upper-class status undisturbed. Not until the 1920's did Charleston Negroes enter into the "co-operative" businesses dependent on the Negro market and not until after World War II did the dispersal of the better-educated descendants of the old families pave the way for the rise to upper-class status of those descendants of the old house-slave class who now moved into the professional and business positions that accorded them higher social status.

New Orleans also had a large ante-bellum group of free people of color, and the Negro Creoles continued to dominate the building and other trades for many years. However, the insurance and other substantial enterprises serving the Negro community were established not by the downtown native New Orleans Creole group (who lived north of Canal Street), but by ambitious members of the uptown group that resided south of Canal Street. This uptown group consisted of Negro Creoles who had come to New Orleans from other parts of the state, and of the Protestant house servants of the wealthy, who—unlike most of the Catholic Creoles—placed a high value on education, sent their children to Methodist and Congregationalist New Orleans and Straight universities and thus were the chief source of the professional Negro elite in the city. New Orleans in effect had at that time two parallel social hierarchies—Creole and non-Creole; and it was among the latter that the new business elite first appeared.

In Nashville at the turn of the century, a light-skinned elite of barbers, contractors, and merchants in the city market was gradually giving way to a darker-skinned group consisting chiefly of physicians and dentists associated with the Meharry Medical School, along with some businessmen and professors. The more important business enterprises included two banks, and two publishing boards—the Baptist and the A.M.E. Sunday School Union. Some members of the old elite made the transition—such as J. C. Napier, the son of an antebellum deliveryman, who became a banker and lawyer, while his brother maintained a fashionable livery stable.

In cities of the New South, especially in Durham and Atlanta, there was developing a substantial entrepreneurial class on the basis of the "group economy," though enterprises like the Fitzgerald brickyards in Durham and certain contractors and real estate dealers in Atlanta continued to depend on the white market. But John Merrick of Durham and A. F. Herndon, the wealthiest Negro in Atlanta, both of whom moved from barbering for prominent whites to founding insurance companies for Negroes (the North Carolina Mutual and the Atlanta Life respectively), illustrated the shift from the older service occupations catering to whites to the newer type of "co-operative" enterprise catering to Negroes. Durham was so new as a city that it had no older upper class; in addition to a blacksmith, and the brickyard owner, the elite of the early twentieth century consisted principally of Merrick and his associates and one or two others engaged in successful business dependent on the Negro market. In Atlanta, the late nineteenth-century elite was composed primarily (as was the Durham group) of ex-slaves of mixed ancestry and their descendants—a contractor, two real estate dealers, some of the barbers, grocers, and draymen, several politicians, one or two undertakers, a lawyer, a few doctors, at least one minister, sometimes the resident bishop of the A.M.E. Church, several college professors, and postmen and teachers. Success in business and family and educational background were important criteria of the upper class. Of this group the undertaker, lawyer, doctors, clerics and professors, and some grocers derived their livelihood from the segregated Negro community. Two insurance companies (the Atlanta Life and the Standard Life) were the most conspicuous evidence of the shift toward the "co-operative" type of enterprise; and ultimately it was through them and related enterprises that after World War I a group of men, most of whom were not born into upper-class Atlanta families, became the core of the newer upper class, in many cases marrying descendants of the older elite.

In Philadelphia, where coachmen, barbers, and head waiters and bellmen held high status into the twentieth century, successful caterers and their families remained at the pinnacle of the social pyramid even when their economic base began to crumble. Du Bois in 1898 reported that the highest class of Philadelphia Negroes was Philadelphia born, lived in well-appointed homes with hired servants, and held themselves aloof from the Negro masses. During the next ten years there was a rapid development of a business and professional class whose economic base was in the stream of migrants coming from the South; many of this class, probably chiefly of middle-class status before World War I, later achieved upper-class status, though here as elsewhere a doctor, no matter what his origins, was considered upper class.

Chicago was to be a conspicuous example of the philosophy of self-help and racial solidarity during the 1920's and even before the War was one of two Northern cities with a Negro bank. Previous to 1900, however, the Negro market (serviced by the less lucrative restaurants, barber shops, and small stores in Negro enclaves) was relatively unimportant in comparison to the white market which Negroes served as tailors, liverymen, draymen, barbers, hairdressers, and caterers. And even during the next fifteen years, while Negroes were losing many of their white customers (barber shops, for example, the largest category of business, came to serve an entirely Negro clientele), men like the lawyer E. H. Morris and the physician Daniel Hale Williams continued to enjoy professional and social relationships with leading whites. Down to the Great Migration the upper class in Chicago consisted of the house servants of the wealthy, Pullman porters, successful politicians, and a few business and professional men. It was, observed Drake and Cayton, "the Negro market created by the Great Migration [that] resulted in the expansion of the business and professional classes who gradually displaced the Old Settlers as 'the cream of colored society.' "

In Boston, lingering abolitionist and equalitarian traditions created a situation where an older upper class consisting of professional and businessmen catering largely to whites, to a considerable extent identified itself with the white community, and provided the leadership in the anti-Washington protest movement. John Daniels in a sociological study published in 1914 said that above the rank and file who formed 80 per cent of the city's Negro population, came a middle-class group of widely varying occupations and statuses ranging from waiters, Pullman porters, janitors, and artisans, who by thrift and industry were making a modest, steady living, up to well-salaried white-collar workers and some of the leading business and professional people. In education and manner much closer to the masses than the upper-class Negroes, they maintained a strong feeling of group solidarity. About 2 per cent of the population, mostly of Northern birth or long Northern residence, and with considerably more white ancestry than the other classes, formed the real upper class of lawyers, physicians, salaried employees, business proprietors, and literary and musical people, characterized by superior education and refinement. In their work they often came in contact with whites more than they did with Negroes, and many were members of white organizations and churches, lived in white neighborhoods, and had many friends among the whites. They had little contact and failed to identify themselves with the masses and were, in Daniels' words, "disposed to cast aspersion on most forms of separate union among the Negro people along the lines of voluntary segregation." While they acted as race spokesmen in demanding full citizenship rights, and while they were in the forefront of the opposition to Booker T. Washington, many who were socially beneath them often accused them of lacking race pride.[36]

Thus, the Boston upper class, dependent on white customers, opposed the doctrines of racial solidarity, economic chauvinism, and segregated institutions espoused by the middle class. And this middle class and the respectable majority of the lower classes were the chief supporters of Negro churches, lodges, business and welfare organizations.[37] In other cities some of the middle class were rising into upper-class status after 1900; and with the increasing discrimination from upper-class whites and the influence of Washington even some of this older Boston upper class was being forced to revise its philosophy.

There is evidence that elsewhere in the North there tended to be a correlation between membership in the older upper class and opposition to Booker T. Washington, though the correlation is far from complete. In Cleveland, for example, the lawyer Charles W. Chesnutt

and H. C. Smith, editor of the *Gazette,* enunciated a philosophy practically identical with that of the Boston "radicals" (except that Chesnutt, while disagreeing with Washington, always remained on friendly
terms with him). Such opposition as there was to Washington among
the ministers seemed to be concentrated among the clergymen of
certain Northern and border-state upper-class churches; and despite
the bait of political office which Washington held out to Northern
lawyers, there was a significant relationship between old upper-class
membership and opposition to the Tuskegeean among them. Even
in the South this may have been true to some degree, though undoubtedly most of the entrepreneurs with white customers supported
Washington, perhaps largely because of that side of his philosophy
which talked of getting along with Southern whites and held that a
competent Negro businessman would have plenty of economic opportunity in the South, even among whites. In Augusta such members of the light-skinned elite as Judson Lyons and the Reverend
W. J. White, editor of the *Georgia Baptist,* were all associated with
the anti-Bookerite protest movement, while members of the rising
group of dark-skinned men, such as the Reverend C. T. Walker, a
close associate of the Tuskegeean, were rivals of the White group
and fostered the ideals of race solidarity and self-help.[38]

All in all, between 1890 and the 1920's, the process occurring at
different rates and times in different cities, and more markedly in
cities where the most substantial in-migration was taking place,[39]
the forces of segregation and discrimination were instrumental in
creating a Negro petit bourgeoisie of business and professional men
who depended on the Negro masses for their livelihood, and this
group was gradually assuming upper-class status—either merging
with or replacing in status the older upper class whose leading members were often or usually business and professional men serving
the white community. By and large it was the older pre-1900 entrepreneurial and professional upper class that tended to be indifferent
or opposed to the philosophy of racial solidarity, even though members of this group came to favor it to the extent that they were forced
(and able) to turn to the Negro market. Self-made men for the most
part, their economic roots in the newly urbanized Negro masses, the
new bourgeoisie, or middle status group, naturally found the philosophy of self-help and racial solidarity—and consequently the philosophy of Booker T. Washington—congenial to their experience and

interests, and they easily appropriated the symbols of American individualism and Social Darwinism to explain and rationalize their social role. This group was especially instrumental in the burgeoning of the philosophy of racial solidarity, self-help, and the group economy, of the rationalization of the economic advantages of the disadvantages in segregation and discrimination. Washington's National Negro Business League was the platform on which this group expressed its point of view.[40]

PART FIVE

The Divided Mind of the Negro, 1895–1915

There are two views of the Negro question. One is that the Negro
should stoop to conquer; that he should accept in silence the denial
of his political rights; that he should not brave the displeasure
of white men by protesting when he is segregated in humiliating ways.
. . . There are others who believe that the Negro owes this nation
no apology for his presence . . . ; that being black he is still no
less a man; that he should refuse to be assigned to an inferior place
by his fellow-countrymen.

> REVERDY C. RANSOM at Harper's
> Ferry Meeting of the Niagara
> Movement, 1906
> *The Spirit of Freedom and Justice*
> (Nashville, 1926), 12–13.

Effective horsemanship is accomplished by straddling.

> KELLY MILLER
> "Come Let Us Reason Together,"
> *Voice of the Negro,* III (Jan. 1906),
> 67.

INTRODUCTION

During the two decades of Washington's ascendancy, Negroes continued to accumulate property and education, but in other respects their status, North and South, actually deteriorated.[1] Southern opinion was becoming more extreme than ever, and Northerners were becoming increasingly indifferent and even hostile toward Negroes. In the South a spate of ultraracist books appeared, from the melodramatic novels of Thomas Dixon (whose views received extraordinary publicity when his *The Clansmen* was made into the noted movie, *The Birth of a Nation* in 1915) to such lurid titles as Charles Carroll's *The Negro a Beast* (1900) and Robert W. Shufeldt's *The Negro: A Menace to American Civilization* (1907). Southern polemicists generally held not only that Negroes were an innately inferior, immoral, and criminal race that could never catch up with the whites in civilization, but that in fact freedom caused a reversion to barbarism. Many propagandists justified lynching on the basis of the Negro's allegedly increasing tendency toward rape and believed colonization the only alternative to violent extermination. There were differences in degree, but scarcely in basic outlook between conservatives like Thomas Nelson Page, who glorified the aristocratic plantation tradition, and extremists like James Vardaman and Hoke Smith, who voiced the hatreds of the lower class. Some, it is true, maintained a sense of *noblesse oblige,* but even the most sympathetic Southerners [2] accepted the idea of innate racial differences and the inferiority of the Negro. In the North weighty scholarly opinion in the biological sciences supported Southern racist doctrines, and eminent historians and political scientists reinterpreted Reconstruction and the triumph of white supremacy in a manner favorable to the white South. Almost alone among prominent social scientists, the anthropologist Franz Boas maintained that innate racial differences were inconsequential. Tangible evidence of attitudes in both parts of the country was the rising tide of mob violence. While the annual number of lynchings declined from over 150 in the early 1890's to victims numbering usually between sixty and eighty after 1905, the number of race riots increased in both sections—from the Wilmington, North Carolina, riot of 1898 and the New York riot of 1900 to a bloody climax in Atlanta in 1906 and Springfield, Illinois, in 1908.

By 1895 disfranchisement had been pretty well accomplished by various devices—legal and extralegal—in most of the South;[3] by 1908 another half dozen states had imitated Mississippi and South Carolina in enacting constitutional provisions; and by 1915 practically all of the Southern states provided for white primaries. In *Williams v Mississippi,* 1898, in *Giles v Harris,* 1903, and in *Giles v Teasley,* 1904, the Supreme Court refused to intervene, though in 1915, in *Guinn v U.S.,* it did declare the grandfather clauses unconstitutional. While the Court upheld the Negroes' rights to jury services (*Rogers v Alabama,* 1903) and while it declared peonage unconstitutional (*Bailey v Alabama,* 1911), in 1896 it upheld the legality of segregation on the basis of the separate-but-equal doctrine (*Plessy v Ferguson,* 1896). Subsequently, Southern states and cities expanded their segregation regulations. Most of the states had passed Jim Crow railway laws by the end of the century and streetcar segregation laws by 1908. Negroes were excluded or segregated in municipal parks, and beginning in 1910 residential segregation ordinances appeared in a number of Southern and border cities—a practice outlawed by the Supreme Court in 1917.

The condition of Negro education reflected the trend toward discrimination. School appropriations for Negro children were in many localities actually reduced; the average per capita expenditure for Negro children rose slightly but the divergence in per capita appropriations between Negro and white students grew rapidly. By 1910 in most of the Southern states at least twice as much was spent per pupil on whites as on Negroes. Conservatives acceded to the desirability of industrial education for the uplift of a "backward race," but extremists like Governor Vardaman of Mississippi objected to any sort of education for Negroes.

Perceptive observers like the Southern educator, Thomas Pearce Bailey and the Northern journalist, Ray Stannard Baker, regarded the increasing oppression as related to the rise of the poorer whites. Yet Baker also recognized that the larger landowners and employers liked the Negro only as long as he remained faithful, obedient, and unambitious. When he became prosperous or educated, or a landowner, many whites turned hostile. Bailey noted, moreover, that it was becoming increasingly difficult for Negroes to purchase land. In the Atlanta riot, Baker pointed out, it was the industrious, respectable, and law-abiding Negroes who were attacked. Evidently, Washington's optimism was somewhat misplaced.

In the North, even in Cleveland and Boston, where abolitionist traditions lingered longest, white attitudes were shifting in an unfavorable direction. This shift was illustrated by the diminution in political participation from the high point about 1890. In Illinois there continued to be one or two Negroes in the legislature, but in Massachusetts, for example, though Negroes still received appointive offices, W. H. Lewis was the last one to sit in the General Court (1902), none served on the Cambridge city council after 1901, and in Boston where there had been three Negroes on the common council in 1894–95, there was but one in 1909. More and more, also, Negroes were experiencing violations of Northern civil rights laws. Court cases involving discrimination on the part of hotels, restaurants, and theaters were frequently decided against the plaintiff, and even where litigation was successful the fines imposed were usually small. Consequently, Negroes ordinarily preferred not to risk further insults. Many communities provided separate schools in defiance of state law, and there was increasing agitation for them in communities with mixed schools.

At the very time that Negro entrepreneurs were losing their white customers, both white employers and white unions depressed the lot of the Negro worker. The condition of the exploited Southern tenant farmer often merged into a state of peonage. Having lost their dominant position in the skilled trades by 1890, Southern Negroes did at least hold to their reduced position in some of them—particularly in the building trades and as printers and machinists. But they were gradually excluded from certain industries in which technological innovation made the work more attractive to whites, as in the tobacco factories, and their numbers increased chiefly in rough and unskilled laboring jobs in the saw mills, cottonseed oil mills, coal mines, and railroads of the New South. Northern Negroes never had a solid footing in the skilled trades, and after 1900 their stronghold in domestic, hotel, and restaurant work was being undermined. By the turn of the century also Negroes found themselves excluded from most trade unions. A few unions however—the cigarmakers, the coal miners, the garment workers, and longshoremen—did not discriminate; and others, especially some of the craft unions in the building trades in the South, fearful of Negro competition, did admit them in varying degrees. Of the labor federations, only the I.W.W. had an explicit philosophy of interracial solidarity which it applied even in the Deep South.

The deteriorating status of the Negro throughout the nation was reflected in the policies of the national administrations at Washington. Roosevelt's actions alternately pleased and angered Negroes. His praise for Negro soldiers fighting alongside the Rough Riders in Cuba was, eighteen months after the event, replaced by charges of cowardice. He won approval for inviting Booker T. Washington to dinner, for closing the Indianola, Mississippi, post office rather than acceding to white demands that he replace the Negro appointee with a white person, and for insisting on appointing W. D. Crum as collector of the Port of Charleston in the face of powerful Southern and senatorial opposition. Meanwhile, he played a shifty game with the lily-white Republicans and Gold Democrats of the South. By 1905 he was speaking favorably of Southern traditions and urging Negroes to ignore classical for industrial education. In 1906 he summarily discharged three companies of the 25th army regiment on unproven charges of rioting in Brownsville, Texas. No action of the President hurt and angered Negroes more than this one. Outrageous also was Roosevelt's message to Congress in 1906, in which he falsely asserted that lynchings were caused by Negro men assaulting white women.

Taft's pronouncements between 1906 and 1908 were also unfortunate, for they favored industrial education almost to the exclusion of higher education and supported ballot restrictions consistent with the literal wording of the fifteenth amendment. Critics pointed also to his close connection, as secretary of War, with the Brownsville affair. Negroes had been elated over Roosevelt's well-publicized appointments (though his policy was to appoint fewer colored men to office), but they became upset over the loss of positions under Taft and his frank declaration that he would not appoint Southern Negroes to office where whites objected. The lily-whites made even greater headway under Taft than they had under Roosevelt; and segregation was introduced in a few of the federal offices in Washington. By the election of 1912 Negroes were faced with a sorry choice: a Democratic candidate, Wilson, born in the South, who would make only the vaguest concessions to Negroes in his campaign promises; Taft, who had thoroughly alienated Negroes during his administration; and Roosevelt, who, while appealing to Negro voters in the North, refused to seat Negro delegates from the South at the Progressive Party convention. Under the circumstances, most voted for Roosevelt. Those who supported Wilson soon found that they had made a mistake, for executive appointments were almost nil, and the policy of segregation in the federal offices was greatly widened.

It appeared that Negroes were practically omitted from the Progressive era's program of reform. Direct primaries might be more democratic, but white primaries were less so. As C. Vann Woodward has pointed out, the Progressive Movement in the South was for whites only. "Progressive" Roosevelt utilized "conservative" Washington, and acted quite conservatively on racial matters. Wilson had no interest in the welfare of the Negro. In most respects, indeed, the outlook appeared to become constantly more dismal during the ascendancy of Washington and the vogue of reform. Yet out of the ferment of the Progressive era, in large part out of the work of a small minority of prominent liberals whose interest in reform included Negroes as well as whites, developed the most effective organization yet established for the agitation of Negro rights—the National Association for the Advancement of Colored People.

One may distinguish perhaps four factors of particular importance in determining the course of Negro thought during the two decades of Washington's ascendancy: the prestige and the influence of Washington himself, the background of deteriorating race relations, the impact of the Progressive Movement (both negative and positive) upon Negro aspirations, the steady rise of education and property accumulation and of Negro entrepreneurial and professional classes.

It is largely against the background of increasing prejudice and discrimination that the ideologies of the period must be considered. White hostility called forth a defensive philosophy of self-help and racial solidarity, frustration of political ambitions caused a redirection of energies toward economic accumulation, and the closing of economic opportunities strengthened the ideology of a segregated economy championed by the newer business and professional men. Naturally, the acceptance of Washington's philosophy was largely determined by these conditions. Not only did his espousal of economic advancement and self-help make sense to a substantial and growing element, not only did Southern Negroes find an opportunistic accommodation advantageous if not necessary, but many leaders in all sections, even those who basically nourished a deep-seated protest philosophy, discouraged as they were by the trend of events, hopefully supported the Tuskegeean and his program in their eagerness to somehow stem the seemingly irresistible tide of racial proscription.

Important also in accounting for the influence of Washington's philosophy among the articulate were the tremendous prestige and power he wielded. Office seekers and money-hungry newspapers, schools that needed funds, ministers who desired the aid of white philanthropy or advancement within their denominations—all found Washington's assistance useful, if not essential. Men of initiative and ambition were thus encouraged to espouse his cause—and often to convince themselves of its correctness—in order to assure their own success. This situation, combined with Washington's deliberate and often devious use of his power in politics, philanthropy, and elsewhere to undermine his critics and destroy what he referred to as "the opposition," undoubtedly inclined overt ideological expression in a more conservative direction than would have otherwise been the case.

On the other hand, the failure of Washington's program to halt the deterioration of race relations and resentment at what was regarded as the abuse of his immense powers over political appointments and philanthropy were the chief factors in the creation of an organized opposition to him. Some had raised their voices against him from the beginning, but it was only after 1900, when Washington reached the zenith of his power, that the sharp division of Negroes into Bookerites and anti-Bookerites, or Conservatives and Radicals became especially pronounced.

Until the formation of the N.A.A.C.P., and quite possibly for some time afterward, Washington's critics consisted of a minority of the intellectual and professional men. The majority of the articulate, of what Du Bois called the "talented tenth," appeared to support Washington to a greater or lesser degree. Many, however, were divided in their loyalties, attempting to maintain friendly relations with both sides in the bitter quarrel, and to essay a compromise position. Large numbers of those who supported Washington did not personally follow his accommodating tactic, which they regarded as necessary for him or for any Negro leader in the South. Some were even more obsequious to the white South than Washington was. And the divided loyalties of many of Washington's supporters were exhibited by inconsistencies and shifts of view. Much of this shifting around was due to personal opportunism, reflecting the desire for preferment which could be obtained only through his powerful aid. But much of it was a sort of ideological opportunism, a desperate attempt to find some solution for what appeared to be an increasingly hopeless situation.

Perhaps an even more fundamental dichotomy than the conflict between Washington and his critics, between the accommodators and the agitators, was the ethnic dualism of American Negroes. Correlated to a considerable extent with the other alignment was a contrast between emphasis on self-help, race pride, and solidarity on the one hand, and immediate assimilation on the other; between stress on Negro ethnocentrism as compared with a complete identification with the American nationality. In their extreme manifestations the doctrines of racial self-help and solidarity involved all-Negro communities or colonization. Ordinarily, however, ethnocentrism in the age of Washington took the form of ethnic pluralism rather than an exclusive nationalism, of giving special emphasis to the support of Negro business and the cultivation of a pride in racial history. It implied that Negroes should remain a distinctively separate group in American society but that they should also enjoy the rights of citizenship. At the other extreme were those who regarded Africa as only another interesting foreign land, declined to support racial institutions or racial business as such, and regarded amalgamation as the appropriate and ultimately the only solution to the race problem. Those who adopted the latter point of view consistently voiced a protest philosophy.

It should be emphasized that even those most articulate in defense of rights and integration were likely to insist also on the necessity of group pride and co-operation in order to attain those goals, and, in some cases, to advocate a group economy as an indirect means of uplifting Negroes economically to the point where they would be freely integrated into the larger American economy. The cleavage between the conciliators and the agitators, between the allies of Washington and his critics, was only roughly correlated with the division between those who emphasized racial solidarity and those who insisted on immediate and complete assimilation. Moreover, here too, one finds inconsistencies and changes of viewpoint and emphasis. A single individual might favor racial solidarity at one time and consider it an evil at another—as did Douglass. The sense of "two-ness" as Du Bois called it, the dual identification with race and with nation, is a fundamental quality in the thinking of the great majority of Negroes—though they vary in the degree of emphasis upon one extreme or the other—and it was particularly important during the period under discussion.

There were two other dichotomies that were more clearly correlated with the Bookerite-anti-Bookerite split, and these encompassed economic doctrines. In the first place the conservatives put greatest emphasis on moral and economic improvement, while the radicals stressed agitation, political action, and civil rights. Here again the degree of emphasis upon one or the other or both of these approaches varied widely, and many of the articulate gave approximately equal emphasis to both. Yet the economic approach was more characteristic of the Washington circle and of the accommodators generally (Washington himself classifying as conservative those who placed primary stress on economic and moral uplift and self-help, even when they clearly indicated full citizenship rights as their ultimate goal), while the politics-and-agitation approach was more characteristic of the radical anti-Bookerites, who insisted upon immediate attainment of citizenship rights. In the second place the anti-Bookerites tended to lean toward economic radicalism—toward Bryanism, interracial trade unionism, and socialism. While the majority of Washington's critics maintained their faith in laissez-faire individualism and were suspicious of labor unions because of their discriminatory policies, those who did lean toward economic radicalism were drawn from the ranks of the racial radicals.

Actually, we are dealing with two types of dichotomies—between different factions and within individuals themselves. There were clear-cut distinctions between conciliators and agitators; between those who placed chief reliance upon the indirect economic approach to full citizenship and those who championed protest and political action as a direct route to the same goal; between those who stressed their affinity with the Negro race and those who insisted upon their full identity with the American nation only; and most dramatically between the Bookerites and the anti-Bookerites. These lines of cleavage were roughly correlated with each other, so that gradualism, conciliation, the middle-class virtues, racial solidarity, self-help, and sympathy for Washington tended to cluster together to form a "conservative" outlook, while agitation for civil and political rights, advocacy of immediate and complete integration, interest in the labor movement, and opposition to the Tuskegeean also tended to cluster together to form a "radical" outlook.[4] However, it cannot be overemphasized that this correlation or clustering is far from a complete description of the situation; that there were the inconsistencies, the twistings and turnings, the attempts to hold to both clusters of ideologies—or to parts of both—or to shift from one to the other that were characteristic of probably the majority of the articulate.

And it was natural for the views of the articulate to present a picture about which it is impossible to make precise generalizations, a picture full of contradictions and changes. There were many factors and variables involved: the equalitarian ideals of American society and the actuality of the American race system; the Utopian vision of a land of brotherhood and the practical benefits to be derived from Washington's influence; the democratic political tradition of American culture and its moral and economic orientation; individual ambition and personal idiosyncrasies; color distinctions among Negroes [5] and the evolving class structure of the Negro community; regional differentiation in the race system and in the Negro class structure, and the beginnings of urbanization and northward migration; the intensification of overt manifestations of discrimination and prejudice, and the growing interest of a few white philanthropists and social reformers in the race problem. All of these impinged upon each other and upon the attitudes of Negroes in a complex web of causation that produced a wide variety of thought patterns, whose threads the following chapters will attempt to disentangle by citing illustrative examples. Certain main trends emerge, but equally significant are the questionings, the shifts, the searchings, the compromises and inconsistencies, the inner conflicts exemplified by individuals and groups.

Gunnar Myrdal has summed up this situation perceptively in observing that for Negroes who "are denied identification with the nation or with national groups . . . social speculation, therefore, moves in a sphere of unreality and futility. . . . *Negroes seem to be held in a state of eternal preparedness for a great number of contradictory opinions*—ready to accept one type or another depending on how they are driven by pressures or where they see an opportunity." [6] There is something pragmatic about the ideologies of American Negroes. They will take the path that seems most likely to eliminate or at least minimize the discrimination involved in the American race system.

In the following pages we will first trace the crystallization of the opposition to Washington and the rise of the N.A.A.C.P. and discuss the philosophy of Tuskegee's critics. We shall then survey the thought of the articulate classes during the period of Washington's ascendancy, and, finally, make an interpretive summary of the outlook of articulate Negroes at about the time of Washington's death in 1915—just prior to the Great Migration, which after emancipation was the great watershed in American Negro history.

CHAPTER X

"RADICALS AND CONSERVATIVES" [1]

At no time were Booker T. Washington's policies favored by all Negroes. Opposition to Washington existed from the time of the Atlanta Address, became more marked after 1900, and culminated in the founding of the National Association for the Advancement of Colored People.

While most articulate Negroes appear to have welcomed Washington's speech, it had a mixed reception among the elite of the national capital,[2] and a significant segment of the press was at first reticent and then broke into criticism. It was three weeks before the Cleveland *Gazette* mentioned the address, but once it had done so it reported receiving a torrent of abuse from other papers for its criticism, to which it replied by charging that Washington's actions were motivated by his desire for money and praise. The Washington *Bee* also failed to print the address and declared a few weeks later that "Prof. Washington's speech suited the white prejudiced element of the country." H. T. Johnson of the A.M.E. Christian *Recorder* expressed himself guardedly at first, but two months later said he believed the Tuskegeean's views to be incorrect.[3]

As the century drew to a close, support for Washington increased. W. E. B. Du Bois later recalled that criticism, at first widely voiced, largely disappeared. In those dreary years the advancing tide of segregation and disfranchisement made protest seem futile, and even some who, like the Grimké brothers, were later numbered among the Tuskegeean's most distinguished opponents, supported his program. Characteristically, the *Bee* was inconsistent in its attitude, but as early

171

as 1897 the *Recorder* declared Washington "endorsed by his people" after a period of misunderstanding.[4]

Perhaps the extent to which Washington's philosophy was accepted among the articulate during the late 1890's was best illustrated by the conventions of the Afro-American Council, attended as they were by the most distinguished leaders. At the December 1898 meeting, Alexander Walters, president of the Council, employing a judicious combination of militance and accommodation, seemed to sum up the thinking of the majority of leaders in that period of extreme discouragement. He insisted that there could be no real peace in America until Negroes were accorded equal rights, but he also thought the race would have done well if these were attained in a hundred years. He believed it would be unwise for Southern Negroes to withdraw from politics altogether, yet he did not object to educational and property qualifications for voting as long as the poor and illiterate of both races were disfranchised. He delivered a peroration on behalf of agitation, for to remain silent in the face of continued outrages and discrimination would be advertising Negroes as unworthy of freedom, but he also counseled reliance on the school house, hard work and moral improvement, and the creation of a group economy. He approved all types of education, but criticized those who after the Civil War had avoided manual labor and entered the professions. In short, "Let us improve our morals, educate ourselves, work, agitate and wait on the Lord."

The speech's enthusiastic reception indicated that here was something that appealed to all sides and to that large middle ground of opinion that held to a broad spectrum of ideologies. Yet the meeting was marked by a sharp clash between the "conservatives" and "radicals" that was precipitated by Ida Wells-Barnett. In her talk on mob violence she charged that Washington was greatly mistaken in thinking that Negroes would gain their rights merely by making themselves a significant element in the nation's economy, and criticized President McKinley for failing to give attention to the matter of the race's rights. These statements naturally displeased Tuskegee supporters and federal office holders—both chiefly from the South. Henry Plummer Cheatham, recorder of deeds, not only defended McKinley, but made a strong plea for conservatism and moderation, asserting that "hot-headed meetings in the North are making it impossible for the Negroes of North Carolina to live peaceably in their Southern home." Thus opened a contentious discussion on political activity in which the Southerners and officeholders were ranged against Northern agitators and opponents of the administration.

Some Northerners were scathing in their attack upon accommodating Southerners, and Dr. N. F. Mossell of Philadelphia denounced "the utterance made by a Southern Negro that the ballot had been given too soon, as the most damnable heresy." The convention's address to the country reflected a distinct compromise. It declared that no one method would achieve the desired ends, that in the North agitation and political activity were essential, while in the South education and internal development would pave the way for citizenship rights. It specifically affirmed that Negroes claimed all rights guaranteed by the Constitution and contended that manhood suffrage was the most effective safeguard of liberty, but did not oppose "legitimate restriction" in the form of an educational or a property qualification, or both, applied to both races. It also attacked segregation, lynch law, and penal conditions and urged federal aid to education and both higher and industrial schools.[5]

Succeeding conventions displayed a similar view. Generally, as a New York daily reported, the Council was "conservative in all of its actions," though the Northern radicals continued to criticize Washington. At Chicago in 1899 a minority group vigorously attacked his political doctrines and charged that he favored industrial to the exclusion of higher education. At the Indianapolis convention in 1900 the conservative element won the day only after a committee report dealing harshly with Southern whites had been modified under pressure from Southern delegates, one of whom, R. R. Wright, Sr., denounced the report as "a lie." It should be noted, however, that a legal bureau, created early in 1899, within a year had taken up the work of testing the franchise provisions of the Louisiana constitution in the courts.[6] Subsequently, this bureau was responsible for most of the Council's significant work.

Meanwhile, Washington had been moving secretly toward control of the Council. During 1901 and 1902 he was anonymously making major financial contributions toward the legal bureau's work and was, in fact, clandestinely directing its course of action. At the rather stormy 1902 St. Paul convention the Washington group secured Fortune's election as president over determined opposition. The convention's manifesto was even more conciliatory than usual, and the elected officials were clearly almost entirely in the Washington orbit. As Washington's secretary, Emmett J. Scott said, "We control the Council now." Yet the situation was unstable. When the executive committee met in Washington in January, conflict was in the air. Both the committee's address to the country and the speeches by its chairman, Bishop Walters, and by James H. Hayes of the recently organized National Negro Suffrage League, had a decidedly radical tone. Hayes asserted that if the intolerable Southern conditions continued, Negroes "must resort to the torch," and both speakers ridiculed the notion that acquisition of wealth and education would solve the problem.[7]

As a matter of fact by 1903 it was evident that there had been a recrudescence of the opposition to Washington. In addition to the handful of older journals that generally criticized the Tuskegeean during the first years of the century—most notably the Cleveland *Gazette* and the Chicago *Conservator*—there appeared in 1901 the most famous of all the anti-Tuskegee papers, the Boston *Guardian,* edited by William Monroe Trotter. The son of Cleveland's recorder of deeds, James Trotter, and the first Negro elected to Phi Beta Kappa at Harvard, he had imbibed from his father—who would not live in a segregated neighborhood and who did not become a minister because he would not be a pastor in a segregated church—an uncompromising hatred of all forms of discrimination. The *Guardian's* articles, editorials, and cartoons flayed Washington and Roosevelt. Trotter called Washington a "self-seeker" who had endorsed Jim Crow cars and disfranchisement, a "coward that . . . skulked all his life far from the field of combat." The Tuskegeean's antipolitical line was "a remarkable piece of deception in view of the fact that Mr. Washington is claiming in private that he, and he alone, is responsible for the president's Colored appointments, and his lily-white policy." When Washington contended that the revised constitutions of the Southern states had put a premium upon intelligence, ownership of property, thrift, and character, Trotter charged that Washington had deliberately made a false statement and had thus given a fatal blow to the Negro's liberty and political rights. Indeed, all the talk of education, wealth, and morality solving the problem was mere "twaddle." Actually, in the South Negroes with these things were disliked; and all the wealth and intelligence acquired by Negroes before the Civil War did less toward freeing the slave than did the agitation of the abolitionists.[8]

Boston in fact was the center of the most vehement agitation. Among Trotter's leading associates there were the lawyer and former minister to Santo Domingo, Archibald Grimké, president of the Massachusetts Suffrage League, and the attorney Clement Morgan, a holder of degrees from Atlanta and Harvard universities, and a member of the Cambridge City Council, 1896–98. Other significant Northern centers of anti-Bookerite agitation were Chicago, where the two lawyers Ferdinand Barnett and E. H. Morris led a group organized around the *Conservator,* and Philadelphia, where Dr. N. F. Mossell, founder of Douglass Hospital, was a central figure. In New York, however, it appears that the influence of men like Fortune and later of Charles W. Anderson, collector of internal revenue, minimized anti-Tuskegee expression.

In the South protest activity had not entirely disappeared. Undoubtedly the best examples of it had been the boycotts organized in various cities against the Jim Crow streetcars. Between 1898 and 1904 citizens of Augusta, Atlanta, Columbia, New Orleans, Mobile, and Houston boycotted the streetcars. In Houston and in 1906 in Austin, Nashville, and Savannah, Negroes even organized their own shortlived transportation companies. In 1905 Jacksonville residents temporarily held the line by securing a court decision declaring the segregation ordinance illegal. And as late as 1910, the Reverend W. H. Steward of Louisville, editor of the *National Baptist,* was credited with defeating an attempt to institute Jim Crow cars in that city.[9] Not unexpectedly, therefore, in a few places—chiefly Richmond and Atlanta—anti-Washington groups did appear. In Richmond, with its noted liberal arts college, Virginia Union University, the *Planet* for a few years had attacked the Tuskegeean, and James H. Hayes, an attorney who had carried the fight against disfranchisement in the Old Dominion to the Supreme Court, provided a focus of dissident activity through his Suffrage League. And in the intellectual atmosphere at Atlanta, with its half dozen institutions of higher learning, at least two leading figures, President John Hope of Atlanta Baptist College and W. E. B. Du Bois came out against Washington. Atlanta continued to be a stronghold of radicalism. In 1905 when the noted magazine the *Voice of the Negro* started to criticize Washington openly, Atlanta obtained its own radical journal. And in 1906 several hundred Georgia Negroes at a state convention in Macon, under the leadership of William Jefferson White, adopted a stirring address of protest and formed an Equal Rights Association.[10] Meanwhile, in the spring of 1903, there had appeared Du Bois' *Souls of Black Folk* with its critical essay about Booker T. Washington, an important work that helped to crystallize the anti-Tuskegee sentiment that became evident at the Afro-American Council meeting at Louisville in July of that year.

Fearful of a combination of dissidents from various cities coalescing around Hayes and Trotter, the Tuskegee circle had worked feverishly during the spring of 1903 to keep control of the Council and assure Fortune's re-election. As a matter of fact delegates from New York, Virginia, New Jersey, and New England held a rival meeting with Hayes' Equal Suffrage League, and only after much negotiation were they brought into the Convention. Washington was bitterly attacked on the floor of the convention by Trotter and two of his associates. Later, there was an undignified struggle over the election of officers, though Fortune won easily. Trotter conceded that most of the resolutions he submitted were rejected. The Convention's "Address" tactfully deplored the influences at work throughout the country to destroy the "friendly" relationships that had always existed between the best people of both races. In Tuskegeean tones it pointed out that lynching was demoralizing to whites. And though it did assert that the disfranchisement laws, originally designed ostensibly to prevent only ignorant Negroes from voting, actually were now openly directed at all Negroes, it made the usual statement accepting restrictions on the ballot.[11]

Opposition editors now regarded the Council, which had been founded as a protest organization, as clearly dominated by Tuskegee. Washington himself felt that he had retained control.[12] But at the end of July more excitement occurred when Washington spoke at a meeting sponsored by the Boston Business League. Heckling and hissing interrupted the speakers, and when Trotter and a friend of his attempted to make Washington reply to questions from the floor, the uproar was so great that Washington was temporarily silenced. The police were called, the two men were arrested, and later they were sentenced to a fifty dollar fine and thirty days in jail for their role in this "Boston Riot." While some were alienated by Trotter's tactics, to others, like Du Bois, he became a martyr.[13]

With the opposition active, Washington, as early as February, had been thinking of a conference of race leaders as a means of effecting an understanding. And it was high time he did so, for as acute an observer as Kelly Miller commented that "few thoughtful men espouse what passes as Mr. Washington's policy without apology or reserve." Finally, a secret meeting, called by Washington and financed by Andrew Carnegie, was held at Carnegie Hall, New York, in January, 1904. Some reports did leak out. The hostile *Bee* revealed that at the end of the conference Washington said that he favored "absolute civil, political and public equality," higher education, and the abolition of Jim Crow cars, and that Du Bois declared himself ready to work with Washington as long as he lived up to this statement. The confidential summary of the conference's proceedings, drawn up by Kelly Miller, also revealed a wide range of agreement among the leaders. They held that most Negroes should stay in the South, that Negroes should at all times work to protect and exercise their right to vote, that lawsuits should be instituted to secure "absolutely equal accommodations" in transportation and public facilities, and that Negro education should include both industrial and higher training.[14]

The Committee of Twelve for the Advancement of the Interests of the Negro Race, established by the Carnegie Hall Conference, existed for several years. Its first important effort was an unsuccessful attempt to negotiate with the Pullman Company in regard to the latter's complying with the separate-but-equal laws by excluding Negroes altogether. Du Bois soon withdrew because he felt that the committee's activities were being dictated by the chairman, Booker T. Washington. Subsequently, committee members, with money secretly supplied by Washington, discreetly employed a lobbyist to work against the proposed Warner-Foraker Amendment to the Hepburn Railway Rate Bill and worked to defeat disfranchisement in Maryland. The committee's work consisted chiefly of publishing a number of pamphlets, which were financed by Carnegie. Most of the pamphlets dealt with Negro self-help and economic achievement or were reprints of speeches by distinguished, but conservative whites whom Washington regarded as sympathetically interested in the race problem. But the committee also published pamphlets on how to vote and obtain jury representation, and even one entitled *Why Disfranchisement is Bad* by Archibald Grimké.[15]

Despite Washington's efforts, the rift grew wider. Directly after the Carnegie Hall meeting one of the conferees, E. H. Morris, precipitated an acrimonious debate at the Bethel Literary Society with an address in which he charged Washington with believing in Negro inferiority, racial segregation, and the relegation of the franchise to a secondary position. The speech caused considerable agitation in the Tuskegee circle, and in March Washington spoke in the same church defending his program as the best way to achieve the higher aims of the race. But this and similar speeches to Northern audiences over the next few years failed to mollify the opposition.[16]

Meanwhile, at least as early as 1902, Washington had been utilizing his reservoirs of power to silence the opposition. He used personal influence to wean people away from the radicals, attempted to deprive opponents of their government jobs, where possible arranged to have his critics sued for libel, placed spies in radical organizations, employed his influence with philanthropists as an effective weapon in dealings with educators and others, deprived critics of participation and subsidies in political campaigns, and subsidized the Negro press to support him and to ignore or to attack the opposition.[17]

In spite of these tactics, some of Washington's critics formed a national organization—the Niagara Movement—in 1905. In response to a call issued by Du Bois, twenty-nine delegates from fourteen states attended the meeting at Fort Erie in July. All but five were from the North or from Washington and its environs. Most of the remainder were from the two chief Southern centers of anti-Bookerite sentiment—three from Atlanta and one from Richmond. The address adopted by this group insisted that Negroes should protest emphatically and continually against the abridgment of political and civil rights and against inequality of economic opportunity. It called for all types of education, including college training. It refused to allow the impression to remain that "the Negro-American assents to inferiority, is submissive under oppression and apologetic before insult." Above all, it stated, "We do not hesitate to complain, and to complain loudly and insistently."

The Niagara Movement, aiming to combat Washington's policy, made clear the split that was to cause the bitterest acrimony for over a dozen years. Washington was clearly upset by the movement and, as earlier, he exerted multifarious and even devious pressures against the movement and its members. Though the Niagara Movement created a considerable stir, its maximum membership was only about 400, and beyond agitation its accomplishments were relatively limited. At Boston in 1907, Du Bois exulted in the movement's sheer survival and reported helping the Brownsville soldiers and winning a segregation case in which the claimant had been awarded one cent in damages. Thereafter, the movement was in decline, its last meeting being held in 1909. Nevertheless, particularly in view of Washington's opposition, it was significant because, as Ray Stannard Baker reported, "it represents, genuinely a more or less prevalent point of view among many coloured people." [18]

Meanwhile, Du Bois and others had established first the *Moon* (published in Memphis, 1906) and then the *Horizon* (published in Washington, 1907–10) as unofficial organs of the Niagara Movement. The latter, a sprightly tabloid, engaged in heavy-handed satire at the expense of "King Booker" and his allies, and in a more serious vein projected its own protest philosophy. In attacking Washington the magazine hit at a wide range of issues: the centering of race interests at Tuskegee, thus making the Institute "a kind of capital for the American Negro with Dr. Washington as king without constitutional limitations"; the fear people had of joining the Niagara Movement because of Washington's influence; Washington's alliance with Roosevelt and Taft and his subsidizing the Negro press. And there was ceaseless criticism of Washington's ideological viewpoint, well summed up in March 1908:

If there is anything dominant in the South that Booker Washington is not a warm supporter of, either expressly, by words written and spoken, or implicitly, by silence kept and maintained, his friends would do well to point it out. He has accepted the revised constitutions . . . ; he has acquiesced in the "jim crow" car policy . . . ; he has kept dumb as an oyster as to peonage . . . ; he has even discovered that colored people can better afford to be lynched than the white people can afford to lynch them. . . . [19]

The radicals were not evenly distributed among all groups in the population. They were more numerous in the North than in the South. Ray Stannard Baker characterized the Northern radicals as being highly educated individuals who held themselves aloof from the masses and tried to avoid or deny the existence of the color line. "Their associations in business are largely with white people and they cling passionately to the fuller life," he observed.[20] Though the whole matter is extremely complicated, it appears, as suggested in chapter IX, that many radicals belonged to that older upper class which believed in immediate integration because its roots were to a large extent in the white community. The Niagara Movement's members were drawn almost entirely from the ranks of the college-educated professional men. Those attending its meetings included Dr. C. E. Bentley of Chicago, Northern lawyers like Clement Morgan, F. L. McGhee of St. Paul, George H. Jackson of Cincinnati, and George W. Crawford of New Haven; ministers such as Byron Gunner of Newport, Reverdy Ransom of Boston and New York, J. Milton Waldron of Jacksonville and Washington, George Freeman Bragg of Baltimore, and Sutton E. Griggs of Nashville; a handful of college educators like W. H. H. Hart of Howard University, President J. R. L. Diggs of Kentucky State College and John Hope; an occasional government employee, and a few editors like Trotter, Harry Smith and J. Max Barber of the *Voice of the Negro*. Other radicals had a similar background. In Baltimore, a stronghold of radical sentiment, the leadership of the anti-Bookerite movement was in the hands of men like the attorney, W. Ashbie Hawkins, the high-school teacher Mason Hawkins, and the Episcopal rector George F. Bragg, and its supporters in that city seem to have been chiefly a college-educated elite of ministers, high-school teachers, and lawyers. Yet, as pointed out in chapter XII, it is not possible to say that the majority of college graduates and professional men supported the Niagara Movement.

Although the Niagara Movement failed it did chalk up one significant victory against Tuskegee when it ousted Washington from control of the Afro-American Council. As early as 1905 the Council appears to have given up its support of a restricted franchise—in fact it urged Negroes toward collective action in testing the disfranchisement laws in the courts. At the October 1906 convention in New York, it was clear that Washington's control was slipping. Though the majority of men elected to office were friendly with the Tuskegeean, and though Washington personally urged calmness and self-control, the delegates, stirred by the Atlanta riot and other outrages, vigorously condemned ballot restrictions, Jim Crow, and mob violence. Walters, having flirted with both sides, had been returned to the presidency the preceding year, and now charged that "it is nonsense for us to say Peace! Peace! when there is no peace. . . . We use diplomatic language and all kinds of subterfuges, but the fact remains that the enemy is trying to keep us down and we are determined to rise or die in the attempt."

In the following months the Niagara Movement came to play a significant role in Council affairs. The 1907 convention actually marked the end of Washington's power in the Council. The anti-Bookerites eliminated several Tuskegee stalwarts from positions of influence, and the outspoken "Report to the Country" not only lacked the usual tactful phrases that would have counterbalanced its attack on the increasingly "bitter and relentless race hatred and contempt," but condemned those Negroes in high places who were "base enough" to urge silence and patience "in obedience to American color-phobia." [21] But victory for the radicals resulted in disruption of the Council whose 1908 meeting was scarcely reported in the press, and no evidence was found to indicate that it even met in 1909.

Despite the increasing dissatisfaction among Negro leaders that this state of affairs undoubtedly represented, the parallel decline of the Niagara Movement made it clear that Washington's critics were not yet in a position to make themselves the ideological spokesmen of the race. Indeed, given the power structure and the nature of American race relations at the time, it was exceedingly unlikely that the Negro radicals, limited in funds and influence, would have been victorious alone against the Tuskegeean and his powerful white allies. It was in large part the fact that the radicals were able to enlist the aid of a small group of prominent white progressives that enabled them—even during Washington's lifetime—to achieve a significant measure of success.

Among this group two men especially stand out—John Milholland and Oswald Garrison Villard, and both were originally supporters of Washington. Milholland, a manufacturer of pneumatic tube equipment and a Progressive Republican with a variety of reform interests, was the leading spirit behind the interracial Constitution League which aimed to attack disfranchisement, peonage, and mob violence by means of court action, legislation and propaganda. At first Milholland and Washington worked together informally on certain matters, but frictions arose, and in 1906 the Brownsville episode led to a permanent break. Washington had himself done all he could do to dissuade Roosevelt from discharging the accused soldiers, but once the President and Secretary of War Taft had taken their action, Washington remained loyal to them, on the ground that they had made a sincere, though unfortunate mistake.[22] Most Negroes, however, did not see the matter in this light. Consequently, while the Niagara Movement seemed to be declining the Constitution League (whose members included Walters and radicals like Ransom, Barber, and Trotter) kept the pot boiling, and in the Brownsville case it had an effective issue. As Washington worked to swing Negroes behind Taft in 1908 he found his chief difficulty was with the League. All in all it was a troublesome period for Washington, who came to admit that the initiative had largely passed from his hands into those of the "black-legs" and "schemers" on the payroll of the League, which he regarded as the headquarters of all the opposition to him.[23]

Villard had long been friendly with Washington and had raised over $150,000 for the Tuskegee endowment. But he was not isolated from Washington's critics, and he was not entirely satisfied with current efforts for the advancement of colored people. In 1908 he disclosed to Washington his belief that a vigorous central defense committee was necessary. Not surprisingly, therefore, he willingly complied when three socialists—the writer William English Walling and the social workers, Dr. Henry Moskowitz and Mary White Ovington—prompted by the Springfield, Illinois riot of 1908, urged him to issue a call for a national conference on the Negro question to be held on Lincoln's birthday in 1909.

Washington declined Villard's invitation to attend the conference. Walters and radical leaders like Ida Wells-Barnett, Barber, and Du Bois came, and in their speeches stressed the importance of the ballot. The conference denounced outrages, persecution, and segregation; demanded academic and professional education for the gifted; and insisted on the right to vote. Out of a second conference a year later developed the formal organization of the National Association for the Advancement of Colored People.[24] The N.A.A.C.P. did not actually unite with the Niagara Movement or with the Constitution League, but most of their members joined the new movement. The interracial character of the N.A.A.C.P. was fundamental to its success, for it gave the agitation for Negro rights a wider audience, better financial support, and the prestige of the names of well-known white progressives like Villard, Milholland, Lillian Wald, Jane Addams, John Haynes Holmes, Franz Boas, Moorfield Storey, and Clarence Darrow. Except for Du Bois, all of the chief officials of the organization at first were whites. But the backbone of the organization, the branches and their membership, consisted chiefly of elite, college-educated Negroes. By 1914 the organization had 6000 members in fifty branches, and a circulation for the *Crisis,* edited by Du Bois, of 31,540.[25] From the beginning largely a legal action organization, the N.A.A.C.P. achieved its first important victory just a few months before Washington's death, when the Supreme Court declared the Oklahoma grandfather clause unconstitutional.

Tuskegee was not slow in taking steps against the new organization, and the old pattern of using various forms of pressure was repeated. Officially, the Association was not anti-Washington. Villard, who continued to correspond with Washington, encouraged the efforts of R. R. Moton of Hampton Institute to effect an understanding between the two groups. Others, however, did not hesitate to attack Washington. In October 1910 during Washington's lecture tour in England, a group headed by Du Bois circulated a statement in London criticizing the Tuskegeean. The signers contradicted the pleasant picture described by Washington, denied that the problem was being solved, and accused Washington of misrepresenting the truth because of his dependence on certain powerful interests for philanthropy.[26] Washington was deeply troubled by such attacks and even more by defections to what Charles W. Anderson referred to as the "Vesey Street crowd." But tensions were relieved considerably when Washington was severely beaten in New York in 1911, allegedly for approaching a white woman. All factions rushed to his defense, and an era of temporary reconciliation followed which included all but Du Bois. During 1913, however, new tensions arose and though Moton continued to negotiate, cordial relationships do not appear to have been restored before Washington died late in 1915.

But by that time various individuals friendly to Washington were working with the N.A.A.C.P. Influential among them were middle-of-the-roaders like the noted Mary Church Terrell and Dean Kelly Miller of Howard University, both of whom had become associated with the organization rather early. Washington in 1914 might crow over the internal feuds in the N.A.A.C.P., such as Walters' desertion, Mossell, Mrs. Barnett, and Trotter quarreling with the others, and the split between Villard and Du Bois that later led to Villard's withdrawal from active participation. But the fact was that by 1914 two of Washington's most loyal supporters, S. Laing Williams of Chicago and John Quincy Adams of St. Paul, were officials of their local branches.[27] Washington's death helped to smooth things over, and the selection of Moton to succeed him at Tuskegee meant that a moderate who had long attempted to work with the opposition led the Hampton-Tuskegee group. In 1916 Joel Spingarn, the president of the N.A.A.C.P., sponsored the Amenia Conference attended by representatives of all points of view ranging from Emmett Scott to Monroe Trotter. This conference reached virtual unanimity of opinion in regard to certain principles—the desirability of all types of education, the importance of the ballot, and the necessity of replacing ancient suspicions and factions with respect for the good faith and methods of leaders in all parts of the country.[28] And then, in the very same year, the N.A.A.C.P. played an ironic masterstroke in inviting the author and diplomat James Weldon Johnson, one of the most capable figures in the Washington orbit, to become its national organizer.

In spite of all that Washington did the opposition triumphed. Probably nothing Washington could have done would have prevented the rise of the N.A.A.C.P. For the continued deterioration of conditions during the period of his ascendancy led to ideological disillusionment with his program, and this fact, coupled with the reform spirit of the Progressive Era, encouraged the rise of protest organizations. Undoubtedly also, the decline of Washington's political power after 1909 and especially after 1913 worked to lessen the support he received from other leaders; his death removed him entirely as an element in the power structure. Nothing could illustrate better than Johnson's selection as national organizer of the N.A.A.C.P. the large shift that had taken place in the less than a dozen years since the founding of the Niagara Movement in 1905.

The radical Negroes were chiefly "radical" on the race question, and most of them remained "conservative" in their broader economic and social outlook. Yet it was among them that economic and social radicalism found something of a foothold. The Niagara Movement, at its 1906 meeting, asserted that "we want the laws enforced against rich as well as poor; against Capitalists as well as Labor; against white as well as black," and the *Horizon* expressed a broadly radical social view that only a few Negroes shared. As it said in November, 1909: "THIS IS A RADICAL PAPER. . . . It advocates Negro equality and human equality; it stands for universal manhood suffrage, including votes for women; it believes in the abolition of war, the taxation of monopoly values, the gradual socialization of capital and the overthrow of persecution and despotism in the name of religion."

True, this was not the first time a Negro advocated socialism. As early as 1897 the Niagarite orator the Reverend Reverdy Ransom had suggested that since the great majority of Negroes belonged to the proletarian class, it would be the socialists who, believing like Jesus "that the rights of men are more sacred than the rights of property," would bring about the solution of the race problem. Other Niagarites who espoused socialism included J. Milton Waldron, J. Max Barber, and, most notably, Du Bois. As he put it in the *Horizon* of February, 1907, he was a "Socialist-of-the-path," for while he did not favor the complete socialization of property, he felt that progress lay in more public ownership of wealth. After all the Negro's natural allies were not the rich, but the poor. In socialism therefore, he believed, with its "larger ideal of human brotherhood, equality of opportunity and work not for wealth but for weal," lay the best hope for American Negroes.[29]

In part because of Washington's close ties with Presidents Roosevelt and Taft, in part because of the increasing disregard in which the Republican party held Negroes, and in part because they found the platforms of Bryan and Wilson more appealing than that of Taft on nonracial matters, the leaders of the rising protest movement were the source of a significant sentiment in the North that favored the Democratic party in the elections of 1908 and 1912.[30]

A few distinguished Negroes who were not "radicals" did, it is true, support the Democrats at times, as did Bishops Abraham Grant, W. B. Derrick, and Henry M. Turner in 1900, and Turner, as previously, continued to support the party as late as 1908 and 1912. Much of the sentiment leading Negroes to support the Democratic party in 1900 appeared to be its anti-imperialist stand. John B. Syphax, a prominent Washingtonian, speaking before the United Colored Democracy in Brooklyn, rang the changes on the treachery of the carpetbaggers, the imperialism of the Republicans, and their oppression of colored Filipinos.[31] An important source of Democratic support in the North was that in many instances Democratic politicians proved more sympathetic toward Negro aspirations than did Republicans. Thus, F. L. McGhee of St. Paul wrote Washington on September 14, 1904, that while he hoped to see Roosevelt re-elected, he would vote for the Democrats because in Minnesota they were better to Negroes than Republicans were. In Chicago and Boston Democratic machines courted Negroes with considerable success beginning in the middle 1890's, and in New York Tammany Hall made a gesture toward giving Negroes some political patronage through the establishment of the United Colored Democracy. In 1910 over a third of the Boston Negroes voted for the Democratic gubernatorial candidate, and Charles Anderson reported from New York that he had never before seen so many Negroes displaying Democratic badges.[32]

With Roosevelt's second administration Negroes grew increasingly disillusioned with the Republicans. Even organs close to Tuskegee soundly berated Roosevelt for his stand on Brownsville and his message to Congress in 1906, and some were lukewarm toward Taft in 1908. George L. Knox, editor of the Indianapolis *Freeman,* and a good friend of Washington, had been irked in 1904 by the Tuskegeean's insistence that he not run for Congress lest he jeopardize Roosevelt's chances in Indiana. He therefore came to criticize the Negro's gullibility in politics, and for the next several years urged independence at election times.[33]

By 1908 substantial elements of the Niagara Movement had come out for the Democrats. At a stormy convention in April, Trotter, Walters, and the radical clergymen S. L. Corrothers and J. Milton Waldron of Washington emerged as the group that came to be the backbone of the National Negro American Political League organized in June. This group, reported to consist of representatives of organizations like the Afro-American Council, the Niagara Movement, and the Constitution League, took a strong stand against Roosevelt's policies. In fact a significant segment of thoughtful Negroes supported Bryan in 1908. The *Gazette* followed the other radical leaders in deserting "Mr. 'Disfranchisement, Jim Crow Car' Taft"; it urged its readers to vote for anyone else, and thus "preserve your self-respect, manhood, and race respect." [34]

Du Bois presented the best rationale of those economic and racial radicals who hoped that the Democrats might move toward both racial and economic justice. Though at first he said that Bryan was just as bad as Taft and that the Socialist party was the only one which treated the Negroes as men, he soon regarded Bryan's silence on the Negro as infinitely better than the statements of the "Coward of Brownsville." Northern Democrats treated Negroes better than did the reactionary Republicans who had sided with Southern Democrats in depriving Negroes of their rights. Whether or not Bryan would appoint Negroes to office, Negroes would benefit from a Democratic victory, for the Democratic party stood for the regulation of corporate wealth, for freedom for brown and black men in the Philippines and the West Indies, for the rights of labor, and for the elimination of all special privileges. Negroes held a balance of power in twelve Northern states, and if they used their vote properly they had it in their power to end "the impossible alliance of radical and socialistic Democracy at the North with an aristocratic caste party at the South," and to make the Democrats truly the party of the working men of both races.[35]

After the election the National Negro-American Political League, rechristened as the National Independent Political League, remained active under the leadership of Walters and Niagarites like Waldron, Trotter, and Byron Gunner. In 1912 the Independents worked closely with the Colored National Democratic League, of which Walters was president, and published a series of pamphlets and broadsides which rehearsed the arguments about Republican hypocrisy, Cleveland's appointments, and the role of Negroes as a balance of power in key states, pointed to the appearance of segregation in the federal offices at Washington, and described Wilson as a Christian gentleman who had never harmed the race.[36] Du Bois, after toying with the idea of working with the Progressives, withdrew from the Socialist party in order to support Wilson. He rationalized his action:

As to Mr. Wilson, there are, one must confess, disquieting facts; he was born in Virginia, and he was long president of a college which did not admit Negro students. . . . On the whole, we do not believe that Woodrow Wilson admires Negroes. . . . Notwithstanding such possible preferences, Woodrow Wilson is a cultivated scholar and he has brains. . . . We have, therefore, a conviction that Mr. Wilson will treat black men and their interests with farsighted fairness. He will not be our friend, but he will not belong to the gang of which Tillman, Vardaman, Hoke Smith and Blease are the brilliant expositors. He will not advance the cause of an oligarchy in the South, he will not seek further means of "jim crow" insult, he will not dismiss black men wholesale from office, and he will remember that the Negro ... has a right to be heard and considered, and if he becomes President by the grace of the black man's vote, his Democratic successors may be more willing to pay the black man's price of decent travel, free labor, votes and education.

Du Bois felt that Debs was the ideal candidate but that Wilson was the only realistic choice.[37]

Despite some misgivings the anti-Roosevelt, anti-Taft, anti-Tuskegee group swallowed Wilson upon his own profession of being a Christian gentleman and his promise of fair dealings, even though he refused to make a forthright statement. Only a minority went along with the Walters-Du Bois-Trotter-Waldron group. The Cleveland *Gazette,* for example, though it was a decidedly radical organ, and though it had supported Bryan in 1908, felt that Taft was the least of the three evils that had a chance of winning. Yet, though not all of the radicals favored Wilson, outside of the professional Democrats, it was among this group that the party found its chief supporters.

The majority of Negroes, perhaps 60 per cent, voted for Roosevelt, the remainder being about evenly divided between Wilson and Taft. Kelly Miller represented the political outlook of many in his discussion of this state of affairs. He exulted in Negro independence from the Republican party, which he believed little different from the Democrats on racial matters. He was sympathetic toward the Progressive party, for as the most disadvantaged group in America, Negroes had the most to gain from its program. He explained away evidence of Roosevelt's opportunism in regard to the Negro as political maneuvering that was intended in the long run to bring Negroes a square deal. "In any event," concluded Miller, "the black man's political emancipation is now complete." Never again would he be regarded as indissolubly linked to any party.[38]

Miller's enthusiasm was premature. The Progressive party collapsed and disillusionment with Wilson set in quickly, so that Negroes drifted back to the Republican fold. Walters, feted as the successful leader of the Colored Democracy, soon found that the President evidently did not intend to appoint many Negroes to office. Wilson even failed to keep his promise of awarding the traditionally Negro posts of minister to Haiti, register of the Treasury, auditor for the Navy, and recorder of deeds to colored men. So bad were conditions that when Robert H. Terrell was renominated by Wilson and confirmed by the Senate, after a difficult battle, the event was hailed as a major victory for the race. Under Wilson also the policy of segregation in federal offices was greatly broadened. In 1914 matters came to a head on this issue when a delegation headed by Trotter obtained an audience with the President. The conference closed unpleasantly when Wilson ordered Trotter out of his office for what he deemed insulting language.[39] Thus, by at least tacit approval of the " 'Jim Crow' insult," by "dismiss[ing] black men wholesale from office," and by seemingly failing "to remember that the Negro has a right to be heard and considered," Wilson had almost step by step refuted Du Bois' campaign estimate of him. So ended the honeymoon between the radical Negroes and the Democrats. The paradoxical union of office seekers and anti-Bookerites, disillusioned Republicans and economic radicals, was unable to weather the chilling realities of the Wilson administration, in which Southern whites played such a large role.

Actually, few Negroes—indeed only a few of the radicals on racial matters—ever embraced socialism, and only a minority ever favored the Democrats. Negroes remained by and large conservative in their political and economic orientation during the Progressive Era of the Square Deal and the New Freedom. In fact, in the face of increasing trade-union discrimination they were becoming more rather than less hostile to organized labor. In spite of some exceptions, most remained at least lukewarm Republicans in their allegiance. Only the temporary swing toward the Progressives in 1912 gave any indication that "left-of-center" reformism would some day have a profound impact upon the Negro vote and upon Negro thought.

CHAPTER XI

THE PARADOX OF W. E. B. DU BOIS [1]

If, of the great trio of Negro leaders, Frederick Douglass best expressed the aspirations toward full citizenship and assimilation, and Booker T. Washington the interest in economic advancement, it was Du Bois who most explicitly revealed the impact of oppression and of the American creed in creating ambivalent loyalties toward race and nation in the minds of American Negroes. As Du Bois said in 1897:

> One feels his two-ness—an American, a Negro, two souls, two thoughts, two unreconciled strivings, two warring ideals in one dark body. . . .
> The history of the American Negro is the history of this strife,—this longing to attain self-conscious manhood, to merge his double self into a better and truer self. . . . He would not Africanize America for America has too much to teach the world and Africa. He would not bleach the Negro soul in a flood of white Americanism, for he knows that Negro blood has a message for the world. He simply wishes to make it possible for a man to be both a Negro and an American, without being cursed and spit upon. . . .

More than any other figure Du Bois made explicit this ambivalence —an ambivalence that is perhaps the central motif in his ideological biography. Even Du Bois has described himself as integrally a part of European civilization, and "yet, more significant, one of its rejected parts; one who expressed in life and action and made vocal to many, a single whirlpool of social entanglement and inner psychological paradox." [2]

A proud and sensitive youth reared in a western Massachusetts town, Du Bois had occasion to know the sting of prejudice and early realized that "I was different from others; or like, mayhap in heart and life and longing, but shut out from their world by a vast veil." Subsequently he therefore found the segregated community of Fisk University, which he attended from 1885 to 1888, an enriching experience. Though he yearned for the full recognition of his American citizenship, he was also, he later recollected, "thrilled and moved to tears," and recognized "something inherently and deeply my own" as a result of his association there with a "closed racial group with rites and loyalties, with a history and a corporate future, with an art and a philosophy." By the time he received his A.B. from Fisk and entered Harvard as a Junior in 1888, "the theory of race separation was quite in my blood," and the lack of social acceptance he experienced at Harvard, he recalled later, did not disturb him. Yet it certainly was his sensitivity to discrimination that led him at this time to view Negroes as a "nation"—Americans, but rejected in the land of their birth.[3]

Meanwhile, Du Bois had been expressing himself on other subjects. As a correspondent for Fortune's New York *Globe* during the early 1880's and as editor of the Fisk *Herald,* he displayed an interest in industriousness and ambition. Furthermore, as a student at Fisk and at Harvard—where he received his Ph.D. in 1895—and as a professor at Wilberforce University (1894–96), Du Bois proved more than willing to meet Southern whites half way. He told both Fisk students and his white associates in the Tennessee prohibitionist movement that the interests of the two races were essentially the same. To his Fisk audience he proposed the admittedly unorthodox idea that Negroes should divide their vote in order not to exacerbate race relations. He assured Southern whites that they could depend on the friendship of Negroes if only the whites would grant them citizenship rights and adequate educational facilities. Since the Negro's condition was such as to encourage prejudice, for their part Negroes must stress duties as well as rights, and work for their own advancement. At both Harvard and Wilberforce he could, in a single speech, lash out at America's immoral and un-American treatment of Negroes (and at Harvard suggest that Negroes would revolt if other means failed) and at the same time adopt a conciliatory position. Since Negroes had not yet achieved what it took the Anglo-Saxons a millennium to do, they were not yet equipped to vote. What he objected to was not the disfranchisement of the Negro masses, but of intelligent, law-abiding Negroes; and what he advocated was a franchise limitation fairly applied to both races along with adequate educational opportunities for all. In 1891 it was even reported in the *Age* that Du Bois had asserted that the whole idea underlying the Lodge Elections Bill was wrong, for it was proposed on the assumption that

> law can accomplish anything. . . . We must ever keep before us the fact that the South has some excuse for its present attitude. We must remember that a good many of our people . . . are not fit for the responsibility of republican government. When you have the right sort of black voters you will need no election laws. The battle of my people must be a moral one, not a legal or physical one.[4]

It was no wonder then that after Washington's address Du Bois wrote the *Age* suggesting "that here might be the basis of a real settlement between whites and blacks." [5]

Meanwhile, Du Bois was formulating his notion of leadership by a college-educated elite, which he regarded as necessary for the advancement of any group. In 1891 he deplored the South's effort to make common and industrial schools rather than colleges the basis of its educational system. For only a liberally educated white leadership could perceive that, despite the justification for overthrowing the Reconstruction governments, to permanently disfranchise the working class of a society in the process of rapid industrialization would, as socialists from Lassalle to Hindman had said, result in economic ruin. And only a liberal higher education could create an intelligent Negro leadership. Thus, while still a student at Harvard, Du Bois had suggested his theory of the talented tenth, foreshadowed his later concern with the working class, and adumbrated the thesis he later stressed so much—that without political rights Negroes, primarily a working group, could not secure economic opportunity. Furthermore, it should be noted that his educational views were not unrelated to his ethnocentric feelings. As he said at Wilberforce, the educated elite had a glorious opportunity to guide the race by reshaping its own ideals in order to provide the masses with appropriate goals and lift them to civilization.[6]

After two years at Wilberforce, Du Bois accepted a one-year research appointment at the University of Pennsylvania. Then in 1897 he became professor of sociology at Atlanta University, where he remained until 1910, teaching and editing the annual Atlanta University Studies on the American Negro.

At no time in his life did Du Bois place greater and more consistent stress upon self-help and racial solidarity than during the last four years of the century. Like many of his contemporaries he fused this emphasis with one on economic advancement; and like a few of them he synthesized it with his educational program for the talented tenth. To Du Bois in fact, the race prejudice which isolated the Negro group and threw upon it "the responsibility of evolving its own methods and organs of civilization" made the stimulation of group co-operation "the central serious problem." [7]

It was his appointment to the University of Pennsylvania that provided Du Bois with his first opportunity to begin a scientific study of the race problem. He had long awaited such an opportunity because he believed that presentation of the facts derived from scientific investigation would go a long way toward solving the race problem. The resulting monograph, *The Philadelphia Negro,* leaned toward the blame-the-Negro, self-help point of view. Yet Du Bois did describe what it meant to be snubbed in employment and in social intercourse, and he judged that the Negro's participation in politics had been, in net effect, beneficial to the city and to the Negro himself. Above all, he felt that Negroes must uplift themselves, and by racial co-operation open enterprises that would provide employment and training in trades and commerce. Whites had their duty to help but society had too many problems "for it lightly to shoulder all the burdens of a less advanced people." Negroes ought to constantly register strong protests against prejudice and injustice, but they should do so because these things hindered them in their own attempt to elevate the race. And this attempt, Du Bois held, must be marked by vigorous and persistent efforts directed toward lessening crime and toward inculcating self-respect, the dignity of labor, and the virtues of truth, honesty, and charity.[8]

Like Washington, then, Du Bois combined an enthusiasm for racial solidarity with one for economic development and the middle-class virtues. In fact, he regarded a college education as "one of the best preparations for a broad business life" and for the making of "captains of industry." Likening Negroes to other nationalities, he chided them for being ashamed of themselves, and held that such success as had been achieved by other nations no larger in population than the American Negroes could be accomplished only through a badly needed co-operation and unity. In view of the poverty of the Negro and the economic spirit of the age, it was most important to achieve success in business. Because of race prejudice the major opportunity for such achievement lay in commercial activity based on Negroes pooling their earnings and pushing forward as a group. Though their collective capital be small, thrift and industry could succeed even under the handicaps of prejudice. Under the circumstances a penny savings bank would be more helpful than the vote. Negroes should patronize and invest their money in Negro-owned enterprises, even at a personal sacrifice. For "we must cooperate or we are lost. Ten million people who join in intelligent self-help can never be long ignored or mistreated." [9]

It should be noted, of course, that Du Bois did not, during the *fin de siècle* years, give up all interest in political rights, though like the majority of articulate Southern Negroes of the day he was willing to compromise on the matter. He was among those who in 1899 petitioned the Georgia legislature not to pass the Hardwick disfranchisement bill, though like Booker T. Washington he was willing to accept an educational and/or property qualification as long as free school facilities were open to all. [10]

During this period Du Bois was more emphatic than at any other time about the value of racial integrity. Speaking on "The Conservation of Races" in 1897 he asserted that there existed subtle psychic differences, which had definitely divided men into races. Like his racist contemporaries, he was certain of the universality of "the race spirit," which he regarded as "the greatest invention for human progress." Each race had a special ideal—the English individualism, the German philosophy and science, and so forth. Therefore, "only Negroes bound and welded together, Negroes inspired by one vast ideal, can work out in its fullness the great message we have for humanity." To those who argued that their only hope lay in amalgamating with the rest of the American population, he admitted that Negroes faced a "puzzling dilemma." Every thoughtful Negro had at some time asked himself whether he was an American, or a Negro, or if he could be both; whether by striving as a Negro he was not perpetuating the very gulf that divided the two races, or whether Negroes "have in America a distinct mission as a race." Du Bois' answer was what is now called cultural pluralism. Negroes were American by birth, in language, in political ideas, and in religion. But any further than this, their Americanism did not go. Since they had given America its only native music and folk stories, "its only touch of pathos and humor amid its mad money-getting plutocracy," it was the Negroes' duty to maintain "our physical power, our intellectual endowment, our spiritual ideas; as a race, we must strive by race organizations, by race solidarity, by race unity to the realization of the broader humanity which freely recognizes differences in men, but sternly deprecates inequalities in their opportunity of development." To this end, separate racial educational, business, and cultural institutions were necessary. Despised and oppressed, the Negroes' only means of advancement was a belief in their own great destiny. No people that wished to be something other than itself "ever wrote its name in history; it must be inspired with the Divine faith of our black mothers, that out of the blood and dust of battles will march a victorious host, a mighty nation, a peculiar people, to speak to the nations of the earth a Divine truth that should make them free." Washington, it should be pointed out, while advocating race pride and race integrity, did not glory so much in the idea of a distinctive Negro culture (though he was always proud of the spirituals or "plantation melodies"). Nor did he exhibit Du Bois' sense of identification with Africans, evident in Du Bois' advocacy of "pan-Negroism" in this same address.[11]

During the last years of the century Du Bois developed his educational theories at considerable length, attempting to construct "A Rational System of Negro Education" by reconciling the two widely diverging tendencies of the day—training for making a living and training for living a broad life. All agreed, he said, on the necessity of universal common school training, and on the contribution Hampton, Tuskegee, and the Slater Fund had made in stressing the building of an economic foundation, the freedmen's primary concern. But unfortunately only three or four schools made broad culture their chief aim. Du Bois criticized the talk of rosewood pianos in dingy cabins, of ignorant farmers, of college graduates without employment, though he agreed that more stress had been placed on college training than the economic condition of the race warranted. But the vogue for industrial education had become so great that the colleges were hard-pressed for funds. This was particularly deplorable because the isolation of the Negro community demanded the creation of an indigenous leadership of college-trained captains of industry and scholars, who would advance the masses economically and culturally, and who could view the race problem from a broad perspective.[12]

There were remarkable similarities between Du Bois and Washington during the late 1890's—a period when more Negro leaders than at any other time adopted a conciliatory tactic. Both tended to blame Negroes largely for their condition, and both placed more emphasis on self-help and duties than on rights. Both placed economic advancement before universal manhood suffrage, and both were willing to accept franchise restrictions based not on race but on education and/or property qualifications equitably applied. Both stressed racial solidarity and economic co-operation. Du Bois was, however, more outspoken about injustices, and he differed sharply with Washington in his espousal of the cause of higher education.

The years from 1901 to 1903 were years of transition in Du Bois' philosophy, years in which he grew more critical of industrial education and more alarmed over disfranchisement. Writing in 1901 he engaged in sharp protest against the Southern race system, even while recognizing that Negroes must adjust to it. He denied that the "many delicate differences in race psychology" excused oppression. He complained of the economic discrimination that retarded the development of a substantial landowning and artisan class. He bemoaned the lack of contact between the races that increased prejudice by preventing the best classes of both races from knowing each other. Yet he felt that, since Negroes must accept segregation, the road to uplift and economic improvement lay in the development of college-educated leaders: "Black captains of industry and missionaries of culture" who with their knowledge of modern civilization could uplift Negro communities "by forms of precept and example, deep sympathy and the inspiration of common kindred and ideals." But while Negroes would have to temporarily acquiesce in segregation, they could not acquiesce in disfranchisement. Du Bois did not object to "legitimate efforts to purge the ballot of ignorance, pauperism and crime," and he conceded that it was "sometimes best that a partially developed people should be ruled by the best of their stronger and better neighbors for their own good," until they were ready to stand on their own feet. But since the dominant opinion

of the South openly asserted that the purpose of the disfranchisement laws was the complete exclusion of Negroes from politics, the
ballot was absolutely necessary for the Negro's safety and welfare.
Moreover, as European experience had demonstrated, workers under
modern industrial conditions needed the vote in order to protect themselves; Negroes, laboring under racial discrimination, needed it even
more.[13]

Du Bois developed further his educational views and the theme
of the talented tenth. He agreed that it was most important to train
Negroes to work, and he conceded that industrial schools would play
an important role in achieving this end. He also approved of the
compromise function of industrial education, which had brought
together races and sections; and although industrial education would
not solve the problem he asserted that "it does mean that its settlement can be auspiciously begun." Yet he had come to criticize the
overinsistence of industrial schools upon the practical, the unfortunate
opposition of their advocates toward colleges, the fact that industrial
schools were preparing their students in obsolete crafts, and the fact
that they produced few actual artisans. Du Bois defended Negro
colleges from charges that they had erred in training school teachers
and professional men before turning to industrial training. He pointed
out that historically the European university had preceded the common school, and that out of the liberal arts institutions came the backbone of the teaching force of the Negro common schools and of industrial schools like Tuskegee, where almost half of the executive
council and a majority of the heads of departments were college
graduates. All races, he held, had been civilized by their exceptional
men; "the problem of education, then, among Negroes, must first
of all deal with the Talented Tenth." [14]

It is evident that Washington and Du Bois had come to disagree
not only in their educational philosophy, but also on the fundamental
question of the immediate importance of the ballot. By 1903 Du
Bois was not only pleading for higher education, but had begun to
criticize the work of the industrial schools. Both men spoke of captains of industry, but where the Tuskegeean emphasized economic
skills, the Atlanta educator stressed a high grade of culture. And unlike Washington, Du Bois had come to believe that educational and
property qualifications for voting would not be equitably applied.
True, Du Bois never gave up his belief that, in the face of white

prejudice and discrimination group solidarity was necessary, especially in economic matters. But all that really remained to make the two men irreconcilable ideological opponents was for Du Bois to advocate the importance of protest rather than accommodation. This he did in his opening attack on Washington in 1903.

During the 1890's Washington and Du Bois had been cordial in their relationships. Upon returning to the United States from Germany in 1894 Du Bois accepted a position at Wilberforce, having had to turn down a somewhat later offer from Tuskegee. Again in 1896, 1899, and as late as 1902 Du Bois seriously considered invitations to Tuskegee.[15] In his correspondence with Washington, through his articles and speeches, and by attending the Hampton and Tuskegee Conferences he exhibited his sympathetic interest in Washington's work. He had, it is true, mildly criticized the Tuskegeean in an article in 1901. In it he said that some of the most prominent men of the race regarded the Hampton-Tuskegee approach as only a partial approach to the race problem, in that they stressed the highest aspirations of the race, advocated college education, and believed that Negroes should enjoy suffrage equally with whites. But as late as July 1902 the *Guardian* denounced Du Bois for siding with Washington at the St. Paul meeting of the Afro-American Council. "Like all the others who are trying to get into the bandwagon of the Tuskegeean, he is no longer to be relied upon," declared the editor, Monroe Trotter.[16]

Kelly Miller has asserted that Trotter wove a "subtle net" around Du Bois and captured him for the radical cause. It would be difficult to test the truth of this statement. Certain it is, however, that by January 1903 Trotter was praising Du Bois as a brilliant leader who, despite temptations, "has never in public utterance or in written article, betrayed his race in its contest for equal opportunity and equal rights." Du Bois himself has recalled that he was gradually growing more disturbed after 1900—less by the ideological difference between him and Washington (which he remembered as mainly one of emphasis) than by the immense power over political appointments, over philanthropic largess, and over the press wielded by what Du Bois has labeled the "Tuskegee Machine." Du Bois found Washington's influence over the press especially deplorable, in view of the Tuskegeean's soft-pedaling of agitation on segregation and disfranchisement.[17] Yet whatever his actual motivation for criticizing Washington, his first public statement on the matter was confined to ideological issues.

This statement was Du Bois' famous essay, "Of Booker T. Washington and Others," in *Souls of Black Folk,* published in the spring of 1903. "Easily the most striking thing," began Du Bois, "in the history of the American Negro since 1876 is the ascendancy of Mr. Booker T. Washington." Others had failed in establishing a compromise between the North, the South, and the Negroes. But Washington, coming with a simple though not entirely original program of industrial education, conciliation of the South, and acceptance of disfranchisement and segregation, had succeeded. For with "singular insight" he had grasped the spirit of the age—"the spirit and thought of triumphant commercialism."

Du Bois went on to criticize the Tuskegeean because his policy "practically accepted the alleged inferiority of the Negro," allowed economic concerns to dominate over the higher aims of life, and preached a "submission to prejudice." Although Washington had made some statements about lynching and the franchise, generally his speeches purveyed the "dangerous half-truths" that the Negro's lowly condition justified the South's attitude and that the Negro's elevation must depend chiefly on his own efforts. Du Bois perceived paradoxes in Washington's attempt to make Negro workers businessmen and property owners when it was impossible for workers to defend themselves without the ballot; in his preaching self-respect while counseling accommodation to discrimination and in his advocacy of industrial and common schools while depreciating the colleges that supplied their teachers. Furthermore, Washington's propaganda had undoubtedly hastened the disfranchisement, the increased segregation, and the decreased philanthropic concern for higher education that accompanied his ascendancy.

Washington's popularity with whites, Du Bois held, had led Negroes to accept his leadership, and criticism of the Tuskegeean had disappeared. The time was ripe therefore for thinking Negroes to undertake their responsibility to the masses by speaking out. In addition to the few who dared to openly oppose Washington, Du Bois thought that men like Archibald and Francis J. Grimké, Kelly Miller, and J. W. E. Bowen could not remain silent much longer. Such men honored Washington for his conciliatory attitude, and they realized that the condition of the masses of the race was responsible for much of the discrimination against it. But they also knew that prejudice was more often a cause than a result of the Negro's degradation; that justice could not be achieved through "indiscriminate flattery"; that Negroes could not gain their rights by voluntarily throwing them away, or obtain respect by constantly belittling themselves; and that, on the contrary, Negroes must speak out constantly against oppression and discrimination.

Du Bois had indeed moved away from his conciliatory ideology of the 1890's. Yet attempts at co-operation between him and Washington were not quite at an end. In the summer of 1903 Du Bois spoke at Tuskegee. The two men also continued their collaboration —begun in 1902—in an effort to prevent the exclusion of Negroes from Pullman cars. Nevertheless, after the "Boston Riot" Du Bois was—with reservations—lining up with Trotter. He did not, he said, agree with Trotter's intemperate tactics, but he admired his integrity and purpose, which were especially needed in view of Washington's backward steps.[18] The Carnegie Hall Meeting of January 1904 and Du Bois' appointment to the Committee of Twelve temporarily restored an uneasy working relationship between him and Washington, but he soon resigned from the Committee and in 1905 was chiefly responsible for inaugurating the Niagara Movement. Meanwhile, he has recollected, he found it increasingly difficult to obtain funds for his work at Atlanta, experienced criticism in the Negro press, and in other ways "felt the implacability of the Tuskegee Machine." [19] He was one of the most active members of the Conference on the Negro in 1909, and when the N.A.A.C.P. was organized in 1910 he became director of publicity and research and editor of the *Crisis*.

Thus by 1905 Du Bois had definitely come to the parting of the ways with Washington. And it is in the Niagara Movement manifestoes and in the pages of the *Horizon* and *Crisis* that one can best observe Du Bois as the consistent agitator, the ardent and brilliant fighter for integration and citizenship rights. For example, he insisted that disfranchisement retarded the economic development of the Negro because the voteless could not protect their property rights. He cited cases of persecution of prosperous Negroes as evidence that Washington's program would not obtain the respect of the white man and the rights of citizenship.[20] In a typical editorial he pointed out that in spite of Washington's conciliatory policy conditions had grown worse. True, as Washington said, Negroes had continued to accumulate property and education, but how Washington could assert that discrimination and prejudice were decreasing was incomprehensible to Du Bois. Horrible as race prejudice was, it could be fought if faced frankly. But "if we continually dodge and cloud the issue, and say the half truth because the whole stings and shames . . . we invite catastrophe." Elsewhere he insisted that opportunism was a dangerous policy that gave moral support to the race's enemies, and he denounced the stress on sycophancy, selfishness, mediocrity, and servility at the expense of the best education, the highest ideals, and self-respect.[21] Naturally he criticized industrial schools. On one occasion he attacked Hampton for its opposition to the work of the Negro colleges, and described it as "a center of that underground and silent intrigue which is determined to perpetuate the American Negro as a docile peasant," lacking political rights and social status. Du Bois was unequivocal in his stand on segregation. He scathingly denounced the separate-but-equal doctrine: "Separate schools for Whites and Blacks, and separate cars for Whites and Blacks are not equal, can not be made equal, and . . . are not intended to be equal." He charged that what the South wanted was not mere separation but subordination, and insisted that no "square deal" was possible as long as segregation existed. And unlike Washington he opposed a colored Episcopal bishop to work only among Negroes, even though this would have elevated a Negro to a high church office.[22]

It is evident from a reading of Du Bois' less publicized scholarly and nonpolemical statements that throughout these years he still maintained his interest in racial solidarity and self-help, in the group economy, and in the American Negro's ties to Africa. On occasion he was most explicit about his concept of economic nationalism. Just as a country can by tariffs build up its separate economy to the point where it can compete in international trade, so the Negro should create a group economy that would "so break the force of race prejudice that his right and ability to enter the national economy are assured." His enthusiasm for the group economy was indeed at times interpreted as implying a favorable attitude toward segregation, and in an exchange of letters on the subject with the editor of the Boston *Transcript,* Du Bois was finally prompted to declare that while opposed to physical separation he was prepared to accept for some time to come a "spiritual" separation in economic life that would involve

Negroes trading only among themselves. True, he shifted his support from the creation of captains of industry who would exploit the Negro proletariat to the building up of a consumers' and producers' cooperative movement among Negroes. But inevitably he had to reconcile his espousal of a group economy with his demands for full integration. In 1913, replying to a communication which claimed it was hard to meet the argument that segregation forced Negroes to develop themselves, Du Bois agreed that undoubtedly thousands of Negro businesses, including the *Crisis,* had developed because of discrimination, capitalizing, in a sense, on race prejudice. But this did not make discrimination a "veiled blessing." While Negro enterprises had done creditable work under the circumstances, and although Negroes must make the best of segregation, turning even its disadvantages to their advantage, they "must never forget that none of its possible advantages can offset its miserable evils, or replace the opportunity . . . of free men in a free world." [23]

A similar paradox was involved in Du Bois' stand on intermarriage. Writing in the *Independent* in 1910 he held that a person had the right to choose his spouse, that the prohibition of intermarriage was not justified when it arbitrarily limited friendships, and that where satisfactory conditions prevailed, race mixture had often produced gifted and desirable stocks and individuals, such as the Egyptians, and Hamilton, Pushkin, Douglass, and Dumas. He believed, however, that for the present widespread intermarriage would be "a social calamity by reason of the wide cultural, ethical and traditional differences" between the races, and predicted that if Negroes were accorded their rights and thus encouraged to build up their racial self-respect, the two races would continue to exist as distinct entities, perhaps forever, and this not "at the behest of any one race which recently arrogantly assumed the heritage of the earth, but for the highest upbuilding of all peoples in their great ideal of human brotherhood." [24]

Nor was Du Bois consistent in his views on race differences. Earlier, while never accepting any idea of Negro inferiority, he had referred to Negroes as a backward, childlike, undeveloped race, and he had accepted the idea of inherent racial differences. But in March 1908 he attacked the "glib" Darwinist interpretations about undeveloped races and the survival of the fittest. After the Universal Races Congress in London in 1911 Du Bois enthusiastically reported its conclusion that there was no proven connection between race and mental or cultural characteristics. Yet in 1913 he harked back to the idea of inherent racial differences and described the Negro as primarily an artist, possessing a "sensuous nature . . . the only race which has held at bay the life destroying forces of the tropics," gaining thereby an unusual aesthetic sensitivity. This quality explained the artistic achievements of the Egyptians and the Ommiads, the literature of Pushkin, the bronze work of Benin, and the "only real American music." [25]

As a matter of fact Du Bois maintained his strong feeling of identification with other colored peoples, especially Africans. At one time he was secretary of a company which aimed to participate in the economic advancement of East Africa. Years before Melville J. Herskovits cited anthropological evidence for African origins of the culture of American Negroes, Du Bois held that their religious life and institutions, family life, burial and beneficial societies, the roots of economic co-operation, and the skill of Negro artisans all had their origins in Africa. Finally, *The Negro,* published in 1915, dealt with Negro history from ancient Egypt to the United States and was especially notable for its discussion of the history and culture of West Africa. In it he also adopted the Italian anthropologist Giuseppe Sergi's thesis that an ancient rather dark-skinned race spawned all of the ancient Mediterranean civilizations. Moreover, he predicted the emergence of a pan-African movement, uniting Negroes everywhere, and a growing unity of the darker races against the intolerable treatment accorded them by the white man. Since the colored races were in a majority, the future world would probably be what colored men make it, and "in the character of the Negro race is the best and greatest hope. For in its normal condition it is at once the strongest and gentlest of the races of men." [26]

A new theme in the pages of the *Horizon* and *Crisis* was Du Bois' interest in the labor movement and in socialism. At one time he had viewed the white working class as the Negro's "bitterest opponent." By 1904 he had come to believe that economic discrimination was in large part the cause of the race problem, and to feel sympathetic toward the socialist movement. Three years later, he was writing favorably of the socialists in the *Horizon.* Elsewhere he advised the socialists that their movement could not succeed unless it included the Negro workers, and wrote that it was simply a matter of time before white and black workers would see their common economic cause against the exploiting capitalists. Though in 1908 Du Bois did not vote for the socialists because they had no chance of winning, in 1911 he joined the party. In a Marxist exegesis in the concluding pages of *The Negro,* Du Bois viewed both American Negroes and Africans, both the white workers and the colored races, as exploited by white capital which employed the notion of race differences as a rationalization of exploitation, segregation, and subordination. And he predicted that the exploited of all races would unite and overthrow white capital, their common oppressor.[27]

Du Bois' espousal of the cause of labor was so deep-seated that he had the *Crisis* printed by members of a union that did not admit Negroes, and in its pages he welcomed the rare signs that white and Negro workers might be getting together. In this regard he was certainly ahead of his time, and even he finally expressed discouragement after the 1917 East St. Louis riot in which white unionists played such a striking role.[28] Thus Du Bois' attempts to woo union labor had succeeded no better than his related attempt to woo the Democratic party which was discussed in the last chapter. But Du Bois never gave up his vision of a union of white and black workers creating a society of economic and racial justice. He had in fact shifted from pinning his faith on the intellectuals or talented tenth of professional and business men to pinning it on the actions of the black working classes, though quite likely they were to be led, as has been suggested, by a talented-tenth intelligentsia.[29]

In W. E. B. Du Bois then, the most distinguished Negro intellectual in the age of Booker T. Washington, we find explicitly stated most of the threads of Negro thought at that time. On the one hand he had a mystic sense of race and of the mission of the Negro, which made him sympathetic toward ideas of racial pride and solidarity as sentiments useful for racial uplift. On the other hand he held explicitly and constantly, especially after 1901, to the ideal of waging a struggle for full acceptance in American society. While at times he seemed to view segregated institutions as good in themselves, actually he regarded them as second-best instruments in the struggle for advancement and citizenship rights. He envisaged not amalgamation but cultural pluralism as the goal. He was inconsistent on the question of innate race differences, but he never admitted that Negroes were inferior. Above all he insisted that Negroes wanted to be both Negroes and Americans, maintaining their racial integrity while associating on the freest terms with all American citizens, participating in American culture in its broadest sense, and contributing to it in fullest freedom.

It is notable that though Du Bois expressed the views held by most of the articulate Negroes of the age of Booker T. Washington, both in his stress on racial solidarity and economic co-operation and in his demand for full citizenship rights, nevertheless he frequently found himself in the minority. Few articulate Negroes exhibited the same extent of political independence; not many Northern Negroes agreed with his accommodating tactic of the late nineteenth century; relatively few championed the cause of liberal education as enthusiastically as he did; few either dared or cared to follow him in the extent to which he championed the protest movement during the first years of the twentieth century; and few embraced socialism or the cause of the black workers and interracial working-class solidarity. It is important to note, however, that many times people, who at heart agreed with his point of view, were not courageous enough to flout the power structure both within and outside of the Negro community as he did.

Of the great trio of Negro leaders, Douglass was the orator, Du Bois the polished writer, and Washington the practical man of affairs. Like Douglass, Du Bois has been known primarily as a protest leader, though he was not as consistent in this role as Douglass. Like Douglass, too, he exhibited a marked oscillation in his ideologies—in fact his was more marked than that of Douglass. Like Douglass he clearly stated the ultimate goals which Washington obscured. Yet Du Bois displayed more of a sense of racial solidarity than Douglass usually did. Nor did he envisage the degree of amalgamation and the loss of racial consciousness that Douglass regarded as the *summum bonum*. On the contrary he, like Washington, emphasized race pride and solidarity and economic chauvinism, though after 1905 he no longer championed support of the individualist entrepreneur but favored instead a co-operative economy. Where Washington wanted to make Negroes entrepreneurs and captains of industry in accordance with the American economic dream (a dream shared with less emphasis by Douglass), Du Bois stressed the role of the college-educated elite and later developed a vision of a world largely dominated by the colored races which would combine with the white workers in overthrowing the domination of white capital and thus secure social justice under socialism. All three emphasized the moral values in American culture and the necessity of justice for the Negro if the promise of American life were to be fulfilled. But of the three men it was Douglass who was pre-eminently the moralist, while Washington and Du Bois expressed sharply divergent economic interpretations. Where Douglass and Washington were primarily petit-bourgeois in their outlook, Du Bois played the role of the Marxist intelligentsia. Where the interest of Douglass and Washington in Africa was largely perfunctory, Du Bois exhibited a deep sense of racial identity with Africans. Above all, though only Douglass favored amalgamation, all three had as their goal the integration of Negroes into American society.

Scholar and prophet; mystic and materialist; ardent agitator for political rights and propagandist for economic co-operation; one who espoused an economic interpretation of politics and yet emphasized the necessity of political rights for economic advancement; one who denounced segregation and called for integration into American society in accordance with the principles of human brotherhood and the ideals of democracy, and at the same time one who favored the maintenance of racial solidarity and integrity and a feeling of identity with Negroes elsewhere in the world; an equalitarian who apparently believed in innate racial differences; a Marxist who was fundamentally a middle-class intellectual, Du Bois becomes the epitome of the paradoxes in American Negro thought. In fact, despite his early tendencies toward an accommodating viewpoint, and despite his strong sense of race solidarity and integrity, Du Bois expressed more effectively than any of his contemporaries the protest tendency in Negro thought, and the desire for citizenship rights and integration into American society.

CHAPTER XII

BOOKER T. WASHINGTON
AND THE "TALENTED TENTH"

Washington's critics were drawn chiefly from the ranks of the college-educated elite, the group which W. E. B. Du Bois labeled the Talented Tenth. Conversely it is also usually said that most members of this group were in the anti-Bookerite camp.[1] Du Bois himself certainly expected that it would be these intellectuals who would espouse the cause of higher education and agitation. The question therefore arises, to what extent did members of this group actually join with Du Bois to agitate the cause of reform? Or did a significant number ally themselves with Tuskegee and adopt a "conservative" point of view?

Most of the college-educated individuals were to be found in the ranks of the professions, and, therefore, we shall examine the views of illustrative figures among the editors, the educators, the ministers, and the lawyers.[2] Actually the number of professional people was extremely small. In 1900 they numbered somewhat over 80,000 or about 1.2 per cent of the gainfully employed population. As late as 1910, though their numbers more than doubled during the decade, only 2.5 per cent of employed Southern Negroes and 3 per cent among Northern Negroes were in the professions, and this number included many ministers and teachers who lacked a college, or even a high school education.[3] Yet this tiny group, as Du Bois emphasized, played a crucial leadership role. Though strictly speaking Du Bois stressed the idea of a college-educated elite, I have included certain important figures who were not college graduates. Du Bois himself

207

certainly regarded Frederick Douglass and H. C. Smith as members of the "Talented Tenth," even though neither went to college. Moreover, a consideration of those men prominent in the professions who did not graduate from college sheds additional light on the ideological trends in the age of Washington. In any case all of the men discussed in this chapter would fit into the category of intellectuals, broadly defined.[4]

Selection of individuals for treatment in this and the following chapter was based upon the two interrelated criteria of eminence and availability of materials.[5] While inferences drawn from the views of the more articulate do not necessarily reflect accurately what even the less vocal among the higher classes were thinking, what they had to say must have borne some relationship to what other members of the intellectual elite believed and quite likely to what other classes were thinking also. Businessmen were rather inarticulate. An important segment of their philosophy has been presented, but it is likely that many also had some interest in matters other than economic self-help and solidarity. Some light is shed upon their attitudes by those entrepreneurs who were able to enter politics (Chapter XIII). While the evidence suggests that Northern businessmen with economic roots in the white community were likely to criticize Washington, Southern businessmen, and businessmen of all sections who depended on the Negro market, probably generally supported him. Quite likely, too, Washington's philosophy in large part accorded with the views of the ambitious and thrifty of all classes. We have no direct evidence on what the masses were thinking, but judging from the statements of those most desirous of appealing to the public —particularly churchmen and editors—it would appear that a stress on self-help and racial solidarity, emphasis on economic development and criticism of labor unions, and a strong plea for political and civil rights all evoked favorable responses from general audiences.

More than any other elite group the educators were subject to forces that compelled an outward conformity to the Tuskegee philosophy. The demands of Southern opinion, the example and prestige of Washington, and the policies of the philanthropic foundations all promoted a conservative spectrum of viewpoints. The characteristic outlook enunciated by Southern public school administrators and industrial school principals was one of self-help and accommodation unrelieved by expressions of the demand for citizenship rights. Presidents of private liberal arts colleges were often somewhat more explicit about the higher aspirations of the race, but a radical like John Hope was clearly exceptional. The declaration of principles adopted by the National Association of Teachers of Colored Youth in 1904 probably represented the general view well enough. It stressed the importance of religion, morality, patriotism, the industrial arts and agriculture, and counseled Negroes to raise money to lengthen the school term. The statement also complained of labor union discrimination, mob violence, peonage, and "whitecapping," but said nothing of segregation and disfranchisement.[6]

Naturally the former students of Hampton and Tuskegee, most of whom became teachers and school principals, generally espoused an accommodating ideology, though there were significant differences between the highly sycophantic attitude of W. H. Holtzclaw at Utica Institute in Mississippi and the more sophisticated point of view of R. R. Moton, commandant of cadets at Hampton Institute, who retained the friendship of a number of the radicals. But the most noted accommodator among Southern educators was William Hooper Councill (d. 1909) of the state normal and industrial school at Huntsville, Alabama.

Few careers illustrate so vividly the transition from agitation and politics to sycophancy, economics, and self-help as do Councill's. Born a slave, he attended a freedmen's school, enjoyed a career as a minor politician and newspaper editor during Reconstruction, served as secretary of the National Equal Rights Convention in 1873, and in 1876 was appointed to the Huntsville institution. Though all along he was conciliatory enough to vote the Democratic ticket, he received national attention in 1887 when he appealed his exclusion from a first-class railway car to the Interstate Commerce Commission. Replaced briefly in his job by Peter H. Clark, Councill had reversed himself by June of the next year, for at a state convention he opposed resolutions memorializing the state legislature for decent railroad accommodations.[7] Typically he combined honeyed words for Southern ears with a message of racial pride and solidarity. Though he did ask for fair treatment in the courts and in economic relations, and though he did object to the filth of the Jim Crow cars, he appeared to accept a secondary place for Negroes in American society, ignored the right to vote, and had no objections to segregation. Even more than Washington he extolled the peaceful relations and the "love and attachment between the races at the South," and the unparalleled economic opportunity the region offered the backward Negroes. He spoke of the wonderful chance for "honorable" domestic work that would make the Negro "the choicest jewel of every Southern home." He justified struggle and suffering as necessary for growth and development and saw advantages in the disadvantages: "Our complaint of American prejudice is rot, mainly." Actually discrimination created economic opportunity, because it was "only friendly advice" to Negroes to support their own enterprises.[8] For Washington's ambiguities Councill substituted oily flattery. Washington never boasted that his school trained domestic servants, nor did he accede to pressure by voting the Democratic ticket.

That such language on the part of a school official did not necessarily reflect his deepest feelings is evident from an examination of the private papers of John B. Rayner, formerly a prominent Texas Populist, and president of the Conroe-Porter Industrial School, which was supported by leading white Texans. His public utterances were extremely sycophantic. But privately he wrote that God did not intend for one part of humanity to feel superior to another part, complained of the limitations upon Negro aspirations and of the deprivation of citizenship rights, and called the Southern whites the most unreasonable of men. On the other hand, he preached to himself a philosophy of resignation. "The art of meekness is the science of Heaven," he wrote. It would solve the race problem, for the meekness of the weak would in time witness the decay of the powerful and the gradual disappearance of all unrighteousness.[9] Perhaps for Rayner the belief that the meek shall inherit the earth proved a satisfying rationale of the Negro's condition and of his own sycophancy.

Of a different stripe was R. R. Wright, Sr., who illustrates perhaps better than anyone else the varied interests and shifting emphases of articulate Southern Negroes between Reconstruction and the Great Migration. Born a slave, he graduated from Atlanta University's classical course in 1876 and accepted a teaching post at Cuthbert, Georgia. Here, in what was later good Booker T. Washington fashion, he began without even a building and created a school with the aid of the community, developed a Farmer's Institute, and demonstrated to farmers how to market co-operatively—all before Tuskegee was founded. Active in Republican circles he was nominated for Congress in 1884 and enjoyed a succession of minor federal offices until the end of the century. Meanwhile, he had been principal of the high school in Augusta and in 1889 became the first president of the state Industrial College for Colored Youth near Savannah, where he started with a classical course and only later added industrial work. While college president he also organized a Civic Improvement League which founded a home for wayward girls. Thus Wright ranged from politics to self-help and co-operative efforts in economics and social welfare. Pressures after 1900 forced him to withdraw from politics. And though his biographer pictures him as a rival of Washington's, the expressed philosophies of the two men were practically identical. Wright thought it "not wise to give any heed to those who advocate that we ought to fight for our rights"; neither complaint nor force would win the race its rightful position, which could be achieved only through winning the respect of whites by the usual program of economics and racial solidarity. He attached value to higher education, but gave prime emphasis to industrial training.[10] Though Wright was a product of Atlanta rather than Hampton, as in Washington's case, the pressures of the times molded an ambitious youth into a conservative educator with an affinity for politics.

Southern educators at private colleges with a liberal arts tradition also tended to be of a conservative frame of mind. One of the most distinguished of these was J. W. E. Bowen of the Northern Methodist Church's Gammon Technological Seminary. The son of a prosperous free Negro contractor in New Orleans, he graduated in 1878 from the Methodist New Orleans University and took his B.D. and Ph.D. (1886) from Boston University. After several years in pastoral and mission work, in 1893 he became a professor at Gammon, where he served as president from 1906 to 1912. During the late 1880's and 1890's it would have been hard to distinguish between the utterances of Washington and Bowen except for the more literary and florid character of the latter's statements. Though in *Souls of Black Folk* Du Bois speculated that Bowen might soon come out against Washington, it would appear that the theologian was sympathetic with Washington's outlook. Yet his relationships with the Tuskegeean became considerably tangled over his role as senior editor of the *Voice of the Negro*. This magazine had been established in 1904 and by the end of that year Bowen found himself held responsible by an incensed Washington for the change of attitude toward

Tuskegee in the magazine's tone—a change which was, in fact, due to the influence of the junior editor, J. Max Barber. But things were smoothed over and beginning in April 1905 Bowen's comments on Washington took on the flavor of panegyrics.[11] After the Atlanta riot, in which Bowen was badly injured, Washington issued a statement praising him and W. H. Crogman, president of Clark University, who was also a Tuskegee supporter, for their courageous actions during the crisis. Within a month Bowen, informing Washington of his appointment as president of Gammon, thanked him "for what you did to bring about my election." With Bowen firmly in the Tuskegee orbit the *Horizon,* citing a recent speech in which the editors felt that Bowen had toadied to Southern whites, called him "a renegade of the most dangerous character." [12]

John Hope of Atlanta Baptist College was among the most distinguished of the anti-Bookerites. The son of a well-to-do white man of Augusta, he found it possible to attend Worcester, Massachusetts, Academy and in 1894 received his A.B. from Brown University and began teaching at the now defunct Baptist school, Roger Williams University, in Nashville. Six months after the Atlanta address he offered his own decidedly radical views, urging Negroes to be discontented and dissatisfied, and insisting that they must agitate for complete equality, even "social equality." On another occasion he asserted that Negroes must pursue the higher fields of learning. Mere wealth would give neither self-respect nor recognition by other peoples of the civilized world. Speaking at the Atlanta University conference in 1899 he disagreed with Washington's thesis that Negro incompetency and lack of industrial skill were the causes of the race's woes, though he did believe it important for Negroes to form their own businesses. Rights were essential, but Negroes must compete with the Anglo-Saxon in his own sphere in order to survive.[13] Moving to Atlanta Baptist College Hope assumed the presidency in 1905. The character of his outlook was exemplified by the fact that under his administration higher education remained the core of the curriculum and by his activity in the Niagara Movement. Consequently he found it difficult to obtain funds for his school, and it was only after considerable soul-searching that he permitted his friend Moton to intervene with Washington in his behalf.

Hope was clearly unusual, if not unique, among educators in the Deep South. As would be expected, schoolmen in the Northern and border states were more likely to exhibit radical tendencies. Yet even here the temper of the times and the power structure within the Negro community frequently operated to elicit conservative ideological expression from men prominently identified with liberal education.

In Baltimore an elite group of well-educated teachers, gathered to staff the Colored High School when Negro teachers were first employed there in 1901, were a central element among the anti-Bookerites. One of them, Mason A. Hawkins, who a few years later became the school's principal, was treasurer of the Niagara Movement. In the nation's capital J. W. Cromwell, who was now an elementary school principal there, first defended Washington before the Bethel Literary Association when the Tuskegeean became famous in 1895. Though Cromwell had never adopted a conciliatory tone toward the white South this action was not surprising since in other respects his ideology had been close to the Tuskegee outlook. Yet by 1903, perhaps partly because Washington had failed to secure for him the presidency of Langston University in Oklahoma, Cromwell became an ardent radical. He even reversed his ideology of the 1880's by declaring that both education and material development "wait on and are subordinate to political life." [14] On the other hand Tuskegee influence led to the appointment of Senator Blanche K. Bruce's son, Roscoe Conkling, a graduate of Harvard, as assistant superintendent of Washington schools (1907–21). Bruce had been director of Tuskegee's Academic Department, and though liberally educated he echoed the Tuskegee philosophy and in Washington gave special attention to industrial training.[15]

That even in the North identification with higher education did not preclude a conservative philosophy is evident from an examination of the views of two of the most prominent administrators in liberal arts schools—W. S. Scarborough, president of the A.M.E. Church's Wilberforce University, and Kelly Miller, dean of Howard University. Scarborough, who was a noted linguist, had been born a slave in Georgia, had graduated from Atlanta University preparatory school and Oberlin College (1875), and a few years later accepted a professorship at Wilberforce which he held until appointed president in 1906. Miller, the son of a South Carolina cash-renting cotton farmer, secured his undergraduate degree from Howard University, and after two years of advanced mathematics at Johns Hopkins University was awarded a professorship at his alma mater in 1890, which he held until appointed dean in 1907. Though Scarborough was generally the more radical of the two men, each represented in his own way the broad shifts in Negro ideologies in the Age of Washington.

During the 1880's and 1890's Scarborough had espoused a protest line. But by the end of the century he was close to the Tuskegee outlook. Although an exemplar of liberal education, he declared that there was "no school in all the land that I would endorse more cordially" than Hampton. At the Hampton Conference in 1900 he said that it would be a blessing to the race if the Negro would adopt Booker T. Washington's "sound philosophy" and follow R. R. Wright's example by withdrawing from politics. He perceived advantages in the disadvantages and thought the salvation of the Negro depended on his own efforts, especially in business. As he said at the 1902 Hampton Conference, co-operation must be the central theme in Negro thought and action if they were to have the unity that made other races strong.

Scarborough never entirely forsook his protest view. In 1900 he denied that the Southern people were the Negro's best friends. He complained in 1901 that the race could not afford to let "this crusade against the higher education" go unchallenged, and by 1903 he was expressing Du Boisian ideas about the talented-tenth and insisting that Negroes must participate in politics. During the period of acute ideological conflict Scarborough followed a middle course. Writing in 1906 he rejected the idea of abandoning politics altogether, but held that Negroes would be in a position to demand more when they possessed more. Politics, property, racial organization, and education, he said, were interdependent instruments of self-help, "and self-help is what we are trying to rely upon." However, by the end of the year his statements had become quite radical.[16] Completely in the anti-Bookerite camp Scarborough was a member of the Committee of Forty created by the National Negro Conference in 1909, and later a member of the N.A.A.C.P. advisory committee.

Of the large group of liberally educated individuals who were at one time or another favorable to Washington, few were as influential as the prolific and perceptive essayist, Kelly Miller.[17] At first Miller was critical of Washington, and at meetings of the Bethel Literary Association following the Atlanta Address was among those who took issue with the Tuskegeean. Yet discouraging conditions at the turn of the century led him to feel that a program of self-help and solidarity, limited political activity, economic and moral virtues, and both industrial and higher education would be thoroughly realistic, whereas an appeal to the moral sense of the nation would avail little. In fact the Wilmington, North Carolina, riot of 1898, by demonstrating the utter helplessness of the Negro, led Miller to propose "political self-effacement." He was not, he said, urging the Negro to surrender his rights, but "to make sensible use of them" by voting for the better element of white Southerners, which had always been ready to work with the Negro to advance the common interest of the region. As he told a hostile audience at the Bethel Literary in 1899, the Negro was "a sheep among wolves," who had to compromise and accept the best terms he could get.[18] In general from 1899 until about 1902 Miller hewed fairly closely to the Tuskegee line, except that he never quite saw eye to eye with Hampton and Tuskegee on educational matters. At the first Hampton Conference in 1897 he replied heatedly to criticisms of higher education made by Hugh M. Browne, a member of the Hampton-Tuskegee circle who was later the principal of Cheyney Institute, Pennsylvania, and secretary of the Committee of Twelve. On this occasion and later Miller consistently favored both industrial and higher training. Higher education was imperative for the development of superior individuals who would lead a backward race upward into civilization. He complained of the philanthropic predilection for industrial education, because both forms of education were "essential to the symmetrical development of any people." The Negro needed to begin at the bottom as well as at the top—he needed training in economic tasks on the one hand and a liberally educated leadership on the other. Higher education was for the few; industrial for the many. "Each is," he was fond of saying, "efficient; neither is sufficient." Thus, combining the economic arguments of Washington with the talented-tenth theme of Du Bois, Miller essayed a compromise of synthesis.[19]

By 1902 Miller was not enthusiastic about Washington. Though he thought him after Douglass the most distinguished member of the race, he nevertheless found his stand too wavering for effective leadership. "Nowhere does one find that Mr. Washington has stated his conviction as to the political and social status of his race in clear and unequivocal terms." Yet, in spite of the critical tone of his remarks, the Boston radicals were displeased with what they regarded as his inconsistency in according importance to Washington while approving of higher education.[20] Similar detachment from both sides was evident in the most celebrated of Miller's essays which appeared the next year, several weeks after the "Boston Riot," in the form of two anonymous articles on "Washington's policy" in the Boston *Transcript* of September 18 and 19, 1903. Miller pointed out that the radicals and conservatives differed not on ends, but on means. He called Du Bois "not an agitator, nor a carping critic . . . but a scholar, a painstaking, accurate investigator . . . and a fearless advocate of the higher aspirations of his race." Washington he described as a first-rate diplomat who did not expressly avow, yet would "not disclaim, in distinct terms, a single plank in the platform of Douglass." True, conditions were growing worse since Washington had become prominent, but his policy would help to mitigate the severity of the blow. Yet Washington did not command an enthusiastic following. Much of his support among Negroes was due to the high regard whites had for him and to his political power. Most thoughtful men, Miller asserted, ranged between the disparate views of Washington and his critics, believing that each had its place.

From then on, during the height of the ideological struggle and the rise and decline of the Niagara Movement, Miller clearly occupied a position in the middle of the road. Though he and Du Bois had been close friends during the 1890's when their views had been similar, the two men now drifted apart.[21] Miller still criticized Washington at times. Once he spoke against the latter's "over-cautiousness of utterance touching the higher claims of the race." In 1907, just when the Tuskegeean was doing his best to allay criticism of the Brownsville action, Miller wrote a pamphlet attacking the chief executive on this and other matters, including his making any one individual, even Washington, the "referee" of Negro appointments. More pleasing to Tuskegee must have been Miller's revision of his Boston *Transcript* articles for his volume *Race Adjustment* in 1908, for it concluded with a panegyric on Washington and had new and unfavorable descriptions of the opposition. Du Bois was now pictured as a frenzied dreamer who had unfortunately turned from scholarship, for which he was fitted, to agitation, for which he was not. Miller dismissed the Niagara platform as "nothing new," and held that many of the movement's members had not, up to that time, been known for their work on behalf of the race.[22]

Basically, Miller's role was that of the pragmatic harmonizer. "Come, Let Us Reason Together," he pleaded in the January 1906 issue of the *Voice of the Negro*. Negroes did not disagree on fundamental principles. Since neither side had been able to bring about the desired results, the ideal approach comprised all movements for the elevation of the race. Miller later recalled that in these years he was roundly attacked by both sides as a "straddler." He was, he has written, an independent rather than an uncritical follower of Washington, not motivated by desire for personal gain. Critics on the left, however, did not believe his stand entirely disinterested. In a thinly veiled reference to the fact that Washington's appointment to the Howard University Trustee Board in the spring of 1907 preceded by a few months Miller's appointment as dean of the College, the *Horizon* concluded that Professor Miller had "found his 'place' and . . . will nestle down into it when school opens in the fall." [23]

By 1910, however, Miller was veering to the left. He addressed the May 1910 conference that formally established the N.A.A.C.P., and in November Charles W. Anderson listed Miller as among those of Washington's friends whom he found wanting "to sit on both sides of the fence and in the middle too." He was one of the few who served on national boards of both the N.A.A.C.P. and the Urban League, and he maintained a working relationship with Washington until the latter's death. And so, though during the first decade of the century Miller does not appear to have made any but the most generalized statements concerning the higher aspirations of the race, during the last five years of Washington's life he more openly asserted the demand for ultimate equality. He maintained his older interests in racial integrity and solidarity, in middle-class virtues and economic advancement, and his sense of "ratio and proportion" about industrial and higher education, but he also denounced segregation in strong terms and, in contrast to his earlier utterances insisted that political participation was prerequisite to the Negro's progress.[24] Miller had moved pragmatically with the times, from verging on calculated conciliation of the white South at the turn of the century to a new militance by the time of the Great Migration. As with many other figures, the chief unifying threads through the years were self-help and racial solidarity. Perhaps more than any other single person Miller can be described as one who typified the thinking of the intellectual and professional elite in the age of Washington.

As Ralph Bunche has observed, by accepting segregation and emphasizing otherworldly matters, the church tended both to play an accommodating role and to stimulate the sentiment of racial solidarity.[25] In accord with the Tuskegee philosophy the segregated church functioned both as an opportunity for racial development and as an accommodating institution in the social order. On the other hand, a perusal of church conference proceedings, collections of sermons, and the material available on the more distinguished clerics indicates significant attention to the ethical message of Christianity in relation to the race problem. In the following pages we shall discuss illustrative figures first from the mass churches—the Baptists and the various Negro Methodist connections—and then the higher status Congregationalist, Presbyterian, and Episcopal churches.[26]

Although the uneven nature of the evidence makes it difficult to arrive at definitive generalizations, it would appear that most of the powerful figures in the mass churches were of a conservative turn of mind. In the case of the A.M.E. Church it is true that scattered evidence indicates that Northern-based bishops such as W. B. Derrick, B. T. Tanner, and L. J. Coppin had proclivities toward radicalism—at least sporadically—though they did not figure as leaders among the anti-Bookerites. The same conclusion is valid for A.M.E. Zion Bishop Alexander Walters of New York, an ex-slave of modest schooling, whose restless quest for racial leadership led to kaleidoscopic changes in ideological expression and a bewildering alternation of alliances with Washington and the anti-Bookerites. The only Southern bishop who could be called an agitator—and he was not identified with the anti-Bookerites—was Henry M. Turner, whose declarations of hatred for "this bloody, lynching nation" were coupled with a nationalistic expression of African colonization. So extreme were his denunciations that President Roosevelt once suggested to Washington that the bishop might be indicted for treason because he had referred to the American flag as a "bloody rag." [27]

Others, such as Bishops Wesley J. Gaines and Abraham Grant in the A.M.E. Church; George W. Clinton and J. W. Hood, along with Walters the most powerful figures in the A.M.E. Zion Church; L. H. Holsey, a prominent bishop in the C.M.E. Church; and E. C. Morris and R. H. Boyd, respectively president of the National Baptist Convention and secretary-treasurer of the Baptist Publishing Board and thus the two most important men among the Baptists, expressed a conservative outlook. All except Hood had been born in slavery, and none of them had more than a secondary school education. As a group they were less well educated than the other men discussed in this chapter and they would hardly be expected to champion the cause of higher education. In general they enunciated a gradualist philosophy of self-help, racial solidarity, and economic progress as the keys to citizenship rights. By the end of the century, however, Holsey had become so discouraged that he proposed a semi-independent Negro state on American soil as the only alternative to extermination. He held that even Washington's policy was not a permanent solution, because as the Negroes acquired wealth and character the greater would be the hostility between the races.[28] Though there were variations among them, as a group these ministers tended to be rather more explicit about ultimate goals than Washington was, and most of them—some frequently, others infrequently—coupled their counsel of thrift, industry, internal development, and cultivating the friendship of the Southern whites with pleas against segregation and disfranchisement. Occasionally, in fact, members of this group were moved to expressions of militant protest. But Washington himself regarded a man as conservative if his call for citizenship rights was dignified—especially if their attainment was placed in the vague future—and if he uttered conciliatory words that stressed that Negroes must bear the chief responsibility for uplifting themselves by accumulating property and getting along with their Southern neighbors. Hood had been a leading politician in North Carolina during Reconstruction, Grant had held minor political jobs while a pastor in Florida and Texas early in his career, and Morris had political ambitions—but they all usually (though not always) soft-pedaled the importance of political participation. Most, if not all, of this group were on personally friendly terms with Washington and worked closely with him in one way or another. Grant was especially close to Washington, who found the bishop useful as a Republican campaigner in 1908; and Clinton was a regular lecturer at Tuskegee's Bible School.

An examination of the official pronouncements of the quadrennial A.M.E. Conferences is perhaps even more significant than an analysis of individual clerics. The 1900 proceedings displayed a more conservative tone than did those of 1912. At the former, the Episcopal address did not regard conditions as satisfactory, but was not specific in its complaints. More forthright, but still quite mild, was the Committee on the State of the Country, whose members included Derrick and Reverdy Ransom. Although they held that "stripped of all disguise, the so-called race problem" was caused by white prejudice, they believed that the South would "continue to yield" to the argument presented by the Negro's economic progress. In 1908 the address of the bishops was again vague. But the 1912 conference reflected the rising radical influence. Washington, it is true, addressed the meeting, and the Committee on the Condition of the Negro, chaired by H. T. Kealing, spoke in enthusiastic generalities about the race's progress. But the Episcopal address criticized those who favored "the policy of non-complaint, non-agitation and non-protest. . . . Only the brave protest, cowards and sycophants never. To accept the doctrine of non-complaint is to court self-disaster." The Committee on the State of the Country paid its respects to the economic virtues and the preferability of rural life, but expressed alarm at the growing tendency to elevate wealth above human welfare. It also spoke of the danger to American institutions involved in the increasing prejudice, discrimination, and mob violence and called on all members of the race to exert themselves like men against those who were cheating the race out of the "priceless heritage of their citizenship." This was the convention that appropriately marked the success of the radicals by electing the Niagara Movement's brilliant orator, Reverdy Ransom, editor of the *Review*.

That Methodist bishops, on the whole notable for conservatism, could at times be moved to dignified but resolute protest is evident from a statement issued by the bishops of all three connections in February 1908. Protesting against "the monstrous injustices" involved in the Brownsville incident and the administration's lily-white policy, they warned the Republicans not to nominate either Roosevelt or Taft. They also specifically attacked disfranchisement, segregation, mob violence, peonage, and convict labor and claimed that as citizens Negroes were entitled as much to equal civil and political rights as all other Americans.[29]

It should also be noted, however, that each of the three mass churches had at least one outstanding example of an anti-Bookerite minister. S. L. Corrothers of Washington was a prominent pastor of the A.M.E. Zion church; J. Milton Waldron and Sutton E. Griggs were Baptist ministers who were active in the Niagara Movement; and most outstanding of all was the brilliant radical orator, Reverdy C. Ransom. While it has not been possible to establish with certainty the social class positions of their congregations, it would appear that usually these men tended to be pastors of the more elite churches within their denominations. Waldron had been a supporter of Washington while he held a post in Jacksonville, but after a disagreement with the Tuskegeean over personal matters,[30] he moved into radical circles and served as president of the Washington, D.C., N.A.A.C.P. Griggs, a consistent proponent of racial solidarity, was a radical during his years in Nashville, but after he moved to Memphis in 1912 the financial difficulties of his church led him to become exceedingly conciliatory toward the white South. Less active in radical circles, but a man who followed a comparable ideological course was the noted Adam Clayton Powell, Sr., of the Abyssinian Baptist Church in New York.[31] Significantly, each of these men who were either consistently or inconsistently in the radical camp were, with the possible exception of Corrothers, the products of higher and professional education. Ransom, who lived all of his life in the North, was a graduate of Wilberforce University; Waldron, who was born in Virginia, had been educated at Lincoln University and Newton Theological Seminary; Griggs graduated from Bishop College in Texas; and Powell, a native of Virginia, had been trained at the Wayland Seminary in Washington.

Even in the Deep South there appears to have been some correlation between social class position and attitude toward Washington among the Baptist ministers. In Augusta, Georgia, William Jefferson White, the son of a planter and a man who had a long and distinguished career dating back to Reconstruction in education, journalism, politics, and the equal rights movement, was a consistent anti-Bookerite. Allied with Washington was Charles T. Walker. Born a slave, Walker was educated at the Augusta Baptist Institute (which was founded by White and which later became Morehouse College), and was subsequently associated with R. R. Wright's Augusta *Sentinel,* a rival of White's Georgia *Baptist.* A local Republican leader, an army chaplain during the Spanish-American War, and an enormously popular religious spellbinder known as the "Black Spurgeon," after 1899 Walker alternated between two large mass-based congregations in Augusta and New York. In his speeches Walker stressed both duties and rights. Washington regarded Walker highly, describing him as a conservative who worked well with the best Southern whites. White presided over the radical Georgia Equal Rights Convention in 1906; Walker also attended, but at Washington's request in order to minimize radical influence.[32]

Yet by and large it was among the more elite Presbyterian, Congregational, and Episcopal churches of the Northern and border states that the protest point of view found its chief strength. This was, naturally, less true of the South. H. H. Proctor, a contemporary of Du Bois at Fisk, a graduate of the Yale Theological School, and pastor of the upper-class First Congregational Church in Atlanta, was known as a moderate. As editor of the Fisk *Herald* he had attacked segregation and had endorsed Fortune's call for an Afro-American League to fight for equal rights. As late as 1895, in speaking of the Jim Crow car he said that Southerners had "better beware or they would find firebrands under their houses and poison in their coffee." After Proctor met Washington at the Atlanta Exposition the Tuskegeean assisted him in raising money for his church work, and subsequently the two men were helpful to each other in various ways. Proctor worked with Du Bois and Washington in the effort to head off Pullman car discrimination in 1903 and 1904. Later he recalled that he was friendly with both men, the work of each being necessary to the advancement of the race.[33]

Among Episcopalians the leading figure until he died in 1898 was the venerable Alexander Crummell, who in his last years practically reversed himself on the matter of industrial education and the gospel of wealth, though he still retained his earlier enthusiasm for race pride and solidarity, and still declined to take an active part in politics.[34] While he did not criticize Washington by name, and although he agreed that most would not go to college, he spoke against "certain pseudo-philanthropists" who wished to bind the Negro to manual labor, and the opportunists who would jump at anything a white man said. Such "leaders for revenue" were unmindful of the fact that labor was always the fruit of civilization, not the basis for it. Well before Du Bois made the theory of talented-tenth leadership famous,

Crummell held that it was the college-educated elite that would raise the Negroes to civilization.[35]

After Crummell's death, perhaps the leading Episcopalian was George Freeman Bragg. Born in North Carolina and educated in the Episcopal Schools at Petersburg, Virginia, he was widely known for his institutional and benevolent work while a rector in Norfolk (1887–91) and Baltimore. He supported the idea of a missionary district for Negroes with a Negro bishop as the best alternate to the Sewanee canon, an idea opposed by the *Horizon,* though supported by Washington. Yet, while Bragg worked with Washington in efforts to prevent disfranchisement in Maryland, he was in fact a member of the Niagara Movement.[36]

But the man who epitomized the upper-class intellectual and religious leader who stood for righteousness above all else was Francis J. Grimké, for years pastor of Washington's fashionable Fifteenth Street Presbyterian Church. The natural son of a wealthy South Carolina planter and brother of the equally noted Archibald Grimké, he was educated at Lincoln University (A.B., 1870), and Princeton Seminary (B.D., 1878). In the late 1890's Grimké was an enthusiastic supporter of Washington who worked to counteract criticisms of the Tuskegeean among his friends, and while he did not flatter the white Southerners, in other respects he generally followed the Tuskegee line of economic and racial Social Darwinism. But as early as 1900 he described as traitors to the Negro those who condoned disfranchisement as justified by the differences in the condition of the two races, and insisted that Negroes should never cease to agitate until their manhood and citizenship were recognized. By 1903 Grimké was clearly of the opposition, and he denounced the "powerful propaganda" emanating from within the race that fostered the notion that if Negroes acquired property everything would be all right. Such a theory was totally false for money would neither break down prejudice nor elevate the Negro's character. From then on Grimké maintained a consistently hostile attitude toward the Tuskegeean's "cowardly, hypocritical course." [37] He signed the call for the National Negro Conference in 1909 and later was president of the N.A.A.C.P.'s Washington branch.

While we have only sampled certain ministers concerning whom considerable information was available, certain tentative conclusions can be drawn. In the first place, the most consistent emphasis was on self-help in various guises. Second, it seems likely that the well-educated Northern ministers of the upper-class denominations were more likely to oppose Washington than were the leaders in the mass churches, most of whom did not go to college. Third, even those who were close to Washington and were regarded as conservative by their contemporaries usually had a significant protest element in their expressed philosophy. Fourth, Washington kept close contact with ministers where possible, and it is evident that much of the support he received was for personal reasons. Moreover, the Baptist minister C. T. Walker certainly put his finger on a crucial point in a letter he wrote Washington from New York in 1901, shortly after it became evident that the Tuskegeean was a power in the Roosevelt administration. Walker regarded it as "amusing" that many of the New York ministers formerly opposed to Washington now wished to hold a reception for him. According to Walker, they said that public sentiment was moving so strongly toward the Tuskegeean that they felt it was useless for prominent Negroes to oppose him any longer.[38] On the other hand, as Ralph Bunche suggests, in view of their social role, ministers were likely to be conservative in their racial pronouncements. Certainly few were active or prominent in the Niagara Movement although they were the most numerous professional group. Only eight attended its Harpers Ferry meeting. Yet it should be emphasized that some at least—most significantly Grimké, whose sincerity cannot be doubted—displayed a genuine instability in their ideologies, unaffected by consideration of the power structure or personal advantage. Broadly speaking the ministers exhibited the same range of ideologies as other leaders, with a strong sentiment in favor of Washington among them, especially among those who were leaders in the mass churches.

The great majority of editors supported Washington, though his assertion that all but three "have stood loyally by me in all my plans and policies" [39] was an exaggeration. The leading consistently anti-Washington journals were the Boston *Guardian* and the Cleveland *Gazette*. Others like the Richmond *Planet*, Chicago *Conservator*, Washington *Bee*, and the A.M.E. *Christian Recorder* opposed Washington at first only to support him later.

That most editors supported Washington, even if, as shall be demonstrated, they did not necessarily employ his accommodating phraseology, was due both to the climate of the age and to other persuasive considerations. Washington himself admitted that he worked to cultivate "in a general and friendly way" almost all of the Negro editors and leaders.[40] His correspondence affords ample evidence of his profound influence over the press and substantiates the charges made during his life time that the Tuskegeean secretly subsidized newspapers and magazines in order to silence criticism of himself. In what ways was this influence maintained and to what extent was Washington able to direct the viewpoint of various journals?

Washington achieved his considerable control over the press by several methods. Some editors were genuinely sympathetic toward him and his policy. Certainly his prestige and power played a large role in attracting support. Indirectly he worked through R. W. Thompson's National Negro Press Bureau in Washington, which sent out Tuskegee-inspired press releases and helped line up editors at election times, and through the Negro press organization which was dominated by Tuskegee supporters. The National Afro-American (after 1907 National Negro) Press Association almost always chose officials who were friendly to Tuskegee, and its president, Cyrus Field Adams, editor of the Chicago *Appeal,* frankly regarded the organization as allied with Tuskegee. Nevertheless its resolutions did not echo the Tuskegee line. For example, those of 1903–1905, drawn up at the zenith of Washington's power, failed to mention economic development or to approve of franchise qualifications, but denounced the malicious movement to destroy the Negro's rights and reaffirmed their unalterable determination to contend for them in all lawful ways. They supported all types of education and placed special emphasis on the ballot, denial of which had inevitably resulted in abridgement of all other citizenship rights.[41]

Washington also exerted a more direct influence. Tuskegee sent out quantities of news releases and at times paid for the cost of printing them. Advertisements were freely placed in a number of journals. Republican party campaign patronage was distributed through Tuskegee. Several journals were assisted by subsidies for particular purposes, such as a special "Tuskegee issue." A few, closer to Washington, received editorial copy. And then there were at least five or six which Washington aided by sustained cash contributions. These were the New York *Age,* the Washington *Colored American,* the Boston *Colored Citizen, Alexander's Magazine,* the *Colored American Maga-*

zine, and in all probability the Washington *Bee.* Two of these, the *Age* and the *Colored American Magazine* were, for a time, partly owned by Washington.

This subsidization of the press, in its various guises, was widespread. Washington of course was not one to spend money foolishly as an examination of the publications to which he gave substantial outright gifts demonstrates. The *Age* was the leading Negro newspaper. Fortune, for years a close friend, proved unreliable and broke with Washington several times. Washington gave generously to the paper's support, made unsuccessful efforts to purchase it in 1903–4, and finally obtained financial control in 1907. In Boston, where Trotter published the *Guardian,* Washington heavily subsidized first the *Colored Citizen* and later *Alexander's Magazine.* He was especially intimate in the *Citizen*'s affairs during the stormy days of 1903, giving advice, criticism, money, and editorial copy. But business in radical Boston was so poor that by 1905 Washington concluded that it was futile to subsidize the paper further, and at his suggestion the editor, Charles Alexander, replaced it with his monthly magazine. Washington continued to accede at times to his constant requests for funds, but Alexander proved disloyal and the magazine failed in 1909. In the nation's capital where Chase used the influential *Bee* to sting Washington, Tuskegee heavily subsidized E. E. Cooper's *Colored American* and supplied editorials from time to time until its demise in 1904. Later, in 1906, Chase became an ardent supporter of Washington, undoubtedly for financial reasons. In Chicago where the *Conservator* was closely connected with the anti-Bookerite circle, Washington toyed with the idea of subsidizing a rival organ, but seems to have given up the project because he could not find a dependable editor. Later the *Conservator* changed hands several times, adopting a more pro-Tuskegee policy and failing entirely in 1909. The evidence concerning the *Colored American Magazine* is less clear, but certainly by 1905 Washington frankly viewed it as a rival of the radical *Voice of the Negro,* founded shortly before he and Fred Moore purchased their organ.[42] Nevertheless, when called on to answer charges as to his subsidization of the press, Washington always denied such activity. He wrote Francis J. Garrison that outside a few shares in the *Colored American Magazine,* which he had sold due to adverse criticism, he did not aid the press except for legitimate advertising. He denied that advertisements were intended to influence editorial policy. But as Judge R. H. Terrell once observed, it was easy to influence Negro newspapers by the use of a little diplomacy and small advertisements.[43]

The importance of Washington's influence with the press lies in large part in his use of this influence as a weapon in his struggle with his critics. Numerous examples can be cited of how at Washington's behest Negro papers either criticized the opposition or ignored it, and of how Washington planted editorials and other materials attacking the radicals in various papers. Nor was it always necessary for him to tell papers dependent on Tuskegee for favors what stand to take.

Let us now turn to an examination of the outlook expressed by several of the leading journals. Special attention will be paid to representative secular and religious journals in the Washington orbit—which included the vast majority of papers and magazines—in order to ascertain how closely their editors adhered to Washington's outlook. Some consideration will also be given to organs of a generally radical persuasion in order to gain additional insight into the way in which conditions in the age of Booker T. Washington influenced editorial policy.

Fortune's *Age* had for years been known for its strong protest position, though by the early 1890's he and Washington had developed a close and paradoxical relationship that came to include financial aid from Tuskegee. Unfortunately the files for most of the 1890's are not extant, but during the early years of the century the *Age* praised Washington and the philosophy of business enterprises, agitated on a variety of issues, was contradictory in its attitude toward the white South, and consistently attacked the anti-Bookerites. Washington, said Fortune, was often misrepresented, for actually he believed that Negroes should strive without ceasing to attain their constitutional rights by obtaining character, education, and wealth. Like many editors in the Tuskegee orbit Fortune did not adopt Washington's position on the Brownsville matter, but bitterly attacked Republican treachery and, in direct contrast to the Tuskegee approach, declined to preach the gospel of good will or to refrain from saying anything that would irritate the situation, since this could be done only by submission to prejudice, discrimination, and mob rule.[44] Thus Fortune continued to be, on occasion, as capable of the most fervid protest as he had been in the 1880's.

Fortune's instability not only involved Washington in heavy financial commitments to the *Age,* whose editorial policy he at times directed personally, but ended in his assumption of financial control in 1907. The new editor and part-owner was Fred R. Moore, a man of modest educational background, whom Washington had previously placed on the *Age* to assist Fortune and whom in 1904 he made editor of the *Colored American Magazine.* The latter journal had been founded in Boston in 1900 by the Colored Co-Operative Publishing Company, with the goal of publishing a literary organ that would foster racial solidarity and advancement. While at first there were some articles supporting protest organizations—and even a vigorous attack on Washington by George W. Forbes, co-editor of the *Guardian*—the editors were basically friendly toward the Tuskegeean and the magazine came to emphasize chiefly two themes dear to him—economic accumulation and Negro support of Negro business. In 1904 the publishers, in serious financial straits, sold the magazine to Moore and Washington, who moved it to New York. Washington gave considerable financial and editorial assistance until, since it was always a losing proposition, the magazine was discontinued in connection with a reorganization of the *Age* in 1909.[45]

Moore, as editor of the magazine, stated his basic aims when he told his readers that the journal sought to publish articles showing the material advancement of the race, believing that Negroes generally are more interested in the doings of the race than in the writings of dreamers or theorists. For the most part, Moore emphasized the virtues of Tuskegee and its founder and the achievements of Negro businessmen, to which he attached more importance than he did to political and civil rights. There were acid articles attacking higher education, and a constant appeal to race pride, self-help, race-solidarity, and economic chauvinism. Only once did he adopt the Tuskegeean's characteristically accommodating phraseology toward the white South.[46] In fact he was, on rare occasions, moved to vigorous criticism, couched in language Washington never employed.[47] The contradictions in Moore's thought are especially well revealed in a comment he made on the Niagara Movement. He welcomed its "abolitionist ring," but he regarded it as fortunate that the masses were willing to toil upward by the slow process of industry, thrift, and sobriety, and he feared that the movement's aggressive attitude would exacerbate racial hostility. Furthermore, Moore's very espousal of race pride and economic solidarity was couched in militant terms. As he realized, there was an important difference between his militance and that of the radicals. Commenting on the *Horizon*'s criticism of his magazine for lack of editorial vigor, Moore insisted that the race needed something other than "vigorous talk and loud-mouthed railing," and he urged the *Horizon* to spend its energies in counseling Negroes to buy homes and educate their children. Instead of fighting one another, Negroes should "punch back" the white man by obtaining property and education.[48] Both magazines were militant, but in different ways.

Moore took over the *Age* with the issue of October 3, 1907, and Tuskegee's hand was evident two weeks later in an editorial reversing the *Age*'s Brownsville policy. Written at Tuskegee's request by Ralph W. Tyler, auditor for the Navy, the "Brownsville Ghouls" editorial pictured Washington's and Roosevelt's critics as "human ghouls, worthless parasites who represent nothing save selfish avarice," who had led "the race into an ambush" by preying upon the misfortunes of the Brownsville soldiers in their greedy desire to further their own political ends.[49] Actually the editorial content of the *Age* remained quite all inclusive, though the emphasis had shifted markedly away from Fortune's radicalism in the direction of stressing Negro business, optimism, and a belief in the advantages of the disadvantages of segregation. Though it criticized the N.A.A.C.P. and the intellectuals it protested on a variety of issues. In fact Washington several times asked Moore to stop discussing political matters and instead discuss more the economic advancement of the race. Once in particular he complained that Moore was giving too much space to lynchings.[50] Moreover, the Tuskegeean could not prevent Moore from opening the pages of the *Age* to anti-Taft writers in 1908 and severely berating the Taft administration as late as 1911. Even worse, he was on close terms with some of Washington's critics, booming his friend Reverdy Ransom for a bishopric at the very time Washington was trying to head off this effort. In the face of all these provocations all that Washington did was to chide Moore occasionally and urge him to be more constructive. On one occasion Washington wrote a close friend that there was little he could do to control *Age* policies unless he was willing to pay the bills. He added that he would not hesitate to do so if he had the cash to support his demands.[51]

An examination of four other journals—one in the South, two in border cities, and one in the North—will complete our sampling of nonreligious publications that were consistent supporters of Washington. All of them were important newspapers, though less influential than the *Age*.

The Atlanta *Independent* was edited by the colorful Benjamin J. Davis, Sr., a leader among Georgia Oddfellows and Republicans, who had attended Atlanta University in 1887–88 and founded the *Independent* in 1903. Publicly he was a fulsome supporter of Washington, was one of the relatively small group to whom Tuskegee supplied editorials on appropriate occasions, and in spite of various evidences of disloyalty was one whom Washington felt "has his faults but has his virtues." [52] Ideologically Davis must be classed with the conservatives. He combined criticism of Negroes with the themes of self-help and racial solidarity in a Social Darwinist ideology of racial elevation through economic progress. Curiously he often clearly stated his goal of full citizenship rights even in extremely accommodating editorials, and he frequently appeared to alternate between abject sycophancy and forthright protest. During the campaign for adoption of the disfranchisement amendment to the Georgia constitution in 1908 Davis' stand shifted back and forth between urging Negroes to eschew politics and insisting that they could and should defeat the proposal by registering and voting against it. Indeed, for one who generally minimized politics, Davis was exceedingly active in Republican circles, serving as chairman of the Republican Committee in the second district of Georgia.

Both E. E. Cooper of Washington and John H. Murphy of Baltimore, though men of relatively limited educational backgrounds, proved themselves able editors. Cooper had founded the Indianapolis *World* and *Freeman* as well as the informative Washington *Colored American*. During the years for which issues are extant (1898–1904) the last-named paper consistently sided with Washington and fostered a philosophy compounded of economic development, self-help, racial solidarity, agitation for civil and political rights, with only an occasional editorial that was accommodating in tone. More staid in style, but of a similar ideology, was Murphy's Baltimore *Afro-American*, which alternated between neutrality and coolness in regard to the radicals but always endorsed the Tuskegeean.

The Indianapolis *Freeman* under George L. Knox, who was very friendly with Washington and occasionally received loans from him, appeared more Southern than Northern in its outlook. Knox, who had been born a slave in Tennessee, after the Civil War became a successful barber and Republican politician in Indiana, and purchased the *Freeman* in 1892. For about three years after the Atlanta Address Knox not only supported Washington and his program of economic chauvinism and the gospel of wealth, but was equally vigorous in protesting against lynching, disfranchisement, and segregation, and defended intermarriage. But from the close of the century until about 1905 Knox was extremely accommodating in tone, agreed with Washington on the advisability of franchise limitations, denied any interest in social equality, and once almost condoned lynching by suggesting that Negroes guilty of assaulting white women were as much at fault as the mob itself.[53] Subsequently, however, Knox was generally—though not always—more outspoken.

Indifference or hostility to the Tuskegeean among southern organs of opinion was a distinct rarity. True, the *Voice of the Negro,* though it originally included Emmett J. Scott on its board of editors, for a couple of years was identified with the radical point of view. During its short span of years (1904–7) it was certainly the most distinguished of Negro periodicals, but it was addressed to a national rather than a local audience. More significant as a genuinely Southern journal was the Richmond *Planet,* whose editor was John Mitchell, Jr. Mitchell began as a crusading journalist and politician, and later turned to banking and business, accompanying this change with an ideological shift. Highly regarded as a courageous and brilliant editor during the 1890's (when he was twice elected president of the Afro-American Press Association), he was also a member of the Richmond City Council (1888–96), founder (1902) and president of the Mechanics Savings Bank, and Grand Chancellor of the Virginia Knights of Pythias. In the pages of the *Planet* during the 1890's he protested frequently against prejudice, lynching, disfranchisement, and segregation; he urged Negroes to practice thrift and industry, support race enterprises, remember their friends among decent whites, and be polite to everyone. On Washington's Atlanta address the *Planet* was silent, and during the next few years only occasionally did it take notice of the Tuskegeean. Yet it was in this period that Mitchell withdrew from politics and turned to fraternal and business activity. Since his interests had shifted from politics to finance, it is not surprising that, as the only Negro attending the American Banking Association meeting in 1904, he enunciated the typical Business League line that the best way for the Negro to reach success was through finance and that "Nowhere in the domain of business have I found a white man other than ready to help us upward." And so, though the files of the *Planet* after 1900 are not available, it is not unnatural that his journal should be reported as supporting Washington in 1905. Yet Mitchell changed his viewpoint again after the N.A.A.C.P. lent respectability to the Negro protest, and before Washington died he saw value in the politics of both the Tuskegeean and his critics. He even went so far as to assert that property rights were based upon the rights of citizenship, whose surrender would soon be followed by "the confiscation of the very material wealth of which Mr. Washington so glibly speaks." [54]

Unlike Mitchell, Calvin Chase of the Washington *Bee* was ordinarily a vitriolic critic of Washington during the first decade of his ascendancy. Then, in September 1906, after a period of silence, Chase came out in support of the Tuskegeean. The *Bee* justified its switch by saying that it was now willing to overlook Washington's past mistakes because his recent speeches had indicated his interest in the franchise and higher education.[55] Subsequently the *Bee,* though in other respects retaining its editorial policy, was lyrical in its praise of Washington and often venomous in its attacks upon the allegedly selfish zealots of the N.A.A.C.P. But during 1915 Chase stopped mentioning the Tuskegeean, and after the latter's death he said that, while Washington deserved some credit, his position as "patronage dictator" had resulted in many inferior appointments, and that because his program to some extent deprived Negroes of their citizenship rights, Washington had actually subordinated the interests of the race for his own personal advancement.[56]

Outstanding if not unique as a uniformly radical paper over the years, and one conducted without the animosity of Trotter's *Guardian,* was the Cleveland *Gazette.* Certainly no journal was conducted with the integrity and consistency displayed by H. C. Smith, and in him the protest tradition, critical of any form of accommodation and segregation, is found in its purest form. Not only did Smith attack Washington and his satellite organizations, but he was one of the most uncompromising foes of segregation, even the quasi-voluntary kind that some Negroes were proposing in connection with schools and the Y.M.C.A.'s. Few were the men in public life who maintained such a consistent philosophy from the early 1880's to the close of the age of Booker T. Washington.

Turning to the religious press, perhaps the two most influential organs were the A.M.E. *Christian Recorder,* edited by H. T. Johnson (1892–1912), and the A.M.E. Church *Review,* edited by Hightower T. Kealing (1896–1912). Johnson, born in South Carolina, had studied at the University of South Carolina, Howard University (A.B.), Lincoln University (B.D.), and Boston University, while Kealing had alternated (1881–95) as a public school official and president of his church's Paul Quinn College in his native Texas, and upon leaving the *Review* became president of the joint church-state Western University at Quindaro, Kansas. At first Johnson was critical of Washington and even Kealing, whose views had been more accommodating than those of Johnson, had been reluctant to endorse him.[57] Yet at the turn of the century it was the *Review* whose editorials agitated as well as enunciated the Tuskegee ideology, while those of the *Recorder* were usually accommodating, Johnson even fulsomely praising the speeches of W. H. Councill. Early in the next century, however, Johnson's editorial policy returned to militant protest, and at the same time continued to support Washington, who in turn assisted him in his campaign for re-election as editor. Both men were at first critical toward the radicals, but beginning in 1905 and 1906 first Kealing and then Johnson grew more favorably disposed toward them and even gave qualified support to the Niagara Movement, while remaining personally loyal to Booker T. Washington. And apparently Kealing declined to serve on the N.A.A.C.P. board in 1910 only at the personal intercession of Washington.[58] The shifting tide of opinion was reflected not only in the changing stands of these men but also in the fact that Ransom was elected to succeed Kealing, while Johnson's successor, R. R. Wright, Jr. (now a bishop), at first taking a fence-sitting position, quickly veered over to the opposition. He attended the 1909 and 1910 conferences on the Negro and became a leader in the N.A.A.C.P.'s Philadelphia branch.

The major publications of the other denominations also supported Washington. W. H. Steward, editor of the *American Baptist* (Louisville), a former slave who became a leader among Kentucky Baptists and in state conventions in the middle 1880's, was a close associate of Washington's, and kept in touch with the Tuskegeean on the progress of attempts to halt disfranchisement and segregation in Kentucky.[59] C. H. Phillips and R. E. Brown, editors of C.M.E. *Christian Index* during the years for which copies are available (1891–1904), failed to take an accommodating line, even though it was the organ of a Southern church with close connections to the white Southern Methodists. They, like others, combined race pride and self-help in economic and social matters with protest in regard to political and civil rights. The A.M.E. Zion *Quarterly Review* was in general a conservative magazine, but as earlier the most accommodating of the church publications was the *Southwestern Christian Advocate* of the Methodist Church, North. Isaiah B. Scott, who edited the paper between 1896 and 1904, was a graduate of the Methodist Central Tennessee College at Nashville who had served as president of Wiley University before being called to the *Advocate,* and in 1904 he became missionary bishop to Africa. His philosophy was almost a replica of Washington's and he made protests only against mob violence. In contrast, his successor, R. E. Jones, a product of Gammon Seminary, started with a militant protest attitude, "commended" the Niagara Movement,[60] and often opposed much that the Tuskegeean approved, though he did not attack Washington directly. But beginning about the time he became president of the Louisiana Business League in 1910 he protested less, spoke more and more about business enterprise, made some highly favorable comments on Washington, and mentioned the N.A.A.C.P. only in incidental references.

    After surveying these examples, one is compelled to conclude that for the most part (except for Scott, Davis, and to a lesser extent Knox and J. C. Dancy [61] of the A.M.E. Zion *Quarterly Review*), Negro editors did not adopt an accommodating line, even when they were close to and heavily subsidized by Tuskegee. In varying degree it is true, and with the conspicuous exception of the consistently radical organs, they placed great reliance on racial solidarity, self-help, and economic accumulation. But most of them did not cease at any time to stress agitation, except in some cases for a brief period in the hopeless years 1899–1900. All explicitly insisted upon political and civil rights—ultimately if not immediately—though the most conservative among them regarded property accumulation and moral virtue as more helpful toward this end than agitation and soft-pedaled the idea of full citizenship rights for the immediate future. Several, such as B. J. Davis on the local level and Dancy on the national scene, enjoyed political careers of some distinction, while Moore, Knox,

Chase, and Fortune dabbled avidly in political waters. Even of the most conservative editors studied—Davis, Knox, Scott and Dancy—three maintained active political interests. And since in spite of Washington's prestige and money, agitation for political and civil rights and against discrimination and oppression filled so many columns in most papers, it seems correct to assume that this was what the editors believed their readers wanted. (This conclusion is fortified by the expressed outlook of the politicians who were not responsible to an electorate but only to Tuskegee, and whose publicly expressed views were therefore more conservative than those of the editors who had to be more responsive to public opinion.) Except for Scott and perhaps Dancy, the editors of the Washington orbit—and there is no reason to believe that a larger sampling would provide a significantly different picture—simply failed to express themselves as Washington did. Even Davis, though his editorials sank to the lowest depths of sycophancy, was more explicit about his ultimate aims than Washington was, and at times breathed a militance that Washington never expressed.

In view of the facts, two pertinent questions suggest themselves: Why did Washington permit the tone of protest to assume the importance it did in journals of his orbit, and why did these journals, several with a militant outlook, support Washington? Either or both of two hypotheses may explain the paradox of Washington's supporting agitating newspapers. He may have been willing to support a journal that did not adopt an accommodating tone as long as that organ supported him personally. It is also possible that Washington was aware that he had to work with people as he found them and could not expect his supporters always to agree with him. There is evidence to support both of these hypotheses.

In the first place Washington's correspondence shows that he was simply unable to commend rigid adherence from the editors he aided. Two striking cases were Fortune and Moore, who in spite of extensive financial assistance and, in Moore's case, Washington's part ownership of the journals he edited, proved unwilling to stick to the Tuskegee line. Washington, of course, was slow to criticize journals less close in their relationships with him. Yet at times he became rather irked. Once he wrote sharply to a western supporter, Nick Chiles of the Topeka *Plaindealer*. Chiles replied vigorously that Washington's program was all right for the South, but not elsewhere.

"We think," he said, "you will finally come to realize that it is not only wealth and education that are needed by the Negro—but a little more manhood and courage to go with it." Washington replied in gentler fashion that while he feared reaction to Chiles' editorial, copies of which had been widely distributed over the South, he agreed that agitation had its uses, and that the different methods of himself and Chiles were both necessary.[62]

It becomes apparent, then, that there were several reasons why editors supported Washington. A few agreed with his conciliatory philosophy. The majority were sympathetic with his emphasis on economic accumulation and racial solidarity. Many stressed the protest implications in his thought and felt that his accommodating tendencies were justified in view of his position. That friendship for Washington was not necessarily associated with an accommodating tone was indicated by a review Cyrus Field Adams wrote of the *Souls of Black Folk* in 1903. Adams saw no contradiction between the ideas of Du Bois and Washington. He praised Du Bois' eloquent and sincere appeal, but thought he had misunderstood Washington and done him a great injustice, as Washington had never advised the race to give up its rights.[63] There were also those, of course, who joined the Washington bandwagon from selfish calculations—not to say dire necessity—and for whatever Washington's cash, prestige, and influence might bring. In many cases the motives were undoubtedly largely mixed.

It is also clear that Washington had more than one motive for allowing the journals in his orbit to protest and agitate. The evidence indicates that Washington recognized some value in agitation and was willing to let his friends use this technique as long as they supported him personally. Furthermore, it is clear that Washington was simply unable to control the activities of even certain of his closest associates. In short, it is apparent that Washington could not exercise a dictatorial policy over the Negro press. While powerful, he needed the support of the press, just as some journals needed him. In such a situation considerable compromise was necessary.

An examination of the role of Negro lawyers in the ideological controversies during the ascendancy of Booker T. Washington is especially illuminating. For, even though they formed but a tiny proportion of the professional class, they were particularly influential in the Negro community and were active among the radicals to an extent well out of proportion to their numbers. Among Washington's leading critics in Chicago were lawyers E. H. Morris and Ferdinand Barnett; Archibald Grimké and Clement Morgan were prominent in the Trotter circle in Boston; Niagarite W. Ashbie Hawkins, who represented the N.A.A.C.P. in its fight against the Baltimore municipal segregation ordinance, was a leading radical there; and F. L. McGhee of St. Paul was credited with suggesting the Niagara Movement. And out of twenty-three signers of Du Bois' London circular attacking Washington in 1910, nine were lawyers.

Particularly evident among the lawyers was the contrast between Northern and Southern leaders in their attitude toward Washington. Due to limited opportunities for legal practice, most of the Southern lawyers—men like the bankers J. T. Settle of Memphis, W. E. Mollison of Vicksburg and J. C. Napier of Nashville—were primarily businessmen or politicians, or both. As Southerners they were likely to agree with the conciliatory tone of Washington's utterances. As businessmen they naturally supported his economic emphasis. As bankers, real estate agents, and professional men dependent upon the support of the Negro community they were sympathetic with Washington's philosophy of economic chauvinism. And as politicians they were compelled to court the favor of the man who held the patronage strings during the administrations of Roosevelt and Taft.

An occasional Southern lawyer was ambivalent toward Washington.[64] However, I have found only two who cared to oppose him openly. One was James H. Hayes of Richmond, who organized a National Negro Suffrage League in 1902 and planned to contest the Virginia disfranchisement laws in the federal courts. Washington objected to the emotional character of Hayes' agitation and through coercion applied by his power over the press, and through the influence of mutual friends, brought Hayes around to his point of view —though only temporarily.[65] The other Southern lawyer who openly opposed Washington was McKinley's register of the Treasury, Judson W. Lyons of Augusta. He had successfully sought Washington's aid for reappointment to his post after Roosevelt became president, but he failed in his bid for a third term in 1905 because he had come to identify himself with Washington's critics.[66]

In contrast to the Southern lawyers, most of the important Northern attorneys and jurists appear to have made law the cornerstone of their careers. Little is known of the lesser lawyers, but it is likely that, like their Southern counterparts, they depended almost entirely on Negroes for their business and eked out a modest living in real estate, insurance, and collecting claims. The more eminent Northern lawyers were, as far as can be ascertained, all men of Northern birth or long Northern residence, often educated at the best Northern colleges, and members of that older upper class that to a considerable extent depended on whites for its livelihood. It would be expected, therefore, that they would be unlikely to champion the doctrines of "no social equality," economic chauvinism, and industrial education, or relegate civil and political rights to a secondary place, as Washington did. Nevertheless, Washington secured the whole-hearted support of some and the half-hearted support of many. Illustrative of the former were Clifford H. Plummer of Boston and Wilford Smith of New York. Trotter hired Plummer as his attorney when Washington sued the editor for the "Boston Riot" incident, but the lawyer was secretly in touch with Tuskegee in the case and later acted as Washington's undercover agent in Trotter's New England Suffrage League. Smith represented Washington in the same case, and was attorney for the Alabama test cases on disfranchisement and jury discrimination financed by Washington.[67]

There were no more consistent opponents of Washington than Morris and Barnett of Chicago. Kentucky-born E. H. Morris, graduate of St. Patrick's College in Chicago, was a distinguished and wealthy corporation lawyer, attorney for Cook County, twice a member of the state legislature, chief figure among Negro Oddfellows, and a valiant defender of Negro rights. When, in his address before the Bethel Literary Association in 1904, he accused the Tuskegeean of believing in Negro inferiority, racial segregation, and eschewing politics, the alarm of the Tuskegee group was therefore eminently justified. Ferdinand Barnett, graduate of Northwestern University and founder of the first Negro newspaper in Illinois (the *Conservator,* 1878), and his wife, the noted anti-lynching crusader, Ida Wells, had both been active in the battle for Negro rights ever since their marriage in 1895. In contrast, Barnett's former law partner, S. Laing Williams, and his wife, the noted club woman, Fannie Barrier Williams, assiduously cultivated Washington. From the time of their marriage in 1887 the Williamses played a leading role in social welfare activities in Chicago's Negro community. During the height of Washington's power, Mrs. Williams was busy writing and talking on the self-help of the Negro women's club movement and other organizations, and the importance of middle-class virtues. Her husband, Washington's closest friend in Chicago, ghost-wrote the Tuskegeean's book on Frederick Douglass, and for his loyalty was rewarded with the post of federal assistant district attorney.[68] Nevertheless we find Williams a vice-president of the Chicago N.A.A.C.P. in 1913.

A third couple were the Terrells of Washington. In almost every respect they epitomized Du Bois' concept of talented-tenth leadership. Raised in Virginia and Washington, D.C., Robert H. Terrell had graduated as commencement orator and the first Negro with an A.B. *cum laude* from Harvard College in 1884. While teaching classics in Washington he obtained a law degree from Howard University, participated in movements for political and civil rights, and encouraged the development of Negro business enterprise, serving as secretary of the ill-fated Capital Savings Bank. Mary Church Terrell, the daughter of a wealthy Memphis real estate dealer, had been educated at Oberlin and had taught at Wilberforce and in Washington before she married her colleague at the M Street High School in 1891. Subsequently she became the first president of the National Association of Colored Women and for a dozen years (1895–1901 and 1906–1911) a member of the Washington Board of Education. In 1901 at the suggestion of his closest friend in the nation's capital, the real estate dealer Whitefield McKinlay, Washington secured the appointment of Terrell, then principal of the high school, as a magistrate in the District of Columbia. From then on Terrell was a member of the Tuskegee circle; he was among those defending Washington when Morris spoke at the Bethel Literary in 1904, and subsequently Washington's opponents seem to have been his chief obstacle in securing reappointments.[69]

Nevertheless, both Terrell and his wife flirted with the opposition. The judge tailored his addresses to suit his audience. As during the 1880's he could either protest vigorously against discrimination and stress the role of the talented tenth and the importance of higher education, or he could enthusiastically endorse the economic formulas of Washington's National Negro Business League.[70] Similarly he tailored his activities in regard to Washington to fit the occasion. By the summer of 1905 Washington felt that Terrell was not behaving as a "supposed friend" should. Soon the exasperating inconsistency of his wife's speeches was arousing Tuskegee ire. On February 19, 1906, Washington wrote Terrell that while he liked her conservative speech at Charlotte, he found it curious that his friends made radical speeches in the North and conservative speeches in the South. In the fall of 1906 Mrs. Terrell was working hand in glove with Washington to prevent Du Bois from securing an appointment as assistant superintendent of schools in the nation's capital—a post awarded to a Tuskegee supporter, Roscoe Conkling Bruce.[71] But the fat was in the fire when she took up the cause of the Brownsville soldiers in co-operation with the Constitution League. Toward the end of 1906 she even indirectly criticized the Tuskegeean by an attack on the race leadership that told dialect stories, counseled an inferior sort of education, and advised accommodation to other discrimination. She was reported as saying privately that this speech was intended to "unshirt" Washington. When Terrell himself was reported shocked at Washington's actions toward the defenders of the discharged soldiers, Collector Anderson thought "Judge Terrell had better take a stitch in his tongue." He accused the judge of posing as a Tuskegee man when Washington was around, and yet managing to support all of Washington's enemies.[72]

Mrs. Terrell further offended Tuskegee by a speech before the American Missionary Association in 1907 in which she caustically criticized the South. R. W. Tyler, fourth auditor of the Treasury, expressed the agitation of the Tuskegee group when he declared that "some one ought to muzzle Mary Church Terrell," and wrote an editorial for the *Age* which closed with the remark that "what we now want as a race, is less agitators and more constructors."

So irritating was her work with the N.A.A.C.P. that Washington wrote Terrell how embarrassing it was to have his wife connected with it. Since the new organization was likely to attack Taft, her activities put those who had worked for Terrell's reappointment in a difficult spot. "Of course," added Washington, "I am not seeking to control anyone's actions, but I simply want to know where we stand." [73] Nevertheless, Mrs. Terrell remained active in the N.A.A.C.P. and became a vice-president of the Washington branch. However, the judge was supported by the Bookerites and was opposed by the anti-Bookerites for appointment to the Howard University Law School. When Anderson called attention to the fact that Terrell was associated with Du Bois in an essay contest sponsored by the N.A.A.C.P., and commented that it was unfortunate that he was one of "our fellows" who "will not 'shinny on their own side,' " Washington apparently thought it desirable to cultivate Terrell by asking him to give the next commencement address at Tuskegee.[74] Indeed, the Judge proved to be an outstanding jurist and a consummate politician, for he remained in office throughout the Wilson administration in the face of opposition from Southern senators and a sharp drop in the number of Negro officeholders.

William H. Lewis, the leading Negro lawyer in metropolitan Boston, was a native of Virginia who had been educated at Amherst and Harvard, and had started out as an ardent agitator and anti-Bookerite. By the time he was elected to the state legislature in 1901, however, he was coming to have respect for Washington to whom he wrote that "while we may differ I trust that we may always be friends." Washington soon recommended Lewis to Roosevelt for the post of assistant district attorney in Boston; Lewis was "very graciously" received by the president, who was glad to hear that the lawyer was more in agreement with Washington than formerly. Lewis was the only one of the five Bostonians at the Louisville Convention of the Afro-American Council who identified himself with Washington, and he further indicated his conservatism by acting as chairman of the "Boston Riot" meeting in August 1903. He received the coveted post in the same year, was appointed special attorney in charge of naturalization affairs for the New England states in 1907, and in 1908 he was chosen by Washington to be the Negro to second Taft's nomination. While the evidence suggests that Lewis cultivated Washington for political reasons, he rationalized his behavior with the remark that the Tuskegeean was trying to bring the wooden horse inside the walls of Troy. Though in his public utterances Lewis made eulogistic references to Washington and usually hewed closely to the Tuskegee line, he still collaborated with members of the opposition on occasion. In October 1907, for example, he held a banquet for Du Bois; and this and similar actions led Anderson to resent his behavior in view of all that Washington had done for Lewis. Yet Washington not only failed to break with Lewis, but in 1911 secured for him the highest federal appointment yet accorded a Negro—that of assistant United States attorney-general.[75]

Frederick L. McGhee (died 1912) of St. Paul, a leader in the civil rights movement of Minnesota during the 1890's, was on friendly terms with Washington at the opening of the century. A leading Catholic layman, he was employed by the Tuskegeean in 1904 as an emissary to the Maryland hierarchy in an effort to secure its opposition to disfranchisement proposals there, and as a lobbyist with Senators on the Crum appointment. Active in the affairs of the Afro-American Council, McGhee had charge first of its legislative committee and then of its legal bureau. He posed as a Washington supporter in Council affairs, yet found it necessary to make unconvincing explanations as to why he opposed Fortune's election to the presidency at both the 1902 and 1903 conventions. Though it was in 1904 that he worked for Washington on his political missions, Du Bois already regarded him as "uncompromisingly" anti-Washington, and by 1905 he was openly allied with the radicals, serving as head of the Niagara Movement's Legal Department.[76]

Two older leaders are especially worthy of consideration—D. Augustus Straker and Archibald Grimké. Straker, a successful jurist in Detroit, maintained, as he had done during the 1880's, that the race problem could be solved only by a two-pronged approach of economic self-help on the part of Negroes, and of whites according Negroes economic opportunity and political rights. He unsuccessfully sought Washington's assistance to obtain a consulship in 1901, and a few years later wrote the Tuskegeean that he would "not stand silently by and see you falsely accused or abused, while I may not agree with you in details." Yet until he died in 1906 Washington's critics considered Straker one of their number, one "who never gave up his ideals and never crawled or kow-towed to the 'New South.' "[77]

Archibald H. Grimké illustrates the oscillation in thought characteristic of some of the intellectuals. A graduate of Harvard Law School in 1874, he established himself in Boston where he married a white woman and became a successful lawyer. An independent in politics he was rewarded with the post of consul in Santo Domingo, 1894–98, and supported the Progressives in 1912–13. During the disturbing years at the turn of the century, when the Hampton-Tuskegee philosophy enjoyed its greatest vogue, Grimké urged Negroes to do well whatever work it fell to them to do, no matter how menial, and by success achieved through industry, thrift, intelligence, and the accumulation of wealth, arrest increasing white indifference. But Grimké was soon associated with the Trotter group, and Washington invited him to the Carnegie Hall Conference only after considerable hesitation, as he thought Grimké "a noisy, turbulent and unscrupulous" man "more bent upon notoriety and keeping up discord than any other motive." Unexpectedly Grimké was impressed by Washington's explanation of his policy, and Moton reported the lawyer as saying that Washington was undoubtedly working for the best interests of the race. Though Emmett Scott learned that Grimké did remain friendly with Trotter, Washington took steps to cultivate him. Grimké temporarily endorsed Washington's views on franchise limitations, though by 1905 he was again opposed to them. Moreover, Washington benefited from the irascible personality of Du Bois who insulted Grimké in 1905. The turning point in the relationship between Grimké and Washington may have come as a result of Grimké's stand on the Brownsville affair; he was reliably reported as "savagely denouncing" the president, the secretary of War, and the Tuskegeean on the matter at a meeting in 1908. From then on Grimké was distinctly of the opposition, serving as president of the N.A.A.C.P.'s Washington chapter and forthrightly attacking all forms of discrimination.[78]

Of those who adopted a consistently uncompromising philosophy of assimilation and protest, few were more respected than the noted author Charles W. Chesnutt. A successful lawyer, accepted in high political and social circles in Cleveland, Chesnutt championed full equality, advocated intermarriage, opposed doctrines of race pride and race solidarity, and believed the solution to the race problem lay in whites living up to their democratic ideas more than in Negroes improving themselves. Even though the two men were thus decidedly in disagreement Chesnutt and Washington maintained a friendly relationship. Washington assiduously cultivated the prominent writer and lawyer, and Chesnutt for his part was of assistance in arranging philanthropic contacts for Washington's Cleveland visits. Nevertheless, Chesnutt always frankly stated his ideological opposition to Washington. He forthrightly told the Tuskegeean that he disagreed with the latter's support of a restricted franchise, his emphasis on economic accumulation rather than on political and civil rights, his tendency to dwell on Negro weaknesses, his overemphasis on industrial education, and his faith in the good will of the Southern white man. The available Chesnutt correspondence with the anti-Bookerites is incomplete, but he undoubtedly maintained cordial relations with members of the radical group, spoke at the Niagara Movement meeting in 1908, and from 1910 on was actively associated with the N.A.A.C.P.[79] Thus Chesnutt, courted by both sides, appears to have been a radical by conviction, but one who respected the views of others. He frankly stated his differences with Washington both publicly and privately, but declined to enter the fray.

It is evident that though lawyers played a prominent role in the opposition, it is likely that the majority of them either passively or actively endorsed Washington's leadership. Practically all of the Southern lawyers did. Though direct evidence is lacking, probably most of the Northern lawyers, who were primarily petty businessmen dependent on the Negro community for their living, also supported Washington, for they would espouse his philosophy of economic accumulation and economic chauvinism. On the other hand, the most distinguished Northern lawyers had been educated at the best Northern universities, and (except for Terrell) appeared to have had their economic and often even their social roots in the white community. These men would therefore, in the normal course of events, be unlikely to favor soft-pedaling political demands, accepting segregation, sneering at "the intellectuals," or emphasizing racial solidarity. And in fact many exhibited strong anti-Bookerite tendencies. It thus is apparent that support of Washington was in part a function of social status and economic interest.

The magnitude of Washington's personal influence cannot be ignored when considering the forces that shaped ideological expression during his ascendancy. People like to be in accord with currently admired figures. Moreover, the evidence is clear that especially after he came to political power, many former critics became supporters. In proportion to their numbers, more eminent lawyers than members of any other professional group dared to publicly oppose Washington. Yet even among those who either opposed him at first, or who might normally been expected to do so, he wielded a substantial influence. Men such as Grimké and Chesnutt wanted to see value in his program and therefore tried to arrive at a *modus vivendi* with him. And this desire undoubtedly influenced others such as Terrell, Straker, and Lewis, who were also largely motivated by personal ambition. It would be a mistake to call these individuals insincere, for self-interest and social idealism are inextricably interwoven in human motivation and the power of rationalization is strong. Moreover, almost anyone, white or Negro, who wanted to do anything about the race problem at least tried to work with Washington. Undoubtedly just as Washington advanced his own career and believed he was serving the best interests of the race by his program, so men like Terrell and Lewis probably justified their action in a similar way. The fact is that these men simply never gave up their relationship with the opposition.

Thus among the lawyers the complex motivations entering into the ideological expression of Negro leaders are made particularly evident. For here a group of outstanding men who clearly met every requirement of Du Bois' definition of the talented tenth cannot be said to have been in the majority clearly for or consistently opposed to Washington. Not only did those dependent on the Negro community for their livelihood naturally espouse much of Washington's philosophy, but the general drift of opinion, the prestige of Washington, the ambitions of individual men, and the configurations of power all served to incline toward Washington the very men who might have been most expected to oppose him.

In reviewing the data we have presented on the thinking of an illustrative sampling of Negro intellectuals, it is evident that most of them—even those with a college education—were at one time or another (if not all the time) either enthusiastic or luke-warm supporters of Booker T. Washington, and that doctrines of racial pride, economics, solidarity, and self-help loomed large in their thinking, though of course their goal was full citizenship rights. This is true even of Du Bois, the most illustrious intellectual of all.

Support for Washington's program was strongest at the turn of the century, when many who later became outspoken critics espoused his program. By 1903, as Kelly Miller pointed out, few thoughtful men endorsed him and his platform unreservedly, and Washington's recognition of this fact was what prompted the Carnegie Hall Conference. During the last decade of Washington's life more and more of the intellectuals drifted into the ranks of the radicals and the N.A.A.C.P.; and even some of his strongest supporters came to give qualified endorsement to the position of the opposition, and themselves came to take a more radical stand, even while remaining personally loyal to Washington.

It is true that the radicals drew most of their support from the college-educated group (though who was more consistently radical than H. C. Smith, who had only a high school education?). It is also evident that conservatism was, by and large, more prevalent among those educators and ministers who themselves lacked a college training, and that the consistent supporters of Washington were largely concentrated in this group. But it is just as true that most of the college-educated elite were either wholeheartedly or partially in support of Washington, at least for a time, and saw at least temporary value in various forms of group separatism; and that some of the chief radical figures themselves at one time or another approved of these things. To assume that, because the leadership of the opposition came from the college-educated elite, more than a small minority of this group were consistently antagonistic to Washington would then be erroneous.

The reasons for the support accorded to Washington by the intellectuals were several. The discouragement characteristic of the period, especially around 1900, certainly swayed many. Washington's money, prestige, and influence were also important factors. Ambitious lawyers, educators, editors, and even ministers felt it worth their while to cultivate the Tuskegeean. Thus the power structure of the Negro community not only strengthened a conservative tendency that was already gaining popularity, but it also contributed substantially to the instability of the ideological expression of many leaders, most notably among the lawyers, editors, and teachers at liberal arts colleges.

Most radical in their expression, by and large, were the lawyers; the ministers and especially the educators were mostly conservative; while the editors were in between. This correlation is undoubtedly related to the social role of the individuals concerned. The radical lawyers and doctors tended to be Northern men with their economic and sometimes their social connections in the white community, though some men of similar background did support Washington.[80] Ministers with their otherworldly interests quite easily fell into an accommodating position. School administrators depended on white public opinion and philanthropy. Even the ministers, who were more directly responsive to Negro rather than white thought, were more outspoken than the school presidents and principals. The newspapers were influenced by Washington directly, and by the general trends of thought. Their dependence on the Negro market seems to have worked in two ways, however. On the one hand they were ordinarily zealous advocates of economic self-help and economic chauvinism. On the other hand their readers apparently did not intend to forget "the promise of American life," and the editors gave considerable emphasis to protest and agitation.

Finally, it cannot be overlooked that the aspirations of the professional men, no matter how conservative their utterances, included integration and the attainment of citizenship rights; and this aspiration they expressed as an ultimate goal where they did not insist upon it as an immediate one. Therefore, although the temporary advantages of the disadvantages in segregation, disillusionment with protest and politics, and the influence of Washington all served to make Negro thought in this period far more separatist, economically orientated, self-helpish, and accommodating than it has been in more optimistic periods, it must be emphasized that the leaders as a group hoped for ultimate equality and citizenship rights, whatever the tactical advantages that might be derived from a conservative program.

It must be concluded that, broadly speaking, while the intellectuals formed the backbone of the Niagara Movement and the N.A.A.C.P., most of them for one reason or another were friendly with Washington, or at least gave him greater or lesser support, though they were not always consistent in doing this. Moreover, to the extent that they were forming the new middle class dependent on the Negro market, they espoused the ideas of race pride and economic solidarity. The assimilationist orientation of the anti-Bookerites is central in Negro thinking, but its fundamental importance should not permit one to minimize the rising tide of sentiment favoring a "cultural pluralism" that was developing in the age of Booker T. Washington and which became the ideological basis of the post-war "New Negro."

CHAPTER XIII

BOOKER T. WASHINGTON
AND THE POLITICIANS

Politicians, though they were frequently college graduates and were often successful editors, lawyers, school presidents, ministers, or businessmen, were not specifically included by Du Bois as members of the talented tenth. And despite their political interests, in overt ideological expression they were, on the whole, the most conservative of the elite groups during the age of Washington.

Of the Reconstruction and late nineteenth-century politicians, only a few remained in office into the Roosevelt-Washington era. Most of those who did not retire into obscurity had turned to the ministry, education, law, or business, even when continuing to play a minor role politically. Generally, whether in or out of office they expressed a conservative point of view. This was true, for example, of the two most prominent officials appointed by President McKinley: Blanche K. Bruce (d. 1897), register of the Treasury; and the lawyer, Henry Plummer Cheatham, recorder of deeds (1897–1901). Cheatham, a graduate of Shaw University, a member of Congress from 1891–93, and after his political career was over the director of an orphanage, pretty well summed up his attitude at the Afro-American Council in December, 1898, when he made a vigorous plea for moderation and conservatism and asserted agitation in the North made it impossible for Negroes in the South to live peaceably with their white neighbors.[1]

Representative of the ex-Congressmen about whom adequate material is available was Thomas E. Miller, a member of the college-educated elite (Lincoln University, 1872), who became the first president of the state college at Orangeburg, South Carolina, in 1896. From then on his tone was even more obsequious than it had been at the time of the constitutional convention of 1895. Speaking in 1902 he expressed a spirit of love and charity for all, played up the themes of Negro military contributions, faithfulness, lawfulness, and obedience, and urged Negroes to stay in the South: "The only thing that surprises . . . is that we have fared so well at the hands of the Southern white man." He spoke in Social Darwinist terms of struggle and asserted that it would take time to achieve full citizenship, which would be accomplished chiefly through frugality and self-help. It was in the race's power, he said, to right every wrong, but it could not be done "by croaking and fault finding, and whining and pining . . . by resolving in meeting or by making bitter speeches." Instead, advancement would have to come through internal means, through the exercises of frugality, buying land, and living in friendship with their white neighbors. Just as the Jews, by unity and economic accumulation, had become practically the rulers of Europe, so also the Negroes could succeed. Yet in 1911 Governor Cole Blease dismissed Miller from his post for opposing him in the previous election.[2]

One man not typical was George H. White, the last Negro to sit in Congress before the late 1920's. Born a slave, he graduated from Howard University in 1877, served in the North Carolina Legislature, and entered Congress (1897–1901) on the wave of the fusion movement. His expressed philosophy was a combination of protest and emphasis on rights along with self-help and economic advancement. Even after the Wilmington riot he failed to adopt the abject tone of many of his contemporaries. In Congress he spoke movingly of the Negro's rights guaranteed by the Constitution, for the treatment of the Negro as a man—for a man's chance to carve out his own destiny as a distinct race—and for "unmitigated justice." Afterwards, since Washington's support for a federal post was necessary, but unavailable, he practiced law in Philadelphia where he continued to urge thoughtful agitation by the best minds of the race, worked with the Constitution League on the Brownsville Case in 1906, and became a member of the executive committee of the N.A.A.C.P.'s Philadelphia branch.[3]

In general, the McKinley-Hanna politicians met disappointment and frustration under Roosevelt and Washington. In the last chapter we discussed the case of Judson W. Lyons, the last Negro to serve on the Republican National Committee, who, though reappointed register of the Treasury when Roosevelt first took office, was not reappointed again in 1905 in large part because of his association with the radicals. Similarly the lawyer Richard T. Greener had continued as consul at Vladivostok until 1906, but was unsuccessful thereafter in his pursuit of political office. This ambition was probably what led him to work for Washington as a spy at the Harpers Ferry Meeting of the Niagara Movement. Though Washington seems to have made some effort to obtain Greener a post, nothing materialized. Greener retired to Chicago an embittered man, privately critical of Washington, though not actively associated with the radicals.[4]

Like Greener, and unlike Lyons, the celebrated William A. Pledger (d. 1904) of Georgia decided it was advisable to cultivate the Tuskegeean. The son of a slaveowner, he studied at Atlanta University, held positions in the customs, land, and immigration offices in various parts of the South, and published a succession of newspapers in Athens and Atlanta. During the 1880's and early 1890's Pledger was the most influential figure among the state's Negro Republicans. He was widely known by his contemporaries as a militant crusader, though a recent study of the Negro in Georgia politics pictures him as chiefly interested in political preferment. At the founding meeting of the Afro-American League in 1890 he made a militant address declaring that disobedience to the constitution was at the bottom of the race question and attacking all the evils of the emerging race system in the still disloyal South. Speaking at the Atlanta Exposition in 1895 his tone was more conciliatory but his message clear: "The Afro-American asks only for justice. He knows that he is entitled to that much . . . and feels that it is his duty to ask for it." Yet he also, as he said before the Bethel Literary Association in 1896, urged the race to upbuilding along business and commercial lines. And in 1900, as chairman of the Republican state executive committee, he even supported the idea of a straight white ticket in order to get whites to vote Republican. Pledger played an active role in the revived Afro-American Council, being elected first vice-president in 1902 and 1903. After the St. Paul meeting in 1902 Pledger complained to Emmett Scott of the hostility of the Tuskegeean, whom he wished would "place him right with the President" as he could not reach Roosevelt even for consultation on Georgia matters. Scott told Pledger that Washington could do no more than suggest that Roosevelt confer with Pledger, but privately advised

Washington that it would be wise to help a man of Pledger's character, since he could "be won away now" as he could "not be perhaps later." By the middle of 1903 Pledger was definitely in the Washington orbit, and at his death in 1904 the pro-Tuskegee Washington *Colored American* commented on his fearless fight for justice and his recently becoming "an ardent champion of Dr. Washington." [5]

P. B. S. Pinchback (along with Robert Smalls, collector of the Port of Beaufort until 1915,[6] one of the handful of Reconstruction leaders who held a significant political position in the twentieth century) perhaps best represented the successful politician who veered with the winds to stay in office. The son of a wealthy planter, Pinchback during Reconstruction was a fearless speaker on behalf of Negro rights, but an unstable politician twisting and turning from faction to faction in the tortured course of Louisiana politics. One-time acting governor of Louisiana, and the unsuccessful claimant in a contested election for the Senate, he held various federal appointments through the years, edited the New Orleans *Louisianian,* and was active in the convention movement. Though his speeches during the early years of the century breathed a spirit of protest and emphasized political rights, it was only natural that he would arrive at an understanding with the Tuskegeean, who by 1902 had started on his ceaseless task of securing federal posts for the "governor." When, in January 1904, E. H. Morris attacked Washington at the Bethel Literary, Pinchback, whom the *Bee* sarcastically noted had some months before bitterly denounced Washington, was now among his defenders. From then on Washington did his best to keep Pinchback in some sort of office.[7]

The paradoxes of Negro thought during Washington's ascendancy are best observed in those of his followers who aspired to political office. Some, such as H. A. Rucker (a McKinley holdover), collector of internal revenue at Atlanta, 1897–1910, who remained consistently loyal to Washington, Whitefield McKinlay, a Charleston-born Washington real estate dealer and the Tuskegeean's most trusted friend in the capital, who became collector of the Port of Georgetown in 1910, and J. C. Napier, the lawyer-banker-politician of Nashville, were conservative businessmen to start with. Others such as W. T. Vernon, who left the presidency of the A.M.E. Church's Western University at Quindaro, Kansas, to replace Lyons as register of the Treasury, and R. W. Tyler, Ohio journalist and minor officeholder who was made auditor for the Navy in 1907 as a reprisal at Senator Foraker for his defense of the Brownsville soldiers, were venal politicians, anxious for political preferment while mouthing the philosophy of moral and economic fundamentals. Moreover, they proved no more loyal to Washington than to anyone else, and flirted with members of the opposition.[8]

In addition to R. H. Terrell and W. H. Lewis, who were discussed in the last chapter, five individuals will be taken as illustrative of Washington's appointees: J. C. Dancy, R. L. Smith, J. C. Napier, Charles W. Anderson, and James Weldon Johnson.

J. C. Dancy, recorder of deeds 1901–10, had been collector of customs at Wilmington, N.C., under Harrison and McKinley, and since 1892 editor of the A.M.E. Zion *Quarterly Review*. Dancy had been a close associate of J. C. Price and in a sense forms a link between the two distinguished conciliators. Friendly with Washington even before Roosevelt became president, Dancy maintained the Tuskegeean's support until the very end when Henry Lincoln Johnson demanded the recordership as his reward from the Taft administration for his role in depriving Lyons of his place on the Republican National Committee in 1908.[9] Washington praised Dancy for being "committed to rational conservatism as a means for solving the great problems now pressing upon us in the South." Just what rational conservatism was can be ascertained from the pages of the A.M.E. Zion *Quarterly Review*. On becoming editor, Dancy asserted: "The race needs more earnest, devoted, determined, active, self-sacrificing men and women, fewer grumblers, and critics, and constant calamity howlers." [10] He consistently urged patience, thrift, industry, frugality, hard work, and Christian character and just as consistently lauded the Tuskegeean. He did, of course, resent segregation, disfranchisement and mob violence, though he expressed himself "conservatively" on these matters.[11] As he said in 1909, no Negro believed in injustice, but experience showed that those who went about improving conditions quietly accomplished far more than those who resorted to denunciation and inflammatory speech-making. Elsewhere he elaborated: "We have learned that prudence is the sheet anchor of a successful life and that rational conservatism is a chief element in the triumph of great principles in the perpetuity of manhood rights and civil liberty." He praised the white citizens of North Carolina and urged Negroes to keep out of the courts, educate their children in the trades and in lessons of honor, virtue, industry, self-respect and piety, and exercise such tact, judgment, and discretion that they would no longer be an object of universal criticism.[12]

R. L. Smith, a native of Charleston and graduate of Atlanta University, founder of the Farmers' Improvement Society, and principal of the Oakland, Texas, Normal School, enunciated an accommodating philosophy but was an active politician. He was elected to the Texas Legislature in 1894 and 1896 from a predominantly white district.[13] Critical of the Reconstruction type of politician, he claimed that the great majority of whites, desirous of preparing Negroes for citizenship, were "perfectly willing to cooperate with any responsible individual . . . whose aim is to make the race better." Norris Wright Cuney's biographer pictured Smith as siding with a lily-white faction against Cuney. Charges that he had worked with the Democrats appeared to be among the reasons that Washington was unable to secure him a collectorship of internal revenue, but finally he was appointed deputy to the U.S. Marshal for the Texas eastern district in 1902. But nothing Washington could do prevented the removal of this "only significant Negro federal officeholder of Texas" in the general dismissal during the first years of the Taft administration.[14] Smith preached the Tuskegee line in public, but he actively engaged in legal action against "those practices which have for twenty years practically decitizenized our race," and privately thought that "Lynch law, peonage, whitecapping and all kindred evils have their root in the rape of the ballot." [15]

J. C. Napier, born near Nashville of an upper-class deliveryman who was closely associated with upper-class whites,[16] received his education at Wilberforce and Oberlin. He held a few minor state offices during Reconstruction, received his law degree from Howard University, and entered upon a career in the treasury service that lasted until 1884. Meanwhile, he had returned to Nashville where he had been elected to the City Council in 1870 and again for three terms 1878–84. He also was a member of the Republican State Executive Committee for sixteen years, usually chairman or secretary. In 1898 he was a candidate for Congress, and in 1900 he led an attack on the lily-white policies of Governor Brownlow. In addition to his political interests, Napier was a leading Nashville businessman and in 1903 helped found the One Cent Savings Bank which he served for many years as cashier. After 1900 Napier actively pushed his political ambitions with Washington, who offered him the presidency of the Business League in 1903; [17] and, finally, he became register of the Treasury in 1911.

Napier's addresses reveal that in spite of his enthusiasm for political activity and opposition to segregation, he expressed an accommodating philosophy. As Washington once said, in the twenty years he had been closely associated with Napier, "I have never heard Mr. Napier express a narrow or bitter thought toward the white race." In a characteristic address before the Bethel Literary Association in 1907 Napier predicted the disappearance of disfranchisement and Jim Crow, but held that this would not be accomplished by legislation, which would only result in "the most bitter opposition." Rather, through good character, intelligence, education, and industry, the Negro "must win the respect and esteem of the people by whom he is surrounded and with whom he comes into contact." [18]

Outside of his secretary, Emmett Scott, no one was closer and more useful to Washington than Charles W. Anderson, collector of internal revenue in New York, 1905–15. Born in Ohio, he made his career in New York State, and all of his adult life was active in politics. Despite a limited education, he was proud of his intellectual interests.[19] In 1889 he wrote to the *Age* expressing discouragement over "the utter lack of interest taken in politics by the younger and better informed men of our race" in New York, and urged a new Republican club to overcome this apathy, do the leg work of politics, and work for civil rights and better government. His efforts were regarded as largely responsible for the New York Civil Rights Law of 1895. He climbed steadily in Republican circles, becoming a state committeeman by 1900, and a member of the state racing commission, 1898–1905, where he was when Washington secured his appointment as collector. As a politician who worked quietly behind the scenes, Anderson was not often given to philosophizing publicly about his racial views. Yet we do have a few illuminating comments. In 1908 he wrote Washington praising the gubernatorial candidate, Charles Evans Hughes, for coming out "flat-footed for an enforcement of the Constitution and the laws. . . . He did not waste any time talking to the brethren about their duties. . . . This is the sort of stuff that rings in the hearts of men. It is too bad that we cannot have more of it." [20]

A close friend of Anderson's was James Weldon Johnson, a native of Jacksonville and graduate of Atlanta University, who had enjoyed a successful career in the early twentieth century as a songwriter and librettist for Broadway musicals. In his autobiography, written after fourteen years as national organizer and executive secretary of the N.A.A.C.P., he recalled how Anderson placed him in charge of the local Republican club and then arranged for his consular appointments first to Venezuela and then to Nicaragua. What Johnson did not tell us is that it was through Washington that Anderson obtained these appointments. Johnson himself felt "deeply indebted" to Washington for the "invaluable service" the latter had done in recommending him to the president and secretary of state; and from time to time he wrote the Tuskegean long, chatty letters about life in Puerto Cabello and Corinto.[21]

In later years Johnson referred to Washington's Atlanta address as illogical, but in the early years of the century the shrewd writer and diplomat referred to the opposition as "the enemy" and Washington regarded him as "a first class man." [22] Johnson, of course, was no rationalizer of discrimination, as is evident from his novel, *The Autobiography of an Ex-Colored Man* (1912). It was Joel Spingarn who, in 1916, had the perspicacity to propose the *"coup d'état"* of securing Johnson, then writing editorials for the *Age,* as national organizer for the N.A.A.C.P. Du Bois, when consulted, also thought he would be "entirely desirable." [23] One suspects that Johnson's desirability was enhanced by his earlier identification with the Washington group.

Unquestionably Negro politicians and ex-politicians desired full constitutional rights, though publicly they almost all expressed a philosophy that must be described as accommodating or "conservative." Men like Judson Lyons and George H. White were clearly exceptional, and naturally they were not in Washington's favor. Of course during Washington's ascendancy politicians found it convenient to express publicly the Tuskegee doctrine—and consequently their expression was remarkably unlike that of the political leaders of the 1870's, 1880's, and even 1890's. Thus the ideological paradox in regard to political activity that is evident in Washington's own career is exemplified also by the careers of his political appointees.

CHAPTER XIV

THE SOCIAL AND INTELLECTUAL ORIGINS OF THE NEW NEGRO

Negro urbanization and northward migration, the flowering of the jazz idiom, the Garvey Back-to-Africa movement, the burgeoning of Negro literature and art, the expanding work of the Urban League, and the anti-lynching campaign and other activities of the N.A.A.C.P. were developments that collectively attracted considerable attention. And when *Survey Graphic* issued its "Harlem" number in 1925 (revised and published in book form as *The New Negro*), it seemed that a "New Negro" had matured and that a "Harlem Renaissance" was under way. Few inquired into his antecedents, but many welcomed the race-conscious, assertive, race-proud New Negro, who was "digging up his past," achieving middle-class status and creating an artistic expression of his separate group life while aiming at integration into American society.

The editor of the New Negro volume was the Harvard Ph.D. and Rhodes scholar Alain Locke. He wrote feelingly of the new cultural expression that was comparable to "those nascent movements of folk-expression and self-determination which are playing a creative part in the world today. . . . As in India, in China, in Egypt, Ireland, Russia, Bohemia, Palestine and Mexico, we are witnessing the resurgence of a people." In fact, American Negroes felt themselves to be "the advance-guard of the African peoples." To Locke, the "old Negro,"—the "Uncle" and the "Mammy"—had long been something of a myth, having given place to a New Negro with "a spirit to seize, even in the face of an extortionate and heavy toll, a chance for the improvement of conditions." So independent and self-directed was the New Negro that he more than fulfilled the dreams of the racial leaders of twenty years before who spoke of developing race pride and stimulating race consciousness and of the desirability of race solidarity. American democratic ideals were the objectives of the Negro's outer life, but those of his inner life, resulting from "an attempt to repair a damaged group psychology and reshape a warped social perspective," took the form of a more positive self-respect and self-reliance, so that there had occurred a "rise from social disillusionment to race pride." The mainspring of Negro life in the post-war generation was a "belief in the efficiency of collective effort, in race cooperation." Yet Locke insisted that the ultimate success of the Negro in "this forced attempt to build his Americanism on race values" was possible "only through the fullest sharing in American culture and institutions."

Other writers in the volume developed the details of this broad theme, especially in literature and the arts. Arthur A. Schomburg, a propagandist for Negro history, declared "The American Negro must remake his past in order to make his future. . . . For him a group tradition must supply compensation for persecution, and pride of race the antidote for prejudice." The volume contained extensive material on Negro folk culture and African cultural origins. It gave considerable attention to the impact of urbanization and northward migration, which Charles S. Johnson said created "a new type of Negro." James Weldon Johnson described the new cultural life arising out of this urbanization in New York, and E. Franklin Frazier contributed an essay on "Durham: Capital of the Black Middle Class."

St. Clair Drake and Horace Cayton, in their study of Chicago Negroes, describe the spirit of the 1920's when leaders in the eight square mile Black Belt fostered the "dream of a Black Metropolis," where Negroes would support their own business and professional class and elect members of the race to high political office—a dream ideologically based on the philosophy of racial pride, solidarity, and self-help. To some this dream was but "a substitute for the real American dream of integration into American life;" but for others this "tactical maneuver within the framework of a broad strategy for complete equality" was itself an inspiring dream.[1]

This cluster of ideas emphasizing race pride, group solidarity, and self-dependence was growing more prominent for over a generation before Locke's book appeared. In fact, the phrase "New Negro" was used at least as early as 1895. The Cleveland *Gazette* on June 28, 1895, in commenting on the success crowning efforts to secure a New York Civil Rights Law, editorialized about "a class of colored people, the 'New Negro,' who have arisen since the war, with education, refinement and money." Refusing to be kept in the status occupied by their ancestors, they insisted upon their civil rights. A few months later J. W. E. Bowen spoke of the New Negro who, though waiting patiently until white Americans were conquered by their love of fair play, would make a great destiny for himself out of "the consciousness of a racial personality under the blaze of a new civilization."

There were indeed varying concepts of the New Negro. Fannie Barrier Williams and Booker T. Washington stressed the economic accomplishments and the efforts for self-help and self-betterment as indicating that the twentieth century would bring forth a New Negro. The white journalist Ray Stannard Baker described the new racial consciousness that resulted from segregation and discrimination. Where "the old-fashioned Negro preferred to go to the white man for everything . . . the New Negro . . . urges his friends to patronize Negro doctors and dentists, and to trade with Negro storekeepers." Du Bois also discerned a "new Negro businessman" developing a group economy.

Radicals, however, usually stressed the protest orientation of the New Negro. Principal Leslie Pinckney Hill of Cheyney Institute insisted that the Negro's ideal must not be the "dispirited or gentle Negroes of the 'mammy' type," who accepted an inferior position, but should be "this New Negro," a man of education who had learned to think and aspire, to feel pride and self-respect, and above all was determined to spare nothing in his effort to attain "full untrammeled American citizenship, or go down in the midst of a glorious warfare for it." William Pickens, dean of Morgan College (and formerly president of the N.A.A.C.P. branch at Talladega College) in his series of essays on *The New Negro,* 1916, enunciated a similar point of view and, like Locke later, held that the Negro stood on the threshold of a renaissance of civilization and culture like the darker and more handicapped peoples throughout the world.

Even some Bookerites spoke of the New Negro's insistence on his rights. S. Laing Williams, writing in 1908, felt that though crowded back and scorned, in the past forty years, by acquiring education and property and creating institutions to advance the race's welfare, the New Negro had risen "from dependence to independence," and hence had become conscious of his worth. This New Negro, "unlike his grandfather, is sensitive to wrongs, writhes under injustice and is fretful under discrimination." Thoroughly prepared to participate in American culture by virtue of his breeding, intelligence, and wealth, convinced that justice would eventually be accorded him, and suspecting "that his heroic patience has invited contempt rather than praise," he would insist on the rights which he had so well earned. Washington himself in an unusual statement once tactfully suggested that the emerging Negro landed proprietor was a new type of freedman, characterized by "sturdy independence," who expected political rights.[2]

While the conceptions varied, it was widely held that a New Negro, self-respecting, educated, prosperous, race-proud, self-dependent, deserving and demanding full citizenship, was arising. To the extent that such a type as the Old Negro had existed, the replacement of plantation and small-town paternalism by the impersonality of an industrialized, urbanized New South; the rise of a group economy in the urban ghettoes; and the growing number of educated, relatively prosperous self-made business and professional men had all worked to foster the change in Negro attitudes just described. Although representatives of the New Negro were certainly not new, the term symbolized the idea that large numbers of ex-slaves and their descendants were becoming proud of their race and self-dependent, and yet were assimilating to American middle-class standards and were anxious to partake of all the rights of American citizens.[3]

It is the thesis of this chapter that, as Locke implied, the roots of the New Negro, both as an artistic movement and as a racial outlook, were in the social and intellectual movements of the age of Washington. They lay in the accumulation of wealth and education, in the literary strivings that began around 1900, in the beginnings of urbanization and northward migration, in the development of the "group economy" and of an entrepreneurial and professional class dependent on that group economy, and above all in the philosophy—itself imbedded in the social situation of the Negro group and in the institutional development of the Negro community—of race pride, solidarity, and self-help. Previous chapters have dealt with the rising tide of racial solidarity in economic and social welfare institutions and in protest organizations, and with the rise of the middle class that exploited the Negro market and championed economic nationalism. This class, having achieved respectable economic and educational status, felt entitled to the rights that Washington said accrued to a race that had accomplished these things. Furthermore, we have dealt with the dualism in Negro thought, the racial consciousness that at once identified Negroes with American society and yet tended toward ethnocentrism. We shall now examine some of the purely intellectual aspects of the movement—the rising interest in Negro history, a new interest in Negro folk culture and in Africa, and the striving for a race literature and cultural life—what might be termed evidence of a cultural nationalism. We shall then examine some of the more extreme ethnocentric sentiments (most notably African emigrationism) and finally the roots of urbanization and northward migration that to a large extent underlay the spirit of the 1920's.

The Negro history movement gained fresh vigor during the age of Washington. Few actually wrote what purported to be history—and these were usually not outstanding in other fields of endeavor—but R. H. Terrell was undoubtedly representative when he expressed the hope that Negro children would be taught something about colored heroes. "It is lamentable," he said, "to see the little they know about their own people who have played such an important part in the development of this country." As Kelly Miller put it: "All great people glorify their history, and look back upon their early attainments with a spiritualized vision." [4]

Representative of the score of historical works that appeared during the age of Washington were W. H. Councill's *Lamp of Wisdom, Or Race History Illuminated,* 1898; Rev. C. T. Walker's *Appeal to Caesar,* 1900, which employed the facts of Egyptian civilization and its influence and of the Negro's progress and contributions to America as an argument for citizenship rights; a pamphlet published in 1901 which by 1913 had reached its ninth edition, entitled *Jesus Christ had Negro Blood in His Veins,* by a Brooklyn physician, W. L. Hunter; the Baltimore minister Harvey Johnson's *The Nations From a New Point of View,* 1903, which rehearsed the old materials regarding ancient civilizations; Pauline Hopkins' *Primer of Facts Pertaining to the Early Greatness of the African Race,* 1905, which aimed to instill race pride as an encouragement to American Negroes to aid in the "restoration" of Africa; Joseph E. Hayne's *The Ammonian or Hametic Origin of the Ancient Greeks, Cretans and all the Celtic Races,* 1905, which held that Greek and Cretan civilizations were created by descendants of Ham and that the Celtic British owed their achievements to their Negro ancestry; Booker T. Washington's *Story of the Negro,* 1909; and James Morris Webb's *The Black Man, The Father of Civilization,* 1910. Less ephemeral because based on better scholarship were *The Aftermath of Slavery,* 1903, by William Sinclair, secretary of the Constitution League, which was notable for its defense of Black Reconstruction; Benjamin Brawley's *Short History of the American Negro,* 1913; J. W. Cromwell's *The Negro in American History,* 1914 (chiefly biographical); and most important of all Du Bois' slim volume, *The Negro,* which appeared in 1915. Du Bois, the most widely learned and most discriminating of Negro scholars and propagandists, brought to bear the latest anthropological theories including the work of Franz Boas. In addition to criticizing the Aryan myth and describing the ancient cultures of Ethiopia and Egypt he devoted five of the book's dozen chapters to a discussion of the history of West and South Africa and the culture of contemporary Africa. Others had specialized concerns. Several dealt mostly with military history, and R. R. Wright, Jr., pioneered in examining the role of Negroes in the discovery and exploration of the New World.[5]

Frequently history was held to be of value in instilling race pride, solidarity, and self-help, whether these might be directed toward agitation for political and civil rights, toward economic co-operation, toward an all-Negro community, or even colonization. Yet those who urged the study of Negro history ranged from amalgamationists [6] to extreme nationalists, and from Booker T. Washington to W. E. B. Du Bois. Interest in race history was most characteristic of those who favored a group economy or other forms of separatism, but even the assimilationist *Gazette* insisted that "Every Afro-American school . . . ought for obvious reasons to compel its students to study Williams' *History of the Negro Race.*" [7] Certainly the interest was widely shared, and about the time of World War I Negro history courses appeared in a few of the colleges.

Unquestionably as the lines of race hardened in the opening years of the century there was an increasing tendency to use Negro history to foster race pride and group solidarity as the basis of advancement by collective action and as an antidote to prejudice and discrimination. This view was perhaps best represented—though in a somewhat extreme form—by Meharry Medical School Professor C. V. Roman, who a few years later was to propose a biracial society and parallel civilizations. To Pennsylvania-born, Canada-reared Roman, past president of the National Medical Association, knowledge of history would foster race pride and solidarity enough "to enable us to spurn as poor relations those unfortunate members of our race" who displayed shame of their ancestry by not wishing to belong to Negro churches, live in Negro neighborhoods, send their children to Negro schools, or patronize Negro business and professional men. Negro children should be taught about the "glorious deeds of Negro men and women first," before they learned of the deeds of the national heroes of the United States. The diffusion of such knowledge would stimulate race pride and would "furnish an atmosphere of mutual cooperation and helpfulness that will change the winter of our discontent into the glorious summer of racial solidarity, that magic alembic in which most of our racial difficulties will disappear." [8]

The increasingly deep-seated historical interest was evident in the formation of historical societies. In 1897 the American Negro Historical Society of Philadelphia was organized to collect relics and facts pertaining to American Negro progress and development.[9] More influential were the Negro Society for Historical Research (1912) and the Association for the Study of Negro Life and History (1915).

The leaders of the former were its president, John Edward Bruce (pseud. Bruce Grit), a free-lance journalist and sometime editor, and its secretary, A. A. Schomburg, a Puerto Rico-born bibliophile. As one member of the society put it, the study of race history would "form an effective breakwater against the ever-increasing and cumulative tide of prejudice and discrimination." Schomburg in a speech at Cheyney Institute urged his listeners to learn Arabic "because much of our life is undoubtedly wrapped up" in Africa's traditions, customs, and history; proposed to stimulate racial patriotism by the study of Negro books; and called for inclusion of Negro history in the curriculum, since "it is the season for us to devote our time to kindling the torches that will inspire us to racial integrity." [10] Bruce, born a slave in Maryland, had received only a public school education, but was an editor before he was twenty-five. He displayed an indefatigable zeal in gathering historical materials, and maintained a consistent enthusiasm for race pride and solidarity—opposing inter-marriage and mixed schools, and apparently accepting the idea of in-herent race differences—but in the protest tradition, and usually openly hostile to (and consistently suspected by) Booker Washington. A member of the extremist school of Biblical interpreters and a later Garveyite, Bruce, in a characteristic speech, insisted that Negroes must fight for their rights by organized resistance, espoused higher education, and called Japan "the logical hope of the darker races in the *inevitable conflict which is to decide the supremacy of nations . . . in the very near future."* Whites, he said, feared contacts with Negroes because, knowing that their history was a "monumental fraud," "a total blank" before 850 B.C., they feared "odious com-parisons." For from ancient African civilization, which was in many ways vastly superior to that of modern Europe, the white man derived his religion and "stole his alphabet" and his knowledge of the basic sciences.[11]

Less chauvinistic and far more scholarly has been the work of the Association for the Study of Negro Life and History founded by Carter G. Woodson, who had worked his way up from the West Virginia coal mines to a Harvard Ph.D. in 1912. Woodson was an anti-Bookerite, though he was not active in radical organizations. According to its constitution, the Association's aim was to collect sociological and historical documents and promote studies bearing on the Negro. Woodson's underlying purpose was succinctly summed up in the objective of preventing the race from becoming "a negligible factor in the thought of the world." [12] Strictly speaking, the work of the Association and its *Journal of Negro History* lies outside the scope of this book, but its philosophy—characterized by the usual ethnic dualism—was rooted in the historical-mindedness of the pre-war generation.

Finally, one must note the compensatory and psychological role the Negro history movement played—no matter what the larger view of its supporters: whether accommodating like Washington, assimila-tionist like Smith, or of the agitation-through-racial-solidarity variety like Bruce. For it gave dignity in the face of insults and provided arguments for equality in the face of assertions of inferiority. Yet even though extreme assimilationists showed interest in it, the movement was chiefly significant as part of the complex of ideas that included self-help, race pride, and solidarity.

The interest in African history was part of a larger identification with Africa shared by the majority of Negroes, however attenuated the feeling might be. Even the anticolonizationist *Christian Recorder* urged the "wide-awake, industrious Negro" to make a fortune out of the economic opportunities in his "fatherland." Yet, despite the widespread pride in the antique African past, generally Negroes accepted white stereotypes as to the primitiveness of its contemporary culture. Both Du Bois' presentation of the culture of contemporary West Africa and Chesnutt's lack of concern about Africa "except as an interesting foreign country" were unusual and extreme viewpoints.[13]

There had been, it is true, occasional evidence of an intelligent interest in African ethnography since the 1880's. A speaker at the Bethel Literary Association in 1881 stirred up considerable enthusiasm by a paper on the Zulus who had thus far held off the British, and scattered articles on specialized phases of African culture appeared from time to time. George Washington Ellis, an official at the American legation in Monrovia, made a careful and sympathetic study of the Vai-speaking people of West Africa. Most significant was the work of Du Bois. Not only was he aware of the complexity and sophistication of contemporary African culture but also—acting more on mystic racial yearnings than on scientific investigation—Du Bois was the precursor of the Africanist Melville J. Herskovits in tracing American Negro culture and institutions to African origins. The sociologist R. R. Wright, Jr., was one of the few to follow in Du Bois' footsteps.[14]

In addition to the interest in African culture, the 1890's witnessed the beginning of an interest in American Negro folk culture. In Boston in 1890 some of the leading socialites organized the Society for the Collection of Negro Folk Lore, and Hampton Institute gave the movement considerable propulsion, involving in it people like Fortune and Crummell. Concerning an important aspect of folk culture, the spirituals, there was some difference of opinion. These Jubilee Songs, or "plantation melodies," had been introduced to the public by the Fisk Jubilee Singers during Reconstruction, and at innumerable occasions they were sung at probably all of the Negro schools. Washington often alluded to them in proud terms. Moton recalled his disappointment at hearing them at Hampton where he hoped to sing "better" things, until Armstrong's constant telling the students to respect their race, its history and its traditions, convinced him of their value. At the Hampton Conference in 1899, there was considerable discussion of the matter. Those present agreed that rag-time and "coon songs" should be discouraged, but that "the beautiful plantation melodies should be preserved." Reverend Ernest Lyon of Baltimore, a minister to Liberia (1903–11), thought Negroes should not seek to imitate the work of white men. He said that "the plantation songs are our own . . . ; they were born out of our sufferings, and . . . express deep things. Never let them go." Kelly Miller also thought the plantation melody should be glorified, despite its "lowly origin." The *Horizon* reported a "revolt" of Howard University students against singing plantation melodies for visitors, and held that they were intended strictly for religious use among Negroes.[15]

There was also developing a definite interest in stimulating creative and intellectual expression in literature and the arts—an interest that paralleled the rise of literary, musical, and artistic organizations discussed in Chapter VIII. This striving for literary and intellectual accomplishment was many-faceted. It was symbolic of the desire to assimilate to American middle-class culture; it was directed toward demonstrating that Negroes did have intellectual and creative abilities; it expressed a belief that only Negro writers could express the aspirations of the race; it was intended to correct the stereotypes of Negro characters in the writings of white authors and to argue the race question from the Negro's point of view; it was an outgrowth of the feeling of race pride; it was connected with the idea that it would be the intellectuals who would, on the basis of racial co-operation, lead the race into achieving higher culture and civilization. Not all of the individuals to be discussed held all of these ideas. It is sometimes hard to see if they advocated cultural activities as a means of assimilating to American culture, or if they were espousing a sort of cultural nationalism. Undoubtedly many were unconsciously striving toward both—as Locke and others did consciously during the Harlem Renaissance.

Evidence of the desire to create a racial literature was not entirely new, but the idea began to take hold during the 1890's. In 1893 H. T. Johnson, editor of the *Recorder,* outlined the need for race authors to express racial aspirations. Five years later, H. T. Kealing wrote of the unique contributions that only Negro authors could make. The literature of any people, he said, had an indigenous quality, "the product of the national peculiarities and race idiosyncrasies" that no alien could duplicate. He called upon the Negro author not to imitate whites, as had been the case hitherto, but to reach "down to the original and unexplored depths of his own being where lies unused the material that is to provide him a place among the great writers." Similarly, W. S. Scarborough, speaking at the Hampton Negro Conference in 1899, called for something higher than the false dialect types depicted by white authors; even Chesnutt's and Dunbar's short stories had not gone far enough in portraying the higher aspirations of the race. Only the Negro author could portray the Negro best—his "loves and hates, his hopes and fears, his ambitions, his whole life, in such a way that the world will weep and laugh . . . , forgetting completely that hero and heroine are God's bronze image, but knowing only that they are men and women with joys and sorrows that belong to the whole human family." In the discussion that followed Scarborough's paper, it was agreed that the types portrayed in vaudeville were false. Lucy Laney, principal of the Haines Normal and Industrial Institute, pre-figured a major interest of the 1920's when she spoke of the material for short stories to be found in the rural South, and called upon Negro writers to go down to the sea islands of Georgia and South Carolina "where they could study the Negro in his original purity," with a culture close to the African.[16]

There was one effort to publish a magazine that would develop a racial literature, *The Colored American Magazine*. Its original editors, whose orientation was indicated by the name of their Colored Co-Operative Publishing Company, were interested in an organ devoted to the higher culture of the race that would also help to "develop and intensify the bonds of that racial brotherhood, which alone can enable a people to assert their racial rights as men."[17] Though the poetry and fiction were by minor figures, the magazine devoted considerable attention to Negro achievement, education, and music and the theater, and was, all in all, the most consciously cultural of the Negro publications until it passed into Tuskegee hands in 1904.

The notion of stimulating Negro cultural development as part of a larger program of racial co-operation and solidarity was evident also in the work of the American Negro Academy, organized in 1897.

Limited to forty members, its aims were the promotion of literature, science, and the arts, the fostering of higher education, the publication of scholarly work, and the defense of the Negro against vicious attacks.[18] Among the most active members were the succession of presidents—Alexander Crummell, Kelly Miller, and W. H. Crogman. By publishing scholarly papers, the Academy planned to counteract both white prejudice and Negro lack of unity. Well before Du Bois popularized the idea the Academy stressed the importance of Talented-Tenth leadership. As Crummell said, it aimed to promote the development of cultured men, because if Negroes, who were too impressed with material things, could not hold their place in the world of culture, they would be relegated to "inferiority . . . and ultimate death." It would be the scholars and thinkers, who by employing their knowledge and culture to guide the crude masses, would "lift up this people of ours to the grand level of civilization." [19] As Du Bois later insisted, cultural achievement was to serve as a basis for race unity and solidarity.

Associated with this cultural striving and groping toward a cultural nationalism was the notion of innate race differences. Their existence was accepted by men as diverse as W. H. Councill, W. E. B. Du Bois, and J. E. Bruce. The accommodating principal of Prairie View State Normal School in Texas, E. J. Blackshear, and the radical apostle of equality, John Hope, both thought that the Negro's real contribution to American culture would derive from his emotional nature. And middle-of-the-roader Kelly Miller voiced the aspiration toward a cultural nationalism not only in his call for the study of Negro history, but also in his belief in a Negro genius in music, literature, and the arts. Rag-time, the plantation melodies with their "inimitable . . . racial quality," and individual achievements in music, poetry, oratory, and painting were due to the fact that the imaginative powers were the first to develop in any race.

Even more explicit than Miller about the idea of a special "Negro Genius" for the arts was Benjamin Brawley, an English professor at Morehouse College and Howard University and an ardent champion of Negro culture and Negro history. The son of a Charleston minister, Brawley had the chance to develop his cultural interests by taking degrees from both Chicago and Harvard universities. He was not primarily interested in the practical, everyday side of racial struggle, though he saw value in the work of both Washington and his critics.

In an article on the subject in 1915 Brawley pointed out that almost all Negro achievements had been in the arts, in the realm of feeling—from the homes of humble Negroes who, unlike poor whites, grew flowers and hung posters on the walls, to the long line of beautiful singers, Douglass' "fervid oratory," Dunbar's "sensuous poetry," Du Bois' "picturesque style," and "the elemental sculpture" of Meta Warrick Fuller. But beyond the Negro's sensuousness of beauty was the soul of the race. Only a race that had yearned and suffered could achieve the greatest heights of art, and the Negro's tragic background was reflected in "the wail of the old melodies and the plaintive quality" of the Negro voice. Moreover, there was "something very elemental about the heart of the race, something that finds its origin in the African forest. . . . There is something grim and stern about it all too, something that speaks of the lash, of the child torn from its mother's bosom, of the dead body riddled with bullets and swinging all night from a limb by the roadside." Negroes could distinguish themselves in all spheres, but each race had its peculiar genius, and as far as one could predict at that time, the Negro was destined to reach his greatest heights in the arts. Even though Brawley later criticized what he regarded as the crudities of the Harlem Renaissance, and though his own poetry was conventional and genteel, his concept of a race soul, his interest in African origins, and his plea for literature based upon the racial experience were all fundamental in the outlook of the Renaissance.[20]

Interestingly enough in these very years, beginning in the late 1890's, there was a significant development in Negro letters. Between Phyllis Wheatley and Dunbar, little of value had appeared except the ex-slave autobiographies. But now there came the first work of Dunbar and Chesnutt, followed by James Weldon Johnson and Du Bois. Yet even this newer literature—the best as represented by these men as well as that of lesser writers—had its deficiencies. Much of the poetry was dialect verse with its limited range of expression, and the rest was mostly imitative of the genteel Victorian tradition. Most of the novels, propagandist in purpose, were highly contrived, often melodramatic stories turning about racial discrimination and miscegenation. Where exploring themes based on Negro life, as did the writers of the Renaissance, these early novelists and dialect poets—with the exception of Johnson's novel and Du Bois' essays—were unable to set forth the inner spirit and strivings of Negro life as it was differentiated from the life of white Americans, nor were they able to rise above their materials so as to make the particular universal in its significance. Generally there was too much emphasis upon the genteel to achieve a genuine racial artistic expression, even among the novelists.[21] Thus we are faced with an interesting example of dualism—a desire to create a Negro literature that would express the true aspirations of Negro life, and at the same time an imitating of contemporary white writers.

Of the major literary figures, we have discussed Chesnutt and Du Bois in other connections. Paul Laurence Dunbar (d. 1906), a citizen of Dayton, Ohio, became famous when William Dean Howells reviewed his *Majors and Minors* in 1896. Dunbar was chiefly interested in writing on nonracial themes. Where dealing with Negro characters, most notably in his short stories, Dunbar, in deference to the white reading public, limited himself almost entirely to the plantation tradition with its stereotypes of carefree slaves and paternalistic masters and Negroes preferring the rural South to the urban North. Even his final novel, *The Sport of the Gods* (1902), while describing how a Southern Negro was railroaded to jail, is mainly concerned with depicting the demoralization of his family in the corrupt life of the Northern city to which they move, and ends on an idyllic note of plantation paternalism. Unlike Chesnutt, Dunbar did not use his writing as an instrument of protest. Nor did Dunbar follow Chesnutt and lesser novelists such as Sutton Griggs and Pauline Hopkins[22] in their emphasis on the middle-class attributes of Negroes. It is doubtful that Dunbar had any real appreciation of the folk Negro—and certainly not of the sporting and Bohemian group described by James Weldon Johnson. Occasionally Dunbar did exhibit protest and race pride. His poem on Frederick Douglass praised that statesman's battle for freedom and his expression of the Negro's highest aspirations; and in "Ode to Ethiopia" Dunbar pledged unwavering faith to his Mother Race. Yet even here he stressed the forgiving nature of the Negro.

One novel that did give a more realistic portrayal of Negro life was Johnson's *Autobiography of an Ex-Colored Man* which appeared anonymously in 1912. Probably the best novel written about "passing," it was more significant for its depiction of life among the sportsmen and theatrical people on Manhattan's West Side and its keen appreciation of the rag-time idiom. There was no pretense of being respectably middle-class, but a frank interest in Negro life as it was and in the value of the Negro's folk contributions. Johnson also wrote dialect poetry and the lyrics for a number of Broadway hits that were in a stereotyped tradition, but this novel was prophetic of the New Negro Harlem Renaissance, of which Johnson himself was a member.

In general the writers and publicists of the early twentieth century prefigured the New Negro Renaissance less in their use of unorthodox, "unrespectable" realistic and folk subject matter than in their insistence upon the Negro's artistic genius and the necessity of fostering a racial culture—however much it might, some hoped, turn out to be like white American culture. Yet there was an incipient interest in folk materials, in the African background, in the mystique of cultural nationalism, and in the insistence on the racial experience as a source of artistic inspiration. In both periods of course the literary propagandists and cultural nationalists were characterized by an ethnic dualism. There was, then, a real connection between the gropings of the first years of the century and the literary outpouring of the 1920's.

Everywhere there appeared to be a rising tide of racial pride and solidarity, a justification of group separatism, a sort of racial nationalism during the generation before World War I. Washington believed that Negroes generally shared his feeling of race pride and race consciousness as a result of the "adverse criticism" they received. Du Bois, writing in 1913 of the increase in racial consciousness and group solidarity, noted that Negroes were "gaining their own leaders, their own voices, their own ideals. Self-realization is thus coming slowly to another one of the world's great races." [23]

Illustrative of this rising racial consciousness was the appearance of Negro dolls and calendars. One observer noted that, whereas about 1890 Negroes were not interested in such things, less than a quarter century later they were willing to pay extra for them. The *Age* applauded the National Baptist Convention for urging all Negro Baptists to buy Negro dolls for their children. And the Baptist leader, R. H. Boyd, whose National Doll Company supplied these toys, advertised in the pages of the *Crisis* that "your child would be happy if it had a Negro doll. . . . The Negro doll is calculated to help in the Christian development of our race." [24]

The collective spirit appeared to be almost as much a hallmark of the fifteen years after 1900 as it was of the New Negro of the 1920's. Observers generally agreed that Negroes were more and more showing evidences of independence and self-help and race pride and solidarity.[25] The advocates of the "group economy" encouraged it under the guise of economic nationalism. Many tended to justify segregated churches and Y's. The argument among Negroes over segregated schools, as old as the 1880's, took on fresh vigor as certain groups in northern cities such as Chicago, Philadelphia, Columbus, and Cleveland urged their establishment. There was the old argument over what Alain Locke later described as the dilemma posed by the conflict between the short-range and the long-range benefits to be derived from segregated or integrated schooling. In Buffalo, there was a movement for what the *Gazette* described as a " 'jim-crow' social center." [26] The all-Negro communities reflected the idea of an *imperium in imperio* as contemporaries referred to it. Closely related to this was the notion of "a nation within a nation." Sometimes this phrase was used loosely—to refer to the fact that American Negroes formed a population larger than that of some independent nations; but at other times it was used with a more precise meaning. In 1913 and 1914 two distinguished men close to Booker T. Washington—his secretary, Emmett Scott, and the sociologist Robert E. Park, co-author of Washington's *The Man Farthest Down*—in practically identical language expressed the view that Negroes were coming to form a distinct nationality. They felt that segregation had stimulated a sense of common interest and solidarity so that Negroes were developing what amounted to a feeling of Negro nationality, comparable to the "racial consciousness" appearing among the peoples of southern Europe.[27] The character of this nationalism is well illustrated by the song, "Lift Every Voice and Sing," which, written by James Weldon Johnson and his brother, J. Rosamond Johnson, in 1900, came to be regarded as the "Negro National Anthem." For this song, not once mentioning the Negro by name, shows a consciousness of suffering in the past, hopefulness for the future, belief in liberty, and faith in God and America. James Weldon Johnson believed that in the last verse, which concludes "May we forever stand, True to our God, True to our native land," "The American Negro was, historically and spiritually, immanent." [28]

In its most extreme form this feeling of racial ethnocentrism rejected the paradoxes of dualism and advocated the creation of an independent national state—usually in Africa. Most articulate Negroes had no interest in colonization. Their characteristic attitude was like that of Bishop Abraham Grant, who declared that since Negroes, here for three hundred years, had discarded their African culture for that of the whites, and had contributed to the nation's economic and military might, they belonged here, for "we have become . . . one people, with one destiny." It would be all right to go to Africa for economic or missionary activity, "but for the masses to talk about going . . . is simply foolishness." [29] Strongly assimilationist journals like the *Gazette* naturally opposed emigration; so did Washington whose general philosophy was contrary to that of the *Gazette*. Du Bois, H. H. Proctor, and John Hope might toy with the idea of an all-Negro community on the Georgia coast,[30] but even Du Bois, with his unusual interest in Africa, never advocated colonization there.

Nevertheless, the persistence of emigrationist sentiment and the later mass appeal of the Garvey Movement suggest that perhaps the desire for colonization was more widespread among the masses than ordinarily believed. Expressions of this desire appeared in places as diverse as Colorado and Richmond. T. McCants Stewart returned with his family to Liberia in 1906, and was quoted as saying, "I watch with great interest the fight which you are making in the United States for equality of opportunity. But I regard it as a hopeless struggle, and am not surprised that many Afro-Americans turn their faces toward Liberia." [31] Similar views were expressed by more obscure would-be-migrants. Yet, though Bishop Turner, the most celebrated advocate of colonization, claimed that between three and four millions were anxious to go, actually his Colored Emigration and Commercial Association was unable to collect dues from its members, much less to enlist many new ones.[32]

Probably the most notable movement toward Africa during Washington's ascendancy appeared in Oklahoma, where disillusionment with the myth of an all-Negro state led to nationalist sentiments of an emigrationist variety. As early as 1897 Liberia Emigration Clubs had been formed "to better our conditions by going to our Native Country," where land and homes awaited the migrants "among our own people and where we can indeed be free and independent." Emigrationist sentiment in Oklahoma came to a climax on the eve of World War I, under the leadership of a supposed Ashanti chief, Alfred C. Sam. Unable to obtain a response in New York, Sam found better recognition in the Midwest, especially Oklahoma. Ashanti rulers were alleged to have provided generous amounts of land, and with a reported $100,000 subscribed, his company purchased a steamship. Though many died on the ill-fated voyage, and though the movement appears to have been fraudulent, it was significant because of the stir it created in Oklahoma and neighboring states.[33]

As suggested in Chapter IV, there is considerable evidence pointing to a close relationship between colonization and migration to other parts of the United States (especially the West), and sentiment for a national state abroad or for an all-Negro state within the United States. As a matter of fact, agitation for migration to the Great Plains and the Far West was fairly continuous, though it seems to have been especially strong around 1900. Some of it was connected with the establishment of all-Negro communities. For example, there was considerable agitation for migration from North Carolina to the North and West in 1899, and soon thereafter George H. White founded the all-Negro Whitesboro, N.J. Elsewhere we have noted such all-Negro towns as Allensworth, California. Migration ideology was naturally expressed at times in nationalist terms. Illustrative of the extreme nationalist fringe was a statement issued about the time of the Chief Sam episode by one Arthur Anderson, the self-appointed "Prophetic Liberator of the Coloured Race." He said he had been advocating his plans for years, and he claimed, like Garvey later, to have been associated with African nationalists abroad, notably those who ran the London *African Times and Orient Review*. He displayed a strong consciousness of a glorious past in Africa, "the mother of civilization, . . . the father of nations, of whom the white man is but a diseased brother, and yet assumes a superiority." He urged racial solidarity; when "firmly united as a people,—a nation apart," Negroes could present their case to the Hague Tribunal and petition Congress for a suitable territory within the United States in which "to develop . . . as a modern nation, a race apart, the people to be free from further oppression," but under American protection. And in a blaze of fantasy he pictured his Utopia as a self-governing monarchy, respected and wealthy—in sharp contrast to the situation in which his followers found themselves. A distinguished cleric such as Bishop Holsey might also advocate a separate all-Negro semisovereign nation under the protection of the United States, but it took the un-grammatical Anderson to paint a vision of kings and palaces, courtiers and ambassadors, and "fetes in magnificient halls and gardens." [34]

Migration enthusiasm also stressed the idea of Negroes owning their own farms, and for the Afro-American Council migration senti-ment was clearly tied up with the continuing desire for land owner-ship and economic independence.[35] The economic motivation behind migration to the farmlands of the Northwest, proposed by the Council, was also related to the continuing migration southwestward and to the beginnings of urbanization. Urbanization of Southern Negroes was proceeding at about the same rate as for Southern whites and for the same economic reasons. So noticeable was this movement that the National Urban League reported in 1912: "The migration of Negroes to the cities, as a part of the general movement . . . to the cities, is a fact of common observation." According to the 1910 census a dozen cities had each over 40,000 Negroes; in 27 leading cities Negroes formed one quarter or more of the population, and in four of them over 50 per cent. The biggest percentage increase be-tween 1900 and 1910 occurred in New South cities like Birmingham (215 per cent), Jacksonville (81 per cent), and Atlanta (45 per cent), and in New York (51 per cent), while Philadelphia, Rich-mond, and Chicago had increases of over 30 per cent.

Moreover, this urban migration was increasingly a northward move-ment. As early as 1903 Du Bois observed that "the most significant economic change among Negroes in the last ten or twenty years has been their influx into northern cities." New York had three-fourths as many Negroes as New Orleans, Philadelphia had almost twice as many as Atlanta, Chicago had more than Savannah. During the next years this development produced even more striking results; accord-ing to the census of 1910 two cities, Washington and New York, had over 90,000 Negroes; and three others, New Orleans, Baltimore, and Philadelphia, over 80,000. Of these five only one was a truly Southern city.[36]

As to the causes of the migration, both before and during World War I, most students have concluded that the basic motivation was economic—the wearing out of the land, the desire for a better living, the promises of Northern employment agents. One investigator found that of several hundred Northern migrants questioned around 1906, over half gave higher wages as their reason for moving North; much smaller numbers desired protection, were tired of the South, came with their parents, wished "opportunity for freer self-expression," or just wanted a change. While people of all classes migrated, he found that the majority were the unskilled laborers and country farm hands; the well-to-do had no desire to leave the South.[37] During the war, too, the masses led the way, professional men following their constituencies when whole communities seemed to be becoming depopulated of Negroes. The economic pinch rather than sensitivity to direct racial insult seems to have been the chief motivating factor. However, the ideological rationale of this wartime movement—a movement that Locke regarded as the social basis of the New Negro —came to emphasize Southern injustices in all spheres of life, even though the fundamental motivation was economic.[38] Moreover, like earlier migration movements, it became associated with ethnocentric tendencies that became evident as disillusionment with the "promised land" set in. For then the Garvey Movement, with its promises of an African Utopia and its psychological support for the oppressed in terms of race pride and race history, achieved mass support when it became evident that bad housing, economic discrimination, and race riots were the order of the day.[39] Thus as Locke indicated, the mass migration of Negroes was certainly related to their higher aspirations and the development of collective feeling, in ideological rationalization if not so much in actual motivation.[40]

What sort of conditions did the early twentieth-century migrants meet when they arrived in the Northern cities? Chesnutt might find life in Cleveland before the war relatively well integrated, with a white clientele for his law practice, social acceptance in exclusive circles, and more than a nodding acquaintance with the city's leaders. But like World War migrants later, most Negroes found themselves in segregated, overcrowded ghettos in deteriorated sections, ghettos that were becoming increasingly isolated and proscribed as their size increased.[41] In the older cities of the South Negroes often lived among whites or in scattered enclaves about the town, but the newer migration, North and South, was generally accompanied by residential segregation—a community pattern that naturally encouraged the development of ethnocentric feelings, and of business and professional classes which catered exclusively to Negroes. Small Negro enclaves had existed for years in Northern cities, and the ghetto phenomenon became greatly accentuated after 1900 in both sections. As the Fisk University sociologist and Urban League official, George Edmund Haynes, said in 1913: "New York has its 'San Juan Hill' in the West Sixties and its Harlem district of over 35,000 within about eighteen city blocks; Philadelphia has its Seventh Ward; Chicago has its State Street; Washington its Northwest neighborhood, and Baltimore its Druid Hill Avenue. Louisville has its Chestnut Street and its Smoke-town; Atlanta its West End and Auburn Avenue." [42]

Drake and Cayton have described the evolution of the Negro community in Chicago as one of a growing population in an expanding ghetto that gradually developed a business and professional class and its own community institutions. In the 1880's Negroes, like foreign immigrants in the city, exhibited an ethnic dualism, but regarded themselves as part of the larger society about them and maintained close connections with powerful and wealthy white citizens who employed Negroes as servants and contributed to Black Belt institutions. But after 1900, as these leaders passed away, as the Negro population grew, and as race proscription increased, Negroes lost their sense of the "interrelatedness of white Chicago and the Negro community" and began to put increasing stress on racial self-reliance—on the development of political power and a strong business and professional class based on the collective power of the Negro community. [43]

Urbanization served as the chief basis of the new group life which Du Bois and others perceived as developing and which formed the basis of the Dream of Black Metropolis in Chicago and elsewhere; which created a new race consciousness, a new racial solidarity and self-reliance, a new middle class that depended for its support upon the Negro community, and ultimately the cultural flowering of the Harlem Renaissance. [44] Du Bois perceived clearly the city's role in its positive and constructive aspects, in spite of the segregation imposed there; and how segregation was causing a collective counter-movement:

It is the city group . . . that is the most civilized and advancing and it is that group whose social structure we need to study. It is in the South above all a segregated group, and this means that it is the group that lives to itself, works by itself, worships alone, and finds education and amusement among its own. This segregation is growing, and its growth involves . . . greater differentiation and greater integration. Greater differentiation from the white group in, for instance . . . the ideals which inspire it and the traditions which it inherits. On the other hand greater integration in the sense of a strong self-consciousness, more harmonious working together with a broader field for such cooperation.[45]

Du Bois thus advanced the thesis that, given the American race system, with its segregation and discrimination, it was in the cities that whatever group advancement was possible would take place, and that it would take place on the basis of collective action, on the basis of group solidarity. Here, indeed, was the climax of that development of racial solidarity and self-help—in the cities where a business and professional class could be supported by the black masses; in the cities of the North where a compact segregated community could elect men to political office. Chesnutt's Cleveland was already being subjected to strains and would soon disappear as a result of the mass migration that created the extensive ghettos which Negro businessmen, politicians, and professional men would exploit under the advantages of the disadvantages. And it was in New York where the race-conscious artists and literati—paradoxically the most interracially integrated group in Negro society (due to their contacts with certain white figures)—produced the proudly race-conscious, race-proud, but largely white-fostered Harlem Renaissance. Of course Negro economic development, cultural expression, and political participation would have achieved far more if the American race system had not existed, but the direction they took and the achievements they did make rested on a rationalization of the value of self-reliance and group solidarity which in turn was based upon the rapidly growing urban ghetto.

Here, then, was the New Negro, resourceful, independent, race-proud, economically advancing, and ready to tackle political and cultural ambitions. He believed in collective economic effort, for the most part denied any interest in social equality, and at the same time denounced the inequities of American racism and insisted upon his citizenship rights. He was interested in the race and its past; he was becoming more conscious of his relationship with other colored peoples and with Africa—an identification which the lower classes perhaps never really lost. In fact, the Garvey Movement was in many ways the lower-class counterpart of the New Negro Movement; both held to a belief in economic chauvinism, an interest in race history, and an identification with Africa; both emphasized race pride and solidarity—though of course the Garvey philosophy lacked the dualistic character of the New Negro outlook.[46] The New Negro regarded the race as a distinct group with a distinct mission, yet part of the United States. He owed an equal debt to Howard, Fisk, Lincoln, and Atlanta and to Hampton and Tuskegee; to the Niagara Movement and to the National Negro Business League; to Booker T. Washington and W. E. B. Du Bois.

ABBREVIATIONS FOR NOTES

Advocate	*Southwestern Christian Advocate*
Age	New York *Age*
A.M.E. *Review*	A.M.E. Church *Review*
Appeal	St. Paul *Appeal*
AUP	Atlanta University Publications
Bee	Washington *Bee*
BTW	Booker T. Washington
Colored American	Washington *Colored American*
Freeman	Indianapolis *Freeman*
Gazette	Cleveland *Gazette*
Guardian	Boston *Guardian*
Hampton Clippings	Hampton Institute Clipping Collection
Independent	Atlanta *Independent*
Index	C.M.E. *Christian Index*
JNE	*Journal of Negro Education*
JNH	*Journal of Negro History*
JSH	*Journal of Southern History*
Planet	Richmond *Planet*
Recorder	A.M.E. *Christian Recorder*

Except where indicated otherwise, all citations to correspondence are to the BTW Papers.

BIBLIOGRAPHICAL NOTE

Since this book is based on a bibliography of nearly twelve hundred titles, it will be possible here only to indicate briefly something of the nature and scope of the sources employed.

The most useful manuscript collection available was the Booker T. Washington Papers, Library of Congress. This very complete and extensive collection sheds a great deal of light on many figures besides Washington. Other useful manuscript collections in the Library of Congress include the Mary Church and Robert H. Terrell Papers and the Carter G. Woodson Collection. At Howard University I used various collections of papers, including those of Kelly Miller, Blanche K. Bruce, P. B. S. Pinchback, George L. Ruffin, and Joel E. Spingarn. At the Schomburg Collection of the New York Public Library papers of John E. Bruce, John B. Rayner (on microfilm), and F. J. Garrison, and the manuscript collection of Alexander Crummell's sermons proved helpful. Yale University has some papers of James Weldon Johnson, and Fisk University has some papers of Charles W. Chesnutt, J. Mercer Langston, and J. C. Napier. The generosity of Dr. Otelia Cromwell and Mrs. Mae Miller Sullivan, both of Washington, D.C., made it possible for me to consult papers in their possession of John W. Cromwell and Kelly Miller, respectively. John C. Dancy, Jr., of Detroit and Mrs. Lilian Dancy Reid of Salisbury, North Carolina, kindly placed papers of their father at my disposal. Microfilm copies of the Frederick Douglass Papers at the Frederick Douglass Home in Washington are readily available. Minutes of meetings of the Freedmen's Aid and Southern Education Society of the Methodist Church, North, were consulted at the Methodist Board of Education in Nashville.

The Negro newspaper microfilm project of the American Council of Learned Societies and the Library of Congress greatly facilitated the research for this book. This microfilm series covers extant copies of newspapers before 1900 and complete serials of journals which were started before 1900 but which have since been discontinued. The most useful of the newspapers included the following: New York *Age*, 1887–1917; Washington *Bee*, 1882–1917; Washington *Colored American*, 1898–1904; Cleveland *Gazette*, 1883–1917; Indianapolis *Freeman*, 1888–1917; Washington *New Era and Citizen* (title varies), 1870–74. Among Drew University's fine holdings of Methodist publications were found copies of journals published by the Negro Methodist Connections—the A.M.E. *Christian Recorder*, 1880–1916; the C.M.E. *Christian Index*, 1891–1904; and the *Southwestern Christian Advocate*, 1883–1917. Among other newspapers that proved helpful special mention should be made of the Boston *Guardian*, 1902–4. I attempted to consult all extant copies of Negro magazines published during the period under consideration. Of these the most useful proved to be *Alexander's Magazine*, 1905–9; the A.M.E. Church *Review*, 1884–1917; the *Colored American Magazine*, 1900–1909; the *Crisis*, 1910–17; the *Horizon*, 1907–10; and the *Voice of the Negro*, 1904–7. Mention should also be made of two magazines edited by whites: the *African Repository*, 1875–92, and the *Southern Workman*, 1873–1917.

The two major collections devoted to Negro materials are the Schomburg Collection of the New York Public Library and the Moorland-Spingarn Collection at Howard University. Using their extensive resources, I made an effort to consult all books and pamphlets written by Negroes during the period covered by this book, and all books and pamphlets about Negroes in this period, no matter when they were written. I also attempted to consult all of the articles by Negroes listed in the standard periodical indices of the period. The large pamphlet holdings of the Library of Congress also proved valuable, and recondite items not available elsewhere were found in the libraries of Atlanta, Fisk, and Harvard universities, and in the main reference collection of the New York Public Library.

As will be apparent to the reader, considerable use has also been made of the standard sociological and historical works on the American Negro. In this connection attention should be called to the Research Memoranda prepared for the Carnegie-Myrdal Study of the Negro in America. These are available at the Schomburg Collection.

Some of the master's theses at Howard University and Atlanta University proved to be of considerable value. Of the doctoral dissertations consulted the following were found to be especially useful: Clarence A. Bacote, "The Negro in Georgia Politics, 1880–1908" (University of Chicago, 1955); Howard H. Bell, "A Survey of the Negro Convention Movement, 1830–1861" (Northwestern University, 1953); Suzanne C. Carson, "Samuel Chapman Armstrong: Missionary to the South" (Johns Hopkins University, 1952); Leslie H. Fishel, Jr., "The North and the Negro, 1865–1900: A Study in Race Discrimination" (Harvard University, 1954, 2 vols.); and Inabel Burns Lindsay, "The Participation of Negroes in the Establishment of Welfare Services, 1865–1900, with Special Reference to the District of Columbia, Maryland and Virginia" (University of Pittsburgh School of Social Work, 1952).

No bibliography of the Negro in the period under consideration is complete without reference to the magnificent collection of several hundred scrapbooks of clippings, on almost every conceivable subject, for the years 1898–1920, at the Hampton Institute Library. Among other clipping collections consulted, the four volumes of J. Mercer Langston clippings at Howard University Library are especially notable.

Only in recent years have most of the major historical journals displayed any considerable interest in Negro history. For scholarly articles, therefore, I have relied chiefly on the files of the *Journal of Negro Education,* the *Journal of Negro History, Phylon,* and, to a lesser extent, the *Journal of Southern History.*

The biographical details on various personalities supplied in this book were gleaned from a wide variety of sources: several formal biographies and autobiographies, numerous sketches in magazines and newspapers, news reports about the doings of important individuals, and a few books that presented short life histories of eminent members of the race. In the last category the most useful volumes included W. J. Simmons, *Men of Mark* (Cleveland, 1887); John W. Cromwell, *The Negro in American History* (Washington, 1914); Joseph R. Gay, *Progress and Achievements of the Twentieth Century Negro* (no imprint, 1913); and J. W. Gibson and W. H. Crogman, *Progress of a Race* (Naperville, Illinois, 1902). Two provocative recent biographies of Du Bois, which should be used to supplement my discussion, are Francis L. Broderick, *W. E. B. Du Bois: Negro Leader in Time of Crisis* (Stanford, 1959), and Elliott M. Rudwick, *W. E. B. Du Bois: A Study in Minority Group Leadership* (Philadelphia, 1961).

NOTES

NOTES TO CHAPTER I

1. *Douglass' Monthly*, August, 1862; September, 1861; *Proceedings of the Fourth Annual Meeting of the Pennsylvania State Equal Rights' League . . . 1868* (Philadelphia, 1868), 35.

2. Howard H. Bell, "A Survey of the Negro Convention Movement, 1830–1861" (doctoral dissertation, Northwestern University, 1953), *passim*.

3. *Proceedings of the National Convention of Colored Men . . . 1864* (Boston, 1864), *passim*.

4. *Convention of the Freedmen of North Carolina: Official Proceedings . . . 1865* (no imprint [1865]), 12–13, 5, 16; *Proceedings of the First Convention of Colored Men of Kentucky . . . 1866* (Louisville, 1866), 24–25, 7–10, 21–22. For Alabama Convention see *The National Freedman*, I (1865), 364–65.

5. *Proceedings of the National Convention of the Colored Men of America . . . 1869* (Washington, 1869), 38–40, 31, 20.

6. *Proceedings of the National Convention of Colored Men . . . 1864*, 13–14; *First Annual Meeting of the National Equal Rights League . . . 1865* (Philadelphia, 1865), 14, 40, 42; *Proceedings of the National Convention . . . 1869*, 32, 37.

7. Sterling D. Spero and Abram L. Harris, *The Black Worker* (New York, 1931), 1–23, 31.

8. Charles H. Wesley, *Negro Labor in the United States* (New York, 1927), 173.

9. *Proceedings of the Colored National Labor Convention . . . 1869* (Washington, 1870), *passim*.

10. *Memorial of the National Convention of Colored People Praying to be Protected in Their Civil Rights*, 43rd Congress, 1st session, Senate Miscellaneous Documents, No. 31. Sumner's Civil Rights Bill was also the occasion for a large number of speeches by Negro congressmen. Generally, Negroes in constitutional conventions, in state legislatures, and in Congress expressed sentiments identical with those of the race conventions which we have thus far discussed. See, for example, *Proceedings of the Constitutional Convention of South Carolina . . . 1868* (Charleston, 1868), 2 vols.; Ethel Maude Christler,

"The Participation of Negroes in the Government of Georgia, 1867–1870" (M.A. thesis, Atlanta University, 1932), *passim; Congressional Globe,* 41st and 42nd Congresses and *Congressional Record,* 43rd and 44th Congresses, *passim.*

11. *Convention of Colored Newspaper Men . . . 1875* (pamphlet without cover in P. B. S. Pinchback Papers), 1–7.

12. Vernon L. Wharton, *The Negro in Mississippi, 1865–1890* (Chapel Hill, 1947), 59.

13. J. W. Alvord, *Letters from the South* (Washington, 1870), 9–10.

14. Roger W. Shugg, *Origins of the Class Struggle in Louisiana* (Baton Rouge, 1939), Chapter viii.

15. J. W. Alvord, *Semi-Annual Report on Schools for Freedmen, No. 3* (Washington, 1867), 12–15, 31; *Ibid., No. 6* (Washington, 1868), 4.

16. Wharton, *Negro in Mississippi,* 246.

17. Some of these, like the International Order of Twelve Knights and Daughters of Tabor, originally founded in 1855 in Illinois; and the Independent Order of Good Samaritans, founded in 1847, did not enjoy rapid growth until able to tap the freedmen after the Civil War. Another order that achieved considerable prominence, the Independent Order of St. Luke (founded in Richmond) was not even established until after emancipation.

NOTES TO INTRODUCTION TO PART TWO

1. The major sources for the following discussion are C. Vann Woodward, *Origins of the New South* (Baton Rouge, 1951); Woodward, *The Strange Career of Jim Crow* (New York, 1955); Gilbert T. Stephenson, *Race Distinctions in American Law* (New York, 1910); Leslie H. Fishel, "The North and the Negro, 1865–1900" (doctoral dissertation, Harvard University, 1953); Rayford W. Logan, *The Negro in American Life and Thought: The Nadir, 1877–1901* (New York, 1954); Paul H. Buck, *The Road to Reunion, 1865–1900* (Boston, 1937). More specialized works of value include James E. Cutler, *Lynch-Law* (New York, 1905); Fishel, "Northern Prejudice and Negro Suffrage, 1865–1870," *JNH,* XXXIX (January, 1954), 8–26; Vincent P. DeSantis, *Republicans Face the Southern Question* (Baltimore, 1959); Stanley P. Hirshon, *Farewell to the Bloody Shirt* (Bloomington, Ind., 1962).

2. Fishel feels, however, that on the whole the Negro's status in the North actually was improving between the end of the depression of the 1870's and 1900. This view is implicit in his "The North and the Negro, 1865–1900" and was expressed in a letter to the author, April 29, 1955.

3. For divergent views on the role of the radical agrarian and conservative groups in passing the disfranchisement amendments and laws see Woodward, *Origins of the New South,* 328–40; and V. O. Key, *Southern Politics in State and Nation* (New York, 1949), 540–50. See also Woodward, *The Strange Career of Jim Crow,* 26–47, 60–64.

NOTES TO CHAPTER II

1. Blanche K. Bruce Papers, correspondence 1876–77, *passim;* Sadie Daniel St. Clair, "The Public Career of Blanche K. Bruce" (doctoral dissertation, New York University, 1947), 96–98.

2. *Report and Testimony of the Select Committee of the United States Senate to Investigate the Causes of the Removal of the Negro from the Southern*

to the Northern States, Senate Report 693, 46th Congress, 2d session, Series 1900, part 2, 584–85; George B. Tindall, *South Carolina Negroes, 1877–1900* (Columbia, S.C., 1952), 66–67.

3. C. Vann Woodward, *The Strange Career of Jim Crow* (New York, 1955), 32, 33, 38, 40; A. A. Taylor, *The Negro in the Reconstruction of Virginia* (Washington, 1926), 268–74; Julian C. Ward, "The Republican Party in Bourbon Georgia, 1872–1890," *JSH,* IX (May, 1943), 200; Clarence A. Bacote, "The Negro in Georgia Politics, 1880–1908" (doctoral dissertation, University of Chicago, 1955), 75–84, 171–82; Jamie L. Reddick, "The Negro and the Populist Movement in Georgia" (M.A. thesis, Atlanta University, 1937), 49–50; Vernon L. Wharton, *The Negro in Mississippi, 1865–1890* (Chapel Hill, 1947), 202–3; Tindall, *South Carolina Negroes,* 62–64. The quotation is from John Hope, "The Negro Suffrage in the States Whose Constitutions Have Not Been Specifically Revised," in American Negro Academy Occasional Papers No. 11, *The Negro and the Elective Franchise* (Washington, 1905), 52.

4. Henry M. Turner, *Speech on Eligibility of Colored Members to Seats in the Georgia Legislature* (Augusta, 1868); *Gazette,* Oct. 5, 1889; William H. Skaggs, *The Southern Oligarchy* (New York, 1924), 111–12.

5. *New National Era and Citizen,* Dec. 18, 1873; *Bee,* March 14, 1885.

6. *Proceedings of the Colored National Labor Convention . . . 1869* (Washington, 1869), 3; New York *Globe,* May 12, 1883.

7. Vincent P. DeSantis, "Negro Dissatisfaction with Republican Policy in the South, 1882–1884," *JNH,* XXXVI (April, 1951), 148–59.

8. New York *Globe,* Sept. 29, 1883; *People's Advocate,* Oct. 6, 1883; *Bee,* Dec. 1, 1883; *Gazette,* May 3, 1884.

9. *Bee,* Feb. 10, 1883.

10. John Daniels, *In Freedom's Birthplace* (Boston, 1914), 119, 129, 454; New York *Freeman,* Dec. 12, 1885, Sept. 25, 1886.

11. New York *Freeman,* April 4, 1885; *Age,* Nov. 19, 1887; Stewart, *The Afro-American in Politics* (Brooklyn, 1891), 6–14; *Proceedings of the Convention of the New York State Cleveland League . . . 1892* (Brooklyn, 1892), 12.

12. *Bee,* April 14, June 23, 1883; April 5, Sept. 6, Nov. 22, 1884.

13. T. Thomas Fortune, *Black and White* (New York, 1885), 93, 99, 104, 117–18, 124, 126, 127–28; New York *Globe,* July 26, 1884; New York *Freeman,* Feb. 7, 1885; Fortune, *The Negro in Politics* (New York, 1886), 58–59, 38; *Age,* July 20, 1889.

14. *Gazette,* Oct. 4, 1892.

15. Taylor, *Whites and Blacks* (Atlanta, 1889), 17, 21, 27, 41; Price, "The Negro in the Last Decade of the Century," *Independent,* XLI (Jan. 1, 1891); W. J. Walls, *Joseph Charles Price* (Boston, 1943), 393.

16. *Freeman,* July 28, 1888; *Bee,* Aug. 4, 1888.

17. *New National Era and Citizen,* Feb. 19, 1874; Douglass to Straker, Aug. 2, 1888, Douglass Papers; Douglass, "The Future of the Negro," A.M.E. *Review,* VI (Oct. 1889), 232–33; "The Cause of Republican Defeat" (1890), MS in Douglass Papers; Benjamin Quarles, *Frederick Douglass* (Washington, 1948), 334. On Straker, see Straker to Douglass, March 22, 1877, Douglass Papers; New York *Globe,* Sept. 1, 1883; Straker, *The New South Investigated* (Detroit, 1888), 75, 225.

18. A.M.E. *Review* XI (April, 1895), 525–26.

19. *Age,* March 28, Oct. 24, 1891; *Freeman,* Nov. 25, 1893.

20. *Bee*, Aug. 24, 1895; *Recorder*, Oct. 31, 1895.
21. *Bee*, Sept. 28, 1894; *Gazette*, March 4, 1895.
22. *Bee*, Aug. 24, 1895; Wisconsin *Afro-American*, Aug. 20, 1892.
23. "The Democratic Return to Power—Its Effect?" A.M.E. *Review*, I (Jan., 1885), 229, 241, 243.
24. A.M.E. *Review*, VI (April, 1890), 303–4; New York *Freeman*, April 4, 1885; *Age*, April 7, 1889.
25. St. Clair, "Public Career of Blanche K. Bruce," 217; Taylor, *Whites and Blacks*, 44, 45, 50; Stewart, *Afro-American in Politics*, 10; Bowen to Still, ———— 12, 1894, Carter G. Woodson Collection.
26. In addition to titles suggested in Note 3, the following are especially helpful in regard to Negroes and third parties in the South: Jack Abramowitz, "The South: Arena for Greenback Reformers," *Social Education*, XVII (March, 1953), 108–10; Abramowitz, "The Negro in the Populist Movement," *JNH*, XXXVIII (July, 1953), 257–89; Woodward, *Origins of the New South* (Baton Rouge, 1951), 79–80, 254–58, 275–77; Woodward, "Tom Watson and the Negro in Agrarian Politics," *JSH*, IV (Feb., 1938), 14–33; Helen G. Edmonds, *The Negro and Fusion Politics in North Carolina, 1894–1901* (Chapel Hill, 1951).
27. *Age*, Jan. 17, March 28, Aug., 1891; Woodward, *Origins of the New South*, 225. For Congressman Thomas E. Miller of South Carolina see *Age*, Oct. 11, 1890; for J. Mercer Langston of Virginia see *Congressional Record*, 51st Congress, 2d session, 1479–82; for George Washington Murray of South Carolina in 1891 see *ibid.*, 53rd Congress, 1st session, 2147–50.
28. Wharton, *Negro in Mississippi*, 211–12; *Age*, Oct. 11, 1890.
29. Langston, *From the Virginia Plantation to the National Capitol* (Hartford, 1894), 511–12; *Journal of the Proceedings . . . of the National Education Association*, 1890, 271 (for Price); *Age*, Sept. 8, 1893 in Langston Clipping Collection.
30. Tindall, *South Carolina Negroes*, 69–70, 56–58, 76–78, 81–82; Smalls, "Election Methods in the South," *North American Review*, CLI (Nov., 1890) 593–600; Tindall, "The Question of Race in the South Carolina Constitutional Convention of 1895," *Negro History Bulletin*, XV (Jan. 1952), 61–62; Mary J. Miller, ed., *Suffrage Speeches by Negroes in the Constitutional Convention* (no imprint, n.d.).

NOTES TO CHAPTER III

1. Crummell Manuscript Collection, MS No. 49; Crummell, "The Social Principle . . . ," in Crummell, *The Greatness of Christ and Other Sermons* (New York, 1882), 287–88, 294, 296, 301–6, 309–10. For his colonizationist views see e.g., Crummell, *The Future of Africa* (New York, 1862); Crummell MSS No. 317 [1863] and No. 18 [1872]; and *African Repository*, XLIII (1867), 262, and XLVIII (1872), 21, 164–65, 237.
2. *Proceedings of the National Conference of Colored Men . . . Nashville . . . 1879* (Washington, 1879), 96, 85–86.
3. *People's Advocate*, Aug. 30, 1879, Sept. 29, 1883.
4. *Recorder*, Nov. 8, 1883; A.M.E. *Review*, II (July, 1885), 87.
5. *Bee*, May 7, 1892; *Constitution of the Union League of the District of Columbia* (Washington, 1893), 4; Alice M. Dunbar, ed., *Masterpieces of Negro Eloquence* (New York, 1914), 178–79.

6. *Gazette*, Feb. 16, 1889.

7. For Colored Alliance see Jack Abramowitz, "Accommodation and Militance in Negro Life, 1876–1916" (doctoral dissertation, Columbia University, 1950), 34–44; C. Vann Woodward, *Origins of the New South* (Baton Rouge, 1951), 192, 220–21, 236, 255, 256. On Populist Movement see chap. II, above. On Knights of Labor see Sterling D. Spero and Abram L. Harris, *The Black Worker* (New York, 1931), 40–48; George B. Tindall, *South Carolina Negroes, 1877–1900* (Columbia, S.C., 1952), 115–17; Sidney Kessler, "The Negro in Labor Strikes," *Midwest Journal*, XVI (Summer, 1954), 16–35; and Kessler, "The Organization of Negroes in the Knights of Labor," *JNH*, XXXVII (July, 1952), 248–76.

8. Douglass, *Three Addresses* (Washington, 1886), 11–12; Lynch, "Should Colored Men Join Labor Organizations?" A.M.E. *Review*, III (Oct., 1886), 165, 167; *Gazette*, July 17, 1886; *Bee*, Feb. 27, 1886; New York *Freeman*, May 1, 1886.

9. Woodward, *Origins of the New South*, 220; Straker, *The New South Investigated* (Detroit, 1888), 194–95, 74, 91, 94; Stewart, "Popular Discontent," A.M.E. *Review*, VII (April, 1891), 365–69.

10. Fortune, *Black and White* (New York, 1884), 34–39, 149–51, 174–75, 217–218, 223, 235–42; New York *Freeman*, March 20, 1886.

11. Bernard Mandel, "Samuel Gompers and the Negro Workers, 1886–1914," *JNH*, XL (Jan., 1955), 234–60.

12. J. W. Cromwell, *History of the Bethel Literary and Historical Association* (Washington, 1896), 7; *Gazette*, March 22, Jan. 26, 1884; *Advocate*, April 29, 1886; *Recorder*, March 26, 1885; *Bee*, March 10, 17, 24, 1884; Cardozo, "Shall Our Schools Be Mixed or Separate?" A.M.E. *Review*, III (Oct., 1886), 160–64; *Index*, March 23, 1895.

13. L. M. Haygood, *The Colored Man in the Methodist Episcopal Church* (New York, 1890), chaps. ix, x, and xiv; George F. Bragg, *History of the Afro-American Group of the Episcopal Church* (Baltimore, 1922), 151, chap. xviii, 271–74.

14. *People's Advocate*, March 3, 1883; R. R. Downs, "Leaders of Thought," A.M.E. *Review*, X (Oct., 1892), 241–42; *Bee*, April 28, 1894.

15. Williams, *History of the Negro Race in America from 1619–1880* (New York, 1883), I, iii ff; Johnson, *School History of the Negro Race in America* (3d ed.; Chicago, 1893), 7; Cromwell, *History of the Bethel Literary and Historical Association*, 4; *Gazette*, Jan. 13, 1895; Straker, *New South Investigated*, 207.

16. *Bee*, June 25, 1887.

17. *Colored American*, Oct. 9, 1898.

18. New York *Globe*, Feb. 2, 1884; George L. Ruffin, "A Look Forward," A.M.E. *Review*, II (July, 1885), 29.

19. Downing, "The Afro-American Force in America," A.M.E. *Review*, I (Oct., 1884), 157–62; Astwood, "Shall Our Schools Be Mixed or Separate?" *Ibid.*, III (April, 1887), 569–71.

20. *Gazette*, Sept. 15, 1894; Alexander, *The Brotherhood of Liberty* (Baltimore, 1891), 46–48; Phillips, *From the Farm to the Bishopric* (Nashville, 1932), chap. xvi; and *Index*, June 28, Aug. 24, 1895; Crummell, "The Need of New Ideas and New Aims for a New Era," 1883, in *Africa and America* (Springfield, Mass., 1891), 21–22, 33–34, 31; *The Echo*, Dec. 1, 1894 (clipping at Howard University Library); Crummell MS No. 25 [1884]; Crummell, *The Race Problem in America* (Washington, 1889), 15.

21. Straker, *New South Investigated*, 51, 167, 100, 49–50, 223–24; Straker, "Lynching Law in the South," A.M.E. *Review*, XI (Oct., 1894), 293.

22. Lucretia H. Coleman, *Poor Ben: A Story of Real Life* (Nashville, 1890), 76–77, 94–96, 115, 154–66; *Gazette*, July 2, 1886; Arnett and Jere A. Brown, *The Black Laws* (No imprint, 1886), 1–18; Coleman, *Poor Ben*, 169, 178–79, 186.

23. Brown, *My Southern Home* (3d ed.; Boston, 1882), 182–83, 233–37, 240–41, 246, 163–65, 248–50.

NOTES TO CHAPTER IV

1. In this chapter the term "migration" refers to migration within the United States, "emigration" and "colonization" to migration from the United States to other countries. Contemporaries frequently used the words interchangeably, the term "emigration" often referring to both types of movement.

2. U.S. Bureau of the Census, *Negroes in the United States* (Washington, 1915), 12, 14, 63–68; Charles S. Johnson, "How Much is the Migration a Flight from Persecution?" *Opportunity*, I (Sept., 1923), 272–74; *Report and Testimony of the Select Committee of the United States Senate to Investigate the Causes of the Removal of the Negroes from the Southern to the Northern States*, 46th Congress, 2d session, Senate Report 693, Series 1899 and 1900 (hereafter cited as *Report and Testimony of the Select Committee*); Frenise A. Logan, "The Movement of Negroes from North Carolina, 1876–1894," *North Carolina Historical Review*, XXXIII (Jan., 1956), 45–65; George B. Tindall, *South Carolina Negroes, 1877–1900* (Columbia, S.C., 1952), chap. ix.

3. *Report and Testimony of the Select Committee*, Series 1900, Part 3, 382, 65–66, 69, 390, and Part 2, 101–104, 39, and Series 1899, Part 1, xxi–xxii; *Proceedings of the State Emigration Convention . . . Raleigh, N.C. . . . 1889* (Wilmington, N.C., 1889), 6–7.

4. *Proceedings of the National Conference of Colored Men . . . 1879* (Washington, 1879), 4, 12, 94, 104, 95; *Age*, Jan. 25, 1890.

5. *Report and Testimony of the Select Committee*, Series 1900, Part 2, 478–88, Part 3, 517–38, and Series 1899, Part 1, 107–108, 49–53; Logan, "The Movement of Negroes from North Carolina," 59–61; Tindall, *South Carolina Negroes*, 178–79. Smalls did give some support to the idea. See Rupert S. Holland, ed., *Letters and Diary of Laura M. Towne* (Cambridge, 1912), 294, and the National League of Boston, *The Wrongs of the Negro: The Remedy* (no imprint, [1888]), 1.

6. Vernon L. Wharton, *The Negro in Mississippi, 1865–1890* (Chapel Hill, 1947), 112–14; William Pickens, *Bursting Bonds* (Boston, 1923), 16–17.

7. Solon J. Buck, *The Granger Movement* (Cambridge, 1913), 32–33.

8. T. J. Woofter, *Negro Migration* (New York, 1920), 14, 41; Johnson, "How Much is the Migration a Flight from Persecution?" 274, 272.

9. U.S. Bureau of the Census, *Negro Population, 1790–1915* (Washington, 1918), 111–14; Kelly Miller, "The Modern Land of Goshen," *Southern Workman*, XXIX (Nov., 1900), 603–604; Du Bois, "The Negro As He Really Is," *World's Work*, II (June, 1901), 864.

10. Alexander Crummell, *Duty of a Rising Christian State to Contribute Toward the World's Well-Being and Civilization* (London, 1856), 31. On the ante-bellum emigration movement see August Meier, "The Emergence of Negro

Nationalism," *Midwest Journal,* IV (Winter, 1951–1952), 98–104; and Howard H. Bell, "A Survey of the Negro Convention Movement, 1830–1861" (doctoral dissertation, Northwestern University, 1953), *passim.*

11. *Report and Testimony of the Select Committee,* Series 1900, Part 2, 194; Wharton, *Negro in Mississippi,* 113; Tindall, *South Carolina Negroes,* 154–63; Walter L. Fleming, "'Pap' Singleton, The Moses of the Colored Exodus," *American Journal of Sociology,* XV (July, 1909), 77–79; Clarence A. Bacote, "The Negro in Georgia Politics, 1880–1908" (doctoral dissertation, University of Chicago, 1955), 27; *African Repository,* LXVII (April, 1891), 36.

12. *African Repository,* LXIII (April, 1887), 35; Tindall, *South Carolina Negroes,* 155–59; *Repository,* LIV (Jan., 1878), 20; Fleming, "'Pap' Singleton," 78; *Repository,* LXIII (April, 1887), 36–37.

13. Scarborough, "The Race Problem," *Arena,* II (Oct., 1890), 561–62.

14. Tindall, *South Carolina Negroes,* 154–56, 180–82; Sir George Campbell, *White and Black* (London, 1879), 347; *African Repository,* LVI (July, 1880), 67–68, and LXVI (April, 1890), 53–54.

15. *African Repository,* LI (April, 1875), 59, and LII (July, 1876), 84–86; J. W. E. Bowen, ed., *Africa and the American Negro,* 195–98 (Atlanta, 1896); *Repository,* LXIV (April, 1889), 51; Turner, *The Barbarous Decision of the United States Supreme Court . . .* (Atlanta, 1893), 3; *Recorder,* April 1, 1886, and Feb. 18, 1892; A.M.E. *Review,* I (Jan., 1885), 246–47.

16. Lucretia H. Coleman, *Poor Ben* (Nashville, 1890), 106, 110, 112; Arnett, "Africa and the Descendants of Africa," A.M.E. *Review,* XI (Oct., 1894), 231–38; Stewart, *Liberia: The Americo-African Republic* (New York, 1886), 101–5. On Stewart see also *Freeman,* Nov. 25, 1893, which in addition has similar comments.

17. "What Should be the Policy of the Colored American Toward Africa?" A.M.E. *Review,* II (July, 1885), 68–75; Bowen, ed., *Africa and the American Negro.*

18. *Freeman,* Dec. 9, 1893; A.M.E. *Review,* II (July, 1885), 70.

19. James D. Corrothers, *In Spite of the Handicap* (New York, 1916), 116; *Freeman,* Nov. 25, 1893.

20. See especially editorial by B. F. Lee in *Recorder,* April 28, 1887.

21. The leading authority on Negro thought in the generation before the Civil War has similarly bracketed together migration to the Caribbean, Canada, Africa, and the American frontier as related and "nationalist" movements. See Bell, "A Survey of the Negro Convention Movement," *passim.*

NOTES TO CHAPTER V

1. *Recorder,* Dec. 2, 1886.

2. New York *Globe,* Sept. 29, Oct. 6, 1883; *Proceedings of the State Convention of Colored Men of South Carolina . . . 1883,* [n.p., 1883], 3–5. For Arkansas and Texas Conventions see Mifflin W. Gibbs, *Shadow and Light* (Washington, 1902), 175–76; Herbert Aptheker, ed., *A Documentary History of the Negro People in the United States* (New York, 1951), 686–90.

3. W. M. Alexander, *The Brotherhood of Liberty* (Baltimore, 1891), *passim; Age,* Feb. 4, 1888.

4. *Age,* Feb. 8, 1890; *Bee,* Feb. 22, 1890; *Constitution of the American Citizens' Equal Rights Association* (Washington, 1890), n.p.; *Gazette,* Dec. 2, 1893, and *Freeman,* Dec. 3, 1893.

5. *Proceedings of the Civil Rights Mass Meeting ... October 22, 1883* (Washington, 1883), 5, 7, 8; Arnett and Brown, *The Black Laws* (no imprint, [1886]); New York *Globe,* March 31, 1883.

6. David W. Bishop, "The Attitude of the Interstate Commerce Commission Toward Discrimination on Public Carriers, 1887–1910" (M.A. thesis, Howard University, 1950), 23–24, 26–31, 45–51; *Age,* May 25, 1889; A.M.E. *Review,* VII (April, 1891), 448.

7. John Hope Franklin, "History of Racial Segregation in the United States," in Ira DeA. Reid, ed., *Racial Desegregation and Integration,* Annals of the American Academy of Political and Social Science, XXXIV (March, 1956), 7; Clarence Bacote, "The Negro in Georgia Politics, 1880–1908" (doctoral dissertation, University of Chicago, 1955), 18.

8. *Recorder,* Feb. 16, 1893; Ida Wells (later Ida Wells-Barnett), *Southern Horrors: Lynch Law in All Its Phases* (New York, 1892); *A Red Record* (Chicago, 1894), and *Mob Rule in New Orleans* (Chicago, 1900).

9. New York *Globe,* March 31, 1883; *Gazette,* Oct. 5, 1889; Herbert Renfro, "Is the Afro-American League a Failure?," A.M.E. *Review,* IX (July, 1892), 14–15.

10. *Recorder,* Aug. 9, 1888, May 8, 1891; J. A. Davis, "Who Shall Deliver Us?," A.M.E. *Review,* XI (Jan., 1895), 431–35; Benjamin E. Mays, *The Negro's God as Reflected in His Literature* (Boston, 1938), chap. ii.

11. *Age,* Oct. 11, 1890; A.M.E. *Review,* VIII (April, 1891), 446–49.

12. Douglass, *Life and Times of Frederick Douglass* (Hartford, 1881), 501–2; Douglass, "The Color Line," *North American Review,* CXXXII (June, 1881), 568, 575–76; Douglass, *Three Addresses* (Washington, 1886), 23.

13. Douglass to George L. Ruffin, Jan. 28 [1884], photostat in Ruffin Papers.

14. Douglass, "The Future of the Race," A.M.E. *Review,* VI (Oct., 1889), 234–36, 225, 227–31.

15. Samuel R. Spencer, Jr., *Booker T. Washington and the Negro's Place in American Life* (Boston, 1955), 108; BTW to Douglass, April 2, 1894, in Douglass Papers.

16. Bacote, "Negro in Georgia Politics," 147.

17. A.M.E. *Review,* I (Jan., 1885), 219.

18. For the views of various notable figures on ante-bellum colonization see generally Howard H. Bell, "A Survey of the Negro Convention Movement, 1830–1861" (doctoral dissertation, Northwestern University, 1953), *passim.*

19. Langston, *Freedom and Citizenship: Selected Letters and Addresses* (Washington, 1883), *passim;* Langston, "Address of Welcome to the Colored Press Convention," A.M.E. *Review,* V (April, 1889), 385; Langston Clipping Collection, Vols. II–IV; Langston, "The Negro Problem Solvable," 1890, MS in Langston Papers.

20. Crogman, *The Negro: His Needs and Claims* (Atlanta, 1885), 5, 26–36; Crogman, *Talks for the Times* (no imprint, [1896]), 64–65, 210–11; Johnson, "The Best Methods of Removing the Disabilities of Caste from the Negro," 1892, MS in Johnson Collection; Cyrus F. Adams, "Col. William Pledger," *Colored American Magazine,* V (June, 1902), 147; W. J. Simmons, *Men of Mark* (Cleveland, 1887), 319.

21. *Catalogue of Zion Wesley College, 1884–1885,* 27–38; William J. Walls, *Joseph Charles Price* (Boston, 1943), 252. Actually, without the substantial aid of philanthropists such as William E. Dodge, Leland Stanford, and Collis

Huntington, it is doubtful that the school would have amounted to very much.

22. *Age*, Oct. 11, 1890; Walls, *Joseph Charles Price*, 269–73.

23. Price, "The Race Problem in the South," a frequently repeated address, MS *circa* 1888, in Carter G. Woodson Collection.

24. Walls, *Joseph Charles Price*, 393–94.

25. *Age*, Oct. 11, 1890.

26. W.E.B. Du Bois, *The Souls of Black Folk* (Chicago, 1903), 42, 49.

27. *Gazette*, Dec. 2, 1893; *Freeman*, Nov. 25, 1893.

NOTES TO CHAPTER VI

1. For a discussion of the different aspects of industrial education see especially W.E.B. Du Bois, ed., *The Negro Artisan* (Atlanta University Publications No. 7, 1902), 31–33; Daniel Coit Gilman, *A Study in Black and White* (John F. Slater Fund, Occasional Papers, No. 10, 1897), 9; U.S. Bureau of Education, *Negro Education* (Washington, 1917), I, 85, 90–95.

2. Greater detail and fuller documentation on the development of industrial education in Negro schools down to the 1880's is given in August Meier, "The Beginning of Industrial Education in Negro Schools," *Midwest Journal*, VII (Spring, 1955), 23–44. For ante-bellum period see especially Benjamin Brawley, *Early Efforts for Industrial Education* (John F. Slater Fund, Occasional Papers, No. 22, 1923); *Proceedings of the Annual Conventions of the Free People of Color*, 1831–1835 and 1853 (title and imprint vary); and Douglass' editorials in *Frederick Douglass' Paper* in March 1853.

3. *Second Annual Report of the Western Freedmen's Aid Commission, 1865* (Cincinnati, 1865), 16.

4. Suzanne Carson's "Samuel Chapman Armstrong: Missionary to the South" (doctoral dissertation, Johns Hopkins University, 1952) has proven to be a helpful interpretation and an invaluable reference (though I take responsibility for the above interpretations). See also editorials and annual reports in *Southern Workman*, 1874.

5. Jackson-Coppin, *Reminiscences of School Life* (Philadelphia, 1913), 24–30; *Sixteenth Annual Report of the Freedmen's Aid Society of the Methodist Church* (Cincinnati, 1883), 19.

6. Louis D. Rubin, Jr., ed., *Teach the Freeman: The Correspondence of Rutherford B. Hayes and the Slater Fund for Negro Education*, 2 vols. (Baton Rouge, 1959), which appeared after this book was written, contains materials which further illustrate some of the points made in this chapter in regard to the Slater Fund.

7. *Proceedings of the Trustees of the John F. Slater Fund for the Education of the Freedmen* (hereafter cited as *Proceedings of the Slater Fund*), 1883, 7, 13–14; *ibid.*, 1888, 7–8; *Annual Report of the General Agent of the John F. Slater Fund*, 1886 (Atlanta, 1886), 35.

8. *Atlanta University Catalogues*: 1881–1882, 21; 1883–1884, 23; 1886–1887, 22; 1888–1889, 26, 28; 1890–1891, 29, 36; *Annual Report of the General Agent of the John F. Slater Fund*, 1886, 20.

9. *Annual Reports of the American Missionary Association*, 1870–1890, *passim*.

10. *Bee*, Jan. 31, 1885, Feb. 26, 1887, Feb. 11, 1888; Marion Thompson Wright, *The Education of Negroes in New Jersey* (New York, 1941), 178–80;

J. W. Gibson and W. H. Crogman, *Progress of a Race* (Atlanta, 1902), 325–26.

11. *Proceedings of the Slater Fund,* 1886, 35; and 1891, 53.

12. Washington himself referred to the economic interest of important capitalists and philanthropists in industrial education and Negro uplift.

13. See statements by J. L. M. Curry and Haygood in *Proceedings of the Slater Fund,* 1891, 17–18, 36. Paradoxically, the Fund under Curry's agency concentrated its philanthropy upon those schools that did the most effective training in agriculture and trades.

14. *Catalogues of Howard University,* 1912–1913, 96–101, and 1916–1917, 101.

15. *Official Compilation of the Proceedings of the Afro-American National Convention, 1890* (Chicago, 1890), 36–37; *The Southland,* I (June, 1890), 245, 250, 255, 258, 287.

16. Crummell, "The Necessities and Advantages of Education Considered in Relation to Colored Men," 1844, Crummell Collection, MS No. 45; Crummell, "The Destined Superiority of the Negro," 1881, in *The Greatness of Christ and Other Sermons* (New York, 1882), 382–402; and "Common Sense in Common Schooling," 1886, in *Africa and America* (Springfield, Mass., 1891), 350–54; *Sixteenth Annual Report of the Freedmen's Aid Society of the Methodist Church* (Cincinnati, 1883), 58–59; Fortune, *Black and White* (New York, 1884), 81–82, and New York *Globe,* March 16, 1884.

17. Lynch, "Should Colored Men Join Labor Organizations?" A.M.E. *Review,* III (Oct., 1886), 167; Stewart, "The Afro-American as a Factor in the Labor Problem," *ibid.,* VI (July, 1889), 38; Bowen, "Manual-Training Schools," *Christian Educator,* I (April, 1890), 115–18; Langston, *From the Virginia Plantation to the National Capitol* (Hartford, 1894), 511–12.

18. For representative presentation of this point of view see U.S. Bureau of Education, *Negro Education,* I, 10, 12, 81.

19. *Proceedings of the Slater Fund,* 1891, 35; Du Bois, *Negro Artisan,* 39.

20. *Proceedings of the Slater Fund,* 1891, 25; and 1902, 44.

21. U.S. Bureau of Education, *Negro Education,* I, 257, 87–88, and chap. vi, II, 18–20.

22. *Forty-Eighth Annual Report of the American Missionary Association,* 1894, 26; *Fifty-Fifth Annual Report . . . ,* 1901, 24; W. E. B. Du Bois, *Souls of Black Folk* (Chicago, 1903), 97.

23. *The Christian Educator,* 1895 *et seq., passim.* See also unpublished minutes of the Freedmen's Aid and Southern Education Society, especially the executive board minutes, March 18, 1892, and the minutes of the Board of Managers, July 2, 1895.

24. Kelly Miller, "Education of the Negro," chap. xvi of *Report of Commissioner of Education for 1900–1901* (Washington, 1902), 817–18; *Crisis,* X (July, 1915), 111, and XV (Nov., 1917), 11.

25. BTW, *My Larger Education* (New York, 1911), 131–37.

26. BTW, *Future of the American Negro* (Boston, 1899), 111–12; BTW, *Working with the Hands* (New York, 1904), 16–18.

27. E. Davidson Washington, ed., *Selected Speeches of Booker T. Washington* (New York, 1932), 7–8; BTW, *Working with the Hands,* 24.

NOTES TO CHAPTER VII

Except where otherwise noted, all works cited in this chapter are by BTW, and all citations to correspondence are to the BTW Papers.

1. *Address . . . Delivered at the Opening of the Cotton States and International Exposition, 1895* (no imprint, n.d.), 6–11.

2. Johnson, "The Social Philosophy of Booker T. Washington," 1940, MS lent to the author by the late Dr. Johnson.

3. *Future of the American Negro* (Boston, 1899), 107. Biographical details are supplied in *Up From Slavery* (New York, 1901), and in the more revealing *Story of My Life and Work* (Naperville, 1900).

4. Emmett J. Scott and Lyman B. Stowe, *Booker T. Washington: Builder of a Civilization* (New York, 1916), 3–4.

5. The following discussion of Booker T. Washington's philosophy is based chiefly on *Up From Slavery, Future of the American Negro, My Larger Education* (New York, 1911), *The Case of the Negro* (Tuskegee, 1902), *Sowing and Reaping* (Boston, 1900), and *Selected Speeches of Booker T. Washington,* ed. by E. Davidson Washington (New York, 1932). Also utilized were a number of his other books, pamphlets, and articles in both Negro and white magazines, the clipping books in the BTW Papers, and materials at the Department of Records and Research, Tuskegee Institute.

6. *Future of the American Negro,* 176.

7. "A University Education for Negroes," *Independent,* LXVIII (March 24, 1910), 613–18; "What I am Trying to Do," *World's Work,* XXVII (Nov., 1913), 103.

8. *My Larger Education,* 72–73, 76–77.

9. *Up From Slavery,* 68–69; "The Best Free Labor in the World," *Southern State Farm Magazine* (Jan., 1898), 496–98 (clipping in BTW Papers); "The Negro and the Labor Unions," *Atlantic Monthly,* CXI (June, 1913), 756–67.

10. *The Case of the Negro,* 2.

11. Detroit *Leader,* Sept. 8, 1911 (in BTW Clipping Books).

12. "Is the Negro Having a Fair Chance?" *Century,* LXXXV (Nov., 1912), 50–55, 46; *My Larger Education,* 189, 197–98; "Fundamental Needs for the Progress of the Race" (1904, MS at Tuskegee Institute Department of Records and Research).

13. *Selected Speeches . . . ,* 94–95, 98.

14. "Taking Advantage of Our Disadvantages," *A.M.E. Review,* XX (April, 1894), 480; *Story of My Life and Work,* 265–66, 274–76.

15. *Selected Speeches . . . ,* 2–3; "Taking Advantage of Our Disadvantages," 480; *My Larger Education,* 178.

16. "Is the Negro Having a Fair Chance?" 51; *Report of the Fifteenth Annual Convention of the National Negro Business League . . . 1914* (no imprint [1914]), 82; "My View of Segregation Laws," *New Republic,* V (Dec. 4, 1915), 113–14.

17. *Recorder,* March 17, 1904.

18. *Future of the American Negro,* 141, 13, 153; *An Open Letter to the Louisiana Constitutional Convention, Feb. 19, 1898* (no imprint [1900?]), 1–2; interview reprinted from Atlanta *Constitution,* ————, 1899 in *ibid.,* 6; *Gazette,* Dec. 20, 1902.

19. BTW to Garrison, Sept. 23, 1899, in F. J. Garrison Papers; BTW to Chesnutt, July 7, 1903.

20. BTW to Garrison, Nov. 28, 1899 in Garrison Papers; BTW to T. Thomas Fortune, Nov. 10, 1899, June 23, 1903.

21. BTW to Garrison, Feb. 27, and March 11, 1900, Garrison Papers; Jesse Lawson to BTW, March 29, June 26, July 30, Oct. 2, Dec. 30, 1901; April 30, June 24, 1902; BTW to Lawson, Dec. 11, 1903. On BTW's opposition to reduced representation for Southern states, see BTW to R. C. Ogden, May 15, 1903; BTW to W. H. Baldwin, March 4, 1904.

22. E.g., Correspondence with A. D. Wimbs, 1901.

23. Correspondence of Wilford Smith (alias J. C. May) and Emmett J. Scott (alias R. C. Black) 1903 and 1904; F. L. McGhee to BTW, Jan. 12, 1904; BTW to George F. Bragg, March 10, 1904. For fuller documentation of this and other points made in this section see August Meier, "Toward a Reinterpretation of Booker T. Washington," *JSH*, XXIII (May, 1957), 220–27.

24. BTW to J. W. E. Bowen, Dec. 27, 1904.

25. *My Larger Education*, 159.

26. See especially Roosevelt to BTW, Sept. 14, Dec. 12, 1901; and Roosevelt to James Ford Rhodes, Dec. 15, 1905, in Elting E. Morison, ed., *The Letters of Theodore Roosevelt* (Cambridge, 1951–54), IV, 1072; Roosevelt to Richard Watson Gilder, Nov. 16, 1908, in Roosevelt Papers, Library of Congress.

27. Samuel R. Spencer, Jr., *Booker T. Washington and the Negro's Place in American Life* (Boston, 1955), 136, 138; two letters of BTW to Roosevelt dated Nov. 4, 1902; Roosevelt to John Graham Brooks, Nov. 13, 1908, in Roosevelt Papers.

28. White to BTW, Oct. 7, 1901; Scott to BTW, July 2, 1902; Roosevelt to Silas McBee, Feb. 3, 1903, in Morison, *Letters of Theodore Roosevelt*, III, 419.

29. The correspondence concerning Washington's political activities during the Roosevelt and Taft administrations is enormous. See especially correspondence with Roosevelt, James R. Clarkson, George Cortelyou, William Loeb, and Charles W. Anderson during Roosevelt's presidency, and with Taft, C. D. Norton, C. D. Hilles, and Anderson during Taft's.

30. E.g., J. C. May to R. C. Black, July 15, 1903; BTW to Smith, Feb. 2, March 3, 1904; Smith to BTW, Feb. 4, 1904.

31. BTW to Villard, Sept. 7, 1908; Villard to BTW, Sept. 8, 1908.

32. BTW to Anderson, Jan. 6, 1911; BTW to R. W. Thompson, Jan. 7, 1911; BTW to Hilles, ——, 1911; *Crisis*, II (Aug., 1911), 139.

33. Jackson to BTW, Jan. 24, 1901.

34. Napier to BTW, Oct. 28, Dec. 11, 1903; BTW to Napier, Nov. 2, 1903; BTW to Lawson, Nov. 5, 1903; BTW to Du Bois, Dec. 14, 1903, Feb. 27, June 4, 1904; Baldwin to BTW, Jan. 7, 1904.

35. Miller to BTW, May 22, 1906; Grimké to BTW, May 25, June 10, 1906; BTW to Grimké, June 2, 4, 10, 1906; Scott to Thompson, June 5, 1906.

36. See correspondence with various college presidents 1904 and 1905.

37. BTW to President J. G. Merrill of Fisk, April 26, 1905; James C. Bertram (Carnegie's secretary) to BTW, Jan. 15, 1908; BTW to Carnegie, Oct. 18, 1910; BTW to Bertram, April 28, 1913, etc.

38. Ridgely Torrence, *The Story of John Hope* (New York, 1948), 159–63; correspondence between Hope and BTW, 1909.

39. Spencer, *Booker T. Washington,* chap. x.

40. BTW to Ogden, May 1, 1903.

NOTES TO CHAPTER VIII

1. R. R. Wright for example was holding such conferences during the early 1880's.

2. "The Tuskegee Negro Conference," *Southern Workman,* XXIX (April, 1900), 234.

3. E. g., Richmond *Dispatch,* Nov. 7, 1913; Newport *News-Star,* Oct. 31, 1915 (both in Hampton Institute Clippings).

4. Smith, "The Farmers' Improvement Society of Texas," A.M.E. *Review,* XXV (Jan., 1909), 289–96; J. Mason Brewer, *Negro Legislators of Texas* (Dallas, 1935), 104; Smith, "Village Improvement Among Negroes," *Outlook,* LXIV (March 31, 1900), 736; Holtzclaw, *Black Man's Burden* (New York, 1915), 136–41.

5. Carnegie gave $2700 each year until 1911 and $1500 annually for the next three years. See BTW to Carnegie, Dec. 16, 20, 1910; James A. Bertram to BTW, Dec. 29, 1910, Dec. 20, 1911; BTW to Bertram, Feb. 11, 1911.

6. *Report of the Seventh Annual Convention of the National Negro Business League* (Boston, [1906]), 188–89. However, the Richmond Business League in 1901 exhausted its treasury in taking legal action against Virginia's Jim Crow Car law, apparently with Washington's approval. See Giles Jackson to BTW, March 28, 1901.

7. *Annual Report of the Sixteenth Annual Session of the National Negro Business League* (Nashville, 1915), 20; *Report of the Fifteenth Annual Convention of the National Negro Business League* (No imprint [1914]), 146–48; *Report of the Fourth Annual Convention of the National Negro Business League* (Wilberforce, Ohio, 1903), 24.

8. *Annual Report of the Sixteenth Session . . . ,* 31–32; *Report of the Fifth Annual Convention of the National Negro Business League* (Pensacola, 1904), 69–73, 46–47; *Report of the Fifteenth Annual Convention . . . ,* 66–69; *Report of the Fifth Annual Convention . . . ,* 72.

9. Thomas W. Burton, *What Experience Has Taught Me* (Cincinnati, 1910), 68–69, 71.

10. E. Johnson, *Key to the Negro Problem* (Forest City, Ark., 1898), 1, 3; Negro Protective League of Pennsylvania, *What Will You Do About This?* (Philadelphia, 1914), 3; George E. Taylor, "The National Liberty Party," *Voice of the Negro,* I (Oct., 1904), 479–81.

11. New York *Freeman,* May 28, 1887; *Age,* Sept. 8, Oct. 5, Nov. 9 and 16, Dec. 14 and 21, 1889, Jan. 4, 11, and 25, 1890; Bruce, *The Blot on the Escutcheon* (Washington, 1890), 12.

12. Walters, *My Life and Work* (New York, 1917), 98–110, 134–38; *Colored American,* Sept. 24, Oct. 1, 1898, Jan. 7, 1899; Cyrus F. Adams, *The National Afro-American Council* (Washington, 1902), 5 ff.; Mrs. N. F. Mossell, "The National Afro-American Council," *Colored American Magazine,* III (Aug., 1901), 293–95; and Bruce Grit [J. E. Bruce], *Concentration of Energy* (New York, 1899).

13. R. R. Wright, Jr., *The Negro in Pennsylvania* (Philadelphia, [1909?]), 116–17.

14. Bowen, *An Appeal for Negro Bishops, But No Separation* (New York, 1912), 51–52; Hood, *One Hundred Years of the African Methodist Episcopal Zion Church* (New York, 1895), 12–17, 22, 26; Payne, *Recollections of Seventy*

Years (Nashville, 1888), 9–12; Morris, *Sermons, Addresses and Reminiscences* (Nashville, 1901), 71.

15. W. E. B. Du Bois, ed., *Economic Co-operation Among Negro Americans* (AUP No. 12, 1907), 80–85; Wright, *Self-Help in Negro Education* (Cheyney, Pa. [1908?]), 6–14.

16. *Voice of the Negro,* IV (March, 1907), 122–26; *Catalogue of Livingstone College,* 1888, 8–10; Ridgely Torrence, *The Story of John Hope* (New York, 1948), 137–38.

17. Lucretia H. Coleman, *Poor Ben: A Story of Real Life* (Nashville, 1890), 7, 8.

18. A.M.E. *Review,* XIII (Jan., 1887), 341; Morris, *Sermons, Addresses and Reminiscences,* 56–57.

19. Du Bois, ed., *Some Efforts of American Negroes for Their Own Social Betterment* (AUP No. 3, 1898), 10; Du Bois, ed., *Efforts for Social Betterment Among Negro Americans* (AUP No. 14, 1910), 18–29; Inabel Burns Lindsay, "The Participation of Negroes in the Establishment of Welfare Services, 1865–1900" (doctoral dissertation, University of Pittsburgh School of Social Work, 1952), 121–32; Grace R. Gwaltney, "The Negro Church and the Social Gospel from 1877 to 1914" (M.A. thesis, Howard University, 1949), *passim;* Anderson, *Presbyterianism: Its Relation to the Negro* (Philadelphia, 1897), *passim;* *Hampton Negro Conference No. 4* (Hampton, 1900), 27, 38.

20. W. A. Hunton, "The Colored Men's Department of the Young Men's Christian Association," *Voice of the Negro,* II (June, 1905), 391–94; Leslie H. Fishel, Jr., "The North and the Negro, 1865–1900" (doctoral dissertation, Harvard University, 1953), 209, 420; Du Bois, *Efforts for Social Betterment . . . ,* 95; *Gazette,* July 6, 1912, March 14, 1914.

21. Lindsay, "Participation of Negroes in the Establishment of Welfare Services," 186–91; Williams, "Social Bonds in the 'Black Belt' of Chicago," in Charity Organization Society, *The Negro in the Cities of the North* (New York, 1905), 40; John Daniels, *In Freedom's Birthplace* (Boston, 1914), 213.

22. Du Bois, *Efforts for Social Betterment,* 42, 65–71, 79–95; Lindsay, "Participation of Negroes in the Establishment of Welfare Services," 161–62, 123–24; Du Bois, "Social Effects of Emancipation," *Survey* (Feb. 1, 1913), 572. The two earliest and most noted of the hospitals were the interracially staffed and financed Provident Hospital organized in Chicago in 1891 under the leadership of Daniel Hale Williams (who performed the first successful heart suture), and Frederick Douglass Hospital of Philadelphia, founded in 1895 under the leadership of Dr. Nathan F. Mossell. See Helen Buckler, *Doctor Dan: Pioneer in American Surgery* (Boston, 1954), chaps. vi and vii; Elliott N. Rudwick, "A Brief History of the Mercy-Douglass Hospital in Philadelphia," *Journal of Negro Education,* X (Jan., 1951), 20–21.

23. Du Bois, *Efforts for Social Betterment . . . ,* 100–103; *Annual Report of the White Rose Industrial Association,* 1911 (New York, 1911), 2–4; National League on Urban Conditions Among Negroes, *Report, 1910–1911* (no imprint, [1911]), *passim.* Only five men, John Haynes Holmes, E. R. A. Seligman, Kelly Miller, the New York school principal William Bulkley, and Rev. W. H. Brooks, were listed on the national boards of both the League and the N.A.A.C.P.

24. Du Bois, "Social Effects of Emancipation," 572; Lindsay, "Participation of Negroes in the Establishment of Welfare Services," 168; Williams, "Club Movement Among Colored Women," in J. W. Gibson and W. H. Crogman, *Progress of a Race* (Naperville, Ill., 1902), 203.

25. Lindsay, "Participation of Negroes in the Establishment of Welfare Services," 170–71; Williams, "Club Movements Among Negro Women," 206; Mary Church Terrell, "Club Work of Colored Women," *Southern Workman,* XXX (Aug., 1901), 436; Du Bois, *Efforts for Social Betterment . . . ,* 55.

26. J. H. N. Waring, *Work of the Colored Law and Order League* (Cheyney, Pa., [1908?]); *Crisis,* III (Nov., 1911), 7; *Alexander's Magazine,* II (Oct., 1906), 17.

27. Miles V. Lynk, *The Afro-American School Speaker and Gems of Literature* (Jackson, Tenn., 1896); Isaiah C. Wears, *Polite and Cultured Conversation* ([Philadelphia ?, 1900 ?]); Silas X. Floyd, *Floyd's Flowers, or Duty and Beauty for Colored Children* (Atlanta, 1905); Joseph R. Gay, *Progress and Achievements of the 20th Century Negro . . . A Handbook for Self-Improvement Which Leads to Greater Success* (no imprint, 1913).

28. Du Bois, *Efforts for Social Betterment . . . ,* 117–19, 104–7; James Weldon Johnson, *Black Manhattan* (New York, 1930), 78–80, 109–10, 170–75, 125; Daniels, *In Freedom's Birthplace,* 201.

29. Du Bois, *Some Efforts of American Negroes . . . ,* 18.

30. Du Bois, *Economic Co-operation . . . ,* 115–17, 119, 109, 122, 125–27; M. S. Stuart, *An Economic Detour* (New York, 1940), 23; E. A. Williams, *History and Manual of the Colored Knights of Pythias* (Nashville, 1917); Charles H. Wesley, *History of the Improved Benevolent and Protective Order of Elks of the World, 1898–1954* (Washington, 1955), chaps. ii–v.

31. W. P. Burrell, *Twenty-Five Years History of the United Order of True Reformers* (Richmond, 1909); Du Bois, "Possibilities of the Negro," *Booklovers' Magazine,* I (July, 1903), 5–7; Abram L. Harris, *The Negro as Capitalist* (Philadelphia, 1936), 62–67; *Crisis,* III (Nov., 1911), 9.

32. Du Bois, *Economic Co-operation . . . ,* 108; W. J. Trent, Jr., "Development of Negro Life Insurance Enterprises" (M.B.A. thesis, University of Pennsylvania, 1932, mimeographed copy), 14; St. Luke *Herald,* July 30, 1910 (copy obtained courtesy of Warren Vann, Yeadon, Pa.).

33. *Colored American,* March 19, 1898.

34. Wright, *Negro in Pennsylvania,* 169; *Gazette,* April 29, 1905, Feb. 18, 1911; *Horizon,* V (May, 1910), 5–6.

NOTES TO CHAPTER IX

1. *Southern Workman,* XII (Jan., 1883), 1, 21; *Christian Educator,* V (July, 1894), 167–68; J. W. Gibson and W. H. Crogman, *Progress of a Race* (Naperville, Ill., 1902), 299; James D. Corrothers, *In Spite of the Handicap* (New York, 1916), 83; Jeffrey R. Brackett, *Notes on the Progress of the Colored People of Maryland Since the War* (Baltimore, 1890), 28. The more known among those with fortunes of $200,000 and over included Frederick Douglass, P. B. S. Pinchback, Dr. C. B. Purvis of Washington, Blanche K. Bruce, William Still, the Boston tailor J. H. Lewis, John McKee of Philadelphia, and Lewis Bates of Chicago.

2. *Crisis,* IV (Oct., 1912), 271; *Age,* July 4, 1891; *Bee,* May 7, 1892; Andrew F. Hilyer, "Some Facts Relating to the Rich Negroes of Washington, D. C.," MS (1898), in Hilyer Papers.

3. *Report of the Fifteenth Annual Convention of the National Negro Business League* (no imprint [1914]), 9.

4. Roi Ottley, *New World A-Coming* (Boston, 1943), 171–73.

5. W. E. B. Du Bois, ed., *The Negro in Business* (AUP No. 4, 1899), 10; Ray Stannard Baker, *Following the Color Line* (New York, 1908), 43; Lorenzo Greene and Carter G. Woodson, *The Negro Wage Earner* (Washington, 1930), chaps. vii–ix; Robert A. Warner, *New Haven Negroes: A Social History* (New Haven, 1940), 233–34. For general discussion of Negro business and its problems see Ira DeA. Reid, "The Negro in the American Economic System," unpublished memorandum for the Carnegie-Myrdal Study of the Negro in America, 3 vols. (1940), and Abram L. Harris, *The Negro as Capitalist* (Philadelphia, 1936).

6. Du Bois, "The Economic Revolution in the South," in BTW and Du Bois, *The Negro in the South* (Philadelphia, 1907), 99.

7. For example, the True Reformers' Bank and the People's Insurance Company, whose funds formed the principal deposits of the Nickel Savings Bank in Richmond, were both founded by ministers; the president of the Galilean Fishermen's Bank was a minister, and the St. Luke's Bank and Order were closely connected with the Richmond churches. Rev. Matthew Anderson's Berean Presbyterian Church in Philadelphia organized the largest Negro building and loan association in Pennsylvania. Rev. T. W. Walker of Birmingham founded the important Southern Mutual Aid Association and was president of another insurance company; was active in the Birmingham Penny Savings Bank (founded also by a minister) and a cemetery company, and founded the Birmingham Grate Coal Mining Company.

8. The most celebrated of these earlier enterprises was the Chesapeake Marine Railroad and Dry Dock Company of Baltimore, formed under the leadership of Isaac Myers after a strike against colored mechanics and longshoremen resulted in the dismissal of a thousand Negroes in the Baltimore shipyards in 1865. This concern continued in successful operation—largely on the basis of government contracts—for eighteen years.

9. Du Bois, ed., *Some Efforts of American Negroes for Their Own Social Betterment* (AUP No. 3, 1898), 24; Wright, *Negro in Pennsylvania* (Philadelphia [1909?]) 85; George E. Haynes, *The Negro at Work in New York City* (New York, 1912), 137–39; *Bee,* May 7, 1892.

10. See especially the book by an employee of the Prudential Life Insurance Company: Frederick L. Hoffman, *Race Traits and Tendencies of the American Negro* (Publications of the American Economic Association, XI, 1896, especially chaps. ii and vi), which predicted that the Negro race in America was dying out.

11. W. J. Trent, Jr., "Development of Negro Life Insurance Enterprise" (M.B.A. thesis, University of Pennsylvania, mimeographed copy), 11–45.

12. BTW, *My Larger Education* (New York, 1911), 193; Harris, *Negro as Capitalist,* 46; Du Bois, ed., *Economic Co-operation Among Negro Americans* (AUP No. 12, 1907), 138.

13. *Ibid.,* 138; Harris, *Negro as Capitalist,* 191; *Alabama Penny Savings & Loan Company* (no imprint, n.d.), pamphlet in BTW Papers; correspondence of Pettiford and BTW, 1902 regarding Pettiford's attempt to obtain a collectorship in Alabama; *Hampton Negro Conference No. 7* (Hampton, 1903), 38, 29; Pettiford, "How to Help the Negro to Help Himself," *Southern Workman,* XXX (Nov., 1901), 387–89.

14. Du Bois, *Economic Co-Operation . . . ,* 164; *A.M.E. Review,* XX (April, 1904), 409. For examples of manufacturing concerns such as cotton mills and brickyards, see Du Bois, *Economic Co-Operation . . . ,* 160–61.

15. William K. Boyd, *The Story of Durham* (Durham, 1925), chap. xiv; R. McCants Andrews, *John Merrick* (Durham, 1920), *passim* (quotation on p. 151); Washington, "Durham, North Carolina: A City of Negro Enterprises," *Independent,* LXX (March 30, 1911), 642–50; Frazier, "Durham: Capital of the Black Middle Class," in Alain Locke, ed., *The New Negro* (New York, 1925), 333–40.

16. Du Bois, *The Philadelphia Negro* (Philadelphia, 1899), 123–25, 116, 226, 229; Du Bois, *The Negro in Business,* 10; *Report of the Fifteenth Annual Convention of the National Negro Business League,* 186; Wright, "The Negro in Philadelphia," Part I, A.M.E. *Review,* XXIV (July, 1907), 30–31; *Annual Report of the Sixteenth Annual Session of the National Negro Business League* (Nashville, 1915), 185.

17. Du Bois, *Economic Co-Operation . . . ,* 99–100; Harris, *Negro as Capitalist,* 124, 144; John Daniels, *In Freedom's Birthplace* (Boston, 1914), chap. ix, 114–15, 363–89, 392; Frank U. Quillin, *The Color Line in Ohio* (Ann Arbor, 1913), 154–59; Du Bois, *Negro in Business . . . ,* 50.

18. Du Bois, "Social Evolution of the Black South," *American Negro Monographs No. 4* (1911), 5; St. Clair Drake and Horace Cayton, *Black Metropolis* (New York, 1945), 80–81, 430–33; Frazier, *Black Bourgeoisie* (Chicago, 1957), chap. vii and 150–51; Gunnar Myrdal, *An American Dilemma* (New York, 1944), II, 794–95, 801; Harris, *Negro as Capitalist,* 49.

19. Wright, "Negro Communities in New Jersey," *Southern Workman,* XXXVII (July, 1908), 385–94; Washington *American,* Feb. 25, 1911 in Hampton Clipping Collection. This collection of clippings on all-Negro towns is an invaluable folio of recondite materials.

20. William E. Benson, "Kowaliga: A Community with a Purpose," in Charity Organization Society, *The Negro in the Cities of the North* (New York, 1905), 22–24; Du Bois, ed., *The Negro Artisan* (AUP No. 7, 1902), 84–87; Greene and Woodson, *The Negro Wage Earner,* 107; Du Bois, *Dusk of Dawn* (New York, 1940), 74–75.

21. Mozell C. Hill, "The All-Negro Communities of Oklahoma," *JNH,* XXXI (July, 1946), 254–68; Joseph Taylor, "The Rise and Decline of a Utopian Community, Boley, Oklahoma," *Negro History Bulletin,* III (April, 1940), 105–6.

22. BTW, *My Larger Education,* 210. In general on Mound Bayou see Aurelius P. Hood, *The Negro at Mound Bayou* (Nashville, 1910), and Taylor, "Mound Bayou—Past and Present," *Negro History Bulletin,* III (April, 1940), 105–6.

23. Montgomery even reversed the position he had taken on the franchise in 1890. See Montgomery to BTW, April 5, 1904.

24. Hill, "The All-Negro Society in Oklahoma" (doctoral dissertation, University of Chicago, 1946), especially chap. ix; *Age,* Sept. 26, 1907; *Report of the Fifteenth Annual Convention of the National Negro Business League,* 21.

25. William E. Bittle and Gilbert L. Geis, "Racial Self-Fulfillment and the Rise of an All-Negro Community in Oklahoma," *Phylon,* XVIII (Third Quarter, 1957), 254–58; August Meier, "Booker T. Washington and the Town of Mound Bayou," *Phylon,* XV (Fourth Quarter, 1954), 396–401.

26. Hill found that the Oklahoma communities lacked any real economic base. The material presented by Bittle and Geis suggests that the success of such an undertaking was unlikely without favorable attitudes on the part of neighboring whites and general health in local economy. See also Harris, *Negro as Capitalist,* chap. ix, for critique of the ideology of a segregated economy.

27. Du Bois, *Some Efforts of American Negroes for Their Own Social Better-ment*, 25.

28. Interview with Charles S. Johnson, Oct. 19, 1953.

29. Frazier, *Negro Youth at the Crossways* (Washington, 1940), 193.

30. John Dollard, *Caste and Class in a Southern Town* (New Haven, 1937); Allison Davis and Burleigh and Mary Gardner, *Deep South* (Chicago, 1941); Drake and Cayton, *Black Metropolis;* Frazier, *Negro Youth at the Crossways;* Charles S. Johnson, *Growing Up in the Black Belt* (Washington, 1941); W. Lloyd Warner, *et al., Color and Human Nature* (Washington, 1941). These, the most influential studies analyzing the Negro class structure, pictured Negroes as an endogamous caste divided into social classes—ordinarily three, each sub-divided into two parts. Current usage refers to a dynamic race system rather than a static caste system. Among Negroes, as among whites, the system of stratification is actually a social continuum, class lines being at best somewhat arbitrary. It should also be pointed out that most members of what sociologists have described as the Negro upper class would, because of the lower economic status of Negroes, have been regarded as no higher than middle class among whites. It should be noted, too, that education and skin color have played crucial roles in the Negro class system, though color is rapidly declining in im-portance today.

31. Frazier, *The Negro in the United States* (New York, 1949), 275–76.

32. Studies during the 1930's and early 1940's emphasized that upper-class Negroes had a disproportionate number of light-skinned individuals, though dark-skinned men of attainment were able to enter upper-class circles. See books by Drake and Cayton, Davis and Gardner, Frazier, and Warner in note 30. For recent discussion of this matter see G. Franklin Edwards, *The Negro Professional Class* (Glencoe, Ill., 1959).

33. Du Bois, "The Negro as He Really Is," *World's Work*, II (June, 1901), 848–66; Baker, *Following the Color Line*, 91–92; Enoch M. Banks, *The Eco-nomics of Land Tenure in Georgia* (New York, 1905), 69–70.

34. Du Bois, "The Negroes of Farmville, Virginia," *Bulletin of the Depart-ment of Labor*, No. 14 (1898), 16–18, 36–37; Du Bois, "The Negro in the Black Belt: Some Social Sketches," *Bulletin of the Department of Labor*, No. 22 (1899), 408, 412, 413–14, 415; Warner, *New Haven Negroes*, 189–90.

35. The generalizations in the preceding paragraph, and the accounts of the following cities (except Boston and Chicago) are based chiefly upon interview materials gathered in 1957 and 1958, supplemented by whatever printed and documentary sources were available. On Atlanta see August Meier and David Lewis, "History of the Negro Upper Class in Atlanta, Georgia, 1890–1958," *JNE*, XXVIII (Spring, 1959), 130–39.

36. Wright, "Negroes in Philadelphia," Part I, 29–31, and Part II, A.M.E. *Review*, XXIV (Oct., 1907), 143; Du Bois, *Philadelphia Negro*, 317–19; Drake and Cayton, *Black Metropolis*, 433–34, 543; on Morris and Williams, interview with Charles S. Johnson, Oct. 19, 1953; Daniels, *In Freedom's Birthplace*, 174–83.

37. This was not entirely true. Mrs. Josephine Ruffin was of upper-class status and a member of the white women's club movement, yet she was the chief leader of the Negro women's club movement in Massachusetts.

38. For more details on these figures see Chapter XII.

39. Interview with Charles S. Johnson, Oct. 19, 1953.

40. This interpretation of the relationship of the developing class structure

and ideologies was corroborated in an interview with Charles S. Johnson, October 19, 1953. Johnson observed that the light-skinned upper class lacked a spirit of racial solidarity during the generation before World War I. On the other hand it should be pointed out that Frazier in *Black Bourgeoisie* puts forth the thesis that the Negro bourgeoisie which encourages the ideology of race pride and economic solidarity because it derives its income from the Negro masses, nevertheless looks down upon the masses and scorns their culture and physical characteristics. All this is evidence of the ambivalence in Negro thought.

NOTES TO INTRODUCTION TO PART FIVE

1. The major sources for the following discussion are C. Vann Woodward, *Origins of the New South* (Baton Rouge, 1951); Gilbert T. Stephenson, *Race Distinctions in American Law* (New York, 1910); Ira De A. Reid, ed., *Racial Desegregation and Integration* (Annals of the American Academy of Political and Social Science, CCCIV, 1956); Ray Stannard Baker, *Following the Color Line* (New York, 1908); Albert Bushnell Hart, *The Southern South* (New York, 1910); Thomas P. Bailey, *Race Orthodoxy in the South* (New York, 1914). More specialized works of value include, "Separate-but-Equal," *Race Relations Law Reporter,* I (Feb., 1956), 284–87; Louis R. Harlan, *Separate but Unequal: Public School Campaigns and Racism in the Southern Seaboard States, 1901–1915* (Chapel Hill, 1958); F. E. Wolfe, *Admission to American Trade Unions* (Baltimore, 1912); Sterling D. Spero and Abram L. Harris, *The Black Worker* (New York, 1931); Lorenzo J. Greene and Carter G. Woodson, *The Negro Wage Earner* (Washington, 1930). For conditions facing Northern Negroes, see especially Frank U. Quillin, *The Color Line in Ohio* (Ann Arbor, 1913); Mary White Ovington, *Half a Man* (New York, 1911); R. R. Wright, Jr., *The Negro in Pennsylvania* (Philadelphia [1909?]); John Daniels, *In Freedom's Birthplace* (Boston, 1914). On the Roosevelt and Wilson administrations, see especially Kelly Miller, *Roosevelt and the Negro* (Washington, 1907); *Kelly Miller's Monographic Magazine*, No. 2 (1913); Emma Lou Thornbrough, "The Brownsville Episode and the Negro Vote," *Mississippi Valley Historical Review*, XLIV (Dec., 1957), 469–83; J. A. Tinsley, "Roosevelt, Foraker and the Brownsville Affray," *JNH*, XLI (Jan., 1956), 43–65; George E. Mowry, "The South and the Progressive Lily White Party of 1912," *JSH*, VI (May, 1940), 237–47; Kathleen L. Wolgemuth, "Woodrow Wilson's Appointment Policy and the Negro," *JSH*, XXIV (Nov., 1958), 457–71; and Wolgemuth, "Woodrow Wilson and Federal Segregation," *JNH*, XLIV (April, 1959), 158–73.

2. See especially Edgar Gardner Murphy, *The Basis of Ascendancy* (New York, 1909); W. D. Weatherford, *Present Forces in Negro Progress* (New York, 1912); Howard W. Odum, *Social and Mental Traits of the Negro* (New York, 1910). Both Weatherford and Odum later rejected the idea of innate racial differences.

3. In some instances Negroes did hold elective office after 1895. There were three in the Louisiana state legislature in 1896, and a few in the Texas legislature about the same time; there was one in the Georgia legislature until 1908. Fusion politics in North Carolina sent several Negroes to state office and George H. White to Congress until 1901. On the local level J. Douglas Wetmore was a member of the Jacksonville City Council in 1905, and Negroes were serving in the Nashville and Knoxville city councils as late as 1912 or 1913.

4. For a perceptive contemporary analysis corroborating this point see Ovington, *Half a Man*, 185–87. In other contexts, it should be noted, racial solidarity has been viewed as radical—as when it is associated with extremist colonization schemes. Also the "New Negro" of the 1920's was a "radical" type that insisted upon race pride, group solidarity, and collective action to advance the status of Negroes within American society by agitation and political action as well as economic chauvinism and economic achievement.

5. This has been important in determining both social distinctions and the outlook of individuals, especially in the past, as a number of sociological and social psychological studies have shown. However, evidence on this matter appeared so rarely in the correspondence and published writings available on the period covered by this book that I have been compelled to ignore it here.

6. Myrdal, *An American Dilemma* (New York, 1944), II, 782.

NOTES TO CHAPTER X

1. The title of this chapter was suggested by that of the opening essay in Kelly Miller's *Race Adjustment* (New York, 3d ed., 1910).

2. *Bee*, Oct. 26, 1895; BTW, *The Story of My Life and Work* (Naperville, Ill., 1900), 203, 204; "Report of the Secretary of Bethel Literary and Historical Society, 1895–1896," MS in Cromwell Papers.

3. *Gazette*, Dec. 7, 1895; *Bee*, Oct. 18, 1895; *Recorder*, Sept. 26, Nov. 28, 1895.

4. Du Bois, *The Souls of Black Folk* (Chicago, 1903), 42, 45; *Recorder*, Aug. 9, 1897.

5. *Colored American*, Jan. 7, 1899; *Gazette*, Jan. 7, 1899.

6. New York *Sun*, Aug. 30, 1900 (Hampton Clippings); *Colored American*, March 25, Aug. 26, 1899, Jan. 20, 1900, Aug. 17, 1901; Cyrus Field Adams, *The National Afro-American Council* (Washington, 1902), 8; A.M.E. *Review*, XVI (Oct., 1899), 272.

7. Correspondence of BTW with Jesse Lawson, 1901–2; *Colored American*, July 19, 1902; *Age*, July 21, 1902 (Hampton Clippings); Scott to BTW, July 17, 1902; *Colored American Magazine*, VI (March, 1903), 338.

8. *Guardian*, Feb. 28, 1903, Dec. 6, Dec. 30, Nov. 1, 1902, April 14, 1903.

9. *Gazette*, Sept. 24, 1898, Oct. 26, 1906; *Age*, July 5, 1900 (Hampton Clippings); A.M.E. *Review*, XX (April, 1904), 409; *Bee*, Aug. 12, 1905; *Freeman*, March 8, 1910.

10. *Voice of the Negro*, III (March, 1906), 175–77.

11. BTW to T. Thomas Fortune, Feb. 17, 1903; Charles W. Anderson to BTW, June 8, 1903; *Colored American*, July 11, 18, 1903; *Guardian*, July 11, 1903; *Age*, July 4, 1903 (Hampton Clippings).

12. *Gazette*, July 11, 1903; *Bee*, Aug. 8, 1903; *Guardian*, July 11, 1903; BTW to Emmett J. Scott, July 27, 1903.

13. *Guardian*, Aug. 1, 8, 15, 1903; *Bee*, Aug. 8, 1903; *Gazette*, Aug. 8, 1903; Ruth Worthy, "A Negro in Our History: William Monroe Trotter, 1872–1934" (M.A. thesis, Columbia University, 1952), chap. iv; BTW, *My Larger Education* (New York, 1911), 122–25; Du Bois, *Dusk of Dawn* (New York, 1940), 87–88.

14. BTW to Du Bois, Feb. 12, 1903; [Kelly Miller], "Washington's Policy," Boston *Transcript*, Sept. 19, 1903; Correspondence of BTW and Carnegie, Nov.

1903—Jan., 1904; *Bee*, Jan. 23, 30, 1904; "Summary of Proceedings, Conference of Colored Men, Jan. 7, 8, 9, 1904," BTW Papers.

15. On railroad items see chapter VII; on Maryland see BTW to Charles W. Chesnutt, Jan. 2, 1906; in general see correspondence of BTW with Hugh M. Browne, secretary of the committee.

16. *Gazette*, Jan. 23, 1904; *Bee*, Jan. 16, 1904; Adams to BTW, n.d., 1904; BTW, extracts from MS speeches of BTW, 1904–1906, at Tuskegee Institute Department of Records and Research.

17. For details of Washington's fight with the opposition, 1902–15, see August Meier, "Booker T. Washington and the Rise of the N.A.A.C.P.," *Crisis*, LXI (Feb., 1954), 71–72, 117–22; see also Elliott Rudwick, "The Niagara Movement," *JNH*, XLII (July, 1957), 181–84, 186–87, 190, 196.

18. *Bee*, July 22, 1905; *Horizon*, II (Sept., 1907), 4; Baker, *Following the Color Line* (New York, 1908), 223.

19. *Horizon*, II (Nov., 1907), 15–16; III (March, 1908), 12–13.

20. Baker, *Following the Color Line*, 217–20.

21. A.M.E. *Review*, XXII (Oct., 1905), 183–84; *Age*, Oct. 11, 1906; *Alexander's Magazine*, III (Dec., 1906), 63–64; *Proceedings of the Ninth Annual Session of the National Afro-American Council . . . 1906* (Louisville, 1907), 13, 42, 15–16; A.M.E. *Review*, XXIII (Jan., 1907), 289–90; *Bee*, July 6, 1907; *Horizon*, II (July, 1907), 20.

22. Andrew M. Humphrey to BTW, May 4, 1904; Humphrey to BTW, June 4, 1904; Correspondence of BTW and Anderson, 1905–6. On the League's activity in Brownsville case see Mary Church Terrell, *A Colored Woman in a White World* (Washington, 1940), 269–77; Anderson to BTW, Jan. 4, 1907; *Recorder*, Aug. 8, 1907; *Preliminary Report of Commission of the Constitution League . . . on Affray at Brownsville . . .*, 59th Congress, 2nd session, Senate Document No. 107 (1906). On BTW's stand see BTW to Oswald Garrison Villard, Nov. 11, 1906; BTW to Taft, Nov. 19, 1906; BTW to Anderson, Nov. 7, 1906; Roosevelt to BTW, Nov. 5, 1906 (copy in F. J. Garrison Papers).

23. BTW to Anderson, Feb. 28, Feb. 26, March 8, 1908; BTW to Ralph W. Tyler, April 26, 1908.

24. Villard to BTW, Jan. 27, 1908; Mary White Ovington, *How the National Association for the Advancement of Colored People Began* (New York, 1914), 1–3, 6; *Proceedings of the National Negro Conference* (No imprint, 1909), *passim;* Flint Kellogg, "Villard and the NAACP," *The Nation*, CLXXXVIII (Feb. 14, 1959), 137–40.

25. *Fifth Annual Report of the N.A.A.C.P.* (No imprint, 1914), 5.

26. Circular entitled "Race Relations in the United States," copy in Chesnutt Papers.

27. BTW to Scott, Jan. 6, 1914; *Fifth Annual Report of the N.A.A.C.P.*, 5.

28. Du Bois, *The Amenia Conference* (Amenia, New York, 1923), 14–15.

29. Du Bois, *Dusk of Dawn*, 91; *Horizon*, VI (Nov., 1909), 1; Ransom, "The Negro and Socialism," A.M.E. *Review*, XIV (Oct., 1897), 196–97; *Horizon*, I (Feb., 1907), 7–8.

30. For more details and fuller documentation of material in the following pages see August Meier, "The Negro and the Democratic Party, 1875–1915," *Phylon*, XVII (2d quarter, 1956), 182–91.

31. Brooklyn *Citizen*, Oct. 10, 1900 (Hampton Clippings).

32. Anderson to BTW, Nov. 11, 1910.

33. BTW to Knox, Oct. 17, 1904; *Freeman*, Aug. 25, 1906, Oct. 24, 1908.

34. *Gazette,* Oct. 31, 1908.

35. *Horizon,* III (Feb., 1908), 17–18; III (April, 1908), 4–6; IV (July, 1908), 6–7; IV (Aug., 1908), 2–4; IV (Sept., 1908), 4–6.

36. National Independent Political League, *Pamphlet No. 3* ([1912]); J. Milton Waldron and J. D. Harkless, *The Political Situation in a Nutshell* (Washington, [1912]), 30, 11, 16, 17.

37. *Crisis,* IV (Aug., 1912), 181.

38. Miller, "The Political Plight of the Negro," *Kelly Miller's Monographic Magazine,* I (1913), 1, 6, 8, 10, 11, 14–17, 21.

39. *Bee,* Nov. 21, 1914; A.M.E. *Review,* XXXI (Jan., 1915), 309–18; *Crisis,* IX (Jan., 1915), 12–13.

NOTES TO CHAPTER XI

1. All works cited are by Du Bois unless otherwise stated. The Du Bois Papers have been closed to scholars for some years. All references to letters to and from Du Bois and all references to manuscript materials by Du Bois are to the notes on these materials made by Francis L. Broderick and placed on file at the Schomburg Collection of the New York Public Library.

2. "Strivings of the Negro People," *Atlantic Monthly,* LXXX (Aug., 1897), 194; *Dusk of Dawn* (New York, 1940), 2.

3. "Strivings of the Negro People," 194–95; "Public Rhetoricals," Fisk University, MS [1885–88]; *Dusk of Dawn,* 23–24, 101, 36; "A Vacation Unique," MS, 1889; "What Will the Negro Do?" MS, 1889.

4. New York *Globe,* e.g., Sept. 8, 1883; Fisk *Herald,* V (Dec., 1887), 8 and V (March, 1888), 8–9; "Political Serfdom," MS, 1887; "An Open Letter to the Southern People," MS, 1888 [?]; "What Will the Negro Do?"; "Harvard and the South," MS, 1891; "The Afro-Americans," MS [1894–96]; *Age,* June 13, 1891.

5. *Dusk of Dawn,* 85. Unfortunately the files of the *Age* are not available for the early 1890's.

6. "Harvard and the South"; "The Afro-American"; "The True Meaning of a University," MS, 1894.

7. *Some Efforts of American Negroes For Their Own Social Betterment* (AUP No. 3, 1898), 43.

8. *The Philadelphia Negro* (Philadelphia, 1899), 325, 388–91, chap. xvii, and *passim.*

9. "Careers Open to College-Bred Negroes," in Du Bois and H. H. Proctor, *Two Addresses* (Nashville, 1898), 7, 12; "The Meaning of Business," MS, 1898; quotation at end of paragraph is from resolutions of the Fourth Atlanta University Conference, *The Negro in Business* (AUP No. 4, 1899), 50.

10. Du Bois and others, *Memorial to the Legislature of Georgia Upon the Hardwick Bill,* Pamphlet, 1899, Du Bois Papers; "The Suffrage Fight in Georgia," *Independent,* LX (Nov. 30, 1899), 3226–28.

11. *The Conservation of Races* (American Negro Academy, Occasional Papers No. 2, 1897), 7, 9–13. Nor was Du Bois averse to a considerable number of American Negroes migrating to Africa, uniting for the uplift and economic development of the continent. See "Possibility of Emigration to Congo Free State," Memorial to Paul Hegeman, Belgian Consul-General to the United States [1895–97].

12. "A Rational System of Negro Education," MS [1897–1900]; Du Bois, ed., *The College-Bred Negro* (AUP No. 5, 1900), 29.

13. "The Relations of the Negroes to the Whites of the South" (Annals of the American Academy of Political and Social Science, XVIII, July, 1901), 121–33; "The Case for the Negro," MS, 1901.

14. "The Talented Tenth," in BTW and others, *The Negro Problem* (New York, 1903), 60–61; *The Negro Artisan* (AUP No. 7, 1902), 81; "Of the Training of Black Men," *Atlantic Monthly*, XC (Sept., 1902), 291; "The Talented Tenth," 45, 33–34.

15. Samuel R. Spencer, Jr., *Booker T. Washington and the Negro's Place in American Life* (Boston, 1955), 146, 148–49.

16. "The Evolution of Negro Leadership," *The Dial*, XXXI (July, 1901), 54 (an article which anticipated in several significant respects Du Bois' discussion in "Of Booker T. Washington and Others"); *Guardian*, July 27, 1902.

17. Miller, *Race Adjustment* (3d ed.; New York, 1909), 14; *Guardian*, Jan. 10, 1903; *Dusk of Dawn*, 70–77.

18. Spencer, *Booker T. Washington*, 157; on Pullman Car matter see Chap. VII, above; Du Bois to Clement Morgan, Oct. 19, 1903, and Du Bois to George Foster Peabody, Dec. 28, 1903.

19. *Dusk of Dawn*, 82–83, 86, 95. On embarrassment Du Bois' stand caused Atlanta University, see Horace Bumstead to Du Bois, Dec. 5, 1903 and Jan. 26, 1905.

20. E.g., *Crisis*, VII (Feb., 1914), 189–90; I (Dec., 1910), 27.

21. *Crisis*, II (June, 1911), 63–64; "The Forward Movement," MS, 1910.

22. *Crisis*, XVI (Nov., 1917), 11; *Horizon*, II (Oct., 1907), 16; *Crisis*, I (Feb., 1911), 20–21; *Horizon*, II (Oct., 1907), 7–8.

23. *Negro American Artisan* (AUP No. 17, 1913), 128–29; E. H. Clement to Du Bois [Dec.? 1907], Dec. 18, 1907, and Du Bois to Clement, Dec. 10 and 30, 1907; *Economic Co-Operation among Negro Americans* (AUP No. 12, 1907), 12; *Crisis*, XV (Nov., 1917), 9; *Crisis*, V (Jan., 1913), 184–86.

24. "The Marrying of Black Folk," *Independent*, LXIX (Oct. 13, 1910), 812–13.

25. *Philadelphia Negro*, 359; "Relations of Negroes to the Whites of the South," 121–22; *The Souls of Black Folk* (Chicago, 1903), 50; *Horizon*, III (March, 1908), 5–6; *Crisis*, II (Aug., 1911), 157–58; "The Negro in Literature and Art," in *The Negro's Progress in Fifty Years* (Annals of the American Academy of Political and Social Science, XXXIX [Sept., 1913]), 233–37.

26. Circular of African Development Company, March 1, 1902; Melville J. Herskovits, *Myth of the Negro Past* (New York, 1941); *The Negro Church* (AUP No. 6, 1903), 5–6; *The Negro American Artisan*, 24; *The Negro American Family* (AUP No. 13, 1908), 10–17; *Economic Co-Operation Among Negro Americans*, 12–14; *The Negro* (New York, 1915), chap. ii, 241–42; Sergi, *The Mediterranean Race* (London, 1901).

27. *The Negro Artisan*, 25; Du Bois to I. M. Rubinow, Nov. 17, 1904; *Horizon*, I (Feb., 1907), 7–8; "A Field for Socialists," MS [1907–9]; "The Economic Revolution in the South," in BTW and Du Bois, *The Negro in the South* (Philadelphia, 1907), 116; Du Bois to Mr. Owens, April 17, 1908; Elliott Rudwick to author, July 17, 1954; *The Negro*, 238–41. Note also his Marxist, economic interpretation in his first novel, *The Quest of the Silver Fleece*, 1911.

28. *Crisis,* XVI (1918), 216–17.
29. Elliott Rudwick to author, Nov. 14, 1955.

NOTES TO CHAPTER XII

1. For an authoritative statement of the traditional point of view that most of the intellectuals were hostile to Washington see Wilson Record, "Negro Intellectuals and Negro Movements in Historical Perspective," *American Quarterly,* VIII (Spring, 1956), 3–20.
2. Due to a paucity of evidence I have omitted a discussion of the views of the physicians. Where an individual can be classified under two or more occupational categories, he is discussed where it seems most relevant. In some cases I have reached back to the period before 1895 in order to gain insight into a person's ideological shifts.
3. R. R. Wright, Jr., "The Negro in Unskilled Labor," in *The Negro's Progress in Fifty Years* (Annals of the American Academy of Political and Social Science, XXXIX, 1913), 30; Monroe Work, "The Negro's Industrial Problem," Part II, *Southern Workman,* XLIII (Sept., 1914), 507.
4. In employing the concept "intellectual"—a category difficult to define precisely—I follow the usage of the sociologist Wilson Record, the leading writer on the subject of the role of Negro intellectuals. He defines intellectuals as "those persons who by temperament, and usually by profession, are concerned primarily with ideas. . . . Corollary with this preoccupation with ideas is specialization in the use of words and symbols and high achievement in the arts of communication." See Record, "Role of Negro Intellectuals," *Crisis,* LX (June–July, 1953), 330. Record regards self-educated men like Douglass as intellectuals, whereas Washington, who had more formal education than Douglass, is regarded as a foe of intellectuals. Yet it should be pointed out that Washington was largely concerned with ideas, and was successful in communicating them. Most of the individuals discussed in this book fall within Record's definition of "intellectual." Though it is a bit fuzzy, I employ his definition partly because it is convenient, and partly because it will serve as a useful basis of comparison between the generalizations made in this chapter and those made by Record in his *American Quarterly* article.
5. It should also be noted that due to a lack of space I have not included summaries of the views of a number of significant individuals about whom there are enough data to supply a valid picture. However, their views approximate one or another of the various patterns exemplified by the persons discussed in some detail.
6. J. R. E. Lee, "The National Association of Teachers of Colored Youth," *Voice of the Negro,* II (June, 1905), 383–94.
7. *Bee,* June 9, 1888. On railroad suit see Chapter V.
8. *Freeman,* Jan. 9, 1901; *Colored American,* Aug. 11, 1900; *Voice of the Negro,* II (Jan., 1905), 680–82.
9. For overt ideology see clippings in Rayner Papers; for his private thoughts see MS entitled "Jottings," 4, 32, 39, 67, 60, 65, etc.
10. Elizabeth Ross Haynes, *The Black Boy of Atlanta* (Boston, 1952), 87–89; Wright, "Let Us Make Much of Farming," *Southern Workman,* XXVIII (April, 1899), 129–30; Wright, "The Demands of the Times as to Negro Education," A.M.E. *Review,* XVI (Oct., 1899), 200–203; *Alexander's Magazine,* I (Dec., 1905), 21–22.

11. Bowen, e.g., *What Shall the Harvest Be?* (Washington, 1892); BTW to Bowen, Dec. 24, 1904; BTW to A. N. Jenkins, March 12, 1905; *Voice of the Negro,* II (April, 1905), 248; *Report of the Seventh Annual Convention of the National Negro Business League ... 1906* (Boston, 1906), 65.

12. *Bee,* Oct. 6, 1906; Bowen to BTW, Nov. 2, 1906; *Horizon,* I (Feb., 1907), 15–16.

13. Ridgely Torrence, *The Story of John Hope* (New York, 1948), 114–16, 134–35, 149–51; Du Bois, ed., *The Negro in Business* (AUP No. 4, 1899), 56–60.

14. *Bee,* Oct. 26, 1895; Cromwell to BTW, June 26, 1902; R. H. Terrell to BTW, June 27, 1902, July 8, 1902; Washington *Record,* Nov. 6, Dec. 18, 1903 in Cromwell clipping books (Cromwell edited this paper); Roscoe Conkling Bruce to Major [Moton], Jan. 13, 1904.

15. Bruce, *Service by the Educated Negro* (Tuskegee, 1903); Bruce, *Two Speeches* (no imprint, 1909). On Washington's aid for capital post see James A. Cobb to Scott, Sept. 3, 1906; and in Mary Church Terrell Papers, M. C. Terrell to "Mr. Pinkett," Sept. 5, 1906.

16. Scarborough, "The Negro and the Trades," *Southern Workman,* XXVI (Feb., 1897), 26; *Hampton Negro Conference No. 4* (Hampton, 1900), 52; Scarborough, "The Negro as a Factor in Business," *Southern Workman,* XXX (Aug., 1901), 456–57; *Hampton Negro Conference No. 6* (Hampton, 1902), 60; Scarborough, "The Negro and the Higher Learning," *Forum,* XXXIII (May, 1902), 349–55; *Recorder,* Jan. 3, 1901; Scarborough, "Lawlessness v. Lawnessness," *Arena,* XXIV (Nov., 1900), 481–82; Scarborough, "The Negro's Program for 1906," *Voice of the Negro,* III (Jan., 1906), 47–49; *Proceedings of the Ninth Annual Session Of the National Afro-American Council ... , 1906* (Louisville, 1907), 21–26; and articles by Scarborough in *Voice of the Negro,* 1907.

17. For a more detailed discussion and fuller documentation see August Meier, "The Racial and Educational Philosophy of Kelly Miller, 1895–1915," *JNE,* XXIX (Spring, 1960), 121–27.

18. J. W. Cromwell, MS of address before the Bethel Literary Association, 1896, in Cromwell Papers; Miller, "The Race Problem in the South," *Outlook,* LX (Dec. 31, 1898), 1059–63; *Colored American,* March 25, 1899.

19. *Southern Workman,* XXVI (Sept., 1897), 179; Miller, "The Negro and Education," *Forum,* XXX (Feb., 1901), 694–701; Miller, "The Education of the Negro," *Report of the Commissioner of Education, 1900–1901* (Washington, 1902), 731–859.

20. Miller, "The Anglo-Saxon and the African," *Arena,* XXVIII (Dec., 1902), 580–82; *Guardian,* Nov. 22, 1902.

21. Miller, "Autobiography," chaps. xx, xxiii. (Manuscript in possession of Mrs. Mae Miller Sullivan, Washington, D.C.)

22. Miller, "A Reply to Tom Watson," *Voice of the Negro,* II (Aug., 1905), 537; Miller, *Roosevelt and the Negro* (Washington, 1907); Miller, *Race Adjustment* (3d ed.; New York, 1910), 27–29, 15–17.

23. Miller, "Autobiography," chap. xxiii; *Horizon,* II (July, 1907), 24–25.

24. Anderson to BTW, Nov. 10, 1910; Miller, e.g., *Out of the House of Bondage* (New York, 1914).

25. Bunche, "Conceptions and Ideologies of the Negro Problem," Memorandum prepared for the Carnegie-Myrdal Study of the Negro in America (1940), 135–36, 147.

26. Most of the leading Negroes in the M.E. Church North were editors and school presidents and accordingly they are discussed in other parts of this chapter.

27. BTW to Turner,   , 1906 (date illegible). Another A.M.E. bishop who favored colonization was W. H. Heard, a member of the college-educated elite who had been trained at the University of South Carolina and Atlanta University.

28. Holsey, *The Race Problem* (Atlanta, 1899), 4–8; Baltimore *Afro-American*, Nov., 10, 1906.

29. *Journal of the Twenty-First Quadrennial Session of the General Conference of the African M. E. Church* (Philadelphia, 1900), 357–59, 254–55; A.M.E. *Review*, XXV (July, 1908), 27–38; *Journal of the Twenty-Fourth Quadrennial Session of the African M. E. Church* (Nashville, 1912), 370–72, 84, 215–16; *Gazette*, Feb. 29, 1908.

30. Draft of a letter for Waldron, Aug. 1, 1901, in BTW Papers; J. Douglas Wetmore to BTW, Nov. 16, 1903; BTW to Waldron, Nov. 25, Dec. 24, 1903.

31. T. O. Fuller, *History of the Negro Baptists of Tennessee* (Memphis, 1936), 75–77; Griggs, *The One Great Question* (Nashville, 1907); "Editorial for *Age*," 1913 in BTW Papers; Griggs, *New Thoughts for a New Era* (Memphis, 1913). On Powell's shift of view see Charles W. Anderson to BTW, Aug. 30, 1911.

32. Walker, e.g., *Truth From Another Angle on the Race Question* (Philadelphia, n.d.), 3–7; BTW, *My Larger Education* (New York, 1911), 231–33; *Voice of the Negro*, III (Mar., 1906), 175–77; BTW to Walker (telegram), Feb. 11, 1906; Walker to BTW, Feb. 14, 1906. On Walker's accommodating attitude, see also Clarence A. Bacote, "The Negro in Georgia Politics, 1880–1908" (doctoral dissertation, University of Chicago, 1955), 31.

33. Fisk *Herald*, IV (Aug., 1887), 9–10; V (Sept., 1887), 10–11; Bacote, "The Negro in Georgia Politics, 1880–1908," 19; Proctor, *Between Black and White* (Boston, 1925), 100–102; BTW to Du Bois, Dec. 14, 1903.

34. Privately he declared himself strongly Republican. See Crummell to J. E. Bruce, Feb. 28, 1896, Bruce Collection.

35. Crummell, *Incidents of Hope for the Negro Race in America* (Washington, 1895), 14; Crummell to Frazier Miller, July 28, June 20, 1898, Crummell Papers.

36. Bragg, *History of the Afro-American Group of the Episcopal Church* (Baltimore, 1922), 251, 293–94; BTW to Bragg, e.g., March 10, 1904; *Gazette*, Aug. 25, 1906.

37. Grimké to BTW, Sept. 20, Dec. 12, 1895; *Southern Workman*, XXVI (Sept., 1897), 185–90; BTW, *The Story of My Life and Work* (Naperville, Ill., 1900), 231; BTW to Grimké, Jan. 13, May 8, 1898; Carter G. Woodson, ed., *The Works of Francis J. Grimké* (Washington, 1942), I, 237–39, 256, 379–80, and III, 7–8.

38. Walker to BTW, July 29, 1901.

39. BTW, *My Larger Education*, 39.

40. BTW to F. J. Garrison, May 17, 1905, Garrison Papers.

41. Adams to BTW, June 13, 1904; *Address of the National Afro-American Press Association*, June 23, 1903 (no imprint, n.d.); *Appeal*, Sept. 2, 1905.

42. On *Age* see correspondence with Fortune, *passim*. On Boston journals see correspondence with Peter Smith, e.g., Oct.–Nov., 1903; BTW to Alexander, April 8, 1905; Alexander to BTW, April 15, 1905; correspondence

with Alexander, 1905–8. On *Colored American* see correspondence with Cooper, 1902–4. I was unable to locate material on Washington's relations with Chase in 1906, but in 1907 and 1908 Chase was requesting and receiving financial and editorial help. See Chase to BTW, Aug. 11, 1907, Feb. 7 and 23, 1908; Chase to Emmett J. Scott, Jan. 22, 1908; BTW to Chase, Feb. 23, 1908. On *Conservator* see especially BTW to Scott, July 29, 1903. For secret attempts to influence *Conservator* policy see Helen Buckler, *Doctor Dan: Pioneer in American Surgery* (Boston, 1954), 234, 240, 248. On *Colored American Magazine* see BTW to Fred R. Moore, Oct. 12, 1905 and April 18, 1906.

43. BTW to Garrison. May 17, 1905, Garrison Papers; Terrell to BTW. March 20, 1906.

44. *Age,* Sept. 24, 1905; Nov. 8, 1906.

45. For details and fuller documentation see August Meier, "Booker T. Washington and the Negro Press, With Special Reference to the *Colored American Magazine*," *JNH,* XXXVIII (January, 1953), 68–73, 79–82.

46. *Colored American Magazine,* XIII (Dec., 1907), 413.

47. See especially *ibid.,* XII (May, 1907), *passim.*

48. *Ibid.,* XI (Oct., 1906), 217; XIII (Dec., 1907), 409.

49. *Age,* Oct. 17, 1907; Scott to Tyler, Oct. 12, 1907; "Brownsville Ghouls," in folder in 1908 Correspondence marked "Moore."

50. BTW to Moore, Aug. 29, 1908.

51. BTW to Charles W. Anderson, April 7, 1910. Reports on Moore's activities are to be found in a stream of letters between 1903 and 1913 from Anderson. Washington's guarded replies substantiate the truth of the charges.

52. BTW to Anderson, date cut off, 1911.

53. *Freeman,* July 4, 1903.

54. *Voice of the Negro,* I (Nov., 1904), 515; L. M. Hershaw, "The Negro Press," in Charity Organization Society, *The Negro in the Cities of the North* (New York, 1905), 68; *Planet,* Nov. 21, 1914, cited in *Gazette,* Dec. 5, 1914; *Planet,* n.d., cited in *Crisis,* IX (Feb., 1915), 175.

55. *Bee,* Sept. 29, 1906.

56. *Ibid.,* Nov. 25, 1915.

57. A.M.E. *Review,* XIV (April, 1898), 467–68.

58. *Ibid.,* XX (July, 1903), 97–101; XXII (Oct., 1905), 108; XXII (April, 1906), 357–59; *Recorder,* Aug. 6, 1903, Aug. 20, 1905; Sept. 20, 1906; BTW to Kealing, May 16, 1910.

59. Stewart to BTW, e.g., Feb. 3, 1904.

60. *Advocate,* July 27, 1905.

61. For discussion of Dancy, see next chapter.

62. Chiles to BTW, Nov. 12, 1906; BTW to Chiles, Nov. 19, 1906.

63. Undated clipping from Chicago *Appeal* accompanying letter from Adams to BTW, July 24, 1903.

64. These included E. A. Johnson of Raleigh and J. Douglas Wetmore of Jacksonville (and later, New York). In this connection one might also mention Henry Lincoln Johnson of Atlanta, a political opportunist originally on the fringes of the Washington circle, who in 1910 secured for himself the post of register of deeds at the expense of Washington's appointee, J. C. Dancy.

65. J. C. May (Wilford Smith) to R. C. Black (Emmett J. Scott), June 3, 1903; Anderson to BTW, June 8, 1903; BTW to Fortune, Jan. 14, 1904; For-

tune to BTW, Jan. 21, 1904; J. C. Asbury to Hayes, Jan. 23, 1904; BTW to Asbury, Jan. 26, 1904; BTW to W. H. Steward, Jan. 10, 1904; Steward to BTW, Feb. 2, 1904; BTW to Hayes, Feb. 2, 1904.

66. Elting E. Morison *et al.,* eds., *The Letters of Theodore Roosevelt* (Cambridge, 1951–54), III, 206 n.; Scott to BTW, n.d., 1904; *Bee,* Dec. 16, 1905; Bacote, "Negro in Georgia Politics," 372–73.

67. Plummer to BTW, Sept. 30, Oct. 1, 12, 19, 24, 1904; Scott to BTW, Oct. 2, 1904; Scott to Plummer, Oct. 17, 1904; May (Smith) to Black (Scott), Aug. 31, June 15, 18, July 15, 30, 1903; Black to May, June 25, Sept. 16, 1903; Smith to BTW, Feb. 26, 1904; Smith to Scott, March 1, 1904, etc.

68. Williams to BTW, Nov. 22, 1901, Dec. 4, 1912; BTW to Anderson, June 14, July 21, Sept. 7, 1904; BTW to Williams, July 15, 1904; BTW to Tyler, Jan. 12, 1906.

69. McKinlay to BTW, Oct. 26, 31, Nov. 6, 1901; R. C. Bruce to BTW, Jan. 13, 1904; and materials bearing on Terrell's efforts for reappointment in 1905, 1909, and 1913 in R. H. Terrell Papers.

70. See various speeches in R. H. Terrell Papers; *Age,* Sept. 18, 1905; *Bee,* June 6, 1914; Terrell, *A Glance at the Past and Present of the Negro* (Washington, 1905).

71. BTW to Scott, Aug. 7, 1905; BTW to R. H. Terrell, Feb. 19, 1906; James A. Cobb to Scott, Sept. 3, 1906; M. C. Terrell to "Mr. Pinkett," Sept. 5, 1906; in M. C. Terrell Papers.

72. M. C. Terrell, *A Colored Woman in a White World* (Washington, 1940), chap. xxvii; John E. Milholland to M. C. Terrell, Sept. 19, 1907, in M. C. Terrell Papers; Anderson to BTW, Dec. 11, 1906; Anderson to Scott, Feb. 25, 1907.

73. Tyler to Scott, Nov. 2, 1907; Anderson to BTW, Oct. 29, 1908; *Age,* Feb. 25, 1909; BTW to R. H. Terrell, April 27, 1910. Though Mrs. Terrell later recalled that her husband did not interfere with her activities, despite dire warnings, the Judge must have remonstrated with her on this occasion, for she wrote him that she would not permit the "narrow, mean" character of many of the radicals or their resolutions against Taft to keep her from doing "something to remove the awful conditions" facing the race. See *Colored Woman in a White World,* 194; M. C. Terrell to R. H. Terrell, n.d., in M. C. Terrell Papers.

74. R. H. Terrell to BTW, June 20, 1910; *Bee,* July 11, 18, 1910; Anderson to BTW, Nov. 10, 1910; BTW to Terrell, Nov. 21, 1910, in M. C. Terrell Papers.

75. John Daniels, *In Freedom's Birthplace* (Boston, 1914), 95–96, 360, 101; Lewis to BTW, Sept. 27, Oct. 14, 1901, Dec. 20, 1902; Lewis, cited in letter of J. C. Asbury to Hayes, Jan. 23, 1904; *Age,* Oct. 7, 1907; Anderson to BTW, Jan. 3, 1909; C. D. Hilles to BTW, Jan. 1, 1911; BTW to Taft (telegram), March 1, 1911, etc. For examples of speeches see Daniels, *In Freedom's Birthplace,* 129; Lewis, "An Address before the House of Representatives of Massachusetts," 1913, in Alice M. Dunbar, ed., *Masterpieces of Negro Eloquence* (New York, 1914), 421–22; Commencement Address at Hampton, May, 1916, *Southern Workman,* XLVI (Jan., 1917), 15–16.

76. McGhee to BTW, Jan. 12, 19, April 19, 1904; Nov. 20, 1901, Jan. 27, 1902, July 15, 1903; Du Bois to F. J. Grimké in Grimké, *Works,* IV, 90; Du Bois, "The Niagara Movement," *Voice of the Negro,* II (Sept., 1905), 691; *Bee,* Aug. 12, 1905.

77. Straker, *Negro Suffrage in the South* (Detroit, 1906), 40; Straker to

BTW, Nov. 19, 1896, Nov. 22, 1901, March 14, 1904; *Horizon,* III (March, 1908), 6.

78. *Hampton Negro Conference No. 3* (Hampton, 1899), 48–51; Grimké, "He Who Keeps Increases," *Southern Workman,* XXX (Oct., 1901), 555; BTW to Du Bois, Jan. 2, 1904; Moton to BTW, Jan. 14, 1904; Scott to BTW, March 28, 1904; Charles Alexander to BTW, Dec. 19, 1905 (regarding money supplied by Washington to pay for articles by Grimké); Grimké, "An Education[al] and Property Basis," *Voice of the Negro,* I (Sept., 1904), 384–85; Grimké, "Meaning and Need of the Movement to Reduce Southern Representation," in *The Negro and the Elective Franchise* (American Negro Academy, Occasional Papers No. 11, 1905), 3–14; BTW to Scott, Aug. 7, 1905; Anderson to BTW, April 1, 1908.

79. Correspondence and manuscripts in Chesnutt Papers.

80. Two examples of doctors with a largely white practice who supported Washington were S. E. Courtney of Boston and Daniel H. Williams of Chicago. Courtney had gone to Hampton with Washington, was a graduate of Harvard Medical School, and served on the Boston School Board. Williams at first felt constrained to cultivate the Tuskegeean in an unsuccessful attempt to secure the appointment of an able physician as surgeon-in-chief of Freedmen's Hospital, but later broke with him.

NOTES TO CHAPTER XIII

1. *Colored American,* Jan. 7, 1899.

2. Miller, *Address* (Orangeburg, S.C., 1902); *Crisis,* II (May, 1911), 7.

3. Pittsburgh *Dispatch,* June 20, 1899 (Hampton Clipping Collection); *Congressional Record,* 50th Congress, 2nd session, 1636–37; 55th Congress, 3rd session, 1124–26; White to BTW, Oct. 7, 1901; A.M.E. *Review,* XXXI (July, 1904), 37–38; *Preliminary Report of Commission of the Constitution League . . . ,* 59th Congress, 2nd session, Senate Document No. 107 (Washington, 1906) 18; *Recorder,* Aug. 6, 1906.

4. Emmett J. Scott to Greener, Aug. 2, 1906; Greener to BTW, Aug. 11 and 23, 1906; BTW to Greener, Aug. 11, Dec. 7, 1906; Greener to Whitefield McKinlay, Sept. 5, 1909, and Sept. 15, 1915, in Woodson Collection.

5. Clarence A. Bacote, "The Negro in Georgia Politics, 1880–1908" (doctoral dissertation, University of Chicago, 1955), *passim; Bee,* Feb. 15, 1890; Cyrus F. Adams, "Col. William Pledger," *Colored American Magazine,* V (June, 1902), 148; *Colored American,* March 31, May 12, 1900; Scott to BTW, July 17, 1902; *Age,* June 26, 1902 (Hampton Clipping Collection); *Bee,* July 18, 1903; *Colored American,* Jan. 16, 1904.

6. As far as could be ascertained Smalls' position was due not to Washington's help but to his own popularity.

7. For speeches of early twentieth century see documents in Pinchback Papers; on incident at the Bethel Literary see Roscoe Conkling Bruce to Major [Moton], Jan. 13, 1904 (BTW Papers), and *Bee,* Jan. 13, 1904; on Washington's efforts to obtain government jobs for Pinchback see numerous letters between BTW and Pinchback, BTW and Anderson, and others.

8. On Vernon, who became a bishop in 1920, see *Bee,* July 14, 1907; BTW to McKinlay, March 8, 1908, June 21, 1911; BTW to Anderson, April 25, 1908, June 9, 1911, etc.; W. T. Vernon, *The Upbuilding of a Race* (Quindaro, Kan., 1904). On Tyler see Theodore Roosevelt to BTW, Dec. 25, 1907;

Anderson to BTW, Feb. 6, 1912, Sept. 26, 1913, Jan. 25, 1907, Jan. 12, 1914; BTW to Anderson, Nov. 10, 1910, June 25, 1912, as well as extensive correspondence with Tyler.

9. BTW to Taft, Feb. 19, 1910; Charles W. Anderson to BTW, Sept. 29, Oct. 2, 1908.

10. BTW to Dancy, Sept. 21, 1899; A.M.E. Zion *Quarterly Review,* II (July, 1892), 414.

11. For a rather explicit statement, see *ibid.,* X (Oct.–Dec., 1900), 39–42.

12. *Ibid.,* Third Quarter, 1909, 51; Dancy, "Annual Address to the North Carolina Industrial Fair," 1901 (MS in possession of Mrs. Lilian Dancy Reid).

13. J. Mason Brewer, *Negro Legislators of Texas* (Dallas, 1935), 101–3; Smith, "Village Improvement Among Negroes," *Outlook,* LXIV (March 31, 1900), 733.

14. *The Helping Hand,* II (Feb., 1898), 4 (in BTW Papers); Smith, "Village Improvement Among Negroes," 736; Maud Cuney Hare, *Norris Wright Cuney* (New York, 1913), 188 ff.; correspondence between Smith and BTW, latter part of 1901; Scott to BTW, Dec. 9, 1901; Smith to BTW, May 14, 1906; BTW to Taft, June 18, 1910.

15. Smith to BTW, Nov.   , 1905.

16. Interview with Lewis W. Jones, Nov. 21, 1953.

17. BTW to Napier, July 7, 1903. For Napier's connection with efforts to end Pullman car discrimination in Tennessee see Chapter VII.

18. BTW, *My Larger Education* (New York, 1911), 65; MS speech in Napier Papers.

19. James D. Corrothers to J. E. Bruce, June 28, 1899, Bruce Collection.

20. *Age,* Nov. 2, 1889; *Gazette,* June 29, 1895; Anderson to BTW, Oct. 29, 1908.

21. Johnson, *Along This Way* (New York, 1933), 218–20; Anderson to BTW, Jan. 12, 1906; Robert Bacon to BTW, Feb. 28, 1906; BTW to Bacon, March 2, 1906; BTW to Anderson, March 10, 1906; Johnson to BTW, March 25, Aug. 30, 1906, Aug. 18, 1910; BTW to William Loeb, April 6, 1907; Anderson to BTW, April 9, 1909, and letter, first page missing, 1910 or 1911.

22. Johnson, *Along This Way,* 312; Johnson to BTW, March 25, 1907; BTW to Anderson, March 8, 1906.

23. J. E. S. [Spingarn] to R. N. [Roy Nash] and R. F. N. to Spingarn, notes attached to letter from John Hope to Spingarn, Oct. 21, 1916, Spingarn Papers.

NOTES TO CHAPTER XIV

1. Alain Locke, ed., *The New Negro* (New York, 1925), ix–xi, 14, 3–8, 10–12, 231, 285; Drake and Cayton, *Black Metropolis* (New York, 1945), 80–82.

2. Bowen, *An Appeal to the King* (Atlanta, [1895]), 7–8; BTW, Fannie Barrier Williams, and N. B. Wood, *A New Negro for a New Century* (Chicago, n.d.); Baker, *Following the Color Line* (New York, 1908), 39; Du Bois, "The Economic Revolution in the South," in BTW and Du Bois, *The Negro and the South* (Philadelphia, 1907), 99–100; Hill, "Race Ideals," *Journal of Race Development,* VI (July, 1913), 97; Pickens, *The New Negro* (New York, 1916), 14; Williams, "The New Negro," *Alexander's Magazine,* VII (Nov., 1908), 17–22; BTW, "Land-Hunger in the Black Belt," *Lippincott's Magazine,* LXXVII (June, 1906), 757–63.

3. According to E. Franklin Frazier, those who belong to the Negro bourgeoisie are actually ashamed of their race, though they talk of race pride and solidarity for the sake of economic self-interest and to hide their insecurity. See *Black Bourgeoisie* (Glencoe, Ill., 1957). Robert Bone in *The Negro Novel in America* (New Haven, 1958) advances the thesis that the younger Negro authors who set the tone for the Harlem Renaissance were actually alienated from their bourgeois background, and therefore found inspiration in Africa and Negro folk-culture—interests rejected by most of the bourgeoisie (63–64).

4. Terrell to J. E. Bruce, March 29, 1896, Bruce Collection; Miller, "The Artistic Gifts of the Negro," *Voice of the Negro*, III (April, 1906), 254.

5. Wright, "A Negro Discovered New Mexico," A.M.E. *Review*, XIII (July, 1896), 2–21, and "Negro Companions of the Spanish Explorers," *American Anthropologist*, n.s., IV (April–June, 1902), 217–18.

6. See especially *To Teach the Negro History* (Philadelphia, 1897) by the lawyer John S. Durham, minister to Haiti 1891–93. (Durham was married to a white woman.)

7. *Gazette*, Nov. 12, 1898.

8. Roman, *A Knowledge of History is Conducive to Racial Solidarity* (Nashville, 1911), 25–27, 30, 33. For advocacy of parallel civilizations see Roman, *American Civilization and the Negro* (Philadelphia, 1916).

9. *Colored American Magazine*, VI (Feb., 1903), 287.

10. York Russell, *Historical Research* (Negro Society for Historical Research, Occasional Papers No. 1, 1912), n.p.; Schomburg, *Racial Integrity* (*ibid.*, No. 3), 5–6.

11. *Colored American*, June 18, 1898; Bruce Grit, *Concentration of Energy* (New York, 1899), and *The Blot on the Escutcheon* (Washington, 1890); *Guardian*, June 15, 1903; Melvin Chisum to E. J. Scott, July 23, 1903; BTW to Scott, July 25, 1903; Charles W. Anderson to BTW, June 8, 1903, Oct. 27, 1907, May 6, 1910; BTW to Anderson, Jan. 10, 1909; Bruce, *The Mission and the Opportunity of the Negro Mason* (no imprint, [1908]), 5–7.

12. Rayford W. Logan, "Carter G. Woodson," *Phylon*, VI (Fourth Quarter, 1945), 318–20; L. D. Reddick, "As I Remember Woodson," *Crisis*, LX (Feb., 1950), esp. 77; quotation in *JNH*, e.g., II (Jan., 1917), 105.

13. *Recorder*, May 18, 1904; Chesnutt to Hugh Browne, June 20, 1908, Chesnutt Papers. The conclusions reached in this book in regard to the American Negroes' feeling of identification with Africa were arrived at before the recent emergence of a large number of independent African states had prompted a general re-examination of the historical evidence in order to prove that American Negroes had always been concerned about and interested in Africa. See especially George Shepperson, "Notes on Negro American Influence on the Emergence of African Nationalism," *Journal of African History*, I (1960), 299–312, and various comments in Part III of John A. Davis, ed., *Africa from the Point of View of American Negro Scholars* ([Paris, 1958], a special issue of the magazine *Présence Africaine*).

14. J. W. Cromwell, *History of the Bethel Literary and Historical Association* (Washington, 1896), 5; J. A. M. Jones, "The Proverbial Philosophy of the Colored Race." A.M.E. *Review*, I (Oct., 1884), 126–33; *Age*, Dec. 13, 1890 (paper by J. W. E. Bowen); Orishatukeh Fatuma, "Religious Belief and Worship of the Yorubas," A.M.E. *Review*, XII (July, 1895), 150–68, and other articles in the same magazine by this author; Monroe N. Work, "Some Paral-

lelisms in the Development of Africans and Other Races," *Southern Workman,* XXXVI (Jan., Feb., March, 1907), 37–43, 105–11, 166–75; Ellis, "Justice in the West African Jungle," *Independent,* LXVII (Dec. 23, 1909), 1438–44, and *Negro Culture in West Africa* (New York, 1914); on Du Bois see Chap. XI; Wright, *The Negro in Pennsylvania* (Philadelphia, [1909?]), 110.

15. *Age,* March 8, 1890 (Hampton Clipping Collection); *Southern Workman,* XXIII (Jan., 1894), 5; BTW, e.g., *Story of the Negro* (New York, 1909), I, 13; R. R. Moton, *Finding a Way Out* (New York, 1920), 58–60; *Hampton Negro Conference No. 3* (Hampton, 1899), 69; Miller, "The Artistic Gifts of the Negro," 253; *Horizon,* V (May, 1912), 6–7.

16. *Recorder,* Aug. 1, 1893; A.M.E. *Review,* XV (Oct., 1898), 629–30; *Hampton Negro Conference No. 3,* 64–70.

17. *Colored American Magazine,* I (May, 1900), 3, 6.

18. American Negro Academy, Occasional Papers No. 1 (1897), inside back cover.

19. *Ibid.,* No. 2 (1897), 3; Crummell, *Civilization the Primal Need of the Race* (*ibid.,* No. 3, 1898), 3–6.

20. Blackshear, "Lines of Negro Education," A.M.E. *Review,* XIII (Jan., 1897), 309–11; Du Bois, ed., *The Negro in Business* (AUP No. 4, 1899), 59–60; Miller, "The Artistic Gifts of the Negro," 252–57; Brawley, "The Negro Genius," *Southern Workman,* XLIV (May, 1915), 305–8.

21. Sterling Brown, *Negro Poetry and Drama* (Washington, 1937), 55, 58–59, 45–46; Bone, *The Negro Novel in America,* chaps. i and ii. The criteria for a successful Negro novel were suggested by Ralph Ellison in an address at Fisk University, April 1953.

22. Pauline Hopkins illustrates very well the dualism of the Negro culture propagandists. She displayed an interest in redeeming Africa and, as one of the editors of the *Colored American Magazine,* she pleaded for a racial literature and racial solidarity, but in her writings she tried to show how well Negroes had absorbed American middle-class ideals in home life, education, and cultural accomplishment. See her *Contending Forces* (Boston, 1900), e.g., 371.

23. BTW, *Story of the Negro,* I, 13; Du Bois, "Social Effects of Emancipation," *Survey,* XXIX (Feb. 1, 1913), 570–72.

24. W. D. Weatherford, *Present Forces in Negro Progress* (New York, 1912), 42–43; *Age,* Oct. 8, 1908; *Crisis,* e.g., II (Aug., 1911), inside back cover.

25. Weatherford, *Present Forces in Negro Progress,* 35–36; John Daniels, *In Freedom's Birthplace* (Boston, 1914), 106.

26. E.g., Wright, *Negro in Pennsylvania,* 169; *Gazette,* April 25, 1905, Feb. 18, 1911, and 1910–15 *passim; Horizon,* V (May, 1910), 5–6; *Crisis,* I (Nov., 1910), 10; Locke, "The Dilemma of Segregation," *JNE,* IV (July, 1935), 506; *Gazette,* Sept. 28, 1912.

27. For Park see Monroe Work, ed., *Negro Year Book, 1914–1915* (Tuskegee, 1914), 45; for Scott see *Bee,* April 30, 1914.

28. Johnson and Johnson, *Lift Every Voice and Sing* (New York, 1900); J. W. Johnson, *Along This Way* (New York, 1933), 154–56.

29. Galesburg, Ill., *Mail,* June 21, 1901 (Hampton Clipping Collection).

30. Ridgely Torrence, *The Story of John Hope* (New York, 1948), 135.

31. Salt Lake City *Herald,* Aug. 6, 1901 and Richmond *Planet,* March 9,

April 26, 1907 (both in Hampton Clipping Collection); *Liberia,* Bulletin No. 31 (1907), 30–32.

32. Atlanta *News,* Sept. 23, 1903 (Hampton Clipping Collection); *Liberia,* Bulletin No. 24 (1904), 92–93.

33. Samuel Chapman, *Destiny of the Black Man* (no imprint, [1897]), 3; Colonization Scrapbook, 1913–16, in Hampton Clipping Collection, e.g., New York *Sun,* Feb. 1, Dec. 1, 1913; *Afro-American Ledger,* Jan. 24, 1914; St. Louis *Globe-Democrat,* May 16, 1915; New York *News,* Jan. 27, 1916. See also *Gazette,* May 29, 1915.

34. E.g., *Recorder,* Sept. 26, 1897, Feb. 27, 1900; A.M.E. *Review,* XV (July, 1898), 56–63, and XX (Oct., 1903), 143–48; *Bee,* Feb. 27, 1900; Helen G. Edmonds, *The Negro and Fusion Politics in North Carolina* (Chapel Hill, 1951), 196; Anderson, *Prophetic Liberator of the Coloured Race* (New York, 1913), n.p.; on Holsey, see Chapter XII, above.

35. See esp. *Proceedings of the Ninth Annual Session of the National Afro-American Council . . . 1906* (Louisville, 1907), 20–21.

36. Thomas Jesse Jones, "Negro Population in the United States," in *The Negro's Progress in Fifty Years* (Annals of the American Academy of Political and Social Science, XLIX, 1913), 7, 9; George Edmund Haynes, "Conditions Among Negroes in the Cities," *ibid.,* 105–7; *Bulletin* of the National League on Urban Conditions Among Negroes, II (Oct., 1912), 5; Du Bois, "The Problem of Work," A.M.E. *Review,* XX (Oct., 1903), 162–63.

37. R. R. Wright, Jr., "The Migration to the North," Annals of the American Academy of Political and Social Science, XXVII (1906), 566. For general viewpoint of students of the matter see esp. Johnson, "How Much is the Migration a Flight from Persecution?" *Opportunity,* I (Sept., 1923), 272–74.

38. On causes of Great Migration see *Ibid.,* 272–74; Emmett J. Scott, *Negro Migration During the War* (New York, 1910); U.S. Department of Labor, *Negro Migration in 1916–17* (Washington, 1919); Haynes, "Negroes Move North," *Survey,* XL (May 4, 1918), 115–22 and XLI (Jan. 4, 1919), 455–61; and Thomas J. Woofter, *Negro Migration* (New York, 1920). Haynes and especially Scott also emphasize noneconomic factors.

39. The escapist Utopian character of the Garvey movement as a response to economic deprivation is revealed in the fact that a large number of ex-Garveyites joined the Father Divine movement during the depression of the 1930's. The Black Muslim movement today further illustrates the economic interpretation given to account for extreme Negro nationalist movements. Support for the Black Muslims comes from the economically deprived lower-lower class. Its increasing importance is to be accounted for by the fact that at a time when Negro aspirations have risen markedly, the Negro unemployment rate continues to rise—it is now nearly three times that for whites. The movement appeals chiefly to unemployed and unskilled workers, for whom automation holds out a bleak future, and for whom the civil rights movement has accomplished nothing to date.

40. See also Ralph J. Bunche, "Conceptions and Ideologies of the Negro Problem" (Memorandum prepared for the Carnegie-Myrdal Study of the Negro in America, 1940), 147–48.

41. Chesnutt to E. J. Lilly, July 7, 1916, Chesnutt Papers; Haynes, "Conditions Among Negroes in the Cities," 109–12; *Bulletin* of the National Urban League, II (Oct., 1912), 5.

42. James Weldon Johnson, *Black Manhattan* (New York, 1930), 58–59; Du Bois, *The Philadelphia Negro* (Philadelphia, 1899), 58; Drake and Cayton, *Black Metropolis,* chap. ii; Daniels, *In Freedom's Birthplace,* 17, 22, 85, 102, 143–49; Haynes, "Conditions Among Negroes in the Cities," 109.

43. Drake and Cayton, *Black Metropolis,* 47–57.

44. The artistic roots of the Renaissance undoubtedly go back at least to the "Black Bohemia" on Manhattan's West Side in the 1880's where Negro artists, actors, and literary figures congregated. (Johnson, *Black Manhattan,* chaps. viii–xi). The flowering of the 1920's was due also in part to contact with white writers and artists in New York.

45. Du Bois, "The Social Evolution of the Black South," *American Negro Monographs,* I (1911), 6–7.

46. Similarly, the Black Muslim movement today is the lower-lower class counterpart of the *new* "New Negro" of the direct-action persuasion. On Garvey's viewpoint, see Amy Jacques-Garvey, ed., *Philosophy and Opinions of Marcus Garvey,* 2 vols. (New York, 1923–25).

INDEX

317

Philadelphia Institute for Colored Youth, 89

Philanthropists, role in Negro life and thought, 87–99 *passim*, 104, 111, 114, 117, 134, 145, 147, 149, 166, 178, 183, 199, 208, 222, 290–92

Phillips, C. H., 49, 56, 234

Physical resistance to oppression, 73, 78–79

Pickens, Williams, 62, 258

Pinchback, P. B. S., 27, 78, 251, 297, 311

Pittsburgh, Pa., 29

Plantation system, 11

Plato, 52

Pledger, William A., 32, 37, 79, 250–51

Plessy v *Ferguson*, 1896, 162

Plummer, Clifford H., 238

Political activity, 4, 6, 11–12, 20, 23–24, 26–41, 56–57, 75–76, 78, 83, 88, 100, 102, 109–13, 143, 148, 163, 165, 168–69, 172–73, 186, 188–89, 193, 208–44 *passim*, 248–55, 257, 276–77, 301; *see also* Political rights; Democratic party; Republican party

Political Independence, 186, 188; *see also* Negro vote, division of; Democratic party, Negro support for

Political rights, 4–6, 9–10, 15–16, 20, 26, 37, 39, 44, 55–58, 60, 69–70, 74–75, 99, 101, 103, 107, 109–13, 169, 173, 177–78, 180, 182–84, 192, 194, 196–97, 199, 206, 208–55 *passim*, 259, 261, 299; *see also* Disfranchisement; Franchise Restrictions

Populist Movement, 19, 23, 27–28, 37–38, 46–48, 287

Powell, Adam Clayton, Sr., 221

Power structure, in Negro community, 1895–1915, 114–15, 205, 213, 224–27, 236, 244–46

Prairie View State College, 87, 267

Presbyterian Church, 133, 218, 222–23

Price, J. C., 33, 39, 50, 70, 80–82, 92, 252

Princeton Theological Seminary, 133, 223

Proctor, H. H., 222, 272

Progressive movement, 165, 184

Progressive party, 165, 187–89, 242

Protest, 5–6, 9–10, 24, 32, 35, 44, 55–58, 60, 69–82, 99, 106–10, 116, 121, 124, 128–30, 135, 159, 166–69, 172–76, 178–80, 184, 191, 193, 196–97, 200, 204–5, 207, 209–55 *passim*, 258–60, 263

Provident Hospital, Chicago, 296

Purvis, Charles B., 45, 48, 54, 297

Purvis, Robert, 29

Pushkin, Alexander (Aleksander), 52, 202–3

Race differences, Negro belief in, 42–43, 49, 54, 73, 194–96, 202–4, 206, 266–68, 270

Race pride, 24, 43, 50, 53–56, 68–69, 75, 77, 80, 105–6, 118, 131–32, 167–68, 195, 204–5, 256–59, 261–63, 265, 270–71, 275; *see also* Negro History, interest in; Nationalism; Ethnocentrism

Race riots, 162, 180; *see also* Mob violence

Racial Co-operation, *see* Racial solidarity; Economic Nationalism

Racial discrimination, development of, 19–23, 99, 161–66, 200, 258; *see also* Segregation, system of; Disfranchisement

Racial equality, *see* Equality of races